Great Political Thinkers

Machiavelli
Quentin Skinner

Hobbes
Richard Tuck

Mill
William Thomas

Marx
Peter Singer

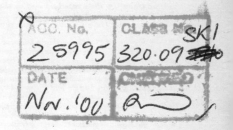
Oxford   New York
OXFORD UNIVERSITY PRESS

Oxford University Press, Great Clarendon Street, Oxford OX2 6DP

Oxford New York
Athens Auckland Bangkok Bogotá Buenos Aires Calcutta
Cape Town Chennai Dar es Salaam Delhi Florence Hong Kong Istanbul
Karachi Kuala Lumpur Madrid Melbourne Mexico City Mumbai
Nairobi Paris São Paulo Singapore Taipei Tokyo Toronto Warsaw
and associated companies in
Berlin Ibadan

Oxford is a registered trade mark of Oxford University Press

British Library Cataloguing in Publication Data
Data available

Library of Congress Cataloging in Publication Data
Great political thinkers / Quentin Skinner . . . [et al.].
p. cm.—(Past Masters)
Includes bibliographical references and index.
Contents: Machiavelli / Quentin Skinner—Hobbes / Richard Tuck—
Mill / William Thomas—Marx / Peter Singer.
1. Machiavelli, Niccolò, 1469–1527—Contributions in political
science.   2. Hobbes, Thomas, 1588–1679—Contributions in political
science.   3. Mill, John Stuart, 1818–1873—Contributions in
political science.   4. Marx, Karl, 1818–1883—Contributions in
political science. [1. Machiavelli, Niccolò, 1469–1527.
2. Hobbes, Thomas, 1588–1679. 3. Mill, John Stuart, 1806–1873.
4. Marx, Karl, 1818–1883. 5. Political scientists.] I. Skinner,
Quentin. II. Series.
320.5′09′2—dc20   JC143.M4G74   1992   91–27678
ISBN 0-19-285254-X

10 9 8 7 6 5

Printed in Great Britain by
Cox & Wyman Ltd, Reading, Berkshire

Great Political Thinkers

Quentin Skinner is Professor of Political Science at the University of Cambridge, and a Fellow of Christ's College. His *The Foundations of Modern Political Thought*, published in two volumes in 1978, won a Wolfson Literary Award.

Richard Tuck is University Lecturer in History at the University of Cambridge and Fellow of Jesus College.

William Thomas is Lecturer in Modern History at Oxford, and Senior Tutor in Modern History at Christ Church. He has edited a selection from James Mill's *History of British India*, and is author of *The Philosophic Radicals*.

Peter Singer is Professor of Philosophy and Director of the Centre for Human Bioethics at Monash University, Melbourne. He is best known as the author of *Animal Liberation*. His other books include *Hegel*, also in the Past Masters series.

Foreword

Wherever political ideas are read or debated, the writings of Machiavelli, Hobbes, Mill and Marx are central to the discussion. Profoundly different from each other, both in outlook and in personality, what these authors have in common is that each of them formulated a classic statement of the nature of political life. In every case it was a view which enraged many of their contemporaries; but in every case it was one which has never ceased to fascinate posterity.

Machiavelli is usually thought to have urged the pursuit of political advantage at the expense of morality. His name has become synonymous with unscrupulous duplicity: to be a Machiavellian is to behave in a way which is not to be trusted. In fact, as Quentin Skinner shows, Machiavelli had lofty political principles. He was the exponent of a distinctive tradition of classical republicanism and he sought by a reinfusion of what he called *virtú* to restore the civic greatness of a state which had succumbed to corruption. His doctrines can only be understood by reconstructing the early sixteenth-century Italian context in which they were formulated.

Hobbes has also had a bad reputation. He too is associated with irreligion and immorality. He portrayed human beings as vain and selfish creatures engaged in a war of all against all which only an omnipotent state could suppress. Yet Richard Tuck reveals him as a humanist, witty and sceptical, and a moralist passionately concerned with the achievement of peace and a good quality of life for everyone. The philosophical foundation of his doctrines has continued to provoke controversy, but about his seriousness and his profundity there can be no doubt.

Mill was more closely in sympathy with the prevailing values of his own day and he is often seen as the quintessential Victorian liberal. In *On Liberty* he attempted to determine the proper boundary between state action and individual freedom, while his *Principles of Political Economy* presupposed a free-market system. Yet William Thomas reminds us that his works betray what his contemporary W. E. Gladstone called 'the high independent thought of a recluse'. Mill cast off much of his early Utilitarian inheritance; he gave sympathetic consideration to the arguments of the early socialists; and he was an eloquent feminist. He was high-minded and earnest, standing aloof from the money-grubbing materialism of his time.

Marx's influence has far surpassed that of the other three; and the passions which his work has aroused are correspondingly intense. The founder of the materialist interpretation of history and the prophet of the class struggle, he has seemed to millions to offer the vital key to the working of human society. His influence upon economics, philosophy and every branch of social thought has been as profound as his impact upon practical politics. Multi-faceted though his achievement was, Marx's central concern was, in Peter Singer's view, the nature of human freedom: he aimed to show how economic relations constrained the liberty of both capitalists and workers; and he looked forward to a communist society which would transform human nature.

Each of these authors has generated an enormous and bewildering literature of commentary and exegesis. Some of that literature is historical in character: like Quentin Skinner's study of Machiavelli, it seeks to clarify the author's meaning and to identify the context in which he wrote. But much of it has been evaluative, aiming, as Peter Singer puts it in his final chapter on Marx, to ascertain which elements of an author's thought remain valuable and which need to be revised or scrapped. These are two different, albeit complementary, ways of approaching the political thought of the past, but the historical approach must come first, for until we have established the author's meaning we cannot know what value to attach to it. Of course, like all texts, political works have more than one meaning. Indeed it is the capacity of successive generations to read new meanings into Machiavelli, Hobbes, Mill and Marx which gives these authors their classic status. But some interpretations are more convincing than others; and it is the object of the four studies which follow to indicate which those interpretations are.

These four self-contained essays were originally written for the Past Masters series, which sets out to expound the ideas of notable thinkers of the past in a lucid, accessible and authoritative manner. Several of them have already achieved classic status as indispensable introductions to their subject. By reprinting them in one volume, the Oxford University Press has provided an invaluable guide to four of the thinkers who have done most to shape the Western political tradition.

KEITH THOMAS
General Editor
Past Masters

Contents

Machiavelli

Quentin Skinner

Preface

It is twenty-five years since a brief outline of Machiavelli's life and writings appeared in English. (The last work comparable in scale to the present one was J. R. Hale's fine study, *Machiavelli and Renaissance Italy*, first published in 1961.) My principal reason for offering this new survey is that in the intervening period a grest deal of fresh information has come to light about Machiavelli's career and thought. Several biographical discoveries have been made; a full critical edition has been issued for the first time; and a new generation of interpreters has been at work, producing a steady stream of commentaries which in some cases have been outstanding in quality. I am greatly indebted to these recent scholarly advances, and have leant heavily on them throughout the following account.

At the same time, however, I have tried to present a view of Machiavelli's political theory that rests at least to some extent on the results of my own research. Building in particular on the work of Hans Baron, Felix Gilbert and J. G. A. Pocock, I have sought to portray Machiavelli essentially as an exponent of a distinctive humanist tradition of classical republicanism. I have argued in addition that the most original and creative aspects of his political vision are best understood as a series of polemical—and sometimes satirical—reactions against the body of humanist beliefs he inherited and basically continued to endorse. Although my primary aim has been to provide a straightforward introduction to his thought, I hope that these conclusions may also be of some interest to specialists in the field.

In quoting from Machiavelli's *Correspondence*, *Legations* and so-called *Caprices* (*Ghiribizzi*), I have made my own translations. In quoting from his other works I have relied (with kind permission) on the excellent English versions in Allan Gilbert, trans.: *Machiavelli: The Chief Works and Others* (3 vols, Duke University Press, 1965) (copyright © 1965 by Duke University Press). When I cite from the *Correspond-*

ence and the *Legations*, I identify the source by placing a 'C' or an 'L' in brackets, as appropriate, together with the page-reference after each quotation. When I refer to other works by Machiavelli, I make it contextually clear in each case which text I am citing, and simply add the page-references in brackets. Full details of all the editions I am using can be found in the list of 'Works by Machiavelli quoted in the text' on p. 98. The references for all other quotations in the body of the text are given in the 'Note on sources' on p. 99.

Two further points need to be made about translations. I have ventured in a few places to amend Gilbert's renderings in order to give a clearer sense of Machiavelli's exact phraseology. And I have held to my belief that Machiavelli's pivotal concept of virtù (*virtus* in Latin) cannot be translated into modern English by any single word or manageable series of periphrases. I have in consequence left these terms in their original form throughout. This is not to say, however, that I fail to discuss their meanings; on the contrary, much of my text can be read as an explication of what I take Machiavelli to have meant by them.

The first three chapters of this book contain—in a greatly abbreviated and revised form—the substance of the Carlyle Lectures on 'The Political Theory of Machiavelli' which I delivered in the University of Oxford during the Michaelmas Term 1980. I am deeply grateful to the University for inviting me to give this series, to Nevil Johnson for taking so much trouble over the arrangements, and to All Souls College for its munificent hospitality.

I am much indebted to Keith Thomas for suggesting that I should contribute this book to his series, and to Henry Hardy of the Oxford University Press for his unfailing patience, as well as for much help and encouragement. I am further indebted to both of them for reading my manuscript and prompting me to revise it at many points. My thanks are also due to the Cambridge University Press for allowing me to borrow several turns of phrase from the chapters on Renaissance political philosophy in volume I of my book *The Foundations of Modern Political Thought*. Finally, my greatest debt of gratitude is owed to John Dunn, Susan James and J. G. A. Pocock, all of whom have read my manuscript with meticulous care and discussed it with me at every stage, offering me numerous valuable suggestions as well as helping me in many other ways.

Contents

Introduction

Machiavelli died over four hundred and fifty years ago, but his name lives on as a byword for cunning, duplicity and the exercise of bad faith in political affairs. 'The murderous Machiavel', as Shakespeare called him, has never ceased to be an object of hatred to moralists of all persuasions, conservatives and revolutionaries alike. Edmund Burke claimed to see 'the odious maxims of a machiavellian policy' underlying the 'democratic tyranny' of the French Revolution. Marx and Engels attacked the principles of machiavellianism with no less vehemence, while insisting that the true exponents of 'machiavellian policy' are those who attempt 'to paralyse democratic energies' at periods of revolutionary change. The point on which both sides agree is that the evils of machiavellianism constitute one of the most dangerous threats to the moral basis of political life.

So much notoriety has gathered around Machiavelli's name that the charge of being a machiavellian still remains a serious accusation in current political debate. When Henry Kissinger, for example, expounded his philosophy in a famous interview published in *The New Republic* in 1972, his interviewer remarked, after hearing him discuss his role as a presidential adviser, that 'listening to you, one sometimes wonders not how much you have influenced the President of the United States, but to what extent you have been influenced by Machiavelli'. The suggestion was one that Kissinger showed himself extremely anxious to repudiate. Was he a machiavellian? 'No, not at all.' Was he not influenced by Machiavelli to some degree? 'To none whatever.'

What lies behind the sinister reputation Machiavelli has acquired? Is it really deserved? What views about politics and political morality does he actually put forward in his major works? These are the questions I hope to answer in the course of this book. I shall argue that, in order to understand Machiavelli's doctrines, we need to begin by recovering the problems

9

he evidently saw himself confronting in *The Prince*, the *Discourses* and his other writings on political philosophy. To attain this perspective, we need in turn to reconstruct the context in which these works were originally composed—the intellectual context of classical and Renaissance philosophy, as well as the political context of Italian city-state life at the start of the sixteenth century. Once we restore Machiavelli to the world in which his ideas were initially formed, we can begin to appreciate the extraordinary originality of his attack on the prevailing moral assumptions of his age. And once we grasp the implications of his own moral outlook, we can readily see why his name is still so often invoked whenever the issues of political power and leadership are discussed.

1 The Diplomat

The humanist background

Niccoló Machiavelli was born in Florence on 3 May 1469. We first hear of him playing an active part in the affairs of his native city in 1498, the year in which the regime controlled by Savonarola fell from power. Savonarola, the Dominican prior of San Marco, whose prophetic sermons had dominated Florentine politics for the previous four years, was arrested for heresy early in April; soon afterwards the city's ruling council began to dismiss his remaining supporters from their positions in the government. One of those who lost his job as a result was Alessandro Braccesi, the head of the second chancery. At first the post was left unoccupied, but after a delay of several weeks the almost unknown name of Machiavelli was put forward as a possible replacement. He was barely twenty-nine years old, and appears to have had no previous administrative experience. Yet his nomination went through without evident difficulty, and on 19 June he was duly confirmed by the great council as second chancellor of the Florentine republic.

By the time Machiavelli entered the chancery, there was a well-established method of recruitment to its major offices. In addition to giving evidence of diplomatic skills, aspiring officials were expected to display a high degree of competence in the so-called 'humane disciplines'. This concept of the *studia humanitatis* had been derived from Roman sources, and especially from Cicero, whose pedagogic ideals were revived by the Italian humanists of the fourteenth century and came to exercise a powerful influence on the universities and on the conduct of Italian public life. The humanists were distinguished first of all by their commitment to a particular theory about the proper contents of a 'truly humane' education. They expected their students to begin with the mastery of Latin, move on to the practice of rhetoric and the imitation of the finest classical stylists, and complete their studies with a close reading of ancient history and moral philosophy. They also popularised the long-standing belief that this type of training offers the best preparation for political life. As Cicero had repeatedly maintained, these disciplines nurture the values we principally need to acquire in order to serve our country well: a willingness to subordinate our private interests to the public good, a desire to fight against corruption and tyranny, and an ambition to reach out for the noblest goals of all, those of honour and glory for our country as well as for ourselves.

As the Florentines became increasingly imbued with these beliefs, they began to call on their leading humanists to fill the most prestigious positions in the city government. The practice may be said to have started with the appointment of Coluccio Salutati as chancellor in 1375, and it rapidly became the rule. While Machiavelli was growing up, the first chancellorship was held by Bartolomeo Scala, who retained his professorship at the university throughout his public career and continued to write on typically humanist themes, his main works being a moral treatise and a *History of the Florentines*. During Machiavelli's own time in the chancery, the same traditions were impressively upheld by Scala's successor, Marcello Adriani. He too transferred to the first chancellorship from a chair at the university, and he too continued to publish works of humanist scholarship, including a textbook on the teaching of Latin and a vernacular treatise *On the Education of the Florentine Nobility*.

The prevalence of these ideals helps to explain how Machiavelli came to be appointed at a relatively early age to a position of considerable responsibility in the administration of the republic. For his family, though neither rich nor highly aristocratic, was closely connected with some of the city's most exalted humanist circles. Machiavelli's father, Bernardo, who earned his living as a lawyer, was an enthusiastic student of the humanities. He was on close terms with several distinguished scholars, including Bartolomeo Scala, whose tract of 1483 *On Laws and Legal Judgements* took the form of a dialogue between himself and 'my friend and intimate', Bernardo Machiavelli. Moreover, it is clear from the *Diary* Bernardo kept between 1474 and 1487 that, throughout the period when his son Niccoló was growing up, Bernardo was engaged in studying several of the leading classical texts on which the renaissance concept of 'the humanities' had been founded. He records that he borrowed Cicero's *Philippics* in 1477, and his greatest rhetorical work, *The Making of an Orator*, in 1480. He also borrowed Cicero's treatise *On Moral Obligation* several times in the 1470s, and in 1476 he even managed to acquire his own copy of Livy's *History*—the text which, some forty years later, was to serve as the framework for his son's *Discourses*, his longest and most ambitious work of political philosophy.

It is also evident from Bernardo's Diary that, in spite of the large expense involved—which he anxiously itemised—he was careful to provide his son with an excellent grounding in the *studia humanitatis*. We first hear of Machiavelli's education immediately after his seventh birthday, when his father records that 'my little son Niccoló has started to go to Master Matteo' for the first stage of his formal schooling, the study of Latin. By the time Machiavelli was twelve he had graduated to the second stage, and had passed into the care of a famous schoolmaster, Paolo da Ronciglione, who taught several of the most illustrious humanists of Machiavelli's generation. This further step is noted by Bernardo in his *Diary* for 5 November 1481, when he proudly announces that 'Niccoló is now writing Latin compositions of his own'—following the standard humanist method of imitating the best models of classical style. Finally, it seems that—if we can trust the word of Paolo Giovio—Machiavelli was sent to complete his education at the university of Florence. Giovio states in his *Maxims* that Machiavelli 'received the best part' of his classical training from Marcello Adriani; and Adriani, as we have seen, occupied a chair at the university for a number of years before his appointment to the first chancellorship.

This humanist background appears to contain the clue to explaining why Machiavelli suddenly received his governmental post in the summer of 1498. Adriani had taken over as first chancellor earlier in the same year, and it seems plausible to suppose that he remembered Machiavelli's talents in the humanities and decided to reward them when he was filling the vacancies in the chancery caused by the change of regime. It is probable, therefore, that it was owing to Adriani's patronage together perhaps with the influence of Bernardo's humanist friends—that Machiavelli found himself launched on his public career in the new anti-Savonarolan government.

The diplomatic missions

Machiavelli's official position involved him in two sorts of duties. The second chancery, set up in 1437, mainly dealt with correspondence relating to the administration of Florence's own territories. But as head of this section Machiavelli also ranked as one of the six secretaries to the first chancellor, and in this capacity he was shortly assigned the further task of serving the Ten of War, the committee responsible for the foreign and diplomatic relations of the republic. This meant that, in addition to his ordinary office work, he could be called on to travel abroad on behalf of the Ten, acting as secretary to its ambassadors and helping to send home detailed reports on foreign affairs.

His first opportunity to take part in a mission of this kind came in July 1500, when he and Francesco della Casa were commissioned 'to proceed with all possible haste' to the court of Louis XII of France (L 70). The decision to send this embassy arose out of the difficulties Florence had been experiencing in the war against Pisa. The Pisans had rebelled in 1496 and over the next four years they succeeded in fighting off all attempts to crush their bid for independence. Early in 1500, however, the French agreed to help the Florentines regain the city, and dispatched a force to lay siege to it. But this too turned out disastrously: the Gascon mercenaries hired by Florence deserted; the Swiss auxiliaries mutinied for lack of pay; and the assault had to be ignominiously called off.

Machiavelli's instructions were 'to establish that it was not due to any shortcoming on our part that this undertaking yielded no results' and at the same time 'to convey the impression' if possible that the French commander had acted 'corruptly and with cowardice' (L 72, 74). However, as he and della Casa discovered at their first audience with Louis XII, the king was not much interested in Florence's excuses for her past failures. Instead he wanted to know what help he could realistically expect in the future from such an apparently ill-run government. This meeting set the tone for the whole of their subsequent discussions with Louis and his chief advisers, Robertet and the archbishop of Rouen. The upshot was that, although Machiavelli remained at the French court for nearly six months, the visit taught him less about the policies of the French than about the increasingly equivocal standing of the Italian city-states.

The first lesson he learned was that, to anyone schooled in the ways of modern kingship, Florence's governmental machinery appeared absurdly vacillating and weak. By the end of July it became obvious that the *signoria*, the city's ruling council, would need to send a further embassy to renegotiate the terms of the alliance with France. Throughout August and September Machiavelli kept waiting to hear whether the new ambassadors had left Florence, and kept assuring the archbishop of Rouen that he expected them at any minute. By the middle of October, when there were still no signs of their arrival, the archbishop began to treat these continued prevarications with open contempt. As Machiavelli reported with obvious chagrin, he 'replied in these exact words' when assured that the promised mission was at last on its way: 'it is true that this is what you say, but before these ambassadors arrive we shall all be dead' (L 168). Even more humiliatingly, Machiavelli discovered that his native city's sense of its own importance seemed to the French to be ludicrously out of line with the realities of its military position and its wealth. The French, he had to tell the *signoria*, 'only value those who are well-armed or willing to pay' and had come to believe that 'both these qualities are lacking in your case'. Although he tried making a speech 'about the security your greatness could bring to the possessions held by his majesty in Italy', he found that 'the whole thing was superfluous', for the French merely laughed at him. The painful truth, he confesses, is that 'they call you Mr Nothing' (L 126 and n.).

Machiavelli took the first of these lessons profoundly to heart. His mature political writings are full of warnings about the folly of procrastinating, the danger of appearing irresolute, the need for bold and rapid action in war and politics alike. But he clearly found it impossible to accept the further implication that there might be no future for the Italian city-states. He continued to theorise about their military and political arrangements on the assumption that they were still genuinely capable of recovering and maintaining their independence, even though the period of his own lifetime witnessed their final and inexorable subordination to the vastly superior forces of France, Germany and Spain.

The mission to France ended in December 1500, and Machiavelli hurried home as quickly as possible. His sister had died while he was away, his father had died shortly before his departure, and in consequence (as he complained to the *signoria*) his family affairs 'had ceased to have any order about them at all' (L 184). There were also anxieties about his job, for his assistant Agostino Vespucci had contacted him at the end of October to convey a rumour that 'unless you return, you will completely lose your place in the chancery' (C 60). Shortly after this, moreover, Machiavelli came to have a further reason for wishing to stay in the vicinity of Florence: his courtship of Marietta Corsini, whom he married in the autumn of 1501. Marietta remains a shadowy figure in Machiavelli's story, but his letters suggest that he never ceased to be fond of her, while she for her part bore him six children, appears to have suffered his infidelities with patience, and eventually outlived him by a quarter of a century.

During the next two years, which Machiavelli spent mainly in and around Florence, the *signoria* became perturbed about the rise of a new and threatening military power on its borders: that of Cesare Borgia. In April 1501 Borgia was created duke of Romagna by his father, Pope Alexander VI. He thereupon launched a series of audacious campaigns designed to carve out for himself a territory to match his new and resounding title. First he seized Faenza and laid siege to Piombino, which he entered in September 1501. Next his lieutenants raised the Val di Chiana in rebellion against Florence in the spring of 1502, while Borgia himself marched north and took over the duchy of Urbino in a lightning *coup*. Elated by these successes, he then demanded a formal alliance with the Florentines and asked that an envoy be sent to hear his terms. The man selected for this delicate task was Machiavelli, who received his commission on 5 October 1502 and presented himself before the duke at Imola two days later.

This mission marks the beginning of the most formative period of Machiavelli's diplomatic career, the period in which he was able to play the role that most delighted him, that of a first-hand observer and assessor of contemporary statecraft. It was also during this time that he arrived at his definitive judgements on most of the leaders whose policies he was able to watch in the process of being formed. It is often suggested that Machiavelli's *Legations* merely contain the 'raw materials' or 'rough drafts' of his later political views, and that he subsequently reworked and even idealised his observations in the years of his enforced retirement. As we shall see, however, a study of the *Legations* in fact reveals that Machiavelli's evaluations, and even his epigrams, generally occurred to him at once, and were later incorporated virtually without alteration into the pages of the *Discourses* and especially *The Prince*.

Machiavelli's mission to Borgia's court lasted nearly four months, in the course of which he had many discussions tête-à-tête with the duke, who seems to have gone out of his way to expound his policies and ambitions underlying them. Machiavelli was greatly impressed. The duke, he reported, is 'superhuman in his courage', as well as being a man of grand designs, who 'thinks himself capable of attaining anything he wants' (L 520). Moreover, his actions are no less striking than his words, for he 'controls everything by himself', governs 'with extreme secrecy' and is capable in consequence of deciding and executing his plans with devastating suddenness (L 427, 503). In short, Machiavelli recognised that Borgia was no mere upstart *condottiere*, but someone who 'must now be regarded as a new power in Italy' (L 422).

These observations, originally sent in secret to the Ten of War, have since become celebrated, for they recur almost word for word in chapter 7 of *The Prince*. Outlining Borgia's career, Machiavelli again emphasises the duke's high courage, his exceptional abilities and tremendous sense of purpose (33–4). He also reiterates his opinion that Borgia was no less impressive in the execution of his schemes. He 'made use of every means and action possible' for 'putting down his roots', and managed to lay 'mighty foundations for future power' in such a short time that, if his luck had not deserted him, he 'would have mastered every difficulty' (29, 33).

While he admired Borgia's qualities of leadership, however, Machiavelli felt an element of uneasiness from the outset about the duke's astounding self-confidence. As early as October 1502 he wrote from Imola that 'as long as I have been here, the duke's government has been founded on nothing more than his good Fortune' (L 386). By the start of the following year he was speaking with increasing disapproval of the fact that the duke was still content to rely on his 'unheard-of good luck' (L 520). And by October 1503, when Machiavelli was sent on a mission to Rome, and again had an opportunity of observing Borgia at close quarters, his earlier doubts crystallised into a strong sense of the limitations of the duke's capacities.

The main purpose of Machiavelli's journey to Rome was to report on an unusual crisis which had developed at the papal court. The pope, Alexander VI, had died in August and his successor, Pius III, had in turn died within a month of taking office. The Florentine *signoria* was anxious to receive daily bulletins about what was likely to happen next, especially after Borgia arrived to promote the candidacy of cardinal Giuliano della Rovere. This development looked potentially threatening to Florence's interests, for the duke's support had been bought with a promise that he would be appointed captain-general of the papal armies if Rovere were elected. And it seemed certain, if Borgia secured this post, that he would begin a new series of hostile campaigns on the borders of Florentine territory.

Machiavelli's earliest dispatches accordingly concentrate on the meeting of the conclave, in which Rovere was elected 'by an enormous majority' and took the name of Julius II (L 599). But once this matter was settled, everyone's attention shifted to the struggle that started to develop between Borgia and the pope. As Machiavelli watched these two masters of duplicity beginning to circle around one another, he saw that his initial doubts about the duke's abilities had been thoroughly justified.

Borgia, he felt, had akeady displayed a lack of foresight in failing to see the dangers inherent in supporting Rovere. As he reminded the Ten of War, the cardinal had been forced 'to live in exile for ten years' under the pontificate of the duke's father, Alexander VI. Surely, he added, Rovere 'cannot have forgotten this so quickly' that he now looks with genuine favour on an alliance with the son of of his enemy (L 599). But Machiavelli's most serious criticism was that, even in this equivocal and perilous situation, Borgia continued to place an altogether hubristic reliance on his uninterrupted run of good luck. At first Machiavelli simply noted, in some apparent surprise, that 'the duke is allowing himself to be carried away by his immense confidence' (L 599). Two weeks later, when Borgia's papal commission had still not arrived, and his possessions in the Romagna had begun to rise in widespread revolt, he reported in more acid tones that the duke 'has become stupified' by 'these blows of Fortune, which he is not accustomed to taste' (L 631). By the end of the month, Machiavelli had come to the conclusion that Borgia's ill Fortune had unmanned him so completely that he was now incapable of remaining firm in any decision at all, and on 26 November he felt able to assure the Ten of War that 'you can henceforth act without having to think about him any more' (L 683). A week later he mentioned Borgia's sffairs for the last time, merely observing that 'little by little the duke is now slipping into his grave' (L 709).

As before, these confidential judgements on Borgia's character have since become famous through their incorporation into chapter 7 of *The Prince*. Machiavelli repeats that the duke 'made a bad choice' in supporting 'the election of Julius as pope', because 'he should never have let the papacy go to any cardinal whom he had injured' (34). And he recurs to his basic accusation that the duke relied too heavily on his luck. Instead

19

of facing the obvious contingency that he might at some point be checked by a 'malicious stroke of Fortune', he collapsed as soon as this happened (29). Despite his admiration, Machiavelli's final verdict on Borgia—in *The Prince* no less than in the *Legations*—is thus an adverse one: he 'gained his position through his father's Fortune' and he lost it as soon as Fortune deserted him (28).

The next influential leader whom Machiavelli was able to assess at first hand was the new pope, Julius II. Machiavelli had been present at several audiences at the time of Julius's election, but it was in the course of two later missions that he gained his fullest insight into the pope's character and leadership. The first of these was in 1506, when Machiavelli returned between August and October to the papal court. His instructions at that point were to keep the *signoria* informed about the progress of Julius's typically aggressive plan to recover Perugia, Bologna and the other territories previously held by the Church. The second chance arose in 1510, when Machiavelli was sent on a new embassy to the court of France. By this time Julius had resolved on a great crusade to drive the 'barbarians' out of Italy, an ambition which placed the Florentines in an awkward position. On the one hand they had no desire to offend the pope in his increasingly bellicose mood. But on the other hand they were traditional allies of the French, who immediately asked what help they could expect if the pope were to invade the duchy of Milan, recaptured by Louis XII in the previous year. As in 1506, Machiavelli thus found himself anxiously following the progress of Julius's campaigns, while hoping and scheming at the same time to preserve Florence's neutrality.

Watching the warrior pope in action, Machiavelli was at first impressed and even amazed. He started out with the assumption that Julius's plan of reconquering the papal states was bound to end in disaster. 'No one believes', he wrote in September 1506, that the pope 'will be able to accomplish what he originally wanted' (L 996). In no time at all, however, he was having to eat his words. Before the end of the month Julius had re-entered Perugia and 'settled its affairs', and before October was out Machiavelli found himself concluding his mission with the resounding announcement that, after a headlong campaign, Bologna had surrendered unconditionally, 'her ambassadors throwing themselves at the feet of the pope and handing their city over to him' (L 995, 1035).

It was not long, however, before Machiavelli began to feel more critical, especially after Julius took the alarming decision to launch his slender forces against the might of France in 1510. At first he merely expressed the sardonic hope that Julius' boldness 'will turn out to be based on something other than his sanctity' (L 1234). But soon he was writing in much graver tones to say that 'no one here knows anything for certain about the basis for the pope's actions', and that Julius's own ambassador professes himself 'completely astounded' by the whole venture, since 'he is deeply sceptical about whether the pope has the resources or the organisation' to undertake it at all (L 1248). Machiavelli was not yet prepared to condemn Julius outright, for he still thought it conceivable that, 'as in the campaign against Bologna', the pope's 'sheer audacity and authority' might serve to convert his maddened onrush into an unexpected victory (L 1244). Basically, however, he was beginning to feel thoroughly unnerved. He repeated with obvious sympathy a remark by Robertet to the effect that Julius appeared 'to have been ordained by the Almighty for the destruction of the world' (L 1270). And he added with unaccustomed solemnity that the pope did indeed 'seem bent on the ruin of Christianity and the accomplishment of Italy's collapse' (L 1257).

This account of the pope's progress reappears virtually unaltered in the pages of *The Prince*. Machiavelli first concedes that, although Julius 'proceeded impetuously in all his affairs', he 'was always successful' even in his most unrealistic enterprises. But he goes on to argue that this was merely because 'the times and their circumstances' were 'so in harmony with his own way of proceeding' that he never had to pay the due penalty for his recklessness. Despite the pope's startling successes, Machiavelli accordingly feels justified in taking an extremely unfavourable view of his statecraft. Admittedly Julius 'accomplished with his impetuous movement what no other pontiff, with the utmost human prudence, would ever have accomplished'. But it was only due to 'the shortness of his life' that we are left with the impression that he must have been a great leader of men. 'If times had come when he needed to proceed with caution, they would have brought about his downfall; for never would he have turned away from those methods to which his nature inclined him' (91–2).

Between his papal legation of 1506 and his return to France in 1510, Machiavelli went on one further mission outside Italy, in the course of which he was able to appraise yet another prominent ruler at first hand—Maximilian, the Holy Roman Emperor. The *signoria*'s decision to send this embassy arose out of its concern about the emperor's plan to march into Italy and have himself crowned at Rome. Announcing this intention, he demanded a large subsidy from the Florentines to help him overcome his chronic lack of funds. The *signoria* felt anxious to oblige him if he were indeed coming; but not if not. So was he in fact going to come? In June 1507 Francesco Vettori was dispatched to find out the answer, but reported in such confusing terms that Machiavelli was sent after him with additional instructions six months later. Both men remained at the imperial court until June of the following year, by which time the proposed expedition had definitely been called off.

Machiavelli's comments on the head of the house of Hapsburg contain none of the nuances or qualifications that characterise his descriptions of Cesare Borgia and Julius II. From first to last the emperor struck Machiavelli as a totally inept ruler, with scarcely any of the right qualifications for conducting an effective government. His basic weakness, Machiavelli felt, was a tendency to be 'altogether too lax and credulous', as a result of which 'he has a constant readiness to be influenced by every different opinion' put to him (L 1098–9). This makes it impossible to conduct negotiations, for even when he begins by deciding on a course of action—as with the expedition to Italy—it is still safe to say that 'God alone knows how it will end' (L 1139). It also makes for hopelessly enfeebled leadership, because everyone is left 'in continuing confusion' and 'nobody knows what he will do at all' (L 1106).

Machiavelli's portrait of the emperor in *The Prince* largely reproduces these earlier judgements. Maximilian is discussed in the course of chapter 23, the theme of which is the need for princes to listen to good advice. The emperor's conduct is treated as a cautionary tale about the dangers of failing to handle one's councillors with adequate decisiveness. Maximilian is described as so 'pliable' that, if ever his plans 'become generally known' and are then 'opposed by those around him', this throws him off course so completely that he is immediately 'pulled away from them'. This not only makes him frustrating to deal with, since 'no one ever knows what he wishes or intends to do'; it also makes him downright incompetent as a ruler, since 'it is impossible to rely' on any decisions he makes, and 'what he does one day he destroys the next' (87).

The lessons of diplomacy

By the time Machiavelli came to record his final verdicts on the rulers and statesmen he had met, he had reached the conclusion that there was one simple yet fundamental lesson which they had all misunderstood, as a result of which they had generally failed in their undertakings, or else had succeeded more by luck than sound political judgement. The basic weakness they all shared was a fatal inflexibility in the face of changing circumstances. Cesare Borgia was at all times overweening in his self-confidence; Maximilian was always cautious and overhesitant; Julius II was always impetuous and over-excited. What they all refused to recognise was that they would have been far more successful if they had sought to accommodate their personalities to the exigencies of the times, instead of trying to reshape their times in the mould of their personalities.

Machiavelli eventually placed this judgement at the very heart of his analysis of political leadership in *The Prince*. However, he first registered the insight much earlier, in the course of his active career as a diplomat. It is clear from his

23

Legations, moreover, that the generalisation first struck him less as a result of his own reflections than through listening to, and subsequently thinking about, the views of two of the shrewdest politicians with whom he came into contact. The point was first put to him on the day of Julius II's election to the pontificate. Machiavelli found himself drawn into conversation with Francesco Soderini, cardinal of Volterra and brother of Piero Soderini, the leader (*gonfaloniere*) of Florence's government. The cardinal assured him that 'not for many years has our city had so much to hope for from a new pope as from the present one'. 'But only', he added, 'if you know how to harmonise with the times' (L 593). Two years later, Machiavelli met with the same judgement in the course of negotiating with Pandolfo Petrucci, the lord of Siena, whom he was later to mention admiringly in *The Prince* as 'a very able man' (85). Machiavelli had been commissioned by the *signoria* to demand the reasons for 'all the tricks and intrigues' which had marked Pandolfo's dealings with Florence (L 911). Pandolfo responded with an effrontery that evidently impressed Machiavelli very much. 'Wishing to make as few mistakes as possible,' he replied, 'I conduct my government day by day, and arrange my affairs hour by hour; because the times are more powerful than our brains' (L 912).

Although Machiavelli's pronouncements on the rulers of his age are in general severely critical, it would be misleading to conclude that he regarded the entire record of contemporary statecraft as nothing more than a history of crimes, follies and misfortunes. At several points in his diplomatic career he was sble to watch a political problem being confronted and resolved in a manner that not only commanded his unequivocal admiration, but also exercised a clear influence on his own theories of political leadership. One such moment occurred in 1503, in the course of the protracted battle of wits between Cesare Borgia and the pope. Machiavelli was fascinated to see how Julius would cope with the dilemma raised by the duke's presence at the papal court. As he reminded the Ten of War, 'the hatred his holiness has always felt' for Borgia 'is well-known', but this hardly alters the fact that Borgia 'has been more help to him than anyone else' in securing his election, as a result of which he 'has made the duke a number of very large promises' (L 599). The problem seemed insoluble: how could Julius hope to achieve any freedom of action without at the same time violating his solemn pledge?

As Machiavelli quickly discovered, the answer came in two disarmingly simple stages. Before his elevation, Julius was careful to emphasise that, 'being a man of great good faith', he was absolutely bound 'to stay in contact' with Borgia 'in order to keep his word to him' (L 613, 621). But as soon as he felt secure, he instantly reneged on all his promises. He not only denied the duke his title and troops, but actually had him arrested and imprisoned him in the papal palace. Machiavelli is scarcely able to conceal his astonishment as well as admiration at the *coup*. 'See now', he exclaims, 'how honourably this pope begins to pay his debts: he simply cancels them by crossing them out.' Nor does anyone consider, he adds significantly, that the papacy has been disgraced; on the contrary, 'everybody continues with the same enthusiasm to bless the pope's hands' (L 683).

On this occasion Machiavelli felt disappointed with Borgia for allowing himself to be so ruinously outflanked. As he typically put it, the duke ought never to have supposed 'that the words of another are more to be relied on than his own' (L 600). Nevertheless, Borgia was undoubtedly the ruler whom Machiavelli found it most instructive to observe in action, and on two other occasions he was privileged to watch him confronting a dangerous crisis and surmounting it with a strength and assurance that earned him Machiavelli's complete respect.

The first of these emergencies arose in December 1502, when the people of the Romagna suddenly voiced their outrage at the oppressive methods used by Borgia's lieutenant, Rimirro de Orco, in pacifying the province in the previous year. Admittedly Rimirro had merely been executing the duke's orders, and had done so with conspicuous success, reducing the whole area from chaos to sound government. But his cruelty had stirred up so much hatred that the continuing stability of the province was now in jeopardy. What was Borgia to do? His solution

25

displayed a terrifying briskness, a quality that Machiavelli mirrors in his account of the episode. Rimirro was summoned to Imola, and four days later 'he was found in the public square, cut into two pieces, where his body still remains, so that the entire populace has been able to see it'. 'It has simply been the pleasure of the duke', Machiavelli adds, 'to show that he can make and unmake men as he wants, according to their deserts' (L 503).

The other point at which Borgia evoked Machiavelli's rather stunned admiration was in dealing with the military difficulties that developed in the Romagna at about the same time. At first the duke had been obliged to rely on the petty lords of the area for his chief military support. But in the summer of 1502 it became clear that their leaders—especially the Orsini and the Vitelli—were not only untrustworthy but were plotting against him. What should he do? His first move was simply to get rid of them by feigning reconciliation, summoning them to a meeting at Senigallia and murdering them *en masse*. For once Machiavelli's studied coolness deserts him as he describes the manoeuvre, and he admits to being 'lost in wonder at this development' (L 508). Next, Borgia resolved that in future he ought never to make use of such treacherous allies, but ought instead to raise his own troops. This policy—almost unheard of at a time when practically every Italian prince fought with hired mercenaries—seems to have struck Machiavelli at once as being an exceptionally far-sighted move. He reports with obvious approval that the duke has not only decided that 'one of the foundations of his power' must henceforth be 'his own arms', but has started the process of recruitment at an astonishing rate, 'having already conducted a review of five hundred men-at-arms and the same number of light cavalry' (L 419). Switching to his most admonitory style, he explains that he is 'writing this all the more willingly' because he has come to believe that 'anyone who is well-armed, and has his own soldiers, will always find himself in a position of advantage, however things may happen to turn out' (L 455).

By 1510, after a decade of missions abroad, Machiavelli had made up his mind about most of the statesmen he had met.

Only Julius II continued to some extent to puzzle him. On the one hand, the pope's declaration of war on France in 1510 struck Machiavelli as almost insanely irresponsible. It required no imagination to see that 'a state of enmity between these two powers' would be 'the most terrifying misfortune that could arise' from Florence's point of view (L 1273). On the other hand, he could not resist hoping that, by sheer impetuosity, Julius might yet prove to be the saviour rather than the scourge of Italy. At the end of the campaign against Bologna, Machiavelli permitted himself to wonder whether the pope might not 'go on to something greater', so that 'this time Italy really may find herself delivered from those who have planned to engulf her' (L 1028). Four years later, despite the worsening of the international crisis, he was still trying to fight off his growing fears with the reflection that, 'as in the case of Bologna', the pope might yet manage 'to carry everyone along with him' (L 1244).

Unfortunately for Machiavelli and for Florence, his fears yielded better predictions than his hopes. After being hard pressed in the fighting of 1511, Julius reacted by concluding an alliance that changed the entire face of Italy. On 4 October 1511 he signed the Holy League with Ferdinand of Spain, thereby winning Spanish military support for the crusade against France. As soon as the new campaigning season opened in 1512, the formidable Spanish infantry marched into Italy. First they pushed back the French advance, forcing them to evacuate Ravenna, Parma and Bologna and finally to retreat beyond Milan. Then they turned against Florence. The city had not dared defy the French, and had failed in consequence to declare its support for the pope. Now it found itself paying a costly penalty for its mistake. On 29 August the Spanish sacked the neighbouring town of Prato, and three days later the Florentines capitulated. The *gonfaloniere* Soderini fled into exile, the Medici re-entered the city after an absence of eighteen years, and a few weeks later the republic was dissolved.

Machiavelli's own fortunes collapsed with those of the republican regime. On 7 November he was formally dismissed from his post in the chancery. Three days later he was sentenced to confinement within Florentine territory for a year, the surety being the enormous sum of a thousand florins. Then in February 1513 came the worst blow of all. He was mistakenly suspected of taking part in an abortive conspiracy against the new Medicean government, and after being put to the torture he was condemned to imprisonment and the payment of a heavy fine. As he later complained to the Medici in the dedication to *The Prince*, 'Fortune's great and steady malice' had suddenly and viciously struck him down (11).

2 The adviser to princes

The Florentine context

Early in 1513 the Medici family scored its most brilliant triumph of all. On 22 February Cardinal Giovanni de' Medici set out for Rome after learning of Julius II's death, and on 11 March he emerged from the conclave of cardinals as pope Leo X. In one way this represented a further blow to Machiavelli's hopes, for it brought the new regime in Florence an unprecedented popularity. Giovanni was the first Florentine ever to become pope, and according to Luca Landucci, the contemporary diarist, the city celebrated with bonfires and ordnance for nearly a week. But in another way the development was an unexpected stroke of good fortune, for it prompted the government to declare an amnesty as part of the general rejoicing, and Machiavelli was freed.

As soon as he came out of prison, Machiavelli began scheming to recommend himself to the city's new authorities. His former colleague, Francesco Vettori, had been made ambassador to Rome, and Machiavelli repeatedly wrote urging him to use his influence 'so that I may begin to receive some employment from our lord the pope' (C 244), However, it soon became clear that Vettori was unable or perhaps unwilling to help. Greatly discouraged, Machiavelli withdrew to his little farm at Sant' Andrea, in order (as he wrote to Vettori) 'to be at a distance from every human face' (C 516). From there he began for the first time to contemplate the political scene less as a participant than as an analyst. First he sent long and powerfully argued letters to Vettori about the implications of the renewed French and Spanish interventions in Italy. And then—as he explained in a letter of 10 December—he started to beguile his enforced leisure by reflecting more systematically on his diplomatic experience, on the lessons of history, and hence on the rules of statecraft.

As Machiavelli complains in the same letter, he is reduced

to living 'in a poor house on a tiny patrimony'. But he is making life bearable by retreating to his study every evening and reading about classical history, 'entering the ancient courts of ancient men' in order 'to speak with them and ask them the reasons for their actions'. He has also been pondering the insights he acquired 'in the course of the fifteen years' when he 'was involved in studying the art of government'. The outcome, he says, is that 'I have composed a little book *On Principalities*, in which I delve as deeply as I can into discussions about this subject'. This 'little book' was Machiavelli's masterpiece, *The Prince*, which was drafted—as this letter indicates—in the second half of 1513, and completed by Christmas of that year (C 303–5).

Machiavelli's highest hope, as he confided to Vettori, was that his treatise might serve to bring him to the notice of 'our Medici lords' (C 305). One reason for wishing to draw attention to himself in this way—as his dedication to *The Prince* makes clear—was a desire to offer the Medici 'some proof that I am your loyal subject' (10). His worries on this score even seem to have impaired his normally objective standards of argument, for in chapter 20 of *The Prince* he maintains with great feeling that new rulers can expect to find 'more loyalty and more assistance in those men who in the beginning of their rule were considered dangerous than in those who in the beginning were trusted' (79). Since this contention is later flatly contradicted in the *Discourses* (236), it is hard not to feel that an element of special pleading has entered Machiavelli's analysis at this point, especially as he anxiously repeats that 'I must not fail to remind any prince' that 'more profit' can always be expected from 'men who were satisfied with the preceding government' than from anyone else (79).

Machiavelli's main concern, however, was of course to make it clear to the Medici that he was a man worth employing, an expert whom it would be foolish to overlook. He insists in his Dedication that 'in order to discern clearly' the nature of a prince, the observer cannot be a prince himself, but 'must be one of the populace'. With his usual confidence, he adds that his own reflections are likely, for two reasons, to be of exceptional value. He stresses the 'lengthy experience with recent matters' he has gained over 'many years' and with 'many troubles and perils'. And he points with pride to the theoretical mastery of statecraft he has acquired at the same time through his 'continual reading' of ancient histories—an indispensable source of wisdom 'which with close attention I have for a long time thought over and considered' (10–11).

What, then, does Machiavelli think he can teach princes in general, and the Medici in particular, as a result of his reading and experience? To anyone beginning *The Prince* at the beginning, he might appear to have little more to offer than a dry and overschematised analysis of types of principality and the means 'to gain and hold them' (46). In the opening chapter he starts by isolating the idea of 'dominion' and lays it down that all dominions 'are either republics or princedoms'. He immediately casts off the first term, remarking that for the moment he will omit any discussion of republics and concern himself exclusively with principalities. Next he offers the unremarkable observation that all princedoms are either hereditary or new ones. Again he discards the first term, arguing that hereditary rulers encounter fewer difficulties and correspondingly stand in less need of his advice. Focusing on new princedoms, he goes on to distinguish the 'wholly new' from those which 'are like members joined to the hereditary state of the prince who conquers them' (11–12). Here he is less interested in the latter class, and after three chapters on 'mixed princedoms' he moves on, in chapter 6, to the topic that clearly fascinates him most of all: that of 'completely new princedoms' (24). At this point he makes one further subdivision of his material, and at the same time introduces perhaps the most important antithesis in the whole of his political theory, the antithesis around which the argument of *The Prince* revolves. New princedoms, he declares, are either acquired and held 'through a man's own armies and his virtú', or else 'through other men's forces and through Fortune' (24, 27).

Turning to this final dichotomy, Machiavelli again exhibits less interest in the first possibility. He agrees that those who have risen to power through 'their own *virtú* and not through

Fortune' have been 'the most admirable leaders', and he instances 'Moses, Cyrus, Romulus, Theseus and the like'. But he is unable to think of any modern Italian examples (with the possible exception of Francesco Sforza) and the implication of his discussion is that such outstanding *virtú* is scarcely to be expected amid the corruption of the modern world (25). He accordingly concentrates on the case of princedoms acquired by Fortune and the aid of foreign arms. Here, by contrast, he finds modern Italy full of examples, the most instructive being that of Cesare Borgia, who 'gained his position through his father's Fortune', and whose career is 'worthy of imitation by all those' who become princes 'through Fortune and by means of another's forces' (28, 33).

This contention marks the end of Machiavelli's divisions and subdivisions, and brings us to the class of principalities with which he is pre-eminently concerned. By this stage it also becomes clear that, although he has taken care to present his argument as a sequence of neutral typologies, he has cunningly organised the discussion in such a way as to highlight one particular type of case, and has done so because of its local and personal significance. The situation in which the need for expert advice is said to be especially urgent is where a ruler has come to power by Fortune and foreign arms. No contemporary reader of *The Prince* could have failed to reflect that, at the point when Machiavelli was advancing this claim, the Medici had just regained their former ascendancy in Florence as the result of an astonishing stroke of good Fortune, combined with the unstoppable force of the foreign arms supplied by Ferdinand of Spain. This does not imply, of course, that Machiavelli's argument can be dismissed as having no more than parochial relevance. But it does appear that he intended his original readers to focus their attention on one particular time and place. The place was Florence; the time was the moment at which *The Prince* was being composed.

The classical heritage

When Machiavelli and his contemporaries felt impelled—as in 1512—to reflect on the immense power of Fortune in human affairs, they generally turned to the Roman historians and moralists to supply them with an authoritative analysis of the goddess's character. These writers had laid it down that, if a ruler owes his position to the intervention of Fortune, the first lesson he must learn is to fear the goddess, even when she comes bearing gifts. Livy had furnished a particularly influential statement of this claim in Book 30 of his *History*, in the course of describing the dramatic moment when Hannibal finally capitulates to the young Scipio. Hannibal begins his speech of surrender by remarking admiringly that his conqueror has so far been 'a man whom Fortune has never deceived'. But this merely prompts him to issue a grave warning about the place of Fortune in human affairs. Not only is 'the might of Fortune immense', but 'the greatest good Fortune is always least to be trusted'. If we depend on Fortune to raise us up, we are liable to fall 'the more terribly' when she turns against us, as she is almost certain to do in the end.

However, the Roman moralists never thought of Fortune as an inexorably malign force. On the contrary, they saw her as a good goddess, *bona dea*, and a potential ally whose attention it is well worth trying to attract. The reason for seeking her friendship is of course that she disposes of the goods of Fortune, which all men are assumed to desire. These goods themselves are variously described: Seneca emphasises 'honours, riches and influence'; Sallust prefers to single out 'glory, honour and power'. But it was generally agreed that, of all the gifts of Fortune, the greatest is honour and the glory that comes with it. As Cicero repeatedly stresses in *Moral Obligation*, man's highest good is 'the attainment of glory', 'the enhancement of personal honour and glory', the acquisition of the 'truest glory' that can be won.

The key question these writers accordingly raise is this: how can we persuade Fortune to look in our direction, to pour out the gifts from her cornucopia on us rather than on others? The answer is that, although Fortune is a goddess, she is still a woman; and since she is a woman, she is most of all attracted by the *vir*, the man of true manliness. One quality she especially likes to reward is thus held to be manly courage. Livy, ple, several times cites the adage that 'Fortune favours ve.' But the quality she admires most of all is *virtus*, the mous attribute of the truly manly man. The idea underl th this belief is most clearly set out in Cicero's *Tusculan Disputations*, in which he lays it down that the criterion for being a real man, a *vir*, is the possession of *virtus* in the highest degree. The implications of the argument are extensively explored in Livy's *History*, in which the successes won by the Romans are almost always explained in terms of the fact that Fortune likes to follow and even wait upon *virtus*, and generally smiles on those who exhibit it.

With the triumph of Christianity, this classical analysis of Fortune was entirely overthrown. The Christian view, most compellingly stated by Boethius in *The Consolation of Philosophy*, is based on denying the key assumption that Fortune is open to being influenced. The goddess is now depicted as 'a blind power', and hence as completely careless and indiscriminate in the bestowal of her gifts. She is no longer seen as a potential friend, but simply as a pitiless force; her symbol is no longer the cornucopia, but rather the wheel of change which turns inexorably 'like the ebb and flow of the tide'.

This new view of Fortune's nature went with a new sense of her significance. By her very carelessness and lack of concern for human merit in the disposition of her rewards, she is said to remind us that the goods of Fortune are completely unworthy of our pursuit, that the desire for worldly honour and glory is, as Boethius puts it, 'really nothing at all'. She serves in consequence to direct our footsteps away from the paths of glory, encouraging us to look beyond our earthly prison in order to seek our heavenly home. But this means that, in spite of her capricious tyranny, Fortune is genuinely an *ancilla dei*, an agent of God's benevolent providence. For it is part of God's design to show us that 'happiness cannot consist in the fortuitous things of this mortal life', and thus to make us 'despise all earthly affairs, and in the joy of heaven rejoice to be freed from earthly things'. It is for this reason, Boethius concludes, that God has placed the control of the world's goods in Fortune's feckless hands. His aim is to teach us 'that sufficiency cannot be obtained through wealth, nor power through kingship, nor respect through office, nor fame through glory'.

Boethius's reconciliation of Fortune with providence had an enduring influence on Italian literature: it underlies Dante's discussion of Fortune in canto VII of *The Inferno* and furnishes the theme of Petrarch's *Remedy of the Two Kinds of Fortune*. However, with the recovery of classical values in the Renaissance, this analysis of Fortune as an *ancilla dei* was in turn challenged by a return to the earlier suggestion that a distinction must be drawn between Fortune and fate.

This development originated in a changing view about the nature of man's peculiar 'excellence and dignity'. Traditionally this had been held to lie in his possession of an immortal soul, but in the work of Petrarch's successors we find a growing tendency to shift the emphasis in such a way as to highlight the freedom of the will. Man's freedom was felt to be threatened, however, by the concept of Fortune as an inexorable force. So we find a corresponding tendency to repudiate any suggestion that Fortune is merely an agent of providence. A striking example is provided by Pico della Mirandola's attack on the alleged science of astrology, a science he denounces for embodying the false assumption that our Fortunes are ineluctably assigned to us by the stars at the moment of our birth. A little later, we begin to encounter a widespread appeal to the far more optimistic view that—as Shakespeare makes Cassius say to Brutus—if we fail in our efforts to attain greatness, the fault must lie 'not in our stars but in our selves'.

By building on this new attitude to freedom, the humanists of fifteenth-century Italy were able to reconstruct the full classical image of Fortune's role in human affairs. We find it in Alberti, in Pontano's treatise *On Fortune*, and most remarkably of all in Aeneas Sylvius Piccolomini's tract of 1444 entitled *A Dream of Fortune*. The writer dreams that he is being guided through Fortune's kingdom, and that he encounters the goddess herself, who agrees to answer his questions. She admits to being wilful in the exercise of her powers, for when he inquires, 'How long do you remain kindly to men?' she replies 'To none for very long.' But she is far from heedless of human merit, and

35

does not deny the suggestion that 'there are arts by which it is possible for your favour to be gained'. Finally, when she is asked what qualities she particularly likes and dislikes, she responds with an allusion to the idea that Fortune favours the brave, declaring that 'those who lack courage are more hateful than anyone else'.

When Machiavelli comes to discuss 'Fortune's power in human affairs' in the penultimate chapter of *The Prince*, his handling of this crucial theme reveals him to be a typical representative of humanist attitudes. He opens his chapter by invoking the familiar belief that men are 'controlled by Fortune and by God', and by noting the apparent implication that 'men have no recourse against the world's variations', since everything is providentially foreordained (89). In contrast to these Christian assumptions he immediately offers a classical analysis of human liberty. He concedes, of course, that man's freedom is far from absolute, since Fortune is immensely powerful, and 'may be mistress of one half our actions'. But he insists that to suppose our fate to be entirely in her hands would be 'to annul our free will'. And since he holds firmly to the humanist view that 'God does not do everything, so as not to take from us free will and part of the glory that pertains to us', he concludes that half our actions 'or almost' must be genuinely under our control rather than under Fortune's sway (90, 94).

Machiavelli's most graphic image for this sense of man as the master of his fate is again classical in inspiration. He stresses that 'Fortune is a woman' and is in consequence readily allured by manly qualities (92). So he sees a genuine possibility of making oneself the ally of Fortune, of learning to act in harmony with her powers, neutralising her varying nature and thus remaining successful in all one's affairs (83, 92).

This brings Machiavelli to the key question the Roman moralists had originally posed: how can we hope to forge an alliance with Fortune, how can we induce her to smile on us? He answers in precisely the terms they had already used. He stresses that 'she is the friend' of the brave, of those who are 'less cautious, more spirited'. And he develops the idea that she

is chiefly excited by, and responsive to, the *virtus* of the true
vir. First he makes the negative point that she is most of all
driven to rage and hatred by lack of *virtú*. Just as the presence
of *virtú* acts as an embankment against her onrush, so she
always 'directs her fury where she knows that no dykes or
embankments are ready to hold her'. He even goes so far as to
suggest that she only shows her power when men of *virtú* fail
to stand up to her—the implication being that she so greatly
admires the quality that she never vents her most lethal spite
on those who exhibit it (90–2).

As well as reiterating these classical arguments, Machiavelli
gives them an unusual erotic twist. He implies that Fortune
may actually take a perverse pleasure in being roughly handled.
He not only claims that, because she is a woman, 'it is
necessary, in order to keep her under, to cuff and maul her'; he
adds that she 'more often lets herself be overcome by men
using such methods than by those who proceed coldly' (92).

The suggestion that men may be able to take advantage of
Fortune in this way has sometimes been presented as a peculiarly Machiavellian insight. But even here Machiavelli is in
fact drawing on a stock of familiar imagery. The idea that
Fortune must be opposed with violence had been emphasised
by Seneca, while Piccolomini in his *Dream of Fortune* had even
gone on to explore the erotic overtones of the belief. When he
asks Fortune 'Who is able to hold on to you more than others?'
she confesses that she is most of all attracted by men 'who
keep my power in check with the greatest spirit'. And when he
finally dares to ask 'Who is most acceptable to you among the
living?', she tells him that, while she views with contempt
'those who run away from me', she is most aroused 'by those
who put me to flight'.

If men are capable of curbing Fortune and thus of attaining
their highest goals, the next question to ask must be what goals
a new prince should set himself. Machiavelli begins by stating
a minimum condition, using a phrase that echoes throughout
The Prince. The basic aim must be *mantenere lo stato*, by
which he means that a new ruler must preserve the existing
state of affairs, and especially keep control of the prevailing

system of government. As well as sheer survival, however, there are far greater ends to be pursued; and in specifying what these are, Machiavelli again reveals himself to be a true heir of the Roman historians and moralists. He assumes that all men want above all to acquire the goods of Fortune. So he totally ignores the orthodox Christian injunction (emphasised, for example, by St Thomas Aquinas in *The Government of Princes*) that a good ruler ought to avoid the temptations of worldly glory and wealth in order to be sure of attaining his heavenly rewards. On the contrary, it seems obvious to Machiavelli that the highest prizes for which men are bound to compete are 'glory and riches'—the two finest gifts that Fortune has it in her power to bestow (91).

Like the Roman moralists, however, Machiavelli sets aside the acquisition of riches as a base pursuit, and argues that the noblest aim for a 'prudent and *virtuoso*' prince must be to introduce a form of government 'that will bring him honour' and make him glorious (93). For new rulers, he adds, there is even the possibility of winning a 'double glory': they not only have the chance 'to begin a new princedom', but also to 'strengthen it with good laws, good arms and good examples' (88). The attainment of worldly honour and glory is thus the highest goal for Machiavelli no less than for Livy or Cicero. When he asks himself in the final chapter of *The Prince* whether the condition of Italy is conducive to the success of a new ruler, he treats this as equivalent to asking 'whether at present in Italy conditions so unite as to offer a new prince honour' (92). And when he expresses his admiration for Ferdinand of Spain whom he respects most of all among contemporary statesmen the reason he gives is that Ferdinand has done 'great things' of such a character as to bring him 'fame and glory' in a high degree (81).

These goals, Machiavelli thinks, are not especially difficult to attain—at least in their minimum form—where a prince has inherited a dominion 'accustomed to the family of one ruler' (12). But they are very hard for a new prince to achieve, particularly if he owes his position to a stroke of good Fortune. Such rulers 'cannot have roots', and are liable to be blown away by the first unfavourable weather that Fortune chooses to send them (28). And they cannot—or rather, they emphatically must not—place any trust in Fortune's continuing benevolence, for this is to rely on the most unreliable force in human affairs (28). For Machiavelli, the next—and the most crucial—question is accordingly this: what maxims, what precepts, can be offered to a new ruler such that, if they are 'carried out prudently', they will make him 'seem an old one' (88)? It is with the answer to this question that the rest of *The Prince* is chiefly concerned.

The Machiavellian revolution

Machiavelli's advice to new princes comes in two main parts. His first and fundamental point is that 'the principal foundations of all states' are 'good laws and good armies'. Moreover, good armies are even more important than good laws, because 'there cannot be good laws where armies are not good', whereas if there are good armies, 'there must be good laws' (47). The moral—put with a typical touch of exaggeration—is that a wise prince should have 'no other object and no other interest' than 'war and its laws and discipline' (55).

Machiavelli goes on to specify that armies are basically of two types: hired mercenaries and citizen militias. In Italy the mercenary system was almost universally employed, but Machiavelli proceeds in chapter 12 to launch an all-out attack on it. 'For many years' the Italians 'have been ruled by mercenary generals' and the results have been appalling: the entire peninsula 'has been overrun by Charles, plundered by Louis, violated by Ferdinand and insulted by the Swiss' (50). Nor could anything better have been expected, for all mercenaries 'are useless and dangerous'. They are 'disunited, ambitious, without discipline, disloyal' and their capacity to ruin you 'is postponed only as long as attack on you is postponed' (47). To Machiavelli the implications are obvious, and he states them with great force in chapter 13. Wise princes will always 'reject these armies and turn to their own'. So strongly does he feel this that he even adds the almost absurd claim that they will 'choose rather to lose with their own soldiers than to win with the others' (52).

Such an intense vehemence of tone stands in need of some explanation, especially in view of the fact that most historians have concluded that the mercenary system usually worked quite effectively. One possibility is that Machiavelli was simply following a literary tradition at this point. The contention that true citizenship involves the bearing of arms had been emphasised by Livy and Polybius as well as Aristotle, and taken over by several generations of Florentine humanists after Leonardo Bruni and his disciples had revived the argument. It would be very unusual, however, for Machiavelli to follow even his most cherished authorities in such a slavish way. It seems more likely that, although he mounts a general attack on hired soldiers, he may have been thinking in particular about the misfortunes of his native city, which undoubtedly suffered a series of humiliations at the hands of its mercenary commanders in the course of the protracted war against Pisa. Not only was the campaign of 1500 a complete disaster, but a similar fiasco resulted when Florence launched a fresh offensive in 1505: the captains of ten mercenary companies mutinied as soon as the assault began, and within a week it had to be abandoned.

As we have seen, Machiavelli had been shocked to discover, at the time of the 1500 débâcle, that the French regarded the Florentines with derision because of their military incompetence, and especially because of their inability to reduce Pisa to obedience. After the renewed failure of 1505, he took the matter into his own hands and drew up a detailed plan for the replacement of Florence's hired troops with a citizen militia. The great council provisionally accepted the idea in December 1505, and Machiavelli was authorised to begin recruiting in Tuscan Romagna. By the following February he was ready to hold his first parade in the city, an occasion watched with great admiration by the diarist Luca Landucci, who recorded that 'this was thought the finest thing that had ever been arranged for Florence'. During the summer of 1506 Machiavelli wrote *A Provision for infantry*, emphasising 'how little hope it is possible to place in foreign and hired arms', and arguing that the city ought instead to be 'armed with her own weapons and with her own men' (3). By the end of the year, the great council was finally convinced. A new government committee—the Nine of the Militia—was set up, Machiavelli was elected its secretary, and one of the most cherished ideals of Florentine humanism became a reality.

One might have supposed that Machiavelli's ardour for his militia-men would have cooled as a result of their disastrous showing in 1512, when they were sent to defend Prato and were effortlessly brushed aside by the advancing Spanish infantry. But in fact his enthusiasm remained undimmed. A year later, we find him assuring the Medici at the end of *The Prince* that what they must do 'before all other things' is to equip Florence 'with her own armies' (95). When he published his *Art of War* in 1521—his only work of political theory to appear during his lifetime—he continued to reiterate the same arguments. The whole of Book I is given over to vindicating 'the method of the citizen army' against those who have doubted its usefulness (580). Machiavelli allows, of course, that such troops are far from invincible, but he still insists on their superiority over any other type of force (585). He concludes with the extravagant assertion that to speak of a wise man finding fault with the idea of a citizen army is simply to utter a contradiction (583).

We can now understand why Machiavelli felt so impressed by Cesare Borgia as a military commander, and asserted in *The Prince* that no better precepts could be offered to a new ruler than the example of the duke's conduct (29). For Machiavelli had been present, as we have seen, when the duke made the ruthless decision to eliminate his mercenary lieutenants and replace them with his own troops. This daring strategy appears to have had a decisive impact on the formation of Machiavelli's ideas. He reverts to it as soon as he raises the question of military policy in chapter 13 of *The Prince*, treating it as an exemplary illustration of the measures that any new ruler ought to adopt. Borgia is first of all praised for having recognised without hesitation that mercenaries are 'uncertain and unfaithful' and deserve to be mercilessly 'wiped out'. And he is even more fulsomely commended for having grasped the basic lesson that any new prince needs to learn if he wishes to maintain his state: he must stop relying on Fortune and foreign arms, raise 'soldiers of his own' and make himself 'sole master of his own troops' (53, cf. 31).

Arms and the man: these are Machiavelli's two great themes in *The Prince*. The other lesson he accordingly wishes to bring home to the rulers of his age is that, in addition to having a sound army, a prince who aims to scale the heights of glory must cultivate the right qualities of princely leadership. The nature of these qualities had already been influentially analysed by the Roman moralists. They had argued in the first place that all great leaders need to some extent to be fortunate. For unless Fortune happens to smile, no amount of unaided human effort can hope to bring us to our highest goals. As we have seen, however, they also maintained that a special range of characteristics—those of the *vir*—tend to attract the favourable attentions of Fortune, and in this way almost guarantee us the attainment of honour, glory and fame. The assumptions underlying this belief are best summarised by Cicero in his *Tusculan Disputations*. He declares that, if we act from a thirst for *virtus* without any thought of winning glory as a result, this will give us the best chance of winning glory as well, provided that Fortune smiles; for glory is *virtus* rewarded.

This analysis was taken over without alteration by the humanists of Renaissance Italy. By the end of the fifteenth century, an extensive *genre* of humanist advice-books for princes had grown up, and had reached an unprecedentedly wide audience through the new medium of print. Such distinguished writers as Bartolomeo Sacchi, Giovanni Pontano and Francesco Patrizi all wrote treatises for the guidance of new rulers, all of which were founded on the same basic principle: that the possession of *virtus* is the key to princely success. As Pontano rather grandly proclaims in his tract on *The Prince*, any ruler who wishes to attain his noblest ends 'must rouse himself to follow the dictates of *virtus*' in all his public acts. *Virtus* is 'the most splendid thing in the world', more magnificent even than the sun, for 'the blind cannot see the sun' whereas 'even they can see *virtus* as plainly as possible'.

Machiavelli reiterates precisely the same beliefs about the relations between *virtú*, Fortune and the achievement of princely goals. He first makes these humanist allegiances clear in chapter 6 of *The Prince*, where he argues that 'in princedoms wholly new, where the prince is new, there is more or less difficulty in keeping them, according as the prince who acquires them is more or less *virtuoso*' (25). This is later corroborated in chapter 24, the aim of which is to explain 'Why the princes of Italy have lost their states' (88). Machiavelli insists that they 'should not blame Fortune' for their disgrace, because 'she only shows her power' when men of *virtú* 'do not prepare to resist her' (89–90). Their losses are simply due to their failure to recognise that 'those defences alone are good' which 'depend on yourself and your own *virtú*' (89). Finally, the role of *virtú* is again underlined in chapter 26, the impassioned 'Exhortation' to liberate Italy that brings *The Prince* to an end. At this point Machiavelli reverts to the incomparable leaders mentioned in chapter 6 for their 'amazing *virtú*'— Moses, Cyrus and Theseus. He implies that nothing less than a union of their astonishing abilities with the greatest good Fortune will enable Italy to be saved. And he adds—in an uncharacteristic moment of preposterous flattery—that the 'glorious family' of the Medici luckily possess all the requisite qualities: they have tremendous *virtú*; they are immensely favoured by Fortune; and they are no less 'favoured by God and by the Church' (93).

It is often complained that Machiavelli fails to provide any definition of *virtú*, and even that (as Whitfield puts it) he is 'innocent of any systematic use of the word'. But it will now be evident that he uses the term with complete consistency. Following his classical and humanist authorities, he treats it as that quality which enables a prince to withstand the blows of Fortune, to attract the goddess's favour, and to rise in consequence to the heights of princely fame, winning honour and glory for himself and security for his government.

It still remains, however, to consider what particular characteristics are to be expected in a man of *virtuoso* capacities. The Roman moralists had bequeathed a complex analysis of the concept of *virtus*, generally picturing the true *vir* as the possessor of three distinct yet affiliated sets of qualities. They took him to be endowed in the first place with the four 'cardinal' virtues of wisdom, justice, courage and temperance—the virtues that Cicero (following Plato) begins by singling out in the opening sections of *Moral Obligation*. But they also credited him with an additional range of qualities that later came to be regarded as peculiarly 'princely' in nature. The chief of these—the pivotal virtue of Cicero's *Moral Obligation*—was what Cicero called 'honesty', meaning a willingness to keep faith and deal honourably with all men at all times. This was felt to need supplementing by two further attributes, both of which were described in *Moral Obligation*, but were more extensively analysed by Seneca, who devoted special treatises to each of them. One was princely magnanimity, the theme of Seneca's *On Mercy*; the other was liberality, one of the major topics discussed in Seneca's *On Benefits*. Finally, the true *vir* was said to be characterised by his steady recognition of the fact that, if we wish to reach the goals of honour and glory, we must always be sure to behave as virtuously as possible. This contention —that it is always rational to be moral—lies at the heart of Cicero's *Moral Obligation*. He observes in Book II that many men believe 'that a thing may be morally right without being expedient, and expedient without being morally right'. But this is an illusion, for it is only by moral methods that we can hope to attain the objects of our desires. Any appearances to the contrary are wholly deceptive, for 'expediency can never conflict with moral rectitude'.

This analysis was again adopted in its entirety by the writers of advice-books for Renaissance princes. They made it their governing assumption that the general concept of *virtus* must refer to the complete list of cardinal and princely virtues, a list they proceeded to amplify and subdivide with so much attention to nuance that, in a treatise such as Patrizi's on *The Education of the King*, the overarching idea of *virtus* is eventually separated out into a series of some forty moral virtues which the ruler is expected to acquire. Next, they unhesitatingly endorsed the contention that the rational course of action for the prince to follow will always be the moral one, arguing the point with so much force that they eventually made it proverbial to say that 'honesty is the best policy'. And finally, they contributed a specifically Christian objection to any divorce between expediency and the moral realm. They insisted that, even if we succeed in advancing our interests by perpetrating injustices in this present life, we can still expect to find these apparent advantages cancelled out when we are justly visited with divine retribution in the life to come.

If we examine the moral treatises of Machiavelli's contemporaries we find these arguments tirelessly reiterated. But when we turn to *The Prince* we find this aspect of humanist morality suddenly and violently overturned. The upheaval begins in chapter 15, when Machiavelli starts to discuss the princely virtues and vices, and warns us that although 'many have written about this' already, he is going to 'depart very far from the methods of the others' (57). He begins by alluding to the familiar humanist commonplaces: that there is a special group of princely virtues; that these include the need to be liberal, merciful and truthful; and that all rulers have a duty to cultivate these qualities. Next he concedes—still in orthodox humanist vein—that 'it would be most praiseworthy for a prince' to be able at all times to act in such ways. But then he totally rejects the fundamental humanist assumption that these are the virtues a ruler needs to acquire if he wishes to achieve his highest ends. This belief—the nerve and heart of humanist advice-books for princes—he regards as an obvious and disastrous mistake. He agrees of course about the nature of the ends to be pursued: every prince must seek to maintain his state and obtain glory for himself. But he objects that, if these goals are to be attained, no ruler can possibly 'possess or fully practise' all the qualities that are usually 'considered good'. The position in which any prince finds himself is that of trying to protect his interests in a dark world in which most men 'are not good'. It follows that, if he 'insists on making it his business to be good' among so many who are not, he will not only fail to achieve 'great things' but 'will surely be destroyed' (58).

Machiavelli's criticism of classical and contemporary humanism is thus a simple but devastating one. He argues that, if a ruler wishes to reach his highest goals, he will *not* always find it rational to be moral; on the contrary, he will find that any consistent attempt to 'practise all those things for which men are considered good' will prove a ruinously irrational policy (66). But what of the Christian objection that this is a foolish as well as a wicked position to adopt, since it forgets the day of judgement on which all injustices will finally be punished? About this Machiavelli says nothing at all. His silence is eloquent, indeed epoch-making; it echoed around Christian Europe, at first eliciting a stunned silence in return, and then a howl of execration that has never finally died away.

If princes ought not to conduct themselves according to the dictates of conventional morality, how ought they to conduct themselves? Machiavelli's response—the core of his positive advice to new rulers—is given at the beginning of chapter 15. A wise prince will be guided above all by the dictates of necessity: 'in order to hold his position', he 'must acquire the power to be not good, and understand when to use it and when not to use it' as circumstances direct (58). Three chapters later, this basic doctrine is repeated. A wise prince 'holds to what is right when he can', but he 'knows how to do wrong when this is necessitated'. Moreover, he must reconcile himself to the fact that 'he will often be necessitated' to act 'contrary to truth, contrary to charity, contrary to humanity, contrary to religion' if he wishes 'to maintain his government' (66).

As we have seen, the crucial importance of this insight was first put to Machiavelli at an early stage in his diplomatic career. It was after conversing with the cardinal of Volterra in 1503, and with Pandolfo Petrucci some two years later, that he originally felt impelled to record what was later to become his central political belief: that the clue to successful statecraft lies in recognising the force of circumstances, accepting what necessity dictates, and harmonising one's behaviour with the times. A year after Pandolfo gave him this recipe for princely success, we find Machiavelli putting forward a similar set of observations as his own ideas for the first time. While stationed at Perugia in September 1506, watching the astonishing progress of Julius II's campaign, he fell to musing in a letter to his friend Giovan Soderini about the reasons for triumph and disaster in civil and military affairs. 'Nature', he declares, 'has given every man a particular talent and inspiration' which 'controls each one of us'. But 'the times are varied' and 'subject to frequent change', so that 'those who fail to alter their ways of proceeding' are bound to encounter 'good Fortune at one time and bad at another'. The moral is obvious: if a man wishes 'always to enjoy good Fortune', he must 'be wise enough to accommodate himself to the times'. Indeed, if everyone were 'to command his nature' in this way, and 'match his way of proceeding with his age', then 'it would genuinely come true that the wise man would be the ruler of the stars and of the fates' (73).

Writing *The Prince* seven years later, Machiavelli virtually copied out these 'Caprices', as he deprecatingly called them, in his chapter on the role of Fortune in human affairs. Everyone, he says, likes to follow his own particular bent: one person acts 'with caution, another impetuously; one by force, the other with skill'. But in the meantime, 'times and affairs change', so that a ruler who 'does not change his way of proceeding' will be bound sooner or later to encounter ill-luck. However, if 'he could change his nature with times and affairs, Fortune would not change'. So the successful prince will always be the one 'who adapts his way of proceeding to the nature of the times' (90–1).

By now it will be evident that the revolution Machiavelli engineered in the *genre* of advice-books for princes was based in effect on redefining the pivotal concept of *virtú*. He endorses the conventional assumption that *virtú* is the name of that congeries of qualities which enables a prince to ally with Fortune and obtain honour, glory and fame. But he divorces the meaning of the term from any necessary connection with the cardinal and princely virtues. He argues instead that the defining characteristic of a truly *virtuoso* prince will be a willingness to do whatever is dictated by necessity—whether the action happens to be wicked or virtuous—in order to attain his highest ends. So *virtù* comes to denote precisely the requisite quality of moral flexibility in a prince: 'he must have a mind ready to turn in any direction as Fortune's winds and the variability of affairs require' (66).

Machiavelli takes some pains to point out that this conclusion opens up an unbridgeable gulf between himself and the whole tradition of humanist political thought, and does so in his most savagely ironic style. To the classical moralists and their innumerable followers, moral virtue had been the defining characteristic of the *vir*, the man of true manliness. Hence to abandon virtue was not merely to act irrationally; it was also to abandon one's status as a man and descend to the level of the beasts. As Cicero had put it in Book I of *Moral Obligation*, there are two ways in which wrong may be done, either by force or by fraud. Both, he declares, 'are bestial' and 'wholly unworthy of man'—force because it typifies the lion and fraud because it 'seems to belong to the cunning fox'.

To Machiavelli, by contrast, it seemed obvious that manliness is not enough. There are indeed two ways of acting, he says at the start of chapter 18, of which 'the first is suited to man, the second to the animals'. But 'because the first is often not sufficient, a prince must resort to the second' (64). One of the things a prince therefore needs to know is which animals to imitate. Machiavelli's celebrated advice is that he will come off best if he 'chooses among the beasts the fox and the lion', supplementing the ideals of manly decency with the indispensable arts of force and fraud (65). This conception is underlined in the next chapter, in which Machiavelli discusses one of his favourite historical characters, the Roman emperor Septimius Severus. First he assures us that the emperor was 'a man of very great *virtù*' (72). And then, explaining the judgement, he adds that Septimius' great qualities were those of 'a very savage lion and a very tricky fox', as a result of which he was 'feared and respected by everybody' (73).

Machiavelli rounds off his analysis by indicating the lines of conduct to be expected from a truly *virtuoso* prince. In chapter 19 he puts the point negatively, stressing that such a ruler will never do anything worthy of contempt, and will always take the greatest care 'to avoid everything that makes him hated' (67). In chapter 21 the positive implications are then spelled out. Such a prince will always act 'without reservation' towards his allies and enemies, boldly standing forth 'as a vigorous supporter of one side'. At the same time, he will seek to present himself to his subjects as majestically as possible, doing 'extra- ordinary things' and keeping them 'always in suspense and wonder, watching for the outcome' (81–3).

In the light of this account, it is easy to understand why Machiavelli felt such admiration for Cesare Borgia, and wished to hold him up—despite his obvious limitations—as a pattern of *virtú* for other new princes. For Borgis had demonstrated, on one terrifying occasion, that he understood perfectly the para- mount importance of avoiding the hatred of the people while at the same time keeping them in awe. The occasion was when he realised that his government of the Romagna, in the capable but tyrannical hands of Rimirro de Orco, was falling into the most serious danger of all, that of becoming an object of hatred to those living under it. As we have seen, Machiavelli was an eye-witness of Borgia's cold-blooded solution to the dilemma: the summary murder of Rimirro and the exhibition of his body in the public square as a sacrifice to the people's rage.

Machiavelli's belief in the imperative need to avoid popular hatred and contempt should perhaps be dated from this moment. But even if the duke's action merely served to corroborate his own sense of political realities, there is no doubt that the episode left him deeply impressed. When he came to discuss the issues of hatred and contempt in *The Prince*, this was precisely the incident he recalled in order to illustrate his point. He makes it clear that Borgia's action had struck him on reflection as being profoundly right. It was resolute; it took courage; and it brought about exactly the desired effect, since it left the people 'gratified and awestruck' while at the same time removing their 'cause for hatred'.

Summing up in his iciest tones, Machiavelli remarks that the duke's conduct seems to him, as usual, to be 'worthy of notice and of being copied by others (31).

The new morality

Machiavelli is fully aware that his new analysis of princely *virtú* raises some new difficulties. He states the main dilemma in the course of chapter 15: on the one hand, a prince must 'acquire the power to be not good' and exercise it whenever this is dictated by necessity; but on the other hand, he must be careful not to acquire the reputation of being a wicked man, because this will tend to 'take his position away from him' instead of securing it (58). The problem is thus to avoid appearing wicked even when you cannot avoid behaving wickedly.

Moreover, the dilemma is even sharper than this implies, for the true aim of the prince is not merely to secure his position, but is of course to win honour and glory as well. As Machiavelli indicates in recounting the story of Agathocles, the tyrant of Sicily, this greatly intensifies the predicament in which any new ruler finds himself. Agathocles, we are told, 'lived a wicked life' at every stage of his career and was known as a man of 'outrageous cruelty and inhumanity'. These attributes brought him immense success, enabling him to rise from 'low and abject Fortune' to become king of Syracuse and hold on to his principality 'without any opposition from the citizens'. But as Machiavelli warns us, in a deeply revealing phrase, such unashamed cruelties may bring us 'sovereignty, but not glory'. Although Agathocles was able to maintain his state by means of these qualities, 'they cannot be called *virtú*' and they 'do not permit him to be honoured among the noblest men' (35–6).

Finally, Machiavelli refuses to admit that the dilemma can be resolved by setting stringent limits to princely wickedness, and in general behaving honourably towards one's subjects and allies. This is exactly what one cannot hope to do, because all men at all times 'are ungrateful, changeable, simulators and dissimulators, runaways in danger, eager for gain', so that 'a prince who bases himself entirely on their word, if he is lacking in other preparations, falls' (62). The implication is that 'a prince, and above all a prince who is new' will often—not just occasionally—find himself forced by necessity to act 'contrary to humanity' if he wishes to keep his position and avoid being deceived (66).

These are acute difficulties, but they can certainly be overcome. The prince need only remember that, although it is not necessary to have all the qualities usually considered good, it is 'very necessary to appear to have them' (66). It is good to be considered liberal; it is sensible to seem merciful and not cruel; it is essential in general to be 'thought to be of great merit' (59, 61, 68). The solution is thus to become 'a great simulator and dissimulator', learning 'how to addle the brains of men with trickery' and make them believe in your pretence (64–5).

Machiavelli had received an early lesson in the value of addling men's brains. As we have seen, he had been present when the struggle developed between Cesare Borgia and Julius II in the closing months of 1503, and it is evident that the impressions he carried away from that occasion were still uppermost in his mind when he came to write about the question of dissimulation in *The Prince*. He immediately refers back to the episode he had witnessed, using it as his main example of the need to remain constantly on one's guard against princely duplicity. Julius, he recalls, managed to conceal his hatred of Borgia so cleverly that he caused the duke to fall into the egregious error of believing that 'men of high rank forget old injuries'. He was then able to put his powers of dissimulation to decisive use. Having won the papal election with Borgia's full support, he suddenly revealed his true feelings, turned against the duke and 'caused his final ruin'. Borgia certainly blundered at this point, and Machiavelli feels that he deserved to be blamed severely for his mistake. He ought to have known that a talent for addling men's brains is part of the armoury of any successful prince (34).

Machiavelli cannot have been unaware, however, that in recommending the arts of deceit as the key to success he was in danger of sounding too glib. More orthodox moralists had always been prepared to consider the suggestion that hypocrisy

51

might be used as a short cut to glory, but had always gone on to rule out any such possibility. Cicero, for example, had explicitly canvassed the idea in Book II of *Moral Obligation*, only to dismiss it as a manifest absurdity. Anyone, he declares, who 'thinks that he can win lasting glory by pretence' is 'very much mistaken'. The reason is that 'true glory strikes deep roots and spreads its branches wide', whereas 'all pretences soon fall to the ground like fragile flowers'.

Machiavelli responds, as before, by rejecting such earnest sentiments in his most ironic style. He insists in chapter 18 that the practice of hypocrisy is not merely indispensable to princely government, but is capable of being sustained without much difficulty for as long as may be required. Two distinct reasons are offered for this deliberately provocative conclusion. One is that most men are so simple-minded, and above all so prone to self-deception, that they usually take things at face value in a wholly uncritical way (65). The other is that, when it comes to assessing the behaviour of princes, even the shrewdest observers are largely condemned to judge by appearances. Isolated from the populace, protected by 'the majesty of the government', the prince's position is such that 'everybody sees what you appear to be' but 'few perceive what you are' (67). Thus there is no reason to suppose that your sins will find you out; on the contrary, 'a prince who deceives always finds men who let themselves be deceived' (65).

The final issue Machiavelli discusses is what attitude we should take towards the new rules he has sought to inculcate. At first sight he appears to adopt a relatively conventional moral stance. He agrees in chapter 15 that 'it would be most praiseworthy' for new princes to exhibit those qualities which are normally considered good, and he equates the abandonment of the princely virtues with the process of learning 'to be not good' (58). The same scale of values recurs even in the notorious chapter on 'How princes should keep their promises'. Machiavelli begins by affirming that everybody realises how praiseworthy it is when a ruler 'lives with sincerity and not with trickery', and goes on to insist that a prince ought not merely to seem conventionally virtuous, but ought 'actually to be so' as far as possible, 'holding to what is right when he can', and only turning away from the virtues when this is dictated by necessity (64, 66).

However, two very different arguments are introduced in the course of chapter 15, each of which is subsequently developed. First of all, Machiavelli is somewhat quizzical about whether we can properly say that those qualities which are considered good, but are nevertheless ruinous, really deserve the name of virtues. Since they are prone to bring destruction, he prefers to say that they 'look like virtues'; and since their opposites are more likely to bring 'safety and well-being', he prefers to say that they 'look like vices' (59).

This suggestion is pursued in both the succeeding chapters. Chapter 16, entitled 'Liberality and stinginess', picks up a theme handled by all the classical moralists and turns it on its head. When Cicero discusses the virtue of liberality in *Moral Obligation*, he defines it as a desire to 'avoid any suspicion of penuriousness', together with an awareness that no vice is more offensive in a political leader than parsimony and avarice. Machiavelli replies that, if this is what we mean by liberality, it is the name not of a virtue but of a vice. He argues that a ruler who wishes to avoid a reputation for parsimony will find that he 'cannot neglect any kind of lavishness'. As a result, he will find himself having 'to burden his people excessively' to pay for his generosity, a policy which will soon make him 'hateful to his subjects'. Conversely, if he begins by abandoning any desire to act with such munificence, he may well be called miserly at the outset, but 'in course of time he will be thought more and more liberal', and will in fact be practising the true virtue of liberality (59).

A similar paradox appears in the following chapter, entitled 'Cruelty and mercy'. This too had been a favourite topic among the Roman moralists, Seneca's essay *On Mercy* being the most celebrated treatment of the theme. According to Seneca, a prince who is merciful will always show 'how loath he is to turn his hand' to punishment; he will resort to it only 'when great and repeated wrongdoing has overcome his patience'; and

53

he will inflict it only 'after great reluctance' and 'much procras-
tination' as well as with the greatest possible clemency. Faced
with this orthodoxy, Machiavelli insists once more that it
represents a complete misunderstanding of the virtue involved.
If you begin by trying to be merciful, so that you 'let evils
continue' and only turn to punishment after 'murders or
plunder' begin, your conduct will be far less clement than that
of a prince who has the courage to begin by 'giving a very few
examples of cruelty'. Machiavelli cites the example of the
Florentines, who wanted 'to escape being called cruel' on a
particular occasion, and in consequence acted in such a way
that the destruction of an entire city resulted—an outcome
hideously more cruel than any cruelty they could have devised.
This is contrasted with the behaviour of Cesare Borgia, who
'was thought cruel', but used 'that well-known cruelty of his'
so well that he 'reorganised the Romagna', united it and
'brought it to peace and loyalty', achieving all these beneficial
results by means of his alleged viciousness (61).

This leads Machiavelli to a closely connected question which
he puts forward—with a similar air of self-conscious paradox
later in the same chapter: 'is it better to be loved than feared,
or the reverse?' (62). Again the classic answer had been furnished by Cicero in *Moral Obligation*. 'Fear is but a poor
safeguard of lasting power', whereas love 'may be trusted to
keep it safe for ever'. Again Machiavelli registers his total
dissent. 'It is much safer', he retorts, 'for a prince to be feared
than loved.' The reason is that many of the qualities that make
a prince loved also tend to bring him into contempt. If your
subjects have no 'dread of punishment' they will take every
chance to deceive you for their own profit. But if you make
yourself feared, they will hesitate to offend or injure you, as a
result of which you will find it much easier to maintain your
state (62).

The other line of argument in these chapters reflects an even
more decisive rejection of conventional humanist morality.
Machiavelli suggests that, even if the qualities usually considered good are indeed virtues—such that a ruler who flouts
them will undoubtedly be falling into vice—he ought not to

worry about such vices if he thinks them either useful or irrelevant to the conduct of his government (58).

Machiavelli's main concern at this point is to remind new rulers of their most basic duty of all. A wise prince 'will not worry about incurring reproaches for those vices without which he can hardly maintain his position'; he will see that such criticisms are merely an unavoidable cost he has to bear in the course of discharging his fundamental obligation, which is of course to maintain his state (58). The implications are first spelled out in relation to the supposed vice of parsimony. Once a wise prince perceives that stinginess is 'one of those vices that make him reign', he will judge it 'of little importance to incur the name of a stingy man' (60). The same applies in the case of cruelty. A willingness to act on occasion with exemplary severity is crucial to the preservation of good order in civil as in military affairs. This means that a wise prince is 'not troubled about a reproach for cruelty', and that 'it is altogether essential not to worry about being called cruel' if you are an army commander, for 'without such a reputation' you can never hope to keep your troops 'united or fit for any action' (61, 63).

Lastly, Machiavelli considers whether it is important for a ruler to eschew the lesser vices and sins of the flesh if he wishes to maintain his state. The writers of advice-books for princes generally dealt with this issue in a sternly moralistic vein, echoing Cicero's insistence in Book I of *Moral Obligation* that propriety is 'essential to moral rectitude', and thus that all persons in positions of authority must avoid all lapses of conduct in their personal lives. By contrast, Machiavelli answers with a shrug. A wise prince 'protects himself from such vices if he can'; but if he finds he cannot, then 'he passes over them with little concern', not troubling himself about such ordinary susceptibilities at all (58).

3 The philosopher of liberty

With the completion of *The Prince*, Machiavelli's hopes of returning to an active public career revived. As he wrote to Vettori in December 1513, his highest aspiration was still to make himself 'useful to our Medici lords, even if they begin by making me roll a stone'. He wondered whether the most effective way of realising his ambition might be to go to Rome with 'this little treatise of mine' in order to offer it in person to Giuliano de' Medici, thereby showing him that he 'might well be pleased to gain my services' (C 305).

At first Vettori seemed willing to support this scheme. He replied that Machiavelli should send him the book, so that he 'could see whether it might be appropriate to present it' (C 312). When Machiavelli duly dispatched the fair copy he had begun to make of the opening chapters, Vettori announced that he was 'extremely pleased with them', though he cautiously added that 'since I do not have the rest of the work, I do not wish to offer a final judgement' (C 319).

It soon became clear, however, that Machiavelli's hopes were again going to be dashed. Having read the whole of *The Prince* early in 1514, Vettori responded with an ominous silence. He never mentioned the work again, and instead began to fill up his letters with distracting chatter about his latest love affairs. Although Machiavelli forced himself to write back in a similar spirit, he was barely able to conceal his mounting anxiety. By the middle of the year, he finally came to realise that it was all hopeless, and wrote in great bitterness to Vettori to say that he was giving up the struggle. It has become obvious, he declares, 'that I am going to have to continue in this sordid way of life, without finding a single man who remembers the service I have done or believes me capable of doing any good' (C 343).

After this disappointment Machiavelli's life underwent a permanent change. Abandoning any further hopes of a diplomatic career, he began to see himself increasingly as a man of letters. The main sign of this new orientation was that, after another year or more of 'rotting in idleness' in the country, he started to take a prominent part in the meetings held by a group of humanists and *literati* who forgathered regularly at Cosimo Rucellai's gardens on the outskirts of Florence for learned conversation and entertainment.

These discussions at the *Orti Oricellari* were partly of a literary character. There were debates about the rival merits of Latin and Italian as literary languages, and there were readings and even performances of plays. The effect on Machiavelli was to channel his creative energies in a wholly new direction: he decided to write a play himself. The result was *Mandragola*, his brilliant if rather brutal comedy about the seduction of an old judge's beautiful young wife. The original version was probably completed in 1518, and may well have been read to Machiavelli's friends in the *Orti* before being publicly presented for the first time in Florence and Rome in the course of the next two years.

It is evident, however, that the most intensive debates at the *Orti* tended to be about politics. As one of the participants, Antonio Brucioli, later recalled in his *Dialogues*, they continually discussed the fate of republican regimes: how they rise to greatness, how they sustain their liberties, how they decline and fall into corruption, how they finally arrive at their inescapable point of collapse. Nor did their interest in civic freedom express itself merely in words. Some members of the group became such passionate opponents of the restored Medicean 'tyranny' that they were drawn into the unsuccessful plot to murder Cardinal Giulio de'Medici in 1522. One of those who were executed after the conspiracy misfired was Jacopo da Diacceto; among those condemned to exile were Zanobi Buondelmonti, Luigi Alamanni and Brucioli himself. All had been prominent members of the *Orti Oricellari* circle—the meetings of which came to an abrupt end after the failure of the attempted coup.

Machiavelli was never so vehement a partisan of republican liberty that he felt inclined to associate himself with any of the various anti-Medicean conspiracies. But it is clear that he was deeply influenced by his contacts with Cosimo Rucellai and his friends. One outcome of his participation in their discussions was his treatise on *The Art of War*, published in 1521. This is actually couched in the form of a conversation set in the *Orti Oricellari*, with Rucellai introducing the argument while Buondelmonti and Alamanni serve as the chief interlocutors. But the most important product of Machiavelli's involvement with these republican sympathisers was his decision to write his Discourses on the first ten books of Livy's *History*, his longest and in many ways his most original work of political philosophy.

Machiavelli had of course been immersed in studying ancient history (including Livy) at least since the summer of 1513, and in his dedication to the *Discourses* he boasts about his 'steady reading' of the best classical authorities. There seems no doubt, however, that the spur to write out his ideas—in the typically humanist form of a commentary on an ancient text—came from his affiliation with the *Orti Oricellari* group. The *Discourses* are dedicated to Rucellai, who initiated their meetings, and to Buondelmonti, one of the conspirators of 1522. Moreover, Machiavelli's dedication not only alludes to their discussions and conveys his 'gratitude for the benefits I have received' from them, but also credits his friends with having 'forced me to write what I of myself never would have written' (188).

The means to greatness

Although Machiavelli ranges widely in his three Discourses over the civil and military affairs of the Roman republic, there is one issue which above all preoccupies him as he sets out to investigate the early history of Rome. He first mentions the topic in the opening paragraph of the first Discourse, and it underlies most of the rest of the book. His aim, he says, is to discover what 'made possible the dominant position to which that republic rose' (192).

There are obvious links between this theme and that of *The Prince*. It is true, of course, that in *The Prince* Machiavelli begins by excluding republics from consideration, whereas in the *Discourses* they furnish him with his main evidence. However, it would be a mistake to infer that the *Discourses* are exclusively concerned with republics as opposed to principalities. As Machiavelli stresses in chapter 2, his interest lies not in republics as such, but rather in the government of cities, whether they are ruled 'as republics or as princedoms' (195). Moreover, there are close parallels between Machiavelli's desire in *The Prince* to advise rulers on how to attain glory by doing 'great things' and his aspiration in the *Discourses* to explain why certain cities have 'come to greatness', and why the city of Rome in particular managed to attain 'supreme greatness' and to produce such 'great results' (207–11, 341).

What, then, were 'the methods needed for attaining to greatness' in the case of Rome (358)? For Machiavelli the question is a practical one, since he endorses the familiar humanist contention that anyone who 'considers present affairs and ancient ones readily understands that all cities and all peoples have the same desires and the same traits'. This means that 'he who diligently examines past events easily foresees future ones' and 'can apply to them the remedies used by the ancients', or at least 'devise new ones because of the similarity of the events' (278). The exhilarating hope that underlies and animates the whole of the *Discourses* is thus that, if we can find out the cause of Rome's success, we may be able to repeat it.

A study of classical history discloses, according to Machiavelli, that the clue to understanding Rome's achievement can be encapsulated in a single sentence. 'Experience shows that cities have never increased in dominion or riches except while they have been at liberty.' The ancient world offers two particularly impressive illustrations of this general truth. First, 'it is a marvellous thing to consider to what greatness Athens came in the space of a hundred years after she freed herself from the tyranny of Pisistratus'. But above all it is 'very marvellous to observe what greatness Rome came to after she freed herself from her kings' (329). By contrast, 'the opposite of all these things happens in those countries that live as slaves' (333). For 'as soon as a tyranny is established over a free

59

community', the first evil that results is that such cities 'no longer go forward and no longer increase in power or in riches; but in most instances, in fact always, they go backward' (329).

What Machiavelli primarily has in mind in laying so much emphasis on liberty is that a city bent on greatness must remain free from all forms of political servitude, whether imposed 'internally' by the rule of a tyrant or 'externally' by an imperial power (195, 235). This in turn means that to say of a city that it possesses its liberty is equivalent to saying that it holds itself independent of any authority save that of the community itself. Liberty thus comes to be equated with self-government. Machiavelli makes this clear in the second chapter of his first Discourse, where he states that he will 'omit discussion of those cities' that started by being 'subject to somebody' and will concentrate on those which began in liberty—that is, on those which 'at once governed themselves by their own judgement' (195). The same commitment is reiterated later in the chapter, where Machiavelli first praises the laws of Solon for setting up 'a form of government based on the people', and then proceeds to equate this arrangement with that of living 'in liberty' (199).

The first general conclusion of the *Discourses* is thus that cities only 'grow enormously in a very short time' and acquire greatness if 'the people are in control of them' (316). This does not lead Machiavelli to lose interest in principalities, for he is sometimes (though not consistently) willing to believe that the maintenance of popular control may be compatible with a monarchical form of government (e.g. 427). But it certainly leads him to express a marked preference for republican over princely regimes. He states his reasons most emphatically at the beginning of the second Discourse. It is 'not individual good but common good' that 'makes cities great', and 'without doubt this common good is thought important only in republics'. Under a prince 'the opposite happens', for 'what benefits him usually injures the city, and what benefits the city injures him'. This explains why cities under monarchical government seldom 'go forward', whereas 'all cities and provinces that live in freedom anywhere in the world' always 'make very great gains' (329, 332).

If liberty is the key to greatness, how is liberty itself to be acquired and kept safe? Machiavelli begins by admitting that an element of good Fortune is always involved. It is essential that a city should have 'a free beginning, without depending on anyone' if it is to have any prospect of achieving civic glory (193, 195). Cities which suffer the misfortune of starting life in a servile condition generally find it 'not merely difficult but impossible' to 'find laws which will keep them free' and bring them fame (296).

As in *The Prince*, however, Machiavelli treats it as a cardinal error to suppose that the attainment of greatness is entirely dependent on Fortune's caprice. He concedes that according to some 'very weighty' writers—including Plutarch and Livy the rise to glory of the Roman people owed almost everything to Fortune. But he replies that he is 'not willing to grant this in any way' (324). He admits that the Romans enjoyed many blessings of Fortune, as well as benefiting from various afflictions which the goddess sent them 'in order to make Rome stronger and bring her to the greatness she attained' (408). But he insists—again echoing *The Prince*—that the achievement of great things is never the outcome merely of good Fortune; it is always the product of Fortune combined with the indispensable quality of *virtú*, the quality that enables us to endure our misfortunes with equanimity and at the same time attracts the goddess's favourable attentions. So he concludes that if we wish to understand what 'made possible the dominant position' to which the Roman republic rose, we must recognise that the answer lies in the fact that Rome possessed 'so much *virtú*' and managed to ensure that this crucial quality was 'kept up in that city for so many centuries' (192). It was because the Romans 'mixed with their Fortune the utmost *virtú*' that they maintained their original freedom and ultimately rose to dominate the world (326).

Turning to analyse this pivotal concept of *virtú*, Machiavelli follows precisely the lines already laid down in *The Prince*. It is true that he applies the term in such a way as to suggest one

61

important addition to his previous account. In *The Prince* he had associated the quality exclusively with the greatest political leaders and military commanders; in the Discourses he explicitly insists that, if a city is to attain greatness, it is essential that the quality should be possessed by the citizen body as a whole (498). However, when he comes to define what he means by *virtú*, he largely reiterates his earlier arguments, coolly taking for granted the startling conclusions he had already reached.

The possession of *virtú* is accordingly represented as a willingness to do whatever may be necessary for the attainment of civic glory and greatness, whether the actions involved happen to be intrinsically good or evil in character. This is first of all treated as the most important attribute of political leadership. As in *The Prince*, the point is made by way of an allusion to, and a sarcastic repudiation of, the values of Ciceronian humanism. Cicero had asserted in *Moral Obligation* that, when Romulus decided 'it was more expedient for him to reign alone' and in consequence murdered his brother, he committed a crime that cannot possibly be condoned, since his defence of his action was 'neither reasonable nor adequate at all'. Machiavelli insists on the contrary that no 'prudent intellect' will ever 'censure anyone for any unlawful action used in organising a kingdom or setting up a republic'. Citing the case of Romulus' fratricide, he contends that 'though the deed accuses him, the result should excuse him; and when it is good, like that of Romulus, it will always excuse him, because he who is violent to destroy, not he who is violent to restore, ought to be censured' (218).

The same willingness to place the good of the community above all private interests and ordinary considerations of morality is held to be no less essential in the case of rank-and-file citizens. Again Machiavelli makes the point by way of parodying the values of classical humanism. Cicero had declared in *Moral Obligation* that 'there are some acts either so repulsive or so wicked that a wise man would not commit them even to save his country'. Machiavelli retorts that 'when it is absolutely a question of the safety of one's country', it becomes the duty of every citizen to recognise that 'there must be no consideration of just or unjust, of merciful or cruel, of praiseworthy or disgraceful; instead, setting aside every scruple, one must follow to the utmost any plan that will save her life and keep her liberty' (519).

This, then, is the sign of *virtú* in rulers and citizens alike: each must be prepared 'to advance not his own interests but the general good, not his own posterity but the common fatherland' (218). This is why Machiavelli speaks of the Roman republic as a repository of 'so much *virtú*': patriotism was felt to be 'more powerful than any other consideration', as a result of which the populace became 'for four hundred years an enemy to the name of king, and a lover of the glory and the common good of its native city' (315, 450).

The contention that the key to preserving liberty lies in keeping up the quality of *virtú* in the citizen body as a whole obviously raises a further question, the most basic one of all: how can we hope to instil this quality widely enough, and maintain it for long enough, to ensure that civic glory is attained? Again Machiavelli concedes that an element of good Fortune is always involved. No city can hope to attain greatness unless it happens to be set on the right road by a great founding father, to whom 'as a daughter' it may be said to owe its birth (223). A city which has not 'chanced upon a prudent founder' will always tend to find itself 'in a somewhat unhappy position' (196). Conversely, a city which can look back to 'the *virtú* and the methods' of a great founder—as Rome looked back to Romulus—has 'chanced upon most excellent Fortune' (244).

The reason why a city needs this 'first Fortune' is that the act of establishing a republic or principality can never be brought about 'through the *virtú* of the masses', because their 'diverse opinions' will always prevent them from being 'suited to organise a government' (218, 240). It follows that 'to set up a republic it is necessary to be alone' (220). Moreover, once a city has 'declined by corruption', it will similarly require 'the *virtú* of one man who is then living', and not 'the *virtú* of the masses' to restore it to greatness (240). So Machiavelli concludes that 'this we must take as a general rule: seldom or never is any republic or kingdom organised well from the beginning, or totally made over' at a later date, 'except when organised by one man' (218).

He then declares, however, that if any city is so imprudent as to rely on this initial good Fortune, it will not only cheat itself of greatness but will very soon collapse. For while 'one alone is suited for organising' a government, no government can hope to last 'if resting on the shoulders of only one' (218). The inescapable weakness of any polity that puts its trust in 'the *virtú* of one man alone' is that 'the *virtú* departs with the life of the man, and seldom is it restored in the course of heredity' (226). What is needed, therefore, for the salvation of a kingdom or a republic is not so much 'to have a prince who will rule prudently while he lives', but rather 'to have one who will so organise it' that its subsequent fortunes come to rest instead upon 'the *virtú* of the masses' (226, 240). The deepest secret of statecraft is thus to know how this can be done.

The problem, Machiavelli goes on, is one of exceptional difficulty. For while we can expect to find a surpassing degree of *virtú* among the founding fathers of cities, we cannot expect to find the same quality occurring naturally among ordinary citizens. On the contrary, most men 'are more prone to evil than to good', and in consequence tend to ignore the interests of their community in order to act 'according to the wickedness of their spirits whenever they have free scope' (201, 218). There is thus a tendency for all cities to fall away from the pristine *virtú* of their founders and 'descend towards a worse condition'—a process Machiavelli summarizes by saying that even the finest communities are liable to become corrupt (322).

The image underlying this analysis is an Aristotelian one: the idea of the polity as a natural body which, like all sublunary creatures, is subject to being 'injured by time' (451). Machiavelli lays particular emphasis on the metaphor of the body politic at the beginning of his third Discourse. He thinks it 'clearer than light that if these bodies are not renewed they do not last', for in time their *virtú* is certain to become corrupt, and such corruption is certain to kill them if their injuries are not healed (419).

The onset of corruption is thus equated with the loss or dissipation of *virtú*, a process of degeneration which develops, according to Machiavelli, in one of two ways. A body of citizens may lose its *virtú*—and hence its concern for the common good—by losing interest in politics altogether, becoming 'lazy and unfit for all *virtuoso* activity' (194). But the more insidious danger arises when the citizens remain active in affairs of state, but begin to promote their individual ambitions or factional loyalties at the expense of the public interest. Thus Machiavelli defines a corrupt political proposal as one 'put forward by men interested in what they can get from the public, rather than in its good' (386). He defines a corrupt constitution as one in which 'only the powerful' are able to propose measures, and do so 'not for the common liberty but for their own power' (242). And he defines a corrupt city as one in which the magistracies are no longer filled by 'those with the greatest *virtú*', but rather by those with the most power, and hence with the best prospects of serving their own selfish ends (241).

This analysis leads Machiavelli into a dilemma. On the one hand he continually stresses that 'the nature of men is ambitious and suspicious' to such a degree that most people will 'never do anything good except by necessity' (201, 257). But on the other hand he insists that, once men are allowed to 'climb from one ambition to another', this will rapidly cause their city to 'go to pieces' and forfeit any chance of becoming great (290). The reason is that, while the preservation of liberty is a necessary condition of greatness, the growth of corruption is invariably fatal to liberty. As soon as self-seeking individuals or sectarian interests begin to gain support, the people's desire to legislate 'on freedom's behalf' becomes correspondingly eroded, factions start to take over and 'tyranny quickly appears' in place of liberty (282). It follows that whenever corruption fully enters a body of citizens, they 'cannot live free even for a short time, in fact not at all' (235, cf. 240).

Machiavelli's dilemma is accordingly this: how can the body of the people—in whom the quality of *virtú* is not naturally to be found—have this quality successfully implanted in them? How can they be prevented from sliding into corruption, how

65

can they be coerced into keeping up an interest in the common good over a sufficiently long period for civic greatness to be attained? It is with the solution to this problem that the whole of the rest of the *Discourses* is concerned.

The laws and leadership

Machiavelli believes that the dilemma he has uncovered can to some extent be circumvented rather than having to be directly overcome. For he allows that, while we can hardly expect the generality of citizens to display much natural *virtú*, it is not too much to hope that a city may from time to time have the good Fortune to find a leader whose actions, like those of a great founding father, exhibit an unforced quality of *virtú* in a high degree (420).

Such truly noble citizens are said to play an indispensable role in keeping their cities on the pathway to glory. Machiavelli argues that if such individual examples of *virtú* 'had appeared at least every ten years' in the history of Rome, 'their necessary result would have been' that the city 'would never have become corrupt' (421). He even declares that 'if a community were fortunate enough' to find a leader of this character in every generation, who 'would renovate its laws and would not merely stop it running to ruin but would pull it backwards', then the outcome would be the miracle of an 'everlasting' republic, a body politic with the ability to escape death (481).

How do such infusions of personal *virtú* contribute to a city's attainment of its highest ends? Machiavelli's attempt to answer this question occupies him throughout the whole of his third Discourse, the aim of which is to illustrate 'how the deeds of individuals increased Roman greatness, and how in that city they caused many good effects' (423).

It is evident that in pursuing this topic Machiavelli is still very close to the spirit of *The Prince*. So it is not surprising to find him inserting into this final section of the *Discourses* a considerable number of references back to his earlier work— nearly a dozen allusions in less than a hundred pages. As in *The Prince*, moreover, he lays it down that there are two distinct ways in which it is possible for a statesman or a general of surpassing *virtú* to achieve great things. The first is by way of his impact on other and lesser citizens. Machiavelli begins by suggesting that this can sometimes produce a directly inspiring effect, since 'these men are of such reputation and their example is so powerful that good men wish to imitate them, and the wicked are ashamed to live a life contrary to theirs' (421). But his basic contention is that the *virtú* of an outstanding leader will always take the form, in part, of a capacity to imprint the same vital quality on his followers, even though they may not be naturally endowed with it at all. Discussing how this form of influence operates, Machiavelli's main suggestion—as in *The Prince* and later in Book IV of *The Art of War*—is that the most efficacious means of coercing people into behaving in a *virtuoso* fashion is by making them terrified of behaving otherwise. Thus he praises Hannibal for recognising the need to instil dread in his troops 'by his personal traits' in order to keep them 'united and quiet' (479). And he reserves his highest admiration for Manlius Torquatus, whose 'strong spirit' and proverbial severity made him 'command strong things' and enabled him to force his fellow citizens back into the condition of pristine *virtú* which they had begun to forsake (480–1).

The other way in which outstanding individuals contribute to civic glory is more immediate: Machiavelli believes that their high *virtú* serves in itself to stave off corruption and collapse. One of his chief concerns in his third Discourse is accordingly to indicate what particular aspects of *virtuoso* leadership tend most readily to bring about this beneficial result. He begins to supply his answer in chapter 23, in which he surveys the career of Camillus, 'the most prudent of all the Roman generals' (462). The qualities that made Camillus seem especially remarkable, and enabled him to achieve so many 'splendid things' were 'his care, his prudence, his great courage' and above all 'his excellent method of administering and commanding armies' (484, 498). Later Machiavelli devotes a sequence of chapters to furnishing a fuller treatment of the same theme. He first argues that great civic leaders have to know how to disarm the envious, 'for envy many times prevents men' from gaining 'the authority necessary in things of importance' (495–6). They also need to be men of high personal courage, especially if called upon to serve in a military capacity, in which case they must be prepared—as Livy puts it—'to show activity in the thickest part of the battle' (515). They must also possess deep political prudence, founded on an appreciation of ancient history as well as modern affairs (521–2). And finally they must be men of the greatest circumspection and wariness, incapable of being deceived by the strategies of their enemies (526).

Throughout this discussion it is clear that the fortunes of Machiavelli's native city are never far from his thoughts. Whenever he cites an indispensable aspect of *virtuoso* leadership, he pauses to indicate that the decline of the Florentine republic and its ignominious collapse in 1512 were due in large part to a failure to pay sufficient attention to this crucial quality. A leader of *virtù* needs to know how to deal with the envious: but neither Savonarola nor Soderini was 'able to overcome envy' and in consequence 'both of them fell' (497). A leader of *virtù* must be prepared to study the lessons of history: but the Florentines, who could easily have 'read or learnt the ancient habits of the barbarians' made no attempt to do so and were easily tricked and despoiled (522). A kader of *virtù* should be a man of circumspection and prudence: but the rulers of Florence showed themselves so naïve in the face of treachery that—as in the war against Pisa—they brought the republic into complete disgrace (527). With this bitter indictment of the regime he had served, Machiavelli brings his third Discourse to an end.

If we revert to the dilemma Machiavelli began by posing, it becomes evident that the argument of his third Discourse leaves it largely unresolved. Although he has explained how it is possible for ordinary citizens to be coerced into *virtù* by the example of great leadership, he has also admitted that the appearance of great leaders is always a matter of pure good Fortune, and is thus an unreliable means of enabling a city to rise to glory and fame. So the fundamental question still remains: how can the generality of men—who will always be prone to let themselves be corrupted by ambition or laziness—have the quality of *virtú* implanted and maintained in them for long enough to ensure that civic glory is achieved?

It is at this juncture that Machiavelli begins to move decisively beyond the confines of his political vision in *The Prince*. The key to solving the problem, he maintains, is to ensure that the citizens are 'well-ordered'—that they are organised in such a way as to compel them to acquire *virtú* and uphold their liberties. This solution is immediately proposed in the opening chapter of the first Discourse. If we wish to understand how it came about that 'so much *virtú* was kept up' in Rome 'for so many centuries', what we need to investigate is 'how she was organised' (192). The next chapter reiterates the same point. To see how the city of Rome succeeded in reaching 'the straight road' that led her 'to a perfect and true end', we need above all to study her *ordini*—her institutions, her constitutional arrangements, her methods of ordering and organising her citizens (196).

The most obvious question this requires us to address, according to Machiavelli, is what institutions a city needs to develop in order to avoid the growth of corruption in its 'inside' affairs—by which he means its political and constitutional arrangements (195, 295). He accordingly devotes the greater part of his first Discourse to considering this theme, taking his main illustrations from the early history of Rome, and continually emphasising 'how well the institutions of that city were adapted to making it great' (271).

He singles out two essential methods of organising home affairs in such a way as to instil the quality of *virtú* in the whole body of the citizens. He begins by arguing—in chapters 11 to 15—that among the most important institutions of any city are those concerned with upholding religious worship and ensuring that it is 'well used' (234). He even declares that 'the observance of religious teaching' is of such paramount importance that it serves in itself to bring about 'the greatness of republics' (225). Conversely, he thinks that 'one can have no better indication' of a country's corruption and ruin than 'to see divine worship little valued' (226).

The Romans understood perfectly how to make use of religion in order to promote the well-being of their republic. King Numa, Romulus' immediate successor, in particular recognised that the establishment of a civic cult was 'altogether necessary if he wished to maintain a civilised community' (224). By contrast, the rulers of modern Italy have disastrously failed to grasp the relevance of this point. Although the city of Rome is still the nominal centre of Christianity, the ironic truth is that 'through the bad example' of the Roman Church, 'this land has lost all piety and all religion' (228). The outcome of this scandal is that the Italians, through being the least religious people in Europe, have become the most corrupt. As a direct consequence, they have lost their liberties, forgotten how to defend themselves, and allowed their country to become 'the prey not merely of powerful barbarians but of whoever assails her' (229).

The secret known to the ancient Romans—and forgotten in the modern world—is that the institutions of religion can be made to play a role analogous to that of outstanding individuals in helping to promote the cause of civic greatness. Religion can be used, that is, to inspire—and if necessary to terrorise—the ordinary populace in such a way as to induce them to prefer the good of their community to all other goods. Machiavelli's principal account of how the Romans encouraged such patriotism is presented in his discussion of auspices. Before they went into battle, Roman generals always took care to announce that the omens were favourable. This prompted their troops to fight in the confident belief that they were sure of victory, a confidence which in turn made them act with so much *virtù* that they almost always won the day (233). Characteristically, however, Machiavelli is more impressed by the way the Romans used their religion to arouse terror in the body of the people, thereby inciting them to behave with a degree of *virtù* they would never otherwise have attained. He offers the most dramatic instance in chapter 11. 'After Hannibal defeated the Romans at Cannae, many citizens met together who, despairing of their native land, agreed to abandon Italy'. When Scipio heard of this, he met them 'with his naked sword in his hand' and forced them to swear a solemn oath binding them to stand their ground. The effect of this was to coerce them into *virtú*: although their 'love of their country and its laws' had not persuaded them to remain in Italy, they were successfully kept there by the fear of blasphemously violating their word (224).

The idea that a God-fearing community will naturally reap the reward of civic glory was a familiar one to Machiavelli's contemporaries. As he himself observes, this had been the promise underlying Savonarola's campaign in Florence during the 1490s, in the course of which he had persuaded the Florentines 'that he spoke with God' and that God's message to the city was that He would restore it to its former greatness as soon as it returned to its original piety (226). However, Machiavelli's own views about the value of religion involve him in departing from this orthodox treatment of the topic in two fundamental respects. He first of all differs from the Savonarolans in his reasons for wishing to uphold the religious basis of political life. He is not in the least interested in the question of religious truth. He is solely interested in the role played by religious sentiment 'in inspiring the people, in keeping men good, in making the wicked ashamed', and he judges the value of different religions entirely by their capacity to promote these useful effects (224). So he not only concludes that the leaders of any community have a duty to 'accept and magnify' anything that 'comes up in favour of religion'; he insists that they must always do so 'even though they think it false' (227).

Machiavelli's other departure from orthodoxy is connected with this pragmatic approach. He declares that, judged by these standards, the ancient religion of the Romans is much to be preferred to the Christian faith. There is no reason why Christianity should not have been interpreted 'according to *virtú*' and employed for 'the betterment and the defence' of Christian communities. But in fact it has been interpreted in such a way as to undermine the qualities needed for a free and vigorous civic life. It has 'glorified humble and contemplative men'; it has 'set up as the greatest good humility, abjectness and contempt for human things'; it has placed no value 'in grandeur of mind, in strength of body' or in any of the other attributes of *virtuoso* citizenship. By imposing this other-worldly image of human excellence, it has not merely failed to promote civic glory; it has actually helped to bring about the decline and fall of great nations by corrupting their communal life. As Machiavelli concludes—with an irony worthy of Gibbon—the price we have paid for the fact that Christianity 'shows us the truth and the true way' is that it 'has made the world weak and turned it over as prey to wicked men' (331).

Machiavelli devotes the rest of his first Discourse to arguing that there is a second and even more effective means of inducing people to acquire *virtú*: by using the coercive powers of the law in such a way as to force them to place the good of their community above all selfish interests. The point is first made in broad terms in the opening chapters of the book. All the finest examples of civic *virtú* are said to 'have their origin in good education', which in turn has its origin 'in good laws' (203). If we ask how some cities manage to keep up their *virtú* over exceptionally long periods, the basic answer in every case is that 'the laws make them good' (201). The pivotal place of this contention in Machiavelli's general argument is later made explicit at the beginning of the third Discourse: if a city is to 'take on new life' and advance along the pathway to glory, this can only be achieved 'either by the *virtú* of a man or by the *virtú* of a law' (419–20).

Given this belief, we can see why Machiavelli attaches so much importance to the founding fathers of cities. They are in a unique position to act as lawgivers, and thus to supply their communities from the outset with the best means of ensuring that *virtú* is promoted and corruption overcome. The most impressive instance of this achievement is said to be that of Lycurgus, the original founder of Sparta. He devised a code of laws so perfect that the city was able to 'live safely under them' for 'more than eight hundred years without debasing them' and without at any point forfeiting its liberty (196, 199). Scarcely less remarkable is the achievement of Romulus and Numa, the first kings of Rome. By means of the many good laws they enacted, the city had the quality of *virtú* 'forced upon her' with such decisiveness that even 'the greatness of her empire could not for many centuries corrupt her', and she remained 'full of a *virtú* as great as that by which any city or republic was ever distinguished' (195, 200).

This brings us, according to Machiavelli, to one of the most instructive lessons we can hope to learn from the study of history. The greatest lawgivers, he has shown, are those who have understood most clearly how to use the law in order to advance the cause of civic greatness. It follows that, if we investigate the details of their constitutional codes, we may be able to uncover the secret of their success, thereby making the wisdom of the ancients directly available to the rulers of the modern world.

After conducting this investigation, Machiavelli concludes that the crucial insight common to all the wisest legislators of antiquity can be very simply expressed. They all perceived that the three 'pure' constitutional forms—monarchy, aristocracy, democracy—are inherently unstable, and tend to generate a cycle of corruption and decay; and they correctly inferred that the key to imposing *virtú* by the force of law must therefore lie in establishing a mixed constitution, one in which the instabilities of the pure forms are corrected while their strengths are combined. As always, Rome furnishes the clearest example: it was because she managed to evolve a 'mixed government' that she finally rose to become 'a perfect republic' (200).

It was of course a commonplace of Roman political theory to defend the special merits of mixed constitutions. The argument is central to Polybius's *History*, recurs in several of Cicero's political treatises, and subsequently found favour with most of the leading humanists of fifteenth-century Florence. However, when we come to Machiavelli's reasons for believing that a mixed constitution is best-suited for promoting *virtú* and upholding liberty, we encounter a dramatic divergence from the conventional humanist point of view.

His argument starts out from the axiom that 'in every

73

republic there are two opposed factions, that of the people and that of the rich' (203). He thinks it obvious that, if the constitution is so arranged that one or other of these groups is allowed complete control, the republic will be 'easily corrupted' (196). If someone from the party of the rich takes over as prince, there will be an immediate danger of tyranny; if the rich set up an aristocratic form of government, they will be prone to rule in their own interests; if there is a democracy, the same will be true of the common people. In every case the general good will become subordinated to factional loyalties, with the result that the *virtú* and in consequence the liberty of the republic will very soon be lost (197–8, 203–4).

The solution, Machiavelli argues, is to frame the laws relating to the constitution in such a way as to engineer a tensely-balanced equilibrium between these opposed social forces, one in which all the parties remain involved in the business of government, and each 'keeps watch over the other' in order to forestall both 'the rich men's arrogance' and 'the people's licence' (199). As the rival groups jealously scrutinise each other for any signs of a move to take over supreme power, the resolution of the pressures thus engendered will mean that only those 'laws and institutions' which are 'conducive to public liberty' will actually be passed. Although motivated entirely by their selfish interests, the factions will thus be guided, as if by an invisible hand, to promote the public interest in all their legislative acts: 'all the laws made in favour of liberty' will 'result from their discord' (203).

This praise of dissension horrified Machiavelli's contemporaries. Guicciardini spoke for them all when he replied in his *Considerations on the Discourses* that 'to praise disunity is like praising a sick man's disease because of the virtues of the remedy applied to it'. Machiavelli's argument ran counter to the whole tradition of republican thought in Florence, a tradition in which the belief that all discord must be outlawed as factious, together with the belief that faction constitutes the deadliest threat to civic liberty, had been emphasised ever since the end of the thirteenth century, when Remigio, Latini, Compagni and above all Dante had issued fierce denunciations of their fellow-citizens for endangering their liberties by refusing to live in peace. To insist, therefore, on the astounding judgement that—as Machiavelli expresses it—the disorders of Rome 'deserve the highest praise' was to repudiate one of the most cherished assumptions of Florentine humanism.

Machiavelli is unrepentant, however, in his attack on this orthodox belief. He explicitly mentions 'the opinion of the many' who hold that the continual clashes between the plebs and nobles in Rome left the city 'so full of confusion' that only 'good Fortune and military *virtú*' prevented it from tearing itself to pieces. But he still insists that those who condemn Rome's disorders are failing to recognise that they served to prevent the triumph of sectarian interests, and are thus 'finding fault with what as a first cause kept Rome free' (202). So he concludes that, even if the dissensions were evil in themselves, they were nevertheless 'an evil necessary to the attainment of Roman greatness' (211).

The prevention of corruption

Machiavelli goes on to argue that although a mixed constitution is necessary, it is by no means sufficient, to ensure that liberty is preserved. The reason is that—as he warns yet again—most people remain more committed to their own ambitions than to the public interest, and 'never do anything good except by necessity' (201). The outcome is a perpetual tendency for over-mighty citizens and powerful interest-groups to alter the balance of the constitution in favour of their own selfish and factional ends, thereby introducing the seeds of corruption into the body politic and endangering its liberty.

To meet this ineradicable threat, Machiavelli has one further constitutional proposal to advance: he maintains that the price of liberty is eternal vigilance. It is essential in the first place to learn the danger-signals—to recognise the means by which an individual citizen or a political party may be able 'to get more power than is safe' (265). Next, it is essential to develop a special set of laws and institutions for dealing with such emergencies. A republic, as Machiavelli puts it, 'ought to have among its *ordini* this: that the citizens are to be watched so that they cannot under cover of good do evil and so that they gain only such popularity as advances and does not harm liberty' (291). Finally, it is then essential for everyone 'to keep their eyes open', holding themselves in readiness not only to identify such corrupting tendencies, but also to employ the force of the law in order to stamp them out as soon as—or even before—they begin to become a menace (266).

Machiavelli couples this analysis with the suggestion that there is one further constitutional lesson of major significance to be learnt from the early history of Rome. Since Rome preserved its freedom for more than four hundred years, it seems that its citizens must have correctly identified the most serious threats to their liberties, and gone on to evolve the right *ordini* for dealing with them. It follows that, if we wish to understand such dangers and their remedies, it will be advantageous for us to turn once more to the history of the Roman republic, seeking to profit from her ancient wisdom and apply it to the modern world.

As the example of Rome shows, the initial danger that any mixed constitution needs to face will always stem from those who benefited from the previous regime. In Machiavelli's terms, this is the threat posed by 'the sons of Brutus', a problem he first mentions in chapter 16 and later underlines at the beginning of his third Discourse. Junius Brutus freed Rome from the tyranny of Tarquinius Superbus, the last of her kings, but Brutus' own sons were among those who had 'profited from the tyrannical government' (235). The establishment of 'the people's liberty' thus seemed to them no better than slavery. As a result, they 'were led to conspire against their native city by no other reason than that they could not profit unlawfully under the consuls as they had under the kings' (236).

Against this type of risk 'there is no more powerful remedy, none more effective nor more certain nor more necessary, than to kill the sons of Brutus' (236). Machiavelli admits that it may appear cruel—and he adds in his iciest tones that it is certainly 'an instance striking among recorded events'—that Brutus should have been willing to 'sit on the judgement seat and not merely condemn his sons to death but be present at their deaths' (424). But he insists that such severity is in fact indispensable. 'For he who seizes a tyranny and does not kill Brutus, and he who sets a state free and does not kill Brutus's sons, maintains himself but a little while' (425).

A further threat to political stability arises from the notorious propensity of self-governing republics to slander and exhibit ingratitude towards their leading citizens. Machiavelli first alludes to this deficiency in chapter 29, where he argues that one of the gravest errors any city is liable to commit 'in keeping herself free' is that of doing 'injury to citizens whom she should reward'. This is a particularly dangerous disease to leave untreated, since those who suffer such injustices are generally in a strong position to strike back, thereby bringing their city 'all the quicker to tyranny—as happened to Rome with Caesar, who by force took for himself what ingratitude denied him' (259).

The only possible remedy is to institute a special *ordine* designed to discourage the envious and the ungrateful from undermining the reputations of prominent people. The best method of doing this is 'to give enough openings for bringing charges'. Any citizen who feels he has been slandered must be able, 'without any fear or without any hesitation', to demand that his accuser should appear in court in order to provide a proper substantiation of his claims. If it then emerges, once a formal accusation 'has been made and well investigated', that the charges cannot be upheld, the law must provide for the slanderer to be severely punished (215–16).

Finally, Machiavelli discusses what he takes to be the most serious danger to the balance of a mixed constitution, the danger that an ambitious citizen may attempt to form a party based on loyalty to himself instead of to the common good. He begins to analyse this source of instability in chapter 34, after which he devotes most of the remainder of the first Discourse to considering how such corruption tends to arise, and what type of *ordini* are needed to ensure that this gateway to tyranny is kept closed.

One way of encouraging the growth of faction is by allowing the prolongation of military commands. Machiavelli even implies that it was 'the power citizens gained' in this way, more than anything else, that eventually 'made Rome a slave' (267). The reason why it is always 'to the detriment of liberty' when such 'free authority is given for a long time' is that absolute authority always corrupts the people by turning them into its 'friends and partisans' (270, 280). This is what happened in Rome's armies under the late republic. 'When a citizen was for a long time commander of an army, he gained its support and made it his partisan', so that the army 'in time forgot the Senate and considered him its head' (486). Then it only needed Sulla, Marius and later Caesar to seek out 'soldiers who, in opposition to the public good, would follow them' for the balance of the constitution to be tilted so violently that tyranny quickly supervened (282, 486).

The proper response to this menace is not to take fright at the very idea of dictatorial authority, since this may sometimes be vitally needed in cases of national emergency (268–9). Rather the answer should be to ensure, by means of the right *ordini*, that such powers are not abused. This can be achieved in two main ways: by requiring that all absolute commands be 'set up for a limited term but not for life'; and by ensuring that their exercise is restricted in such a way that they are only able 'to dispose of that affair that caused them to be set up'. As long as these *ordini* are observed, there is no danger that absolute power will corrupt absolutely and 'weaken the government' (268).

The other principal source of faction is the malign influence exercised by those with extensive personal wealth. The rich are always in a position to do favours to other citizens, such as 'lending them money, marrying off their daughters, protecting them from the magistrates' and in general conferring benefits of various kinds. Patronage of this nature is extremely sinister, since it tends to 'make men partisans of their benefactors' at the cost of the public interest. This in turn serves to 'give the man they follow courage to think he can corrupt the public and violate the laws' (493). Hence Machiavelli's insistence that 'corruption and slight aptitude for free life spring from inequality in a city'; hence too his frequently reiterated warning that 'the ambition of the rich, if by various means and in various ways a city does not crush it, is what quickly brings her to ruin' (240, 274)

The only way out of this predicament is for 'well-ordered republics' to 'keep their treasuries rich and their citizens poor' (272). Machiavelli is somewhat vague about the type of *ordini* needed to bring this about, but he is eloquent about the benefits to be expected from such a policy. If the law is used to 'keep the citizens poor', this will effectively prevent them—even when they are 'without goodness and wisdom'—from being able to 'corrupt themselves or others with riches' (469). If at the same time the city's coffers remain full, the government will be able to outbid the rich in any 'scheme of befriending the people', since it will always be possible to offer greater rewards for public than for private services (300). Machiavelli accordingly concludes that 'the most useful thing a free community can bring about is to keep its members poor' (486). He ends his discussion on a grandly rhetorical note by adding that he could 'show with a long speech that poverty produces much better fruits than riches', if 'the writings of other men had not many times made the subject splendid' (488).

By the time we reach this point in Machiavelli's analysis, we can readily see that—as in his third Discourse—there is a continuing preoccupation with the fortunes of his native city lying beneath the surface of his general argument. He first of all reminds us that, if a city is to preserve its liberty, it is essential that its constitution should embody some provision against the prevalent vice of slandering and mistrusting prominent citizens. He then points out that this 'has always been badly arranged in our city of Florence'. Anyone who 'reads the history of this city will see how many slanders have at all times been uttered against citizens who have been employed in its important affairs'. The outcome has been 'countless troubles', all of which have helped to undermine the city's liberties, and all of which could easily have been avoided if only 'an arrangement for bringing charges against citizens and punishing slanderers' had at some time been worked out (216).

Florence took a further step towards slavery when she failed to prevent Cosimo de' Medici from building up a party devoted to the advancement of his family's selfish interests. Machiavelli has shown what strategy a city needs to adopt if a leading citizen tries to corrupt the people with his wealth: it needs to outbid him by making it more profitable to serve the common good. As it was, Cosimo's rivals instead chose to drive him from Florence, thereby provoking so much resentment among his followers that they eventually 'called him back and made him prince of the republic—a rank to which without that open opposition he never could have risen' (266, 300).

Florence's one remaining chance to secure her liberties came in 1494, when the Medici were again forced into exile and the republic was fully restored. At this point, however, the city's new leaders, under the direction of Piero Soderini, made the most fatal mistake of all by failing to adopt a policy which, Machiavelli has argued, is absolutely indispensable whenever such a change of regime takes place. Anyone who has 'read ancient history' knows that once a move has been made 'from tyranny into republic', it is essential for 'the sons of Brutus' to be killed (424–5). But Soderini 'believed that with patience and goodness he could overcome the longing of Brutus' sons to get back under another government', since he believed that 'he could extinguish evil factions' without bloodshed and 'dispose of some men's hostility' with rewards (425). The outcome of this shocking naïvety was that the sons of Brutus—that is, the partisans of the Medici—survived to destroy him and restore the Medicean tyranny after the débâcle of 1512.

Soderini failed to put into practice the central precept of Machiavellian statecraft. He scrupled to do evil that good might come of it, and in consequence refused to crush his adversaries because he recognised that he would need to seize illegal powers in order to do it. What he failed to recognise was the folly of yielding to such scruples when the city's liberties were genuinely at stake. He should have seen that 'his works and his intentions would be judged by their outcome', and realised that 'if Fortune and life were with him he could convince everybody that what he did was for the preservation of his native city and not for his own ambition' (425). As it was, the consequences of his 'not having the wisdom to be Brutus-like' were as disastrous as possible. He not only lost 'his position and his reputation'; he also lost his city and its liberties, and delivered his fellow-citizens over to 'become slaves' (425, 461). As in his third Discourse, Machiavelli's argument thus culminates in a violent denunciation of the leader and the government he himself had served.

The quest for empire

At the beginning of his second Discourse, Machiavelli reveals that his discussion of *ordini* is still only half-completed. He has so far claimed that, if a city is to achieve greatness, it needs to develop the right laws and institutions for ensuring that its citizens behave with the highest *virtú* in the conduct of their 'inside' affairs. He now indicates that it is no less essential to establish a further set of *ordini* designed to encourage the citizens to behave with a like *virtú* in their 'outside' affairs— by which he means their military and diplomatic relations with other kingdoms and republics (339). The exposition of this further argument occupies him throughout the central section of his book.

The need for these additional laws and institutions arises from the fact that all republics and principalities exist in a state of hostile competition with each other. Men are never 'content to live on their own resources'; they are always 'inclined to try to govern others' (194). This makes it 'impossible for a republic to succeed in standing still and enjoying its liberties' (379). Any city attempting to follow such an eirenic course of action will quickly fall victim to the incessant flux of political life, in which everyone's fortunes always 'rise up or sink down' without ever being able to 'remain fixed' (210). The only solution is to treat attack as the best form of defence, adopting a policy of expansion in order to ensure that one's native city 'can both defend herself from those who assail her and crush whoever opposes himself to her greatness' (194). The pursuit of dominion abroad is thus held to be a precondition of liberty at home.

As before, Machiavelli turns for the corroboration of these

general claims to the early history of Rome. He declares in his opening chapter that 'there has never been another republic' with so many of the right *ordini* for expansion and conquest (324). Rome owed these arrangements to Romulus, her first lawgiver, who acted with so much foresight that the city was able from the outset to develop an 'unusual and immense *virtù*' in the conduct of her military affairs (332). This in turn enabled her—together with her exceptional good Fortune—to rise by a series of brilliant victories to her final position of 'supreme greatness' and 'tremendous power' (337, 341).

As Romulus correctly perceived, two fundamental procedures need to be adopted if a city is to regulate its 'outside' affairs in a satisfactory way. In the first place, it is essential to keep the largest possible number of citizens available for purposes of expansion as well as defence. To bring this about, two related policies have to be pursued. The first—examined in chapter 3—is to encourage immigration: it is obviously beneficial to your city, and especially to its manpower, to preserve 'the ways open and safe for foreigners who wish to come to live in it' (334). The second strategy—discussed in chapter 4—is 'to get associates for yourself': you need to surround yourself with allies, keeping them in a subordinate position but protecting them with your laws in return for being able to call upon their military services (336–7).

The other crucial procedure is connected with this preference for assembling the largest possible forces. To make the best use of them, and hence to serve the interests of your city most effectively, it is essential to make your wars 'short and big'. This is what the Romans always did, for 'as soon as war was declared', they invariably 'led their armies against the enemy and at once fought a battle'. No policy, Machiavelli crisply concludes, could be 'safer or stronger or more profitable', for it enables you to come to terms with your opponents from a position of strength as well as with the minimum cost (342).

Having outlined these military *ordini*, Machiavelli proceeds to consider a series of more specific lessons about the conduct of warfare which he believes can be learnt from a study of Rome's achievement. This topic, introduced in chapter 10, occupies him for the whole of the rest of the second Discourse, as well as being taken up—in a more polished but essentially similar style—in the central sections of his later treatise on *The Art of War*.

It is perhaps an index of Machiavelli's growing pessimism about the prospects of reviving ancient military *virtú* in the modern world that all his conclusions in these chapters are presented in a negative form. Rather than considering what approaches serve to encourage *virtú* and promote greatness, he concentrates entirely on those tactics and strategies which embody mistakes and in consequence bring 'death and ruin' instead of victory (377–8). The result is a long list of admonitions and caveats. It is imprudent to accept the common maxim that 'riches are the sinews of war' (348–9). It is injurious to make either 'hesitating decisions' or 'slow and late ones' (361). It is entirely false to suppose that the conduct of warfare 'will be turned over, in course of time, to the artillery' (367, 371). It is valueless to employ auxiliary or mercenary soldiers—an argument which, as Machiavelli reminds us, he has already presented 'at length in another work' (381). It is useless in time of war, and in peacetime it is actively harmful, to rely on fortresses as a principal system of defence (394). It is dangerous to make it impossible for a citizen to be 'avenged to his satisfaction' if he feels insulted or injured (405). And it is the worst mistake of all 'to refuse every agreement' when attacked by superior forces, and try instead to defeat them against the odds (403).

The reason Machiavelli gives for condemning these practices is the same in every case. They all fail to recognise that, if civic glory is to be attained, the quality that needs most of all to be instilled in one's own armies—and reckoned with in the armies of one's enemies—is that of *virtú*, the willingness to set aside all considerations of personal safety and interest in order to defend the liberties of one's native land.

With some of the policies he lists, Machiavelli argues that the danger involved is that of raising up exceptional *virtú* against those who practise them. This, for example, is why it is a mistake to rely on fortresses. The security they afford you makes you 'quicker and less hesitant about oppressing your subjects', but this in turn 'stirs them up in such a way that your fortress, which is the cause of it, cannot then defend you' against their hatred and rage (393). The same applies to the refusal to avenge injuries. If a citizen feels himself gravely insulted, he may derive such *virtú* from his sense of outrage that he inflicts a desperate injury by way of return, as happened in the case of Pausanias, who assassinated Philip of Macedon for denying him vengeance after he had been dishonoured (405–6).

The danger in other cases is that your fortunes may fall into the hands of people lacking in any *virtuoso* concern for the public interest. This is what happens if you allow political decisions to be made in a slow or hesitating way. For it is generally safe to assume that those who wish to prevent a conclusion from being reached are 'moved by selfish passion' and are really trying 'to bring down the government' (361). The same is true of using auxiliary or mercenary troops. Since such forces are always completely corrupt, they 'usually plunder the one who has hired them as much as the one against whom they have been hired' (382).

But the most dangerous expedients are those based on the straightforward failure to appreciate that the quality of *virtú* matters more than anything else in military just as in civil affairs. This is why it is so ruinous to measure your enemies by their wealth, for what you ought to be measuring is obviously their *virtú*, since 'war is made with steel and not with gold' (350). So too with relying on artillery to win your battles. Machiavelli concedes, of course, that the Romans 'would have made their gains more quickly if there had been guns in those times' (370). But he persists in thinking it a cardinal error to suppose that, 'as a result of these fire-weapons, men cannot use and show their *virtú* as they could in antiquity' (367). He therefore continues to draw the somewhat optimistic conclusion that, although 'artillery is useful in an army where the *virtú* of the ancients is combined with it', it still remains 'quite useless against a *virtuoso* army' (372). Finally, the same considerations explain why it is especially dangerous to refuse negotiations in the face of superior forces. This is to ask more than can realistically be demanded even of the most *virtuosi* troops, and is thus 'to turn the outcome over' to 'the pleasure of Fortune' in a way that 'no prudent man risks unless he must' (403).

As in both his other Discourses, Machiavelli's survey of Roman history prompts him to end with an agonised comparison between the total corruption of his native city and the exemplary *virtù* of the ancient world. The Florentines could easily 'have seen the means the Romans used' in their military affairs, 'and could have followed their example' (380). But in fact they have taken no account of Roman methods, and in consequence have fallen into every conceivable trap (339). The Romans understood perfectly the dangers of acting indecisively. But Florence's leaders have never grasped this obvious lesson of history, as a result of which they have brought 'damage and disgrace to our republic' (361). The Romans always recognised the uselessness of mercenary and auxiliary troops. But the Florentines, together with many other republics and principalities, are still needlessly humiliated by their reliance on these corrupt and cowardly forces (383). The Romans saw that, in keeping watch over their associates, a policy of 'building fortresses as a bridle to keep them faithful' would only breed resentment and insecurity. By contrast, 'it is a saying in Florence, brought forward by our wise men, that Pisa and other like cities must be held with fortresses' (392). Finally—with the greatest anguish—Machiavelli comes to the gambit he has already stigmatised as the most irrational of all, that of refusing to negotiate when confronted by superior forces. All the evidence of ancient history shows that this is to tempt Fortune in the most reckless possible way. Yet this is exactly what the Florentines did when Ferdinand's armies invaded in the summer of 1512. As soon as the Spanish crossed the border, they found themselves short of food and tried to arrange a truce. But 'the people of Florence, made haughty by this, did not accept it' (403). The immediate result was the sack of Prato, the surrender of Florence, the collapse of the republic and the restoration of the Medicean tyranny—all of which could easily have been avoided. As before, Machiavelli feels driven to conclude on a note of almost despairing anger at the follies of the regime he himself had served.

4 The historian of Florence

The purpose of history

Shortly after the completion of the *Discourses*, a sudden turn of Fortune's wheel at last brought Machiavelli the patronage he had always craved from the Medicean government. Lorenzo de' Medici—to whom he had re-dedicated *The Prince* after the death of Giuliano in 1516—died prematurely three years later. He was succeeded in the control of Florentine affairs by his cousin, Cardinal Giulio, soon to be elected pope as Clement VII. The cardinal happened to be related to one of Machiavelli's closest friends, Lorenzo Strozzi, to whom Machiavelli later dedicated his *Art of War*. As a result of this connection, Machiavelli managed to gain an introduction to the Medicean court in March 1520, and soon afterwards he received a hint that some employment—literary even if not diplomatic—might be found for him. Nor were his expectations disappointed, for in November of the same year he obtained a formal commission from the Medici to write the history of Florence.

The composition of *The History of Florence* occupied Machiavelli almost for the rest of his life. It is his longest and most leisured work, as well as being the one in which he follows the literary prescriptions of his favourite classical authorities with the greatest care. The two basic tenets of classical—and hence of humanist—historiography were that works of history should inculcate moral lessons, and that their materials should therefore be selected and organised in such a way as to highlight the proper lessons with the maximum force. Sallust, for example, had offered an influential statement of both these principles. In *The War with Jugurtha* he argued that the aim of the historian must be to reflect on the past in a 'useful' and 'serviceable' way. And in *The War with Catiline* he drew the inference that the correct approach must therefore consist of 'selecting such portions' as seem 'worthy of record', and not trying to furnish a complete chronicle of events.

Machiavelli is assiduous about meeting both these requirements, as he reveals in particular in his handling of the various transitions and climaxes of his narrative. Book II, for example, ends with an edifying account of how the duke of Athens came to rule Florence as a tyrant in 1342 and was driven from power in the course of the following year. Book III then switches almost directly to the next revealing episode—the revolt of the Ciompi in 1378—after a bare sketch of the intervening half-century. Similarly, Book III concludes with a description of the reaction following the revolution of 1378, and Book IV opens after a gap of another forty years with a discussion of how the Medici managed to rise to power.

A further tenet of humanist historical writing was that, in order to convey the most salutary lessons in the most memorable fashion, the historian must cultivate a commanding rhetorical style. As Sallust had declared at the start of *The War with Catiline*, the special challenge of history lies in the fact that 'the style and diction must be equal to the deeds recorded'. Machiavelli again takes this ideal very seriously, so much so that in the summer of 1520 he decided to compose a stylistic 'model' for a history, the draft of which he circulated among his friends from the *Orti Oricellari* in order to solicit their comments on his approach. He chose as his theme the biography of Castruccio Castracani, the early fourteenth-century tyrant of Lucca. But the details of Castruccio's life—some of which Machiavelli simply invents—are of less interest to him than the business of selecting and arranging them in an elevated and instructive way. The opening description of Castruccio's birth as a foundling is fictitious, but it offers Machiavelli the chance to write a grand declamation on the power of Fortune in human affairs (533–4). The moment when the young Castruccio—who was educated by a priest—first begins 'to busy himself with weapons' similarly gives Machiavelli an opportunity to present a version of the classic debate about the rival attractions of letters and arms (535–6). The dying oration pronounced by the remorseful tyrant is again in the best traditions of ancient historiography (553–4). And the story is rounded off with numerous instances of Castruccio's epigrammatic wit, most of which are in fact stolen directly from Diogenes Laertius' *Lives of the Philosophers* and are simply inserted for rhetorical effect (555–9)

When Machiavelli sent this *Life* of Castruccio to his friends Alamanni and Buondelmonti, they accepted it very much in the spirit of a rehearsal for the large-scale historical work that Machiavelli was by then hoping to write. Replying in a letter of September 1520, Buondelmonti spoke of the *Life* as 'a model for your history' and added that for this reason he thought it best to comment on the manuscript 'mainly from the point of view of language and style'. He reserved his highest praise for its rhetorical flights, saying that he enjoyed the invented deathbed oration 'more than anything else'. And he told Machiavelli what he must have wanted most of all to hear as he prepared to venture into this new literary field: 'it seems to all of us that you ought now to set to work to write your *History* with all diligence' (C 394–5).

When Machiavelli duly settled down to compose his *History* a few months later, these stylistic devices were elaborately put to work. The book is conceived in his most aphoristic and antithetical manner, with all the major themes of his political theory reappearing in rhetorical dress. In Book II, for example, one of the *signori* is made to confront the duke of Athens with a passionate oration on 'the name of liberty, which no force crushes, no time wears away, and no gain counterbalances' (1124). In the next Book one of the ordinary citizens declaims an equally lofty speech to the *signori* on the theme of *virtú* and corruption, and on the obligation of every citizen to serve the public interest at all times (1145–8). And in Book V Rinaldo degli Albizzi attempts to enlist the help of the duke of Milan against the growing power of the Medici with a further declamation on *virtú*, corruption, and the patriotic duty to offer one's allegiance to a city that 'loves all her people equally', and not to one that, 'neglecting all the others, bows down before a very few of them' (1242).

Finally, the most important precept the humanists learned from their classical authorities was that the historian must focus his attention on the finest achievements of our ancestors, thereby encouraging us to emulate their noblest and most glorious deeds. Although the great Roman historians had tended to be pessimistic in outlook, and frequently dilated on the growing corruption of the world, this had usually prompted them to insist all the more vehemently on the historian's obligation to recall us to better days. As Sallust explained in *The War with Jugurtha*, it is only by keeping alive 'the memory of great deeds' that we can hope to kindle 'in the breasts of noble men' the kind of ambition 'that cannot be quelled until they by their own *virtus* have equalled the fame and glory of their forefathers'. Moreover, it was this feeling for the panegyric quality of the historian's task that the humanists of the Renaissance chiefly carried away from their study of Livy, Sallust and their contemporaries. This can clearly be seen, for example, in the account of the purpose of history that appears in the Dedication to the *History of the Florentine People* which the chancellor Poggio Bracciolini completed in the 1450s. This affirms that 'the great usefulness of a really truthful history' lies in the fact that 'we are able to observe what can be achieved by the *virtus* of the most outstanding men'. We see how they come to be activated by a desire 'for glory, for their country's liberty, for the good of their children, the gods and all humane things'. And we find ourselves 'so greatly roused up' by their wonderful example that 'it is as if they spur us on' to rival their greatness.

There is no doubt that Machiavelli was fully aware of this further aspect of humanist historiography, for he even refers admiringly to Poggio's work in the Preface to his own *History* (1031). But at this point—after following the humanist approach with such exactitude—he suddenly shatters the expectations he has built up. At the beginning of Book V, when he turns to examine the history of Florence over the preceding century, he announces that 'the things done by our princes, abroad and at home, cannot, like those of the ancients, be read of with wonder because of their *virtú* and greatness'. It is simply not possible to 'tell of the bravery of soldiers or the *virtú* of generals or the love of citizens for their country'. We can only tell of an increasingly corrupt world in which we see 'with what tricks and schemes the princes, the soldiers, the heads of the republics, in order to keep that reputation which they did not deserve, carried on their affairs'. Machiavelli thus engineers a complete reversal of prevailing assumptions about the purpose of history: instead of recounting a story that 'kindles free spirits to imitation', he hopes to 'kindle such spirits to avoid and get rid of present abuses' (1233).

The entire *History of Florence* is thus organised around the theme of decline and fall. Book I describes the collapse of the Roman empire in the west and the coming of the barbarians to Italy. The end of Book I and the beginning of Book II then relate how 'new cities and new dominions born among the Roman ruins showed such *virtú*' that 'they freed Italy and defended her from the barbarians' (1233). But after this brief period of modest success, Machiavelli presents the rest of his narrative—from the middle of Book II to the end of Book VIII, where he brings the story to a close in the 1490s—as a history of progressive corruption and collapse. The nadir is reached in 1494, when the ultimate humiliation occurred: Italy 'put herself back into slavery' under the barbarians she had originally succeeded in driving out (1233).

The decline and fall of Florence

The overriding theme of the *History of Florence* is corruption: Machiavelli describes how its malign influence seized hold of Florence, strangled its liberty and finally brought it to tyranny and disgrace. As in the *Discourses*—which he follows closely— he sees two principal areas in which the spirit of corruption is prone to arise, and after drawing a distinction between them in the Preface he employs it to organise the whole of his account. First there is a perennial danger of corruption in the handling of 'external' policies, the main symptom of which will be a tendency for military affairs to be conducted with increasing indecision and cowardice. And secondly, there is a similar danger in relation to 'the things done at home', where the growth of corruption will mainly be reflected in the form of 'civil strife and internal hostilities' (1030–1).

Machiavelli takes up the first of these issues in Books V and

VI, in which he chiefly deals with the history of Florence's external affairs. However, he does not undertake—as he had already done in the *Discourses*—to provide a detailed analysis of the city's strategic miscalculations and mistakes. He contents himself with offering a series of mocking illustrations of Florentine military incompetence. This enables him to preserve the accepted format of humanist histories—in which there were always elaborate accounts of notable battles—while at the same time parodying their contents. For the point of Machiavelli's military set pieces is that all the engagements he describes are wholly ridiculous, and not martial or glorious at all. When, for example, he writes about the great battle of Zagonara, which was fought in 1424 at the start of the war against Milan, he first observes that this was regarded at the time as a massive defeat for Florence, and was 'reported everywhere in Italy'. He then adds that nobody died in the action except three Florentines who, 'falling from their horses, were drowned in the mud' (1193). Later he accords the same satirical treatment to the famous victory won by the Florentines at Anghiari in 1440. Throughout this long fight, he remarks, 'not more than one man died, and he perished not from wounds or any honourable blow, but by falling from his horse and being trampled on' (1280).

The rest of the *History* is devoted to the miserable tale of Florence's increasing corruption at home. When Machiavelli turns to this topic at the start of Book III, he first makes it clear that, in speaking of internal corruption, what he chiefly has in mind—as in the *Discourses*—is the tendency for civic laws and institutions to be 'planned not for the common profit' but rather for individual or sectarian advantage (1140). He criticises his great predecessors, Bruni and Poggio, for failing to pay due attention to this danger in their histories of Florence (1031). And he justifies his own intense preoccupation with the theme by insisting that the enmities which arise when a community loses its *virtú* in this way, 'bring about all the evils that spring up in cities'—as the sad case of Florence amply demonstrates (1140).

Machiavelli begins by conceding that there will always be

'serious and natural enmities between the people and the nobles' in any city, because of 'the latter's wish to rule and the former's not to be enthralled' (1140). As in the *Discourses*, he is far from supposing that all such hostilities are to be avoided. He repeats his previous contention that 'some divisions harm republics and some divisions benefit them. Those do harm that are accompanied with factions and partisans; those bring benefit that are kept up without factions and partisans.' So the aim of a prudent legislator should not be to 'provide that there will be no enmities'; it should only be to ensure 'that there will be no factions' based on the enmities that inevitably arise (1336).

In Florence, however, the hostilities that have developed have always been 'those of factions' (1337). As a result, the city has been one of those unfortunate communities which have been condemned to oscillate between two equally ruinous poles, varying 'not between liberty and slavery' but rather 'between slavery and licence'. The common people have been 'the promoters of licence' while the nobility have been 'the promoters of slavery'. The helpless city has in consequence staggered 'from the tyrannical form to the licentious, and from that back to the other', both parties having such powerful enemies that neither has been able to impose stability for any length of time (1187).

To Machiavelli, the internal history of Florence since the thirteenth century thus appears as a series of hectic movements between these two extremes, in the course of which the city and its liberties have eventually been battered to pieces. Book II opens at the start of the fourteenth century with the nobles in power. This led directly to the tyranny of the duke of Athens in 1342, when the citizens 'saw the majesty of their government ruined, her customs destroyed, her statutes annulled' (1128). They accordingly turned against the tyrant and succeeded in setting up their own popular regime. But as Machiavelli goes on to relate in Book III, this in turn degenerated into licence when the 'unrestrained mob' managed to seize control of the republic in 1378 (1161–3). Next the pendulum swung back to 'the aristocrats of popular origin', and by the middle of the fifteenth century they were seeking once again to curtail the liberties of the people, thereby encouraging a new form of tyrannical government (1188).

It is true that, when Machiavelli arrives at this final phase of his narrative in Books VII and VIII, he begins to present his argument in a more oblique and cautious style. His central topic is inescapably the rise of the Medici, and he clearly feels that some allowance has to be made for the fact that the same family had made it possible for him to write his *History*. While he takes considerable pains to dissemble his hostility, however, it is easy to recover his true feelings about the Medicean contribution to Florentine history if we simply piece together certain sections of the argument which he is careful to keep separate.

Book VII opens with a general discussion of the most insidious means by which a leading citizen can hope to corrupt the populace in such a way as to promote divisive factions and acquire absolute power for himself. The issue had already been extensively treated in the *Discourses*, and Machiavelli largely contents himself with reiterating his earlier arguments. The greatest danger is said to be that of permitting the rich to employ their wealth to gain 'partisans who follow them for personal profit' instead of following the public interest. He adds that there are two principal methods by which this can be done. One is 'by doing favours to various citizens, defending them from the magistrates, assisting them with money and aiding them in getting undeserved offices'. The other is 'by pleasing the masses with games and public gifts', putting on costly displays of a kind calculated to win a spurious popularity and lull the people into forfeiting their liberties (1337).

If we turn with this analysis in mind to the last two Books of the *History*, it is not difficult to detect the tone of aversion that underlies Machiavelli's effusive descriptions of successive Medicean governments. He begins with Cosimo, on whom he lavishes a fine encomium in chapter 5 of Book VII, praising him in particular for surpassing 'every other in his time' not merely 'in influence and wealth but also in liberality'. It shortly becomes clear, however, that what Machiavelli has in mind is that by the time of his death 'there was no citizen of any standing in the city to whom Cosimo had not lent a large sum of money' (1342). And the sinister implications of such studied munificence have already been pointed out. Next, Machiavelli moves on to the brief career of Cosimo's son, Piero de' Medici. At first he is described as 'good and honourable', but we soon learn that his sense of honour prompted him to lay on a series of chivalric tournaments and other festivities that were so elaborate and splendid that the city was kept busy for months in preparing and presenting them (1352). As before, we have already been warned about the harmful influence of such blatant appeals to the masses. Finally, when Machiavelli comes to the years of Lorenzo the Magnificent—and thus to the period of his own youth—he scarcely troubles to suppress the rising note of antipathy. By this stage, he declares, 'the Fortune and the liberality' of the Medici had so decisively done their corrupting work that 'the people had been made deaf' to the very idea of throwing off the Medicean tyranny, in consequence of which 'liberty was not known in Florence' any more (1393).

The final misfortune

Despite Florence's relapse into tyranny, despite the return of the barbarians, Machiavelli still felt able to comfort himself with the reflection that Italy had been spared the worst degradation of all. Although the barbarians had conquered, they had not succeeded in putting to the sword any of Italy's greatest cities. As he observes in *The Art of War*, Tortona may have been sacked 'but not Milan, Capua but not Naples, Brescia but not Venice' and—finally and most symbolically of all 'Ravenna but not Rome' (624).

Machiavelli ought to have known better than to tempt Fortune with such overconfident sentiments. For in May 1527 the unthinkable happened. During the previous year, Francis I had treacherously entered a League to recover the possessions in Italy which he had been forced to cede after his crushing defeat at the hands of the imperial forces in 1525. Responding to this renewed challenge, Charles V ordered his armies back into Italy in the spring of 1527. But the troops were unpaid and badly disciplined, and instead of attacking any military targets they advanced directly on Rome. Entering the undefended city on 6 May, they put it to the sack in a four-day massacre that astounded and horrified the entire Christian world.

With the fall of Rome, Clement VII had to flee for his life. And with the loss of papal backing, the increasingly unpopular government of the Medici in Florence immediately collapsed. On 16 May the city council met to proclaim the restoration of the republic, and on the following morning the young Medicean princes rode out of the city and into exile.

For Machiavelli, with his staunchly republican sympathies, the restoration of free government in Florence ought to have been a moment of triumph. But in view of his connections with the Medici, who had paid his salary for the past six years, he must have appeared to the younger generation of republicans as little more than an ageing and insignificant client of the discredited tyranny. Although he seems to have nurtured some hopes of regaining his old position in the second chancery, there was no question of any job being found for him in the new anti-Medicean government.

The irony of it all seems to have broken Machiavelli's spirit, and soon afterwards he contracted an illness from which he never recovered. The story that he summoned a priest to his deathbed to hear a final confession is one that most biographers have repeated, but it is undoubtedly a pious invention of a later date. Machiavelli had viewed the Church's ministrations with disdain throughout his life, and there is no evidence that he changed his mind at the moment of death. He died on 21 June, in the midst of his family and friends, and was buried in Santa Croce on the following day.

With Machiavelli, more than with any other political theorist, the temptation to pursue him beyond the grave, to end by summarising and sitting in judgement on his philosophy, is one that has generally proved irresistible. The process began immediately after his death, and it continues to this day. Some of Machiavelli's earliest critics, such as Francis Bacon, felt able to concede that 'we are much beholden to Machiavel and others, that write what men do, and not what they ought to do'. But the majority of Machiavelli's original readers were so shocked by his outlook thst they simply denounced him as an invention of the devil, or even as Old Nick, the devil himself. By contrast, the bulk of Machiavelli's modern commentators have confronted even his most outrageous doctrines with an air of conscious worldliness. But some of them, especially Leo Strauss and his disciples, have unrepentantly continued to uphold the traditional view that (as Strauss expresses it) Machiavelli can only be characterised as 'a teacher of evil'.

The business of the historian, however, is surely to serve as a recording angel, not a hanging judge. All I have accordingly sought to do in the preceding pages is to recover the past and place it before the present, without trying to employ the local and defeasible standards of the present as a way of praising or blaming the past. As the inscription on Machiavelli's tomb proudly reminds us, 'no epitaph can match so great a name'.

Works by Machiavelli quoted in the text

The Art of War in *Machiavelli: The Chief Works and Others*, tr. A. Gilbert, 3 vols (Durham, North Carolina, 1965), pp. 561–726.

Caprices [*Ghiribizzi*] in R. Ridolfi and P. Ghiglieri, 'I Ghiribizzi al Soderini', *La Bibliofilia* 72 (1970), pp. 71–4.

Correspondence [*Lettere*], ed. F. Gaeta (Milan, 1961).

Discourses on the first Decade of Titus Livius in *Machiavelli*, tr. Gilbert, pp. 175–529.

The History of Florence in *Machiavelli*, tr. Gilbert, pp. 1025–1435.

The Legations [*Legazioni e commissarie*], ed. S. Bertelli, 3 vols (Milan, 1964).

The Life of Castruccio Castracani of Lucca in *Machiavelli*, tr. Gilbert, pp. 533–59.

The Prince in *Machiavelli*, tr. Gilbert, pp. 5–96.

A Provision for Infantry in *Machiavelli*, tr. Gilbert, p. 3.

Note on sources

The sources for the quotations given in the text, from works other than those by Machiavelli, are as follows:

Bacon (87): *The Advancement of Learning*, ed. G. Kitchen (London, 1973), 165.

Boethius: all quotations from *The Consolation of Philosophy (Philosophiae Consolationis)*, tr. S. Tester (London, 1973). References as follows: 26/177, 179, 197, 221; 27/263.

Bracciolini (81): *A History of the Florentine People (Historiae Florentini Populi)* in *Opera Omnia*, ed. R. Fubini, 4 vols (Turin, 1964), II, 91–4.

Burke (1): *Reflections on the Revolution in France*, Everyman edn. (London, 1910), 78.

Cicero: all quotations from *On Moral Obligation (De Officiis)*, tr. W. Miller (London, 1913). References as follows: 25/199, 211, 217; 36/177–9, 279; 40/45; 44/211–13; 45/231, 253; 46/191; 47/101; 54/163, 300–11.

Giovio (5): *Maxims placed next to the true likenesses of famous men (Elogia veris clarorum virorum imaginibus apposita)* (Venice, 1546), 55b.

Guicciardini (66): *Considerations on the 'Discourses' of Machiavelli* in *Select Writings*, tr. and ed. C. and M. Grayson (London, 1965), 68.

Landucci (32): *A Florentine Diary from 1450 to 1516*, tr. A. Jervis (London, 1927), 218.

Livy (25): the *History (Ab Urbe Condita)*, tr. B. Foster et al., 14 vols (London, 1919–59), VIII, 477–81.

Bernardo Machiavelli (5): *Diary (Libro di Ricordi)*, ed. C. Olschki (Florence, 1954), 11, 31, 35, 58, 88, 123, 138.

Marx (1): *Marx and Engels: 1848, Collected Works*, vol. 7 (London, 1979), 212.

Piccolomini (27–9): *A Dream of Fortune (Somnium de Fortuna)* in *Opera Omnia* (Basel, 1551), 616.

Pontano (34): *The Prince* (*De Principe*) in *Prosatori Latini del quattrocento*, ed. E. Garin (Milan, n.d.), 1042–4.

Sallust is quoted from *The War with Catiline* in *Sallust*, tr. J. Rolfe (London, 1931) as follows: 25/19; 78/9; 79/7; and from *The War with Jugurtha* in *Sallust*, tr. Rolfe, as follows: 78/137; 81/139.

Seneca is first quoted (25) from *The Epistles* (*Ad Lucilium Epistulae Morales*), tr. R. Gummere, 3 vols (London, 1917–25), II, 117; and later (45) from *On Mercy* (*De Clementia*), tr. J. Basore (London, 1928), 397–9, 435.

Strauss (88): *Thoughts on Machiavelli* (Glencoe, Ill., 1958), 9.

Whitfield (35): *Machiavelli* (Oxford, 1947), 105.

Further reading

Bibliography

There are several excellent surveys of the recent literature: E. Cochrane, 'Machiavelli: 1940–1960', *Journal of Modern History* 33 (1961), pp. 113–36; C Goffis, 'Gli studi Machiavelliani nell' ultimo ventennio', *Cultura e scuola* 33–4 (1970), pp. 34–55; F. Gilbert, 'Machiavelli in modern historical scholarship', *Machiavelli nel V° centenario della nascita* (Biblioteca di cultura, 2) (Bologna, 1973), pp. 155–71; and J. Geerken, 'Machiavelli Studies since 1969', *Journal of the History of Ideas* 37 (1976), pp. 351–68.

Biography

R. Ridolfi, *The Life of Niccolò Machiavelli*, tr. C. Grayson (London, 1963) is the standard authority. For a briefer account, see J. Hale, *Machiavelli and Renaissance Italy* (London, 1961). Hale is especially interesting on Machiavelli's diplomatic career. On this topic, see also F. Chabod, 'Il Segretario Fiorentino' in *Opere di Federico Chabod*, Vol. I: *Scritti su Machiavelli* (Turin, 1964), pp. 241–368.

Several recent biographical discoveries have been made. There is new and important information (on which I have drawn in chapter 1) about Machiavelli's humanist educational background in F. Gilbert, *Machiavelli and Guicciardini* (Princeton, N.J., 1965), pp. 318–22. See also S. Bertelli and F. Gaeta, 'Noterelle Machiavelliane', *Rivista Storica Italiana* 73 (1961), pp. 544–57. On the 'silent years' before 1498, D. Maffei, *Il giovane Machiavelli, banchiere con Berto Berti a Roma* (Florence, 1973) has advanced the startling claim that Machiavelli went to work in a bank at Rome at the age of eighteen, became a cashier in 1493 and remained there until his chancery appointment. But M. Martelli has demonstrated in 'L'altro Niccolò di Bernardo Machiavelli', *Rinascimento* 14 (1974), pp. 39-100, that the documents cited by Maffei refer to a different Niccolò Machiavelli. On Machiavelli's entry into the chancery, and on the nature of his duties there, the fundamental study remains N. Rubinstein, 'The beginnings of Niccolò Machiavelli's career in the Florentine chancery', *Italian Studies* II (1956), pp. 72–91. But see also R. Black, 'Florentine political traditions and Machiavelli's election to the Chancery', *Italian Studies* 40 (1985), pp. 1–16. Machiavelli's dispatches from the imperial court in 1508 have lately been minutely scrutinised by R. Jones. See 'Some Observations on the relations between Francesco Vettori and Niccolò Machiavelli during the Embassy to Maximilian I', *Italian Studies* 23 (1968), pp. 93–113. This article establishes that not all the reports were written by Machiavelli, as had previously been supposed; many were jointly composed by Machiavelli and Vettori. (In the text I have quoted only from those now known to be in Machiavelli's hand.) On Machiavelli's relations with the *Orti Oricellari* circle after his dismissal in 1512, two important studies are relevant: D. Cantimori, 'Rhetoric and politics in Italian humanism', *Journal of the Warburg Institute* 1 (1937–8), pp. 83–102; and F. Gilbert, 'Bernardo Rucellai and the Orti Oricellari: a Study on the Origin of Modern Political Thought' in his *History: Choice and Commitment* (London, 1977), pp. 215–46. Finally, the letter describing Machiavelli's deathbed 'conversion' has recently been proved to be a late eighteenth-century forgery. See R. Ridolfi, 'La "mancata conversione" del Machiavelli', *Archivo Storico Italiano* 127 (1969), pp. 383–95, and E. Levi, 'Nota su di un falso Machiavelliano', *Pensiero Politico* 2 (1969), pp. 459–63. For additional details and documents about various phases of Machiavelli's career, see also J. Stephens and H. Butters, 'New Light on Machiavelli', *English Historical Review*, 97 (1982), pp. 54–69.

The historical background

For a general introduction to fifteenth-century Florence, see G. Brucker, *Renaissance Florence* (London, 1969). The standard work on the ascendancy of the Medici is N. Rubinstein, *The Government of Florence under the Medici 1434-1494* (Oxford, 1966). For the whole Medicean story, see J. Hale, *Florence and the Medici* (London, 1977). On the relations between government and warfare in this period, see C. Bayley, *War and Society in Renaissance Florence* (Toronto, 1961) and M. Mallett, *Mercenaries and their Masters* (London, 1974). On the 'barbarian' invasions after 1494, Francesco Guicciardini's account in *The History of Italy*, tr. S. Alexander (London, 1969), has never been surpassed. For a lucid modern introduction, see chapters 6 and 9 of V. Green, *Renaissance and Reformation*, 2nd ed. (London, 1964).

The intellectual background

The great work is J. Burckhardt, *The Civilisation of the Renaissance in Italy*, tr. S. Middlemore (London, 1960). Also indispensable are the essays collected in P. Kristeller, *Renaissance Thought*, 2 vols (New York, 1961–5). For the general humanist background to Machiavelli's thought, see F. Gilbert, 'The Humanist Concept of the Prince and *The Prince* of Machiavelli' in his *History: Choice and Commitment*, pp. 91–114; J. Seigel, *Rhetoric and Philosophy in Renaissance Humanism* (Princeton, N.J., 1968); and Q. Skinner, *The Foundations of Modern Political Thought*, 2 vols (Cambridge, 1978). On the development of Florentine humanism in the fifteenth century, the crucial work is H. Baron, *The Crisis of the Early Italian Renaissance*, 2nd ed. (Princeton, N.J., 1966). See also E. Garin, 'I Cancellieri Umanisti della Repubblica Fiorentina da Coluccio Salutati a Bartolomeo Scala', *Rivista Storica Italiana* 71 (1959), pp. 185–208, and the same author's *Italian Humanism*, tr. P. Munz (Oxford, 1965). On humanist ideas about history and historical writing, see D. Wilcox, *The Development of Florentine Humanist Historiography in the Fifteenth Century* (Cambridge, Mass., 1969), and L. Green, *Chronicle into History* (Cambridge, 1972). F. Gilbert relates this background to Machiavelli's *History* in 'Machiavelli's *Istorie Fiorentine*: An Essay in Interpretation' in *History: Choice and Commitment*, pp. 135–53, a discussion to which my own analysis in chapter 4 is greatly indebted. For a general study of Machiavelli's relationship to 'civic humanism', see M. Hulliung, *Citizen Machiavelli* (Princeton, 1983).

Machiavelli's political thought

F. Gilbert, *Machiavelli and Guicciardini* (Princeton, N.J., 1965) is an outstanding study. J. Pocock, *The Machiavellian Moment* (Princeton, N.J., 1975) is another major contribution, especially valuable on the *Discourses*. G. Sasso, *Niccolò Machiavelli: storia del suo pensiero politico*, nuova editione (Bologna, 1980) provides the fullest chronological outline of Machiavelli's ideas, but stops short of the *History*. For briefer surveys see S. Anglo, *Machiavelli: a Dissection* (London, 1969) and N. Borsellino, *Niccolò Machiavelli* (Letteratura Italiana Laterza, 17) (Rome, 1973), which incorporates many findings of recent research. See also the important essays collected in C. Dionisotti, *Machiavellerie* (Turin, 1980).

The dating of several of Machiavelli's works remains a matter of scholarly controversy. In the case of *The Prince*, I accept that it was probably begun and completed in the second half of 1513. This is classically argued in F. Chabod, 'Sulla composizione de "Il principe" di Niccolò Machiavelli' in *Opere*, vol. I, pp. 137–93. In the case of the *Discourses*, I incline to the view that Machiavelli only began it after completing *The Prince*, was probably spurred into action by the *Orti Oricellari* group, and finished it before 1519. These claims are defended in an important article by H. Baron, 'Machiavelli: the Republican Citizen and the Author of "The Prince"', *English Historical Review* 76 (1961), pp. 217–53. In the case of *Mandragola*, I have followed R. Ridolfi, 'Composizione, rappresentazione e prima edizione della *Mandragola*', *La Bibliofilia* 64 (1962), pp. 285–300; Ridolfi proposes early 1518 as the date of composition. However, the songs were definitely added in 1526, and S. Bertelli, 'When Did Machiavelli Write *Mandragola*?', *Renaissance Quarterly* 24 (1971), pp. 317–26, has suggested that some of the text may have been drafted as early as 1504. Finally, in the case of Machiavelli's 'Caprices', two unequivocal discoveries have been made. Machiavelli is generally assumed to have written this letter to the former *gonfaloniere* Piero Soderini in January 1513. But R. Ridolfi and P. Ghiglieri, 'I *Ghiribizzi* al

Soderini', *La Bibliofilia* 72 (1970), pp. 53–74, have shown that the correct date is September 1506, while M. Martelli, '"I Ghiribizzi" a Giovan Battista Soderini', *Rinascimento* 9 (1969), pp. 147–80, has added that the intended recipient was Giovan Soderini, the *gonfaloniere*'s nephew.

A major focus of recent research has been the study of Machiavelli's political vocabulary. For his views on liberty, see M. Colish, 'The Idea of Liberty in Machiavelli', *Journal of the History of Ideas* 32 (1971), pp. 323–50 and Q. Skinner, 'The idea of negative liberty: philosophical and historical perspectives' in *Philosophy in History*, ed. R. Rorty et al. (Cambridge, 1984), pp. 193–221. On ambition, see R. Price, 'Ambizione in Machiavelli's thought' in *History of Political Thought* 3 (1982), pp. 383–445. On his concept of glory, see R. Price, 'The Theme of *Gloria* in Machiavelli', *Renaissance Quarterly* 30 (1977), pp. 588–631, and V. Santi, '"Fama" e "Laude" distinte da "Gloria" in Machiavelli', *Forum Italicum* 12 (1978), pp. 206-15. For his views about Fortune, see T. Flanagan, 'The Concept of *Fortuna* in Machiavelli' in *The Political Calculus*, ed. A. Parel (Toronto, 1972), pp. 127–56; R. Orr, 'The Time Motif in Machiavelli' in *Machiavelli and the Nature of Political Thought*, ed. M. Fleisher (New York, 1972), pp. 185–208; and the important general article by R. Wittkower, 'Chance, Time and Virtue', *Journal of the Warburg Institute* I (1937–8), pp. 313–21. See also H. Pitkin, *Fortune is a Woman* (Berkeley, 1984), and (more sceptically) Q. Skinner, 'Ms. Machiavelli', *The New York Review of Books*, March 14 1985, pp. 29–30. Finally, on the pivotal concept of *virtú*, see I. Berlin, 'The Originality of Machiavelli' in his *Against the Current*, ed. H. Hardy (London, 1979), pp. 25–79; I. Hannaford, 'Machiavelli's Concept of *Virtú* in *The Prince* and *The Discourses* Reconsidered', *Political Studies* 20 (1972), pp. 185–9; J. H. Hexter, 'The Loom of Language and the Fabric of Imperatives: the Case of *Il principe* and *Utopia*' in *The Vision of Politics on the Eve of the Reformation* (London, 1973), pp. 179–203; G. Paparelli, 'Virtú e Fortuna nel medioevo, nel rinascimento e in Machiavelli', *Cultura e scuola* 33–4 (1970), pp. 76–89; R. Price, 'The Sense of *Virtú* in Machiavelli', *European Studies Review* 3 (1973), pp. 315–45; and N. Wood, 'Machiavelli's Concept of *Virtú* Reconsidered, *Political Studies* 15 (1967), pp. 159–72.

Hobbes

Richard Tuck

Though words be the signs we have of one another's opinions and intentions; yet, because the equivocation of them is so frequent according to the diversity of contexture, and of the company wherewith they go (which the presence of him that speaketh, our sight of his actions, and conjecture of his intentions, must help to discharge us of): it must be extreme hard to find out the opinions and meanings of those men that are gone from us long ago, and have left no other signification thereof but their books; which cannot possibly be understood without history enough to discover those aforementioned circumstances, and also without great prudence to observe them. (Hobbes, *The Elements of Law, Natural and Politic* I.13.8)

Preface

Hobbes created English-language philosophy. Before his work, there was little written in English on the more technical areas of philosophy—on metaphysics, physics, and even ethics. Only Richard Hooker can count as a precursor, and then merely in one limited branch of philosophy, that of jurisprudence. But after Hobbes, there was no area of human enquiry deemed inappropriate for the English language. This was a remarkable achievement, and one which we tend to take for granted; but it was possible for Hobbes only because he had a thorough mastery of the contemporary debates in the traditional language of philosophy—Latin—and in the new language—French. He wrote continually in both Latin and English, and we cannot really understand his finest achievement (which was to produce, in *Leviathan*, the first unquestionably great philosophical work in our language) without surveying the full range of his intellectual activity.

This has seldom been done: of all the great philosophers, Hobbes has arguably been the most neglected by posterity. As we shall see in Part III, there are clear historical reasons for this; but the fact remains that he has suffered in many ways. He devoted at least half his time and energy to trying to understand modern science, at the moment at which it was first emerging; his understanding of it was certainly as acute as any of his contemporaries; yet because his ideas on this subject are not fully discussed in *Leviathan* his theories are disregarded. The works in which he set them out are scarcely read today, and some of them have not even been translated from their original Latin. Though *Leviathan* is remarkable in many ways, it was not actually intended by him to be his principal statement even on political and moral matters, and our (understandable) concentration on that single work has distorted many accounts of what Hobbes was trying to do.

Hobbes is thus a peculiarly appropriate figure to be discussed in a book of this kind, for the resurrection of what he was trying to do yields intellectual dividends well beyond the area of pure historical enquiry. But he is also an unusually difficult figure, for most present-day readers of Hobbes approach him with expectations formed either wittingly or unwittingly by the unsatisfactory traditions of interpretation which have developed about him during the last two centuries. I have therefore divided the body of the book into three parts. In the first, I have described his life (an astonishing and often tumultuous one) and the broad intellectual contexts in which he operated at different phases of his life. This part offers in effect a brief, synoptic view of Hobbes's philosophy. The second part then focuses more closely on the arguments advanced in his philosophical works, considering them as contributions to contemporary debates on science, ethics, politics, and religion. The last part considers in more detail the post-Hobbesian interpretations of these arguments, and compares them with the account of the arguments I have offered in Part II. Hobbes's modern commentators have, I believe, made him both more difficult and less interesting than he deserves, and locating him more firmly in the debates of his own time emphasizes rather than diminishes his importance in the debates of our century.

Many people have helped in the construction of this book, notably the undergraduates with whom I have discussed Hobbes over the past fifteen years (especially my present Special Subject group of historians in Cambridge), and my former colleague Noel Malcolm, whose knowledge of Hobbes is unparalleled. But I owe the following a particular debt for reading the manuscript of the book and commenting on it: Quentin Skinner, James Tully, Anne Malcolm, J. P. Tuck, and the general editor of the Past Masters series, Keith Thomas. All of them made me think again about important aspects of the work, and prevented many errors and infelicities from reaching a wider audience.

Contents

I Hobbes's life

The life of a humanist

It is sometimes tempting to think that the heroes of the various histories of philosophy or ethics—men as different as St Thomas Aquinas, Machiavelli, Luther, Hobbes, Kant, or Hegel—were all in some sense engaged on a common enterprise, and would have recognized one another as fellow workers. But a moment's reflection reminds us that it is we who have made a unity of their task: from their own point of view, they belonged to very different ways of living and had very different tasks to perform. They would have seen themselves as intellectually kin to men who do not figure in these lists— priests or scholars who had on the face of it no great philosophical interest. This is particularly true of the major philosophers of late sixteenth- and seventeenth-century Europe; many of them were trained as what were termed 'humanists', and their intellectual origins lay in the study of the classics and in the stylish and imaginative use of language characteristic of the early Renaissance humanists, rather than in the laborious philosophizing of their medieval precursors. The life of an intellectual in seventeenth-century Europe, in both its material conditions and its theoretical concerns, would have been immediately recognizable to a humanist of the early sixteenth century, but would have seemed very strange to a scholastic philosopher of the late Middle Ages.

Of no one is this truer than Hobbes. He was born into a relatively poor family, like many seventeenth-century writers—only Descartes and Robert Boyle, of all the throng of philosophers and scientists which the century produced, came from unimpeachably upper-class backgrounds. His father was an impoverished minor clergyman in the town of Malmesbury (Wiltshire), the kind of ecclesiastic left over from pre-Elizabethan times who was not even (almost certainly) a graduate. He was also an alcoholic who deserted his family when Thomas

115

was sixteen, to die (as Aubrey, Hobbes's wonderful biographer, and friend, recorded rather oddly) 'in obscurity beyond London'. Hobbes was born on 5 April 1588, and he seems to have been fond of repeating the joke that his mother fell into labour with him on hearing a rumour that the Spanish Armada was coming—'so that fear and I were born twins together'.

He was clearly recognized very early as an extremely clever boy, particularly at mastering the Renaissance curriculum of a sixteenth-century grammar school with its emphasis on a fluent and stylish grasp of Latin and, though to a lesser extent, Greek. Hobbes was a very fine linguist who could both speak and read Latin, Greek, French, and Italian as well as English. While still at school he translated Euripides' *Medea* from Greek into Latin iambics, and an interest in and a proficiency at translation accompanied him for the rest of his life. His first publication was in fact a translation into English of Thucydides (1629), and one of his last was a translation of the *Odyssey* into English verse. This also reflects the other skill which a Renaissance grammar school sought to impart to its pupils, and in which Hobbes was again spectacularly fluent—the writing of poetry. His first known written work to survive is a Latin poem on 'the Wonders of the English Peak in Darby-shire', and all his life he wrote Latin and English verse. He was, it should be said, in general an extremely quick writer of both prose and verse, once he put his mind to any project (though he also accused himself of laziness)—we know, for example, that he wrote the last ten chapters of *Leviathan* (about 90,000 words) in considerably less than a year.

These skills were not, in sixteenth- and seventeenth-century Europe, what they subsequently became—the resolutely impractical badge of a social élite. They had become embedded in the school curriculum since the Renaissance because they had a use, and were in fact highly marketable; proficiency at them offered a fine means of social advancement for a bright, lower-class boy. Clearly, the ancient professions—the Church, the Law and Medicine—recruited people of this sort; but there was a much wider demand for them, since anyone who was engaged in public life (particularly if that public life involved a knowledge of or participation in the wider European context) needed men about him who were good linguists and fluent and persuasive writers, capable of conducting correspondence, drafting speeches, giving advice, and training up children in the same skills. This was the market for 'humanism' as the word had been understood since the Renaissance, and it was the prevalence of such people in the city states and princely courts of Italy which had first fostered the development of Renaissance culture. But the same kind of men existed in Northern Europe, particularly in the great aristocratic families, and surprisingly many major seventeenth-century writers lived as the pensioners of such families (John Locke and John Selden are two notable examples).

It was into the household of one of these aristocrats that Hobbes was recruited, after passing from the Malmesbury school to an Oxford 'hall' (a kind of college entirely devoted to the general Arts course, rather than the specialized postgraduate professional courses). It may well be that, like Locke later, Hobbes felt a strong and principled reluctance to enter a profession, and particularly the largest employer of graduates, the Church; his hostility to all the professions was later most marked, and was something which earlier humanists too had often exhibited (it is no accident that most of the famous early Italian humanists were laymen). The household of a great English nobleman offered a different kind of life, though one with some social costs: it made a married life virtually impossible, and it is striking how many of the great seventeenth-century theorists were bachelors, living a life without close ties of affection; Locke is again an obvious case. Such households would disengage a theorist not merely from family ties, but from many of the institutions in which most people lived their lives, and would naturally breed a radical and self-confident race of intellectuals. And while they also continually emphasized the difference in social status between nobleman and employee—Hobbes referred to himself on occasion as a 'domestic' in the household of his employer—they did so while simultaneously putting the servant and the master on an intellectual level, leading to (in our eyes) a strangely ambiguous relationship.

The nobleman to whom the recently graduated Hobbes was recommended in February 1608 by the Principal of his hall was William Lord Cavendish, created Earl of Devonshire in 1618, who despite his title lived principally at Hardwick Hall in Derbyshire. The rest of Hobbes's life was spent in the employment either of the Earls of Devonshire, or their neighbours and cousins the Earls of Newcastle (or, briefly, another of their neighbouring families). He acted as secretary, tutor, financial agent, and general adviser, and we have one or two vivid glimpses of his life during the next twenty years. Like all such servants, he spent a lot of time sitting in anterooms while his master and other great men discussed state affairs (or merely gossiped), and Aubrey recorded that to while away the time he would read the pocket-sized editions of classical texts produced by the Dutch printers Elzevir. In the anterooms he would meet the secretaries of other noblemen, and some of Hobbes's disappointingly scanty correspondence from this period is with such secretaries and tutors, full of private jokes about their masters' doings. Because his master disliked financial affairs, Hobbes sat as his nominee on the board of the Virginia Company in which the Devonshires had a substantial holding. And when Lord Cavendish sent his son off on what would later be called 'the Grand Tour' between 1610 and 1615, Hobbes accompanied him as a tutor, though only three years separated pupil and tutor—another finely-judged and ambiguous relationship.

Touring round Europe as what one of his French friends later called the 'conducteur d'un Seigneur' became in fact one of Hobbes's major activities: in addition to the 1610–15 trip, he took the son of another family round Europe in 1630, and in 1634–6 he took the son of his pupil of 1610 on a journey similar to the one he had gone on with his father. These tours gave Hobbes an opportunity to meet both politicians and intellectuals throughout Europe which probably no other major thinker has ever enjoyed; by 1636 he had met most of the leading philosophers of his time, from Galileo (whom he probably met at Florence in the spring of 1636) to the Frenchmen Pierre Gassendi and Marin Mersenne—the latter was the only effective channel of communication with René Descartes (who was virtually in hiding in The Netherlands at the time), and he put Hobbes and Descartes in touch, though they did not actually meet until 1648.

But Hobbes was not particularly interested in such figures until the 1630s; what seems to have had the greatest impact on him in his early trips was his visit to Venice, where his master became acquainted with some of the principal writer-politicians of the Republic, who had recently defended its independence from the Papacy and the Hapsburgs in the 'Interdict Crisis' of 1606. When Hobbes and Cavendish returned to England, they kept in touch with these Venetians (Hobbes, characteristically, translating their letters from Italian to English so that his master could read them), and for some time the Venetians' concerns became those of the Cavendish household also. Many of the themes which emerged at this time were to play an important part, though often metamorphosed, in Hobbes's later works.

Venice was the only survivor from the great days of Italian republicanism, and the men who controlled it were obsessed, reasonably enough, with the question of what had led other Italian republics such as Florence to collapse into principalities effectively under the domination of Spain—which since its victory in the Italian wars of the early sixteenth century had imposed a system of formal and informal imperial control across the Peninsula, pulling the city-states into line with a combination of financial bribery, military intimidation, and propaganda about the threat from the Turkish Empire. Seen from Venice, and indeed from many other vantage points in Europe, this process (together with the comparable attempt by the Spaniards to maintain control of The Netherlands) was the quintessence of modern politics, and a whole *genre* of works on politics developed to analyse it. This was the kind of political literature with which the young Hobbes was most familiar; it was a particularly appealing *genre* for a humanist since it continually deployed classical themes and quoted ancient authors—and indeed some of the contributors to it were among the leading classical scholars of their time.

The central feature of this literature was a pervasive scepticism about the validity of the moral principles by which an earlier generation had lived. For writers of that earlier generation, in the late fifteenth or early sixteenth centuries, an effective public life lived by honourable men was still a possibility; and whether they were citizens of a republic such as Florence before the Medici, or advisers to a prince such as the Duke of Milan, the King of France or the Emperor Charles V, they found models for what they sought in the works of ancient writers who had followed the same vision—notably Cicero and Seneca. The idea that something like the Ciceronian republic could be reconstructed in modern Europe took an extraordinary hold on the imagination of many men at the beginning of the sixteenth century, and led some people (like the Italian Cardinal Bembo) to purge even their language of all post-Ciceronian accretions (which made writing a history of Venice, as Bembo did, rather difficult—for example, the Turks had become 'Thracians', and the nunneries of the city 'temples of vestal virgins').

But this Ciceronian ideal, vividly though it is expressed in the art and literature of Renaissance Italy, came by the end of the century to seem nothing more than a fantasy. The reality of modern politics was manipulation, deceit, and intimidation, and the classical author who captured this was not Cicero but Tacitus. One of the major theorists of this new attitude was the Netherlander Justus Lipsius, who said of Tacitus in 1574:

> this writer deals with princely courts, with the inner life of princes, . . . and he teaches us, who have noticed the similarity in many respects with our own times, that the same effects may come from the same causes. You will find under a tyrant flattery and treachery not unknown in our age; nothing sincere, nothing straightforward, and not even good faith amongst friends; constant accusations of treason . . .; mass slaughter of good men, and a peace more brutal than war.

Machiavelli, though himself in many ways an authentic Ciceronian, was reread by a new audience in the last decades of the
sixteenth century as a kind of Tacitist, and his fellow-country-
man Guicciardini was admired even more—largely because, far
more than Machiavelli, he expressed a sceptical disengagement
from politics. A term that Guicciardini first used became in
time a watchword for this new movement: it was *ragion di
stato*, 'reason of state', which appears in the titles of books and
pamphlets all over Europe from about 1590 onwards.

However, the sense that honour and morality had departed
from the world had wider implications than the merely political. Not only had the practical circumstances of modernity
rendered traditional ethics irrelevant, they had called into
question the validity of ethical commitments *as such*. Right
across Europe, for example, the Wars of Religion after the
Reformation had been fought to a standstill, with neither side
achieving an outright victory: almost all European countries
were now going to have to live with a substantial degree of
fundamental ideological conflict within their boundaries. It
would be hard to overestimate the shock which the warfare
between religious fanatics caused to disengaged contemporary
observers; as Lipsius said,

> Good Lord, what firebrands of sedition hath religion kindled
> in this fayrest part of the world? The chiefe heads of our
> christian commonwealths are at strife amongst them selves,
> and many millions of men have bin brought to ruine and do
> dayly perish, under a pretext of piety.

The response of many of Lipsius's generation (he was born in
1547) was to give up strongly held and publicly defended beliefs
of all kinds, and to retreat to a dispassionate and sceptical
stance. Here, too, they found ancient exemplars: the collapse
of the free Greek city-states of antiquity in the face of the
empires first of Alexander and his successors, and then of
Rome, had engendered a very similar set of attitudes. The
sceptics in the ancient world such as Pyrrho or Carneades
argued that nothing could be known securely about either the
moral or the physical world: knowledge of the former was

vitiated by irresolvable disagreement between different cultures and ages, while knowledge of the latter was prevented by the varying and inaccurate character of human observation (optical illusions, etc.). They urged instead the cultivation of what they called *ataraxia*, the complete suspension of belief and consequently of all emotional involvement with anything. To an extent, scepticism of this kind joined hands with another ancient philosophy, Stoicism: for while the Stoics did not rule out the possibility of knowledge, they also stressed that the path of wisdom was the elimination of emotion and passionate commitment, and the entering into a state of *apatheia*.

In the late sixteenth century, both sceptical and Stoic texts were widely read; Lipsius made himself an expert not merely on Tacitus but on Stoicism also, and he often expressed a sympathy with the ancient sceptics. His closest intellectual ally, the Frenchman Michel de Montaigne (about whom Lipsius once said, 'I have found no one in Europe whose way of thinking about things is closer to my own'), achieved great fame in his *Essais* of 1580–8 precisely by blending Tacitism, scepticism, and Stoicism in an enticing and persuasive mixture; he provided what might stand as a summary of the fundamental attitude when he said in a rightly famous passsage,

> what goodnesse is that, which but yesterday I saw in credit and esteeme, and to morrow, to have lost all reputation, and that the crossing of a River, is made a crime? What truth is that, which these Mountains bound, and is a lie in the World beyond them?

One universal principle of human conduct remained intact after this sceptical onslaught, however. It was that men both do and must seek their own *self-preservation*. Both Montaigne and Lipsius condemned public-spiritedness and patriotism, for such feelings exposed their possessor to great danger: the wise man took his own survival to be his central obligation, and would do nothing and cultivate no feelings which might endanger it. Moreover, if he had in the end to choose between his own survival and that of another, he must choose his own.

Here, again, they were echoing antiquity: the second-century B.C. sceptic Carneades had argued forcefully that in the event of a shipwreck, the wise man would be prepared to seize the only plank capable of bearing him to shore, even if that meant pushing another person off it.

A further parallel between the ancient world and the modern lay in the character of the target against which these arguments were levelled. In the ancient world, the most complete and systematic body of knowledge or 'science' was represented by the works of Aristotle, and it was against Aristotle and his followers that both sceptic and Stoic repeatedly turned. Aristotle had, for example, asserted that, all other things being equal, human perceptions of the external world were *correct*: if something *looks* white to an ordinary, healthy observer, then it *is* white. The sceptical stress on optical illusion and the generally unreliable character of sense-perception obviously undermined the whole of Aristotelian science. Likewise, Aristotle had expressed great confidence in the universality of (roughly) the conventional moral beliefs of a middle-class Athenian of his day, and it was easy to cast doubt on this by pointing to the astonishing diversity of ethical belief and conduct in the world.

For the writers of the late sixteenth century, too, Aristotle was one of the principal targets; both Protestant and Catholic had sought to align their certainties with his, and the whole Aristotelian enterprise gave people confidence that a determinate and valid body of knowledge was possible. Though the Ciceronians of Renaissance Italy had condemned the medieval Aristotelians, they had not in general condemned the historical Aristotle, and a new school of post-Renaissance Aristotelian studies sprang up in the early sixteenth century. But Lipsius, Montaigne, and their followers were intemperate in their attacks on Aristotle himself; as one of these followers, the Frenchman Pierre Charron, said in 1601, Aristotle 'hath uttered more grosse absurdities than [any other philosopher], and is at no agreement with himself, neither doth he know many times where he is'.

These, then, were the attitudes to modern politics which

seemed to many people early in the seventeenth century best to capture the realities of their situation. In Venice, all these themes were discussed: Paolo Sarpi, leader of the Republic during the Interdict Crisis, was a keen reader of Montaigne and a clear sceptic in his own right, while another propagandist for Venice (Trajano Boccalini) praised both Lipsius and Tacitus extensively. What in particular they found admirable in these modern authors was their disengagement from *religious* belief: Venice was struggling to maintain its independence in religious matters from the Papacy, and the Venetian state sought to keep a firm grip on religious enthusiasm in the city. Sarpi, despite being a Servite friar, went so far as to argue that a community of atheists could funtion perfectly well as a civil society, and he and his fellows were impressed when they read Francis Bacon's *Essays* (modelled on Montaigne, and influenced by Lipsius) to discover that he thought the same: 'atheism leaves a man to sense, to philosophy, to natural piety, to laws, to reputation; all which may be guides to an outward moral virtue, though religion were not; . . . we see the times inclined to atheism (as the time of Augustus Caesar) were civil times' (Essay XVII, 'Of Superstition').

Accordingly, they urged the translation of Bacon's *Essays* into Latin so that a wider European audience could read them, and were keen to keep in touch with Cavendish and Hobbes in order to use them as a channel of communication with Bacon. A letter of 1623 asked Cavendish to find someone who could act as an amanuensis for Bacon and then send information about his new ideas out to Venice. It is no surprise, therefore, to find Aubrey recording that Hobbes both translated several of Bacon's *Essays* into Latin, and took down his thoughts as Bacon dictated them while walking in his garden at Gorhambury. The Cavendish household also went in for writing Bacon-like essays on various subjects, a volume of which survives; it was once thought to be by Hobbes, but it is now thought that it was in fact by his pupil.

The Venetians were also keen on the study of the Greek historian Thucydides. While admiring Tacitus, they recognized that he dealt with the affairs of a monarchy, not a republic; in

Thucydides' history of the war between Athens and Sparta they found the appropriate text for a modern republic—far from the noble tone of Cicero, and suitably sceptical and relativist about human affairs. One of Sarpi's friends tried to persuade scholars throughout Europe to study Thucydides, and again it is no surprise to find that in 1629 Hobbes appeared in print for the first time with an English translation of Thucydides dedicated to the young third Earl of Devonshire in memory of his father (Hobbes's pupil on the Venetian trip), who had died prematurely the previous year, and that in the introduction to it he praised Lipsius.

The culture of modern humanism into which he had thus incorporated himself was to remain important to Hobbes for the rest of his life, though, as we shall see, he distanced himself from many of its specific elements, and in particular its openness to classical republicanism. Indeed, in one sense his life's work, at least in political theory, can be read as a transformation of this culture from within: what for Lipsius and Montaigne had been an ineluctable and natural principle of human conduct, namely self-preservation, becomes in Hobbes the fundamental *right* upon which a new kind of ethics can be constructed. But he embarked on this enterprise only after assimilating a rather different kind of intellectual culture, in which the study of metaphysics and physics played a far more prominent role than they had done in the humanist circles of his youth.

The life of a philosopher

The second Earl of Devonshire having died shortly before the translation of Thucydides was published, Hobbes found himself effectively without employment: the third Earl was only eleven on his father's death, and Hobbes did not belong in a fatherless household of young children. For a couple of years he acted as tutor in a neighbouring house, and then returned to the Devonshires to act as adviser to the Dowager Countess and tutor to the Earl. At the same time he came to be more closely associated with another branch of the Cavendish family, settled at Welbeck, about eight miles from Hardwick, and headed by

125

the Earl of Newcastle. He now began to act as agent and adviser for these Cavendishes also, and their interests pushed him in a new direction, away from his purely humanistic skills.

Both the Earl of Newcastle and his younger brother Sir Charles Cavendish were primarily concerned with military affairs: the Earl, indeed, became one of the principal Royalist generals on the outbreak of the Civil War in 1642. In early seventeenth-century Europe, there was virtually an entire way of life centred on the army: the war against Spain in The Netherlands, which had led to the independence of the Dutch republic in the late sixteenth century, gradually spread out across the Continent and became enmeshed with other wars and revolutions against Hapsburg power such as the Bohemian Revolt of 1618, until almost the whole of Europe was caught up in what was later termed the Thirty Years War (1618–48). England is usually thought to have been only marginally involved in this conflict, but in fact there was a substantial English army in Holland almost continuously from 1584 to 1642.

The miliary culture of early seventeenth-century Europe owed a lot to the modern humanism surveyed in the previous section. Lipsius, once again, was a leading theorist of both the Roman and the modern army, his works on military organisation and discipline being eagerly read even by field commanders. A contemporary critic of Tacitism even observed that Tacitus's prose style sounded like the clipped commands of a soldier, quite different from the orotund and peaceful prose of Cicero. But the military culture went beyond humanism in its interest in science and technology (though Lipsius did write a book on Roman military machines). The great new armies of the period fought with up-to-date weapons, particularly battle-field artillery, and a proper understanding of how the new technology worked was vital to effective soldiering.

The Earl of Newcastle and his brother had a consuming interest in military technology. The Earl was particularly concerned with horses (which were of course still centrally important in warfare), but he was also interested in the modern study of *optics*, especially its application to the development of an effective telescope—a tremendously important military prize for the first nation to develop one. It should be remembered that the very first, primitive telescope was constructed as late as 1608, by the Dutchman Lippershey. Sir Charles was himself a competent mathematician, and interested in both optics and ballistics (the development of modern mathematical dynamics and military fire-power going hand in hand). But the two brothers were also clearly interested in some of the fundamental theoretical issues thrown up by the new technologies, and corresponded with or helped financially philosophers and scientists both in England and on the Continent.

As an intermittent servant of the Earl of Newcastle, Hobbes found himself during the 1630s pursuing his master's interests in these areas. Thus he was sent off to look at horses and buy them on Newcastle's behalf; one of the odder productions of his pen was a theoretical analysis of the gaits of a horse which he produced for the Earl, but never published. In January 1634, while visiting London with 'My Lady' (that is, the Dowager Countess of Devonshire), Hobbes was commissioned by Newcastle to buy a copy of Galileo's *Dialogue Concerning the Two Chief Systems of the World* (1632), the foundational work of modern physics—the first indication that Hobbes was becoming involved in these concerns. During 1634 he discussed problems of optics and physics with people associated with the Welbeck Cavendishes, and when he took the young third Earl of Devonshire off on his Grand Tour later that year he also took with him letters of introduction from the Cavendishes to various French mathematicians and philosophers. Because of the importance of his young charge, he even obtained an invitation to meet Galileo himself at Arcetri near Florence. This journey, which lasted until October 1636, seems to have been one of the key periods in Hobbes's life, overshadowing even the Venetian visit of 1610.

It was at this time that he became aware of what was happening in French philosophical circles. The heart of French philosophy at this time was in a chamber of the convent of the Minim Friars in Paris, occupied by Father Marin Mersenne, whom Hobbes later described as 'the pole round which revolved every star in the world of science'. Mersenne both kept in touch with savants all over Europe, and seems to have had a clear vision himself of what a new philosophy must consist in. All the philosophers whose work he applauded and orchestrated differed from the humanist sceptics of the previous generation in that they believed that science of various kinds was possible. As we saw in the previous section, late sixteenth-century scepticism had called into question the possibility of ever having a true and systematic knowledge of *anything*: both the natural and the moral world were seen as essentially unknowable. But the philosophers round Mersenne rejected this pessimism, without in any way wishing to revert to traditional Aristotelianism. They had before them an example of a new kind of science, explicitly anti-Aristotelian but also transcending scepticism, in the shape of Galileo's physics; the philosophers following in his wake sought, in effect, to retain the critical insights of late Renaissance humanism (and much of its substantive content in the way of theories of language, political conduct, etc.), but to marry to them the new natural science of Galileo. Although, as we shall see, they came to hope that a new *ethical* science could be developed too, this seems to have been initially less important for them.

Mersenne himself published in 1625 a book on *Scientific Truth: Against the Sceptics or Pyrrhonians*, in which he sought to answer the sceptical case against the possibility of a wide range of sciences without returning to Aristotelianism; but his arguments were *ad hoc* and clearly unsatisfactory. However, one of his friends was able to accomplish what Mersenne hoped for: this was the famous René Descartes, who had actually been at school with Mersenne. Descartes was from a noble family, and had followed the calling of a soldier; indeed, he later alleged that his fundamental philosophical idea came to him while in winter quarters on one of the campaigns of the Thirty Years War. During the 1630s he was effectively in hiding in Holland, working on his philosophy and communicating with the outside world only through Mersenne. Between 1629 and 1633 he composed his first major work, *The World*, in which some of his ideas were put forward; but in it he committed himself to supporting Galileo's theory that the earth rotated, and news of Galileo's condemnation at the hands of the Roman Inquisition in 1633 led him to abandon publication of the book. However, much of the material that would have been in it appeared four years later in a collection of essays prefaced by *A Discourse on the Method for Rightly Conducting the Reason and Searching for Truth in the Sciences*, one of the most famous pieces of philosophical writing.

To understand Descartes's arguments (and, later, the comparable arguments of Hobbes), we must remember that the sceptical attack on natural science had emphasized the impossibility of accurate observation of the external world: since we are familiar with optical illusions, dreams, and so on, how do we know that what we see *really* has the properties which we ascribe to it? And if we cannot know that, how can we know the truth about anything? The answers these seventeenth-century philosophers gave to these questions might seem very simple to us, but that is because they have become the foundational presuppositions of our scientific culture. Descartes and his contemporaries were living in a culture saturated by Aristotelianism, where, if one was not a total sceptic, one was likely to believe that the external world actually possessed the properties ascribed to it by an observer, so that anything which, for example, looked red was really red, in the same sense that it might be said to be really a certain size or shape.

Descartes, however, denied this, without becoming a complete sceptic. Instead, he insisted that there need be no resemblance between what we experience and the external world: the sequence of images that constitutes our continuous life of perception does not necessarily represent in a picture-like way the world outside us. In *The World* he used the analogy of language: words refer to objects, but they do not *resemble* them; in the same way, he argued, visual images or other sensory inputs relate to objects without depicting them. The external world is in fact incapable of being experienced in its true character. By contrast, we can have an absolutely compelling knowledge of our own internal life, and of the images which flicker in front of us.

129

The difference between Descartes and a sceptic arose from this last point, and it is a subtle but nevertheless crucial divergence. For the sceptics, the fact that one person thought an apple was green and another thought it was brown illustrated our incapacity to know the truth: the apple, they believed, must be a determinate colour, but human perception could not decide what it was. To that extent, the sceptic was still a kind of Aristotelian, who simply insisted on the irremediable character of human fallibility: an ideal, non-human observer might see the world as it really was, and it would still be a world of colours, smells, tastes, and so on. Descartes, on the other hand, argued that we have no reason to suppose that there are colours, etc., in the real, external world *at all*, and therefore no reason to conclude that colour-blindness (for example) means that we cannot know the truth about that world. Colour is solely an internal phenomenon, caused no doubt by something external, but neither fallibly nor infallibly representing it.

Descartes was not actually the first person to come up with this idea. Something quite like it appears in a book which another friend of Mersenne's, Pierre Gassendi, wrote in 1625, but did not publish until 1649, while Hobbes also persistently claimed that he had had the same idea independently of both Descartes and Gassendi, in 1630. But though none of these three ever acknowledged as much, the idea in fact first appeared in print (applied to the sensation of heat rather than colour, but the principle is the same) in a work by Galileo of 1623, *The Assayer*. Descartes himself alleged in *A Discourse on the Method* that he had first had the idea in 1619, partly perhaps to register a prior claim to Galileo. Unfortunately, there is no corroboration for the claims of either Hobbes or Descartes. What is clear, however, is that like scientists today competing for a Nobel Prize, these philosophers were conscious of the great importance of the discovery and anxious to claim unique credit for it.

In one sense this idea answered the sceptic, but in another it engendered a new kind of scepticism, throwing doubt even on the *existence* of properties like colour. There is no question but that it was Descartes who was chiefly responsible for seeing this and exploring its implications. Between writing *The World* and *A Discourse on the Method* he was led to consider further the sceptical aspect of his idea, and in the latter work he was to present a notorious new doubt. Perhaps not only colours are non-existent, but also the material objects in which they seem to inhere? Perhaps there is *nothing* out there: after all, we can imagine a language which is complete in itself but which does not refer to any real objects (like the languages which Tolkien invented to accompany *The Lord of the Rings*), so why can we not imagine an orderly and systematic sequence of images which do not refer to anything? Dreams, Descartes pointed out, are precisely such sequences. The consequences of abandoning both Aristotelianism and traditional scepticism thus appeared vertiginous, leading to a form of scepticism more alarming than any before, in which the entire external world melted away.

At the beginning of *A Discourse* Descartes presented this doubt, along with more traditional doubts culled from the sceptical literature; he then sought to answer it, claiming that if this 'hyperbolical' doubt could be answered, the traditional ones would also collapse—though he had actually little reason to suppose this was the case. His answer rested on two arguments. The first was expressed in the slogan *Cogito ergo sum* ('I think therefore I am'): though there may be nothing outside, we know there is something inside, for we have direct experience of the interior world of colours, sounds, and so on. The puzzle is, does this interior world relate to anything external? Here Descartes used his second argument, which was an a priori 'proof' of God's existence (that is, a 'proof' which purports to need no information about the external world for its validity). Having to his own satisfaction established the existence of a God of a familiar kind—that is, a benevolent creator—Descartes concluded that such a God would not mislead his favoured creation, man. What we genuinely think we perceive must therefore be more or less what is actually out there.

The elegance with which Descartes presented his doubt

excited readers all over Europe; but the cogency of his answer was less apparent. As both Gassendi and Hobbes later pointed out, the argument for God's existence was very shaky, and if that was removed Descartes turned out to be a super-sceptic. Instead of doing the work Mersenne and the others hoped for, of vindicating the natural sciences, *A Discourse on the Method* then looked more like a demonstration of their wholly imaginary character. Science would (in our terms) be indistinguishable from science fiction. So a major task still remained for modern philosophy, and Hobbes, with characteristic intellectual self-confidence, appears to have decided after reading *A Discourse on the Method* that he would shoulder the burden.

What he produced at this point remained in manuscript, in some cases down to the twentieth century, and much has also been lost, so the true story of his first attempts at philosophy will probably never be known. The story in modern works on Hobbes is unnecessarily complicated by the fact that one of the great Hobbes scholars, the German Ferdinand Toennies, attributed to Hobbes in 1889 a manuscript in the British Museum known as 'A Short Tract on First Principles', and dated it to *c*.1630—the time when Hobbes claimed to have first thought of his theory of perception. Unfortunately, though all subsequent writers have followed Toennies, there is in fact no evidence that the manuscript is by Hobbes, let alone that it dates from *c*.1630; it also contains some arguments which directly contradict what Hobbes said was his fundamental idea. For these reasons I shall not refer to it again.

The secure evidence points to the following account. In the mid-1630s Hobbes followed the lead of the Earl of Newcastle and Sir Charles Cavendish into the modern study of optics and ballistics, becoming in the process as dissatisfied with conventional Aristotelian physics as he had earlier been with Aristotelian ethics. Even before reading Descartes, he had come to fundamentally the same conclusion as Descartes and Gassendi about perception; in a letter to the Earl in October 1636 about light passing through a pinhole, he remarked that 'whereas I use the phrases, the light passes, or the coulor [sic] passes or diffuseth itselfe, my meaning is that the motion is only in the medium, and light and coulor are but the effects of that motion in the brayne'. A year later a friend in Paris sent Hobbes a copy of Descartes's *Discourse,* in which Hobbes read of the sceptical use to which this idea could be put.

During the next three years Hobbes worked away on his philosophy, and by the end of 1640 (when, as we shall see, he had to flee to France) he had written two drafts. One was a fairly substantial work in Latin, divided into three 'Sections'. Section One was devoted to the fundamentals of metaphysics and physics—to such questions as the nature of space, matter, motion, and so on. Section Two was concerned with perception, and included a long discussion of the principles of optics (reflection, refraction, etc.), as well as other aspects of human conduct such as the desire for what is perceived and the judgement that it is 'good'. Section Three dealt with the political implications of these arguments. Hobbes seems to have intended that the overall title of the work should be *The Elements of Philosophy.* All that clearly survives of this early draft is part of Section Two (a manuscript formerly in Sir Charles Cavendish's possession and now in the British Museum), but we can tell from that fragment that a critique of Descartes was fundamental to it: Descartes's optics are criticized on almost every page.

The second of these two early drafts survives entire, indeed in many manuscript copies. It was a work in English which essentially put into a single compass what Hobbes had put in Sections Two and Three of the Latin *Elements of Philosophy;* he gave it the title *The Elements of Law, Natural and Politic.* It is characteristic of Hobbes that he should have worked on the same material simultaneously in English and Latin: this bilingual approach remained a feature of his work, and reflects his fluency and interest in translation. The *Elements of Law* was apparently written quite quickly, with the political events of 1640 very much in his mind, and it was widely circulated among his English friends; in the eyes of many of them, and of many subsequent readers, it remains one of the best statements of Hobbes's philosophy.

From the point of view of his French friends, for whom the

Latin *Flements of Philosophy* was presumably intended, the most striking thing about both drafts would have been the last sections, on politics. Though Descartes had rather vaguely proclaimed his intention of putting both ethics and politics on a new foundation, he conspicuously failed to do so, and remained one of the few major philosophers never to write on politics. Nor is there much indication, in Hobbes's correspondence with Newcastle and Newcastle's scientists in the mid-1630s, that he was then vitally concerned with political matters. But his move to include politics in his survey of philosophy is not in fact surprising, particularly given the form he gave to it—that is, an account of the elements of *law*, with the principles of *natural law* at its heart.

It is not surprising because there already existed a major work of legal philosophy which was extremely well suited in a number of respects to Hobbes's general purpose of transcending scepticism. It could play the same role for him as Galileo's *Dialogues* did for all the members of the Mersenne circle, as a representation for them of the kind of science which was to be put on their new, post-sceptical foundations. This work was Hugo Grotius's *The Laws of War and Peace*, published in 1625. Grotius was a Dutchman; only five years older than Hobbes, he already had an immense reputation across Europe. Like Hobbes, he had been a skilled humanist in his youth, and had been recruited to serve as an aide to one of the statesmen of his nation. But a remarkable career in Dutch politics culminated in 1619 with his being tried for treason, and nearly condemned to death; he escaped from prison, and spent the rest of his life in exile. As a young man he had been open to the humanism of Lipsius and Montaigne, but he gradually came to see that something new was required; in a series of works drafted in the first and second decades of the century he developed a new ethical theory, and from 1625 that theory was fully in the public domain.

Though *The Laws of War and Peace* is a long and discursive work, its fundamental argument is quite simple. It begins by posing the sceptical challenge to conventional ethics, through a summary of the views of the ancient sceptic Carneades, and then tries to answer the challenge—just as Descartes began by raising his doubt and then replied to it. Grotius's answer was in effect that whatever else they believed or had believed in the past, all men would agree that everyone has a fundamental *right* to preserve themselves, and that wanton or unnecessary injury to another person is unjustifiable. No social life was possible if the members of a society denied either of these two propositions, but no other principles were necessary for a social existence, at least on a rudimentary level.

Grotius made it clear that this theory was directed both at the sceptic and at the Aristotelian. It answered the sceptic because it showed that the multiplicity of beliefs and practices around the world was compatible with a minimal common core of morality, and it rebutted the Aristotelian because it disregarded the elaborate accounts of the virtues and the principles of natural law which Aristotelians had always sought to develop. Such things as *benevolence*, for example—actually helping one's neighbour, as distinct from not injuring him—were put by Grotius on a higher level than the minimal core: one could envisage a society of rather stand-offish individuals who had no sense of common welfare beyond the common security of their own persons. International relations, according to Grotius, provided an example of just such a society: nation-states were under no obligation to help one another, but they were obliged not to harm each other; and much of his book was devoted to exploring the implications of this observation.

Three features of Grotius's work were particularly significant for Hobbes's enterprise. The first was that Grotius had in a sense converted the sceptical humanist's language of self-preservation into a language of *natural rights*—that is, into a genuinely *moral* language—without abandoning much of the actual content of the theories put forward by men such as Lipsius and Montaigne. Theories based on natural rights were to be the principal vehicles for the discussion of ethical issues for the rest of the century. Second, Grotius (unlike Descartes) had accomplished this conversion without talking about God; in fact, in a notorious passage he said that his thesis would hold good 'even if we should concede (what cannot be conceded without great wickedness) that there is no God'. Grotius had met the sceptic on his own ground: if the source of the sceptic's dismay was his perception of the multiplicity of human beliefs, that dismay could be countered simply by pointing to something all human beings must have in common.

But in some ways it was the third feature which was most significant. Grotius's minimal core of rights and duties gave rise to a 'state of nature' (though he did not himself often use this term), a state in which *all* men must find themselves simply *qua* men, and on to which would be grafted the various appurtenances of developed civil life, including benevolence. Thus whatever rights or duties were claimed by governments must have arisen from or be compatible with the rights and duties of the state of nature. In this sense Grotius was a thorough-going individualist: no political community could have any moral hold over its members unless those members had in some way given it that moral hold. This, too, was to be chracteristic of much political thought in' the course of the century.

The use to which Grotius put his new theory of natural rights was also suggestive. We are accustomed, perhaps, to thinking of natural rights as a *liberal* doctrine, and to associating them with such things as the American Declaration of Independence—the 'rights of man'. But for Grotius, as for many of his early followers, the implications of the minimalist theory of natural rights were *illiberal*. *All* we have the fundamental right to do is to preserve ourselves; whatever is necessary to our preservation (without, at least according to Grotius, endangering other people's preservation) is *ipso facto* legitimate. He gave two examples of this: one was voluntary slavery, in which someone on the verge of starvation or execution sells himself to a master in return for his life and food, and the other was absolute monarchy, where an entire population might renounce their civil rights in order to achieve social peace or prosperity. It is worth remembering that the latter was precisely the justification used both by the Roman emperors and by modern absolute rulers for their despotic powers, while the former was believed by many Europeans (not unjustifiably) to be the means by which the native slave traders of West Africa had acquired their prisoners. Grotius's theory thus fitted neatly into the actual practices of his time—something for which Jean-Jacques Rousseau was later vehemently to denounce him.

It was these illiberal implications of the Grotian theory which were especially relevant to Hobbes's view of the English political scene in the late 1630s. Hobbes later said that he had developed his political ideas at this time because his native country was 'burning with the questions of the rights of rulers and the duties of subjects, forerunners of an approaching war' (*De Cive*, Preface 19), and indeed some fundamental political issues were being raised in England between 1637 and 1640. For fifty years England's stance in European politics had been as the ally of Holland in its struggle with the Spanish empire (an alliance which had led to the Armada War itself); now Charles I, alarmed by the developing imperial hegemony of his erstwhile ally, was trying to shift England more into the Spanish camp. His alarm was well founded: the Dutch were creating a formidable empire based on commerce and military power, and even under Cromwell the English were to find themselves fighting against them. But public opinion in England during Charles's reign was very unwilling to sanction such a shift, and Charles knew that the military expenditure necessary could not be funded by a parliamentary grant: for a variety of reasons he had been unprepared to summon a Parliament since 1629. So from 1635 onwards he tried to raise money for a new anti-Dutch fleet through 'Ship Money', an ancient and contentious right of the Crown to tax communities specifically in order to pay for a navy.

There was considerable opposition to this tax, and a famous legal case in 1637 ('Hampden's Case') argued out the issues. The Crown claimed both that any sovereign must have the power to raise military forces for the defence of the realm, and that it must be the sole judge of whether a threat to the realm existed; the opposition conceded the first claim, but denied the second, arguing that public opinion, particularly when represented in a Parliament, could also be the judge of whether a threat existed—and manifestly England's security was not endangered by the Dutch. As we shall see, these must have been the 'questions' to which Hobbes was referring—the argument of the *Elements of Law* is particularly well judged as a contribution to the Ship Money debate, on the King's side. In England as on the Continent, the language of 'natural rights' was thus to be used first as a defence of the established authority.

By 1640 opposition to Charles's policies was getting out of hand. The Scots dealt the final blow by raising an army to resist his ecclesiastical programme in their country, and defeating the English army sent against them. The military débâcle forced Charles to call two Parliaments in 1640, first the 'Short' Parliament and then, in November, the famous 'Long' Parliament. It was clear that when the Parliaments met they would turn against the King's ministers; indeed the Long Parliament passed an Act of Attainder against his principal minister, the Earl of Strafford, who was executed in May 1641. Strafford was an old patron of the Earl of Newcastle, and Newcastle's circle obviously felt both the need to come to his support, and fear lest they be caught up in his downfall. There may even have been a move to have Hobbes stand as a candidate for the Short Parliament—a transition from humanism to politics by no means unprecedented (Grotius is an obvious parallel). Though Hobbes was not himself in the end present in the Parliament, he wrote the *Elements of Law* as a kind of brief for the Earl and his supporters to use in the debates. But when the Long Parliament met, Hobbes's dominant emotion was fear that the *Elements of Law* might be used against him in some future prosecution; accordingly, he suddenly fled to France in November 1640, and stayed there until the winter of 1651–2, throughout the bitter campaigns of the English Civil War.

A few days before going, he decided to let his French friends know how his philosophy had developed, and sent Mersenne what may have been a summary of the *Elements of Philosophy*. Mersenne, as requested, sent the critical sections on Descartes on to Descartes himself, who responded extremely coolly to this unknown opponent. On the strength of this summary, Mersenne also persuaded Hobbes to contribute to a set of objections to a work by Descartes (the *Meditations on First Philosophy*), which was to be published alongside the work itself in 1641. Once settled in Paris, Hobbes busied himself getting ready for the publication in Latin of Section Three of the *Elements of Philosophy*, which naturally included much of the material which had appeared in the political chapters of the *Elements of Law*, and which shared with the English work an obvious and immediate relevance to the political situation. He finished the text in November 1641, and it was printed in April 1642 under the title *Section Three of the Elements of Philosophy: The Citizen (De Cive)*. As the title indicates, Hobbes clearly intended to follow it up reasonably quickly with Sections One and Two, but a number of things delayed him.

The first is that he was now daily in touch with French philosophy, and becoming more aware of the complexities of modern physics and metaphysics. From being a critic of Descartes rather outside the Mersenne circle, he was now more of an ally in a common struggle; thus (probably at Mersenne's request) he devoted much time in 1643 to a critique of an anti-Cartesian and anti-Galilean work by another English exile, Thomas White. A summary of this critique appeared the following year in a volume edited by Mersenne; this was the first public appearance of Hobbes's general philosophy, as distinct from his political theory. By 1646 Hobbes could speak quite warmly of Descartes, depicting himself as a kind of under-labourer to him. They eventually met in 1648, shortly before Descartes emigrated to Sweden, where he died in 1650.

The second reason for the delay was Hobbes's new poverty. Like the other Royalist exiles who joined him in Paris as the war increasingly went against the King, he was cut off from his English income—in his case, the income of the Cavendishes from their estates. In 1646 poverty obliged him to accept the post of tutor in mathematics to the Prince of Wales, later Charles II, who had also arrived in Paris (the Prince later described Hobbes as 'the oddest fellow he ever met with'). This job apparently took up a lot of time, and Hobbes claimed that it prevented him from finishing the *Elements of Philosophy*;

he was also paid extremely erratically for his labours. Nevertheless, by May 1646 he had drafted (in English) a lot of what
would later appear as Section Two of the *Elements*, and was
well on the way to finishing Section One. However, the fact
that when he sanctioned a new edition of *De Cive* that year he
amended the title simply to *Philosophical Elements of the
Citizen*, and thus avoided committing himself to further instalments, may perhaps be an indication of a new sense of
realism. The new edition appeared early in 1647 from the
Elzevir Press in Amsterdam, a mass-market publishing house,
whose imprint set Hobbes firmly before the international
audience. The first edition of *De Cive* had been on a very small
scale, and not until 1647 was his name known outside his own
circle of friends. Hobbes added to the second edition a number
of lengthy explanatory footnotes which often illuminate puzzling areas of his argument better than anything else he ever
wrote.

In 1647 he was very ill for some months, and was indeed so
close to death that he was given the last rites. He was never to
be wholly well again, though his remarkable constitution gave
him another thirty years of life; from about 1648 he began to
exhibit symptoms which modern scholars have thought indicated Parkinson's disease, and he increasingly came to rely on
amanuenses rather than write out his manuscripts personally.
This, together with the difficulties consequent upon his move
back to England in 1651 (see next section), delayed the completion of the *Elements of Philosophy* even more; as a result
Section One did not finally appear until 1655, under the title
Matter (De Corpore), and Section Two only appeared in 1658
under the title *Man (De Homine)*. The three sections were not
printed together in a single volume until the publishers Blaeu
of Amsterdam (another mass-market house) produced a collected edition of Hobbes's Latin works in 1668. Hobbes may
have mentally slowed down too: both *De Corpore* and *De
Homine* were far from satisfactory in many respects, and have
never commanded the enthusiastic following of his earlier
works. The story of Hobbes's construction of a philosophical
system is thus in the end a story of compromise and tiredness:

the freshness of his early ambitions turned to a weary dogmatism in the printed volumes which eventually appeared.

The life of a heretic

Though his illness in 1647 may have slowed him down, and though it would not have been surprising for someone in the mid-seventeenth century to have died at the age he was then (fifty-nine), it is a remarkable fact that very soon afterwards he was able to compose his most famous work, *Leviathan*, which appeared from an English publisher in April 1651. Hobbes sent instalments of his manuscript for setting in type each week from Paris to London, with proofs being sent back each week in return—an astonishing method of publishing. It was *Leviathan* which quickly gained for Hobbes the reputation of 'the Beast of Malmesbury'—a reputation which he has never altogether lost, and which led to a long period in which he was under threat from men who had once been his friends. They believed that the book was in many ways a repudiation of all that Hobbes had formerly stood for, and in particular a piece of treachery to the cause of royalism in England—a cause which was in need of redoubled support after the execution of Charles I in January 1649. After the restoration of the monarchy in 1660, Hobbes persistently denied these charges, but they were not wholly unfounded.

One indication of this is the fact that a year after Charles's execution, Hobbes's early works began to be pirated by English publishers, anxious to use them to establish a wholly royalist case against the new republican regime, but Hobbes quite clearly and deliberately refused to allow *Leviathan* to be used in this way. Thus the *Elements of Law* was published (in two parts) early in 1650, and an unauthorized translation of *De Cive* was registered by its publisher in November 1650, actually appearing in the shops in March 1651, at about the same time as *Leviathan* itself. These unauthorized publications were read enthusiastically by Royalists; one of them, an old friend of Hobbes called Robert Payne, after finding the *Elements* in an Oxford bookshop and erroneously taking it to be a pirated translation of *De Cive*, wrote to Hobbes in May 1650 urging him to produce an authorized translation.

The answer he received greatly disconcerted him, for Hobbes replied that he already had 'another trifle on hand' in the shape of an English work on politics, almost two-thirds completed, and being translated into French as he wrote it by a friend of his—a translation which has disappeared. This 'trifle' was, of course, *Leviathan*. When Hobbes told Payne what the new work contained, his old friend was even more disconcerted, for he learned that it involved an explicit attack on the Anglican ecclesiastical order and a defence of what was known as 'Independency'. The attack was contained in Parts Three and Four of the book; Parts One and Two were a restatement of Hobbes's psychological and political ideas, and were substantially the same as the earlier versions. What was significant about *Leviathan*, and the reason why Hobbes wrote it, was the argument embedded in the parts of the book which few modern readers have ever read.

To understand Payne's horror, we have to remember that one of the central issues in the Civil War was the status and organization of the Church. After attainting Strafford and repudiating Charles's policies during the 1630s, the Long Parliament had turned its attention to the Church and proposed the abolition of bishops and their replacement by a system of lay commissioners. For Charles and the Royalists, the preservation of the episcopal Church of England was an issue almost as worth fighting over as the question of who should control the army, though it was the latter issue which actually tipped the nation into open war in 1642; for their parliamentary opponents the reconstruction of the Church was equally important. In 1643 the King looked close to winning the war through his control of the coalfields of north-eastern England, which cut off the energy supplies of London; in order to break this control, Parliament needed to bring the Scots into the war, but the Scots were prepared to come in only if the English agreed to introduce a Presbyterian system of church government, in which clergymen and bodies of lay elders exercised a formidable moral and religious control over the population and over the institutions of the State.

From 1644 until 1649 Parliament was formally committed to such a system, but many English parliamentarians feared it as much as they feared the disciplines of episcopacy. What they wanted was something more like the practice in parts of New England, in which congregations were relatively independent in doctrinal and disciplinary matters, and the State exercised only a loose, supervisory role. Cromwell and the soldiers under him came to represent this Independency, and their military triumph against both the King and, later, the Scots ensured that it was their vision of church government which would prevail in the new republic.

Given this background, it is easy to see why Payne was horrified, for Hobbes was endorsing precisely the principles held by the men who had executed the King. From the time when they came to know what *Leviathan* contained, his old Royalist friends would have nothing more to do with him, and began to accuse him of 'atheism', 'heresy', and 'treachery'— accusations which, it must be stressed, were only rarely levelled at him on account of his earlier works. Even Clarendon, minister to both Charles I and Charles II, admired the *Elements of Law* and *De Cive*, though he too was repelled by *Leviathan*.

Furthermore, Hobbes was not content merely to defend a particular system of church government. When the book was finally published, his former friends were shocked to discover that it also contained what one of them described as 'a farrago of Christian atheism'—a most idiosyncratic version of Christian theology designed to fit in with a materialist philosophy. Though his materialism had never been concealed, and was particularly obvious in his published objections to Descartes's *Meditations*, it had never been so gratuitously offensive to orthodox theology as it was presented in *Leviathan*. The very title of the book was chilling: it was a reference to chapter 41 of the Book of Job in the Bible, in which the 'leviathan' (or sea monster) is described in terms of his absolute and terrifying power—'upon earth there is not his like, who is made without fear'. This was the State as depicted by Hobbes, with absolute power even over God's servants such as Job. The message was rubbed in still more by an astonishing title page (probably designed by the artist Wenceslas Hollar) in which a giant figure composed entirely of a mass of smaller figures is shown looming, sword and crozier in hand, over a settled countryside.

Hobbes quite clearly intended *Leviathan* to be offensive to contemporary, particularly Anglican, sensibilities; he even added a 'Review and Conclusion' in which he explicitly aligned his book with the recent pamphlet literature in England defending the new regime on the basis of its actual possession of power. Why, then, did Hobbes write it? Payne's explanation was that he had been offended in some way by the Anglican clergy gathered at the exile court in Paris, and there may have been something in that. Certainly, Hobbes seems to have been a constant source of irritation to them. This irritation found a relatively honourable expression in a controversy between Hobbes and Bishop John Bramhall in 1645 over free will and determinism, but it may have had a less honourable side— Hobbes seems to have thought that the machinations of the clergy kept him from receiving the full payment for his work as the Prince's tutor.

But we must also remember that the ecclesiastical regime put into place by the new republic after 1649 was very close to what Hobbes seems to have wanted on general grounds, and which he may well have enthusiastically preferred to traditional episcopacy. This is because, like almost all the most interesting seventeenth-century political theorists (including Grotius and Locke), he seems to have feared the moral and intellectual disciplines of Presbyterian Calvinism far more than anything else. It was the Calvinists of Holland who drove Grotius into exile, and who seemed to be a threat to modern sceptical and post-sceptical philosophy; for their opponents, episcopacy was useful as a bulwark against Presbyterianism, but it had a disciplinary structure of its own which might one day be used against philosophy. The relatively tolerant and lay-influenced episcopacy of England in the 1630s was not necessarily to be relied on. But a system of Independency had no general ecclesiastical discipline: all was made free within a structure imposed purely by the State. As we shall see, this corresponded precisely to what Hobbes deeply desired, but which he had presumably thought impossible until 1649.

Indeed, as early as September of that year he told Gassendi that he was inclined to go back to England, and at the end of 1651 (after presenting Charles II with a manuscript copy of *Leviathan*) he slipped across the Channel, never to return to France. The Earl of Devonshire had 'compounded' for some of his estate earlier in the year (that is, had paid the government a lump sum in return for repossessing land of which he had been deprived for supporting the King), and was thus able to pay Hobbes a stipend again; in 1653 Hobbes moved back into his old way of life, living mainly at Devonshire House in London.

His life under the Commonwealth and, later, the Protectorate of Cromwell, was relatively untroubled. He had various friends and supporters under the new regime, of whom perhaps the most interesting was John Selden, who was in many ways the closest English equivalent to Grotius—a lawyer and political theorist who had eagerly taken up the Grotian theory of a minimalist, post-sceptical morality, and who had always been a dedicated opponent of ecclesiastical authority and discipline. Though in the 1620s he had led the parliamentary opposition to the Crown, and to many of Hobbes's friends, in the 1630s he mixed with men like Clarendon and written in defence of the anti-Dutch policies of Charles I. But after being elected to the Long Parliament he committed himself to Parliament's cause during the Civil War, largely because he always believed that he and his friends could eventually secure the kind of ecclesiastical settlement they wanted, with the Church firmly under state control—and so it proved. Many of the leading politicians under both the Commonwealth and the Protectorate admired him; John Milton praised him, and Cromwell at one point considered asking him to write a new constitution for England. Though he and Hobbes did not meet until Hobbes sent him a complimentary copy of *Leviathan*, Hobbes had long respected his work, and he is almost the only person mentioned without cavil in *Leviathan*. Hobbes was allegedly present at his deathbed in 1654, and urged him not to see a priest, remarking (according to Aubrey), 'Will you that have wrote like a man, now dye like a woman?'

But though men like Selden were in power, and Presbyterianism had not triumphed, it had also not conclusively been defeated; some clergymen still wanted to see a national Presbyterian church. Moreover, there were still spokesmen for traditional episcopacy to be found. During the 1650s Hobbes found himself drawn into confrontations with both groups. Against the latter, he published the papers exchanged between himself and Bramhall ten years earlier, to which Bramhall replied with a defence of his own position which went well beyond sober philosophizing.

Much more important, however, was his confrontation with the Presbyterians. This took the form of participating in the struggle between Independents and Presbyterians at Oxford during the middle years of the decade, an involvement which took two forms. On the one hand, he engaged in an acrimonious controversy with a prominent Oxford Presbyterian, John Wallis; this arose from Wallis's objections to some of Hobbes's geometrical arguments in *De Corpore* but quickly spread to cover (in the words of the title of one of Hobbes's contributions) 'the Absurd Geometry, Rural Language, Scottish Church-Politicks and Barbarismes of John Wallis'—a fine catalogue of everything Hobbes detested most. On the other, he provided aid and advice to the Independents at Oxford fighting against men such as Wallis, a group which ranged from a young don called Henry Stubbe (who began to translate *Leviathan* into Latin) to the Vice-chancellor himself, an Independent who had been put into place by the republican government.

The weight of the English political establishment at this time was on Hobbes's side. This was not to be true, however, after the Restoration in 1660. When the republic collapsed in internal feuding after Cromwell's death, it was a hastily constructed coalition of Hobbes's adversaries—the Presbyterians and Anglicans—which paved the way for the return of the King. They were duly rewarded with the establishment of a Presbyterian regime in Scotland and the restoration of the Anglican order in England, in which dissenters were penalized in a variety of ways. Moreover, the men who returned to power from exile with Charles II were in many cases men who had known and admired Hobbes before the war, but now detested him for his apparent treachery. The most spectacular instances of this were two of the principal ministers in the new government, Edward Hyde, Earl of Clarendon, and Gilbert Sheldon, Bishop of London 1660–3 and Archbishop of Canterbury 1663–77. Both men saw themselves as heirs to the Anglican royalism of the late 1630s, which they took Hobbes too to have endorsed at the time; in his autobiography Clarendon depicted the Anglican culture of that age in his idyllic portrayal of the circle of friends who met at Lord Falkland's house at Great Tew in the years before the Civil War, a circle which included Sheldon and many other former friends of Hobbes. They wished now to reinstate the values of Great Tew, and to punish Hobbes for his repudiation of them.

On the other hand, neither Clarendon nor Sheldon had unquestionable power within the new regime. The King himself was by no means a committed Anglican (indeed, he became a secret convert to Roman Catholicism), and many of his courtiers and advisers were either rather raffish libertines or survivors from the Protectorate, neither of which groups were particularly wedded to Clarendon's vision, and both of which were prepared to allow more toleration to dissenters. Hobbes's 'atheism' or 'heresy' in fact became an issue in the struggle within the government between these various figures, which culminated in the impeachment and exile of Clarendon in November 1667. This was because Clarendon repeatedly accused his tolerationist opponents of atheism or profanity, and in October 1666 allowed a Bill to be introduced into the Commons which would for the first time since the Reformation have made Christian heresy a criminal offence. The Commons committee considering the Bill was specifically empowered to gather information about the atheistical implications of *Leviathan*.

Fortunately for *Leviathan*'s 78-year-old author, the Bill failed in the Lords despite the efforts of the bishops, and a second attempt to introduce it the following year also failed—though it kept being reintroduced (in 1674, 1675, and 1680). From 1666 until his death Hobbes was therefore faced by the frightening prospect of being either imprisoned or forced into exile for his beliefs. It must have seemed like a replay of 1640, when he fled to France to avoid the hostility of the House of Commons. The threat of official sanctions against him persisted for some time: in March 1668 a Fellow of Corpus Christi College, Cambridge, named Daniel Scargill was deprived of his fellowship for, as his recantation in 1669 put it, 'professing that I gloried to be an *Hobbist* and an *Atheist*'.

These terrifying experiences coloured the rest of Hobbes's life, and drove him to a last burst of composition in order to vindicate himself. He had been told that nothing by him in English would be licensed by the English censors; but in 1668 he published (in the Blaeu edition of his collected Latin works) a translation into Latin of *Leviathan* with an appendix defending his materialism and insisting that under English law there could be no punishment for heresy. He also butchered the sections of the book concerned with ecclesiastical government, dropping his former defence of Independency. At the same time he drafted six works in English, though none were published in his lifetime.

The first was *A dialogue between a philosopher and a student of the common laws of England*, which Hobbes probably wrote in 1666; the second was entitled *An Historical narration concerning heresy, and the punishment thereof*, which he composed in 1668; the third was a new reply to Bramhall (also 1668), and the fourth (which has disappeared) was a comment by Hobbes on the Scargill affair. At some point before the end of 1670 he also composed *Behemoth; or, the Long Parliament*, while the last English manuscript which we know about was a short note on heresy discovered at Chatsworth in 1968. In addition, he is likely to have written during these years his Latin verse *Historia Ecclesiastica*, which is also largely concerned with the theme of heresy.

Heresy is the central theme of all these works: even *Behemoth*, though in form a history of the Civil War, begins with an account of the history of persecution for heresy and then proceeds to argue that it was the evil desire for intellectual control on the part of the Calvinist clergy which precipitated the war. Cromwell is treated with considerable respect, and the restoration of Anglicanism under Clarendon is not even mentioned; in a way, the Restoration is depicted as the culmination of the lay attack on Presbyterian Calvinism begun during the war. Moreover, the point of the first English work, the *Dialogue of the common laws*, was to show that on Hobbes's interpretation of the source of English law, there could be no valid actions against anyone for heresy. In the process, however, he provided some fine general discussions of the nature of law in general and the English common law in particular, which have made the work deservedly popular with modern readers. It is also worth remarking that many of Hobbes's post-Restoration works are couched in the form of dialogues, an interesting return to a deeply humanist practice (though Wallis, for one, complained that they were dialogues 'between Thomas and Hobbes').

Neither the Earl of Devonshire nor the Earl of Newcastle could be of much use to Hobbes in this crisis, since both had substantially retired from public life after the Restoration. He did, however, find a patron who could assist him; this was Henry Bennet, Earl of Arlington, who was one of Clarendon's leading opponents, and whom Hobbes may have met when he was attached to the exiled court. Like the King, Arlington was more sympathetic to Catholicism than to Anglicanism, and favoured loosening the restrictions on dissenters of all kinds; he helped Hobbes to evade the wrath of the Commons in 1666–7, and provided some helpful comments on the *Historical narration concerning heresy* (though he was unable to get it passed by the censors). *Behemoth* was dedicated to him, as was one of Hobbes's polemical works on geometry; it was probably through his influence that Hobbes was introduced to the Grand Duke Cosimo di Medici of Tuscany on the Grand Duke's state visit in 1669. The Grand Duke was so impressed that he took back with him copies of Hobbes's works and a portrait of the philosopher to hang in the Medici collections in Florence.

Arlington was a particularly useful patron as, after Clarendon's fall, he was one of the five ministers who formed a new
government (known after their initials as the Cabal—Clifford,
Arlington, Buckingham, Ashley Cooper, and Lauderdale). They
came to power with the avowed aim of promoting religious
toleration or comprehension: that is, either an established
Anglican church but with civil rights for non-Anglican
churches, or a national church which contained within itself a
wide range of dissenting opinions; during their years in office
(which lasted roughly until 1674) they attracted about themselves a number of advisers committed to the same project.

Some of the advisers were old friends of Selden—two lawyers, John Vaughan and Matthew Hale, who were given high
legal office and consulted on legal matters concerning toleration, were Selden's executors. Vaughan read Hobbes's *Dialogue
of the common laws* in manuscript, and liked it; Hale also read
it, and though he wrote a critique of it he too was sympathetic
to some of its basic points. Another adviser was John Locke; he
was extremely close at this time to Ashley Cooper, from 1672
the Earl of Shaftesbury. He drafted papers and speeches on
toleration for his master, at the same time as Hobbes was
writing papers on heresy for Arlington—a singular conjunction
of the two great seventeenth-century English philosophers
working in a common cause. We do not know if they met—
though in 1673 Hobbes's friend John Aubrey wrote to Locke
asking him to look at the manuscripts about heresy which
Hobbes had drafted (particularly the *Dialogue of the common
laws* and *Behemoth*), and observing that 'the old gent. is still
strangely vigorous. If you see him (which he would take kindly)
pray my service to him.'

The conjunction of Hobbes and Locke should alert us to the
fact that the Cabal's policies cut across the conventional
categories of English politics. They sought toleration, but they
sought it by and large against the opposition of an Anglican
and anti-tolerationist Parliament, which (for example) in 1673
passed the Test Act, requiring any holder of civil or military
office to be a member of the Church of England. The Cabal
ministers were thus prepared to elevate monarchical power, if

by doing so they undermined the power of the Church; in many ways this was the keynote of 'enlightened despotism', as the term came to be employed to describe the activities of the liberal but despotic rulers of eighteenth-century Europe such as Catherine the Great of Russia. Locke's papers for Shaftesbury at this time wholly endorse such an approach, and it was of course very close to what Hobbes had always wanted. Indeed, one might say that throughout the seventeenth century in England there was an Anglican, Tory majority in the country, and anyone who wanted toleration would be pretty sceptical about Parliaments; Locke, even in his later and more revolutionary phase, remained unenamoured of full parliamentary sovereignty.

But the last of the Cabal ministers fell in 1674 in the face of entrenched Anglicanism and a monarch unwilling in the end to offend the Tory, Anglican order. No long-term change in the ecclesiastical settlement had been achieved, and dissent had only been tolerated through the issue by Charles of declarations of indulgence—acts of pure and arbitrary royal power. By 1675 the resurgent anti-tolerationists were seeking to extend the Test Act by enforcing an oath on all office-holders binding them not to 'endeavour the alteration of the Government either in Church or State'. At this point Locke was driven into exile, and into a new and radical commitment to armed revolution in defence of religious pluralism; but here his path and Hobbes's diverged. The 'old gent.' was eighty-seven in 1675, and no longer particularly frightened for his personal safety; he had returned to his first love, translation, and in 1674 completed an English version of the *Iliad* and *Odyssey*. But he did leave London in 1675, and spent the rest of his life in the country at Hardwick; Cavendish family tradition later held that he also started going to church and taking communion, but always turned his back on the sermon.

Nevertheless, he had one last contribution to make to political debate, though only within the Devonshire household. At the end of 1678 the balance of power in London swung once more against the Anglicans, and the Earl of Danby, their spokesman, was impeached. A move was started to have

Charles's younger brother and heir apparent, James Duke of York, excluded from the succession; this was ostensibly because he was an avowed Catholic, but in reality because Charles's illegitimate son, the Duke of Monmouth (who would, the exclusionists hoped, become his heir), looked like an ideal monarch for the dissenting interest. The issue of 'exclusion' was to dominate English politics until Charles's death in 1685, and it was as a contribution to the debates about it that Locke wrote his famous *Two Treatises of Government*. The Earl of Devonshire's eldest son, Lord Cavendish, who sat in the Parliament of 1675–9, was a keen member of the anti-Danby faction, and a moderate supporter of exclusion; he later became a prominent Whig and the first Duke of Devonshire, having helped to engineer the Revolution of 1688. How far Hobbes would have approved of his later conduct it is hard to say; but he did sketch out, almost certainly for Lord Cavendish's use, some thoughts on the principle of exclusion which must date from early 1679. He concluded that a sovereign could perfectly legitimately exclude his natural heir from succession, but could not be *forced* to do so by his subjects—a position which may well have corresponded quite closely with Cavendish's at the time, given that he was hoping that Charles would agree to the exclusion of the Duke of York.

This was to be Hobbes's last service for the family he had served through four generations, and which now treated him as a cross between a servant and an honoured guest. His standing with them in his old age is vividly illustrated by a memoir compiled from family reminiscences in 1708, in which it was recorded, for example, that after breakfast each day he 'went around the Lodgings to wait upon [i.e. to greet] the Earl, the Countess and the Children, and any considerable Strangers, paying some short Addresses to all of them. He kept these Rounds till about 12 a Clock, when he had a little Dinner provided for him, which he eat always by himself without Ceremony'. In October 1679 he fell ill, and on 3 December he died at Hardwick. A variety of rumours circulated about his state of mind on his deathbed—always a keen source of interest where a suspected atheist was concerned. It is clear that he did not see a priest nor take the sacrament, though his friends explained this by the suddenness of his final seizure; there is also good evidence of his having remarked bleakly that 'he was 91 years finding a hole to go out of this world, and at length found it'. The inscription over his tomb in the parish church of Ault Hucknall, near Hardwick, which he composed himself, is wholly and proudly secular. He allegedly considered seriously but finally rejected the epitaph 'This is the true philosopher's stone'—which, a clerical critic observed, would have had 'as much Religion in it, as that which now remains'. He seems in fact to have died much as he had lived, a witty and sceptical humanist.

II Hobbes's work

Science

As we saw in Part I, there are good grounds for supposing that Hobbes began his philosophical enquiries in the late 1630s because he was intrigued by the philosophical problems raised by modern natural science, and particularly by the possibility of replacing late Renaissance scepticism with a philosophy accommodated to the ideas (above all) of Galileo. The crucial idea, as we also saw, was simply to treat what is perceived by man—the images and so on which are immediately apparent to an internal observer—as bearing no relationship of *verisimilitude* to the external world. Man is effectively a prisoner within the cell of his own mind, and has no idea what in reality lies outside his prison walls. Like Descartes and Gassendi, Hobbes had come to believe this by 1637, and was then spurred on by Descartes's hyper-scepticism into working out a new theory as to what kind of things must lie beyond the prison. This new theory was the basis of the metaphysics and physics which occupied him down to the publication of *De Corpore* in 1655 and *De Homine* in 1658.

Its fundamental propositions hardly altered during that time, and may be found (often expressed in virtually the same words) in his works from the *Elements of Law* and the first draft of the *Elements of Philosophy*, through the *Critique of Thomas White* and *Leviathan* itself, down to the final publication of the *Elements of Philosophy*. Having established the prevalence of optical illusion, and the impossibility of believing that what we think we see, such as colour, is *really* a property of an external object, Hobbes asserted (in the words of the *Elements of Law*, which is often the most accessible statement of his general philosophy) that

> whatsoever accidents or qualities our senses make us think there be in the world, they are not there, but are seemings

and apparitions only. The things that really are in the world without us, are those motions by which these seemings are caused. And this is the great deception of sense, which also is by sense to be corrected. For as sense telleth me, when I see directly, that the colour seemeth to be in the object; so also sense telleth me, when I see by reflection, that colour is not in the object. (I.2.10)

In other words, the senses themselves give us evidence of the unreality of what they present to us as real: we have only to reflect on the implications of such things as a reflected image to realize that seeing something does not in itself give us any grounds for supposing that the thing seen is *really* in the place it appears to be or has the properties which we think it has.

But the important work in this passage is done by the second sentence, which expresses Hobbes's conviction that there is actually something outside us (against Descartes's doubt), and that it consists of 'motions'. The *Elements of Law* and his other ethical and political works merely assume this to be so, but in the first section of the *Elements of Philosophy* Hobbes presents an argument against what is in effect the Cartesian sceptic. Though the original draft of the first section is lost, notes on various early versions survive, and it was clearly drawn on by Hobbes in his Objections to Descartes's *Meditations* of 1641 and his *Critique of Thomas White* in 1643; it is also referred to in the surviving early version of Section Two. The argument began in a wholly Cartesian manner by imagining, in the words of what is probably the earliest set of notes,

the world annihilated except one man to whom there would remain ideas and images of all the things he had seen, or perceived by his other senses . . .: all which though in truth they would be only ideas and phantasms internally happening and falling to the imaginant himself, nevertheless they would appear as if they were external and not depending upon the power or virtue of the mind.

This technique of using the image of a mind left floating in a wholly empty universe was one which Hobbes was still using when he finally published Section One as *De Corpore* in 1655.

The question which Hobbes then put to himself was the same one which Descartes had put about his disengaged mind: what could such a man think, and how could he come to *know* anything about the universe in which he found himself, and about its history (including the fact, as Hobbes believed it to be, that the man's own thoughts must have been the product of a physical process within the universe prior to the annihilation of everything but himself)?

Hobbes's answer went in essence as follows. First, it would be perfectly possible for the man to have a complete language, referring to everything which he believed to exist in the same way as our languages refer to what we think exists outside us. Everything which it is possible for us to think or reason about would be possible for him too, since the actual existence of anything which is the object of our thinking is irrelevant. A language is simply a formal system whose relationship to reality is puzzling and contentious; but it is the only tool we have to *reason* with. Hobbes consistently used the analogy of counting to explain what he meant by reasoning. Just as effective counting consists in understanding the rules of a formal system (the natural numbers) which may not have any precise relationship to reality, so effective reasoning consists in understanding the meanings of words within the system of language without necessarily having any clear belief about what they refer to. As Hobbes said in a famous phrase from *Leviathan*, 'words are wise mens counters, they do but reckon by them: but they are the mony of fooles' (p. 106)—for fools believe words to have some real value.

He believed the same to be true of the only fully satisfactory example of a system of reasoning yet produced, namely Euclidean geometry. The method of exposition employed by Euclid and his successors was to define precisely the meaning of terms such as 'line' and 'point', and to draw conclusions (allegedly) strictly from these definitions. The system was thus self-contained and conventional, as Hobbes believed an ideal language to be. And, like a language, assessing its relationship to reality required some further theory; in the case of geometry, Hobbes argued that the Euclidean definitions were in fact met by the behaviour of a moving body, the *direction* of whose movement could be thought of as a line without breadth (a line without breadth being the famous, and famously puzzling, definition of a line employed by Euclid). Hobbes believed that this approach met the sceptical objections which had been advanced even to geometry in antiquity; he also believed that it could solve the famous 'impossible' problems such as squaring the circle, whose alleged impossibility seemed to him, reasonably enough, to be part of the sceptics' case. He wasted many years in futile attempts to solve these puzzles, his 'theorems' being treated with contempt by men like Wallis, who were better mathematicians but worse philosophers.

Hobbes's solipsist alone in the universe would thus be able to talk and think; he would even have available to him the whole of geometry. But what he would think would be rather different from the musings of Descartes's sceptic. First of all, while Hobbes accepted the validity of the proposition *I think, therefore I am* (acknowledging as much in his Objections to Descartes's *Meditations*), he did not conclude from this that his solipsist would come up with Descartes's idea of a mind separate from its own perceptions and witnessing them like an observer witnesses the events outside him—the famous Cartesian 'Ego'. Instead, he insisted that the solipsist would think of himself just *as* the train of perceptions, because he could not perceive anything (so to speak) doing the thinking.

> Although someone may think that he *was* thinking (for this thought is simply an act of remembering), it is quite impossible for him to think that he *is* thinking, or to know that he is knowing. For then an infinite chain of questions would arise: How do you know that you know that you know . . .? (2nd Objection)

The self in this sense is imaginary, simply a construct arising from our inability to conceive of thinking without a thinker to *do* it.

Second, the perceptions which flit across the solipsist's mind (just as they flit continuously across our minds) would give him the ideas of space and time, but he would, Hobbes argued, come to see that space and time are *also* imaginary. The proposition that space and time are imaginary might seem astonishing, but Hobbes's point was that no one has ever had direct experience of them: they are constructs or deductions from what we do directly experience. Space cannot really be apprehended except as something which a body occupies (even the emptiness of inter-stellar space, he might have said, we really think of as full of something—the kind of black, transparent medium in which planets and spaceships move, and which it is impossible actually to picture as boundless). Similarly time is a 'phantasm of motion': we can directly experience moving objects, but not that they are moving 'in' time any more than that they are moving 'in' space.

So far, the solipsist is in no better position than the Cartesian sceptic, for he is still incapable of coming to any conclusions about what is really to be found in an external universe. He knows what objects in space and time would be, but he does not yet know whether everything he perceives is imaginary or not. In some ways his position is even worse, because he even thinks of his own self as imaginary. It is a vertiginous and disturbing picture, the metaphysical counterpart of the radically individualist political world Hobbes was to depict. But at this point Hobbes brought a new argument to bear on his dilemma. One thing the solipsist does know is that his own thoughts exhibit *change*: he does not gaze out mentally over an unchanging landscape, but is presented with the same succession of images, sounds, and so on with which we are presented every moment of our lives. And it is natural for the solipsist to ask how this can be: what is it which leads him to have *changing* or *moving* images in front of him? This is a question which Descartes's sceptic had failed to ask; Descartes did in a way depict him as someone contemplating a single image in front of his mind's eye rather than the moving pictures postulated by Hobbes.

Hobbes answered the solipsist's question using a number of metaphysical propositions which played an absolutely vital role in both his physics and his psychological theories. The first and most important one was the proposition that *nothing can move itself*, which he asserted on the basis of what is known in the history of philosophy as the 'principle of sufficient reason'—that is, the principle that there has to be some new feature in a situation to explain some new alteration in it. A body which displayed no other alteration in its condition could not therefore start to move. Hobbes always insisted that self-movement was literally inconceivable.

The second proposition was that nothing could be moved except bodies in space, and the third was that only bodies could move other bodies—there can be no explanations of movement involving 'incorporal substances'. Hobbes again presented these propositions as necessarily true, their falsehood being inconceivable: the first because movement *means* alteration in spatial position, and only bodies occupy space, the second because (in the words of the *Critique*) 'we can conceive of only one efficient cause that sets in motion any body initially at rest: the motion of an adjacent body. As the commencement of motion is the quitting of place, we can see that the only reason why a body leaves its place is that another body standing adjacent replaces the first by moving forward' (fo. 300). This was the central plank of Hobbes's philosophical vessel.

The answer to the solipsist was, then, that there must be, or have been, some material object outside himself which was causing him to have the perceptions which he had. He could not be causing them himself, since nothing can cause its own alterations, and he has no 'self' other than the train of perceptions. And the thing outside him must be *material*, since nothing else could produce a change in anything.

But this is actually as far as Hobbes ever went, or intended to go, in answering the solipsist. Everything else—that is, the actual character of the external world and of our relationship to it—must remain conjectural or hypothetical, though some hypotheses are better than others. I will consider two examples of such hypotheses, each of peculiar importance within Hobbes's theory. The first, which also tells us a lot about Hobbes's thinking about *reasoning*, concerns the central Cartesian puzzle about dreaming. While the Cartesian sceptic was particularly troubled by the doubt that everything which we experience while (apparently) awake might merely be a dream, the Hobbesian solipsist was not one bit troubled by his identical fear. As Hobbes said in the *Elements of Law*, it is not

> impossible for a man to be so far deceived, as when his dream is past, to think it real: for if he dream of such things as are ordinarily in his mind, and in such order as he useth to do waking, and withal that he laid him down to sleep in the place where he findeth himself when he awaketh (all which may happen) I know no *criterion* or mark by which he can discern whether it were a dream or not . . . (I.3.10)

But from Hobbes's point of view that simply did not matter: our thoughts while asleep are *caused* in exactly the same way as our thoughts while awake, that is to say, by the bombardment of external objects upon our senses and by the resonances set up inside our brain by the bombardment; and it may well be that we are asleep and dreaming, or that the world outside ourselves no longer exists.

There are, however, some lower-level considerations which might in general recommend to us the hypothesis that we have been dreaming and are now awake. The principal one, which Hobbes made much of in his discussions of human psychology, is that there are obvious differences between an *ordered* and a *disordered* train of thought. As an example of the latter, Hobbes (with considerable insight into the mind of the mentally disturbed) depicted someone running from one thought to another via a combination of word associations or puns, and the association of objects. Dreams, he believed, normally exhibited a comparable disorder. On the other hand, waking, conscious, and rational thought was characteristically distinguished by a purposive sequencing of ideas: rather than merely being the victim of random associations, the thinker considered a series of images in order to get something he wanted or was interested in. If we are at present running through such a sequence, then we can say we are 'awake' (while leaving open the logical possibility that we are asleep). His picture of rational or ordered thought seems in fact to have been like the modern notion of a properly organized computer program: we can distinguish between a case where the program is functioning smoothly, and the machine is thereby doing something effectively, and a case where there is some malfunction. But in either case the computer remains a machine, and the difference between the cases is a purely formal one.

Hobbes was indeed always at pains to stress that this distinction did not imply that the rational thinker was 'free' in some metaphysical sense to order his thoughts as he wished. Hobbes's ideas about free will and determinism were among the most puzzling and contentious of his views for his contemporaries (witness his prolonged debate with Bishop Bramhall), and they have continued to attract considerable argument. Obviously, his commitment to the propositions that there is no 'self' independent of the activity of thinking, and that nothing moves itself, immediately ruled out any orthodox notion of free will: there was nothing that could *be* free and alter an agent's perceptions and actions in the orthodox way. 'Freedom' for Hobbes was still a meaningful term, but it meant purely the condition of having no hindrance to the securing of what one wants; the will itself, or the act of wanting, could not be free. The idea of the 'free self' was as imaginary as the idea of the self: 'a wooden top that is lashed by the boys, and runs about sometimes to one wall, sometimes to another, sometimes spinning, sometimes hitting men on the shins, if it were sensible of its own motion, would think it proceeded from its own will, unless it felt what lashed it.' ('The Questions concerning Liberty, Necessity, and Chance'). This metaphysical argument gave an additional purchase to the attack on the traditional humanist notion of civic liberty which, as we shall see, Hobbes undertook in his political works—for if no one can be truly free, there is no point in proclaiming that one can be at liberty only under a certain constitutional regime.

The second example of Hobbes's hypotheses about the physical world which I want to consider is his idea about the nature of *light*. Hobbes was always very proud of his theory of light, holding it and his political theory to be his main contributions to modern thought; as we have seen, optics (the analysis of both the transmission of light and of vision) was a subject to which he constantly returned. Descartes's theory of light was once again the target. Descartes believed that the universe was filled with some substance to which any light source applied pressure. This pressure was felt by the eye, which interpreted it very sensitively as a visible emanation from the source. The transmission of light was thus like the transmission of a movement from one end of a stick to the other, and vision was in principle the same as the activity of a blind man feeling his way along a street with his stick. Hobbes never denied that such a theory fitted his metaphysical criteria for a good scientific theory: it involved, after all, purely mechanical effects brought about by material objects. But he once again used a variety of lower-level considerations to suggest a different hypothesis (at least in his works prior to 1645), which later scientists regarded as a major idea.

This different hypothesis was that a light source such as the sun is like the human heart (or indeed any pump), alternately expanding and contracting and sending pulses of matter out towards an observer. For this image Hobbes drew explicitly on the work of William Harvey, whose discovery of the circulation of the blood had been announced in a book published in 1628. Hobbes was greatly impressed by Harvey, whose vision of the human body as constantly in motion corresponded so well with his own metaphysics. The analogy with the circulation of the blood was, however, only partial, since light does not form a closed and circulating system, and Hobbes was always troubled by the problem of how a light source could dilate. To explain this, he insisted (against Descartes) in these early works that a vacuum must be possible, so that a dilating object simply became less dense by virtue of tiny vacuums springing up in its interstices; but he gradually came to be persuaded by experimental evidence and by the force of Descartes's arguments that a vacuum is impossible. The consequence was that he had to abandon his early theory of light, and in *De Corpore* it is replaced by a much less persuasive one (in which a luminous body actually has to move its position in space to produce the sensation of light). Eighteenth- and nineteenth-century scientists, who had only a vague knowledge of Hobbes's early works, had laboriously to reinvent the hypothesis that light is emitted in a pulse-like motion; in this respect Hobbes's instinct for what a good scientific explanation might be was to be shared later by many practising scientists.

Not that Hobbes would have been particularly impressed by this fact. The appearance in his lifetime of something resembling the practice of modern science, notably in the form of what Robert Boyle and the early members of the Royal Society were up to, attracted from him nothing but derision (expressed pungently in his Latin *Physical dialogue on the nature of air* of 1661, one of the contributions to his long controversy with Wallis and Wallis's supporters, and addressed especially to Boyle). The reason for his contempt was twofold. The first was that for political reasons (which I shall outline later) he mistrusted any privileged body of intellectuals who might come to have some kind of independent ideological authority over their fellow citizens—and presciently he saw that modern scientists might form just such a new priesthood.

The second reason was that he mistrusted any great reliance on experimental evidence to prove the truth or falsehood of scientific theories. As he said in the *Elements of Law* (14.10), 'experience concludeth nothing universally'. Every experiment produces information about how human beings perceive their world, and nothing more; consequently, a scientist has to be extremely careful about his interpretation of any experimental results, and must constantly put them in the context of his theory of perception, which in turn must be set in the context of a general metaphysical theory. Unless these backing theories were correct, the experiment could tell the scientist little of use. As an example of fallacious reasoning, he used the proudest claim made by Robert Boyle, that he had succeeded in producing an artificial vacuum by pumping all the air out of a large glass container, in which various experiments could then be performed. As Hobbes observed, all Boyle should in fact have claimed was that he had managed to pump out of his container everything which a pump could extract—and since it remained

163

a wholly open question what sort of thing could *not* be pumped out, it must also remain an open question whether Boyle had in fact produced a vacuum. Hobbes's contempt for experimental machinery of this kind was well expressed in a remark from another work in this controversy, of 1662: 'not every one that brings from beyond seas a new gin [engine], or other jaunty device, is therefore a philosopher. For if you reckon that way, not only apothecaries and gardeners, but many other sorts of workman, will put in for, and get the prize ('Considerations upon the Reputation, Loyalty, Manners, and Religion of Thomas Hobbes').

Despite his contempt for the actual practice of most modern scientists, in many ways Hobbes's philosophy is closer to the assumptions on which modern science rests than any of the competing philosophies on offer in the seventeenth century. It shared with Descartes's the stress on the need to think of the real world as essentially different from how we experience it, and this stress has been characteristic of the most important achievements of the physical sciences—beginning with Galileo pointing out that the experience of someone on the earth itself could not determine whether the earth was rotating, and ending with the utterly unimaginable postulates of modern theoretical physics about the objects which really make up the material universe. But, unlike Descartes, Hobbes was able to make sense of a material world outside our minds without bringing in elaborate theological postulates, which fits the secular cast of mind of many modern scientists. It should be said, however, that Hobbes (despite his own pleas) has rarely been seen as the key theoretician of modern science—which illustrates the dubiousness of the notion that there was a historical link between modern science and the process of secularization. Seventeenth- and eighteenth-century scientists in fact disowned the one truly secular philosophy of science on offer to them, preferring instead the elaborate theological speculations in which Newton indulged. In this respect, Hobbes's theory of science represented an exploration of intellectual possibilities which were not to be opened up again for another two hundred years.

Ethics

Just as Hobbes's philosophy of science was in effect designed to validate and explain the traditional sceptical view that our observation of the world is radically contaminated by illusion, so his philosophy of ethics was intended to underwrite the traditional sceptic's moral relativism. It is important to stress here that Hobbes's writings on politics were intended to elucidate broadly *ethical* issues, and that he was not concerned (at least on the face of it) with explaining political behaviour in the supposedly 'value-free' manner of a modern political scientist. The dedicatory letters to both the *Elements of Law* and *De Cive* make this absolutely clear—particularly perhaps the latter, in which Hobbes remarked that 'what deals with figures, is called *Geometry*, with motion, *Physics*, and with natural right, *Morals*: all of them together are *Philosophy*'. The central problem with which he was concerned in the third section of his philosophy was thus not the explanation of human action (that belonged, if anywhere, in Section Two), but the problem of 'natural right'—the existence or non-existence of common ethical standards by which men should live their lives.

As we saw in Part I, the particular kind of humanism which had been fashionable in Hobbes's youth, and which was represented above all by the figures of Montaigne and Lipsius, stressed the sheer multiplicity of human beliefs and customs and threw up its hands in despair at the prospect of finding any common moral denominator. All that it was safe to say of human beings, these humanists came to believe, was that they are primarily concerned with preserving themselves in a dangerous world—and one made doubly dangerous by the presence of competing ideologies. This impulse to self-preservation, however, was not itself a moral matter. As we also saw in Part I, Hugo Grotius proposed what is in retrospect (like most good ideas) an obvious twist to this argument, namely that self-preservation *is* a moral principle: it is the foundational 'natural right' upon which all known moralities and codes of social behaviour must have been constructed. But it is balanced by a fundamental duty or 'natural law' to abstain from harming other people except where our own preservation is at stake.

Grotius's idea was that there must be a kind of equilibrium of permitted violence for any society to survive. If *too little* violence were permitted—that is, if people were not allowed to defend themselves when wantonly attacked—then a few aggressive individuals would destroy the rest. If *too much* violence were permitted—if people were allowed to attack other members of the society for whatever reasons they themselves thought fit—then this too would wreck the possibility of social life. So whatever the laws and customs of a society (and Grotius was as fully conscious as any earlier relativist of the enormous moral divergences between societies), they must in part be designed to protect this equilibrium of violence. Beyond this common core, however, societies could differ extravagantly in their laws, and anything which was accepted as law in a particular society would be immune to moral criticism coming from someone outside the society.

This was the most up-to-date and appealing moral theory on offer when Hobbes began to write the ethical section of his *Elements of Philosophy*, and it is not surprising that we constantly find echoes of Grotius in his works. It should be said that Grotius is virtually never referred to by *name*; but he shares that characteristic with almost all other philosophers, both past and contemporary—Hobbes being extremely reluctant to locate his own ideas in any familiar intellectual context. Hobbes's first task was to show that the relativist idea was correct, and could be explained by his own philosophy of science; he then had to show that something like the Grotian theory also followed from his fundamental principles—though he introduced into it a new sceptical twist, comparable perhaps to the hyperbolical doubt which Descartes had introduced in the course of his refutation of scepticism, and his answer to this new doubt pushed his political conclusions some way away from Grotius's.

The relativist idea was pungently expressed by Hobbes in the *Elements of Law*:

Every man, for his own part, calleth that which pleaseth, and is delightful to himself, GOOD; and that EVIL which displeaseth him: insomuch that while every man differeth from other in constitution, they differ also one from another concerning the common distinction of good and evil. Nor is there any such thing as ἀγαθὸν ἁπλῶζ [*agathon haplos*], that is to say, simply good. For even the goodness which we attribute to God Almighty, is his goodness to us. And as we call good and evil the things that please and displease us; so call we goodness and badness, the qualities of powers whereby they do it. (I.7.3)

Hobbes, in other words, treated *moral* terms in exactly the same way as he had treated colour terms: though common language and common sense might lead us to think that something is really and objectively good, in the same way as we might think something is really and objectively red, in fact such ideas are illusions or fantasies, features of the inside of our heads only. The sensation of colour is to be understood, as we have seen, as what it feels like to come under the influence of something in the external world which is not itself a colour, but a pulse of light impinging on our eyes; similarly, moral approval or disapproval are to be understood as feelings engendered by the impact of something external on the system of passions and wants which make up the human emotive psychology.

That there is such a system, Hobbes not unnaturally took for granted, regarding it as a matter of direct introspective observation. He equally took it for granted that the system must function in accordance with the general metaphysical principles he had laid down for all scientific explanation—that is, it must take the form of what we might call a *ballistical* system, in which moving bodies interact in various ways. But the specific theory he put forward was, like his optics, a *theory* only, though he claimed that it was superior to all other hypotheses available.

For it, he drew once again on Harvey's discovery of the circulation of the blood, and proposed that it was one part of a complicated system involving 'animal' and 'vital' spirits. To understand this, we have to remember that even schoolchildren nowadays are incomparably better equipped to talk about basic chemistry than the most highly educated intellectual of Stuart England. We possess, for example, the absolutely familiar and useful term 'gas' to describe a particular state in which matter can be found; but the word was only invented by a Flemish medical alchemist in Hobbes's lifetime, and was not in common usage for another hundred years. We also have the notion of electrical transmission through fibres, and an awareness that electricity and chemistry are intimately connected; again, no one in Hobbes's time could have had these ideas. So we must not think that he meant by 'spirit' anything particularly mysterious, and especially that he meant something *incorporeal*—Hobbes always insisted, as we have seen, that there could be no such thing.

What he meant was simply that there is some mechanical system in the body whereby sense-perceptions are transmitted to the brain, and that they there cause perturbations to the 'spirits' which link the brain and the heart, and that the consequent perturbations in the heart affect the circulation of the blood—and *in extremis* would cut it off altogether, killing the animal. The different physiological changes during this process are describable in terms of the familiar language of perception and emotion: thus the alterations in the make-up of the brain are *perceptions*, and the alterations in the behaviour of the blood are *passions*. Both kinds of alteration mistakenly lead people to attribute relevant properties to external objects, so that a spider, for example, can seem both 'black' and 'frightening', and perhaps also 'evil', though none of these terms really refers to anything.

Because moral judgements are a matter of feeling as well as perception, it was reasonable for Hobbes to say on the basis of this theory (as he always did) that the description of something as 'good' must be broadly the same as the description of it as 'pleasurable'—for the feeling of moral approbation is in a way a feeling of pleasure at the action in question. But it would also have been reasonable for him to have pointed out that the two feelings are not quite the same, and that the difference between them needs some explanation (a point made later, in effect, by Hume). That he never did, and persisted in holding that 'the good' and 'the pleasurable' were identical, is best seen as the consequence of his immersion in the scepticism of Montaigne's time, with its standard assumption that people take to be 'good' what is in their own interest (or, in the Latin terminology which they employed, and which went back to comparable arguments to be found in Cicero, that what was *honestum* was what was *utile*).

Having insinuated this identity, Hobbes had both stated and explained moral relativism: there were no objective moral properties, but what seemed good was what pleased any individual or was good *for him*. The implicit 'realism' of ordinary moral language, like that of the ordinary language of colour, was therefore a serious error. Hobbes indeed usually treated this error as the major difficulty in the way of a peaceful life, rather than (as is often supposed) viewing the clash of naked self-interest as the fundamental problem in human social existence.

The account of the passions which Hobbes gave, after all, treated them as broadly beneficial: what men feel strongly about or desire strongly is what helps them to survive, and they cannot for long want a state of affairs in which their survival is endangered. Such a view was common ground between Hobbes and many of his contemporaries, including Descartes: all argued that the traditional idea that reason should control the passions was an error, and that (properly understood) our emotions would guide us in the right direction. Men, on Hobbes's account, do not want to harm other men *for the sake of harming them*; they wish for power over them, it is true, but power only to secure their own preservation. The common idea that Hobbes was in some sense 'pessimistic' about human nature is wide of the mark, for his natural men (rather like Grotius's) were in principle stand-offish towards one another rather than inherently belligerent.

But Hobbes did believe that such creatures could not enjoy a decent social existence unless they were capable of using a common moral language to describe their activities. This is simply a deep-rooted assumption in his work, which is never fully justified, but which is constantly implied by the way in

169

which he described the problem of human conflict. In *De Cive*,
for example, he observed that

> the desires of men are different, as men differ among them-
> selves in temperament, custom and opinion; we see this in
> sense-perceptions such as taste, touch or smell, but even
> more in the common business of life, where what one person
> *praises*—that is, calls *good*—another will *condemn* and call
> *evil*. Indeed, often the same man at different times will
> *praise* and *blame* the same thing. As long as this is the case
> there will necessarily arise discord and conflict. (III.31)

It was conflict over what to *praise*, or morally to approve,
which Hobbes thus isolated as the cause of discord, rather than
simple conflict over *wants*. What he was frightened of, it is
reasonable to assume, were such things as the Wars of Religion,
or other ideological wars; not (say) class wars, in which the
clash of wants could more clearly be seen.

The malleability of opinion by outside forces was part of this
problem: as he said in the passage just quoted, the same man
could often believe quite different things, depending on the
circumstances. In *Leviathan*, indeed, Hobbes describes the
minds of 'the Common-people' as 'like clean paper, fit to
receive whatsoever by Publique Authority shall be imprinted
in them' unless they had already been 'scribbled over with the
opinions of their Doctors' (ch. 30, p. 379). Controlling or
combating the pens which could write on this clean paper was
crucial, and it was this which led him throughout his work
bitterly to condemn the activities of rhetoricians: 'such is the
power of eloquence, as many times a man is made to believe
thereby, that he sensibly feeleth smart and damage, when he
feeleth none, and to enter into rage and indignation, without
any cause, than what is in the words and passion of the speaker'
(*Elements of Law* II.8.14; see also *De Cive* XII.12). This was
despite the fact that he himself, like all humanists, was both
fascinated by and very skilled at rhetoric; indeed he wrote a
couple of works on the subject to be read by his Cavendish
pupils (one was published in 1637). But the power of rhetoric,

and of other outside influences on opinion, made the resolution of conflict a doubly difficult affair.

Nevertheless, Hobbes believed that there was a solution to moral conflict. The traditional moralist's response to ethical disagreement had been to hope that sooner or later everyone would come to see the moral *facts* clearly and rationally, but Hobbes of course could not resort to pious hopes of this kind. Instead, he proposed that the route to agreement must lie through *politics*, and this must count as Hobbes's most distinctive contribution to political theory. He put his idea most clearly, and most sceptically, in a passage of the *Elements of Law* where he contrasted a 'state of nature' (by which he meant the condition of men without some proper political organization) with the state of men under a regime of civil laws—a state later writers standardly termed 'civil society', but which Hobbes (though he did sometimes use that expression) more commonly called a 'commonwealth' or, when he wrote in Latin, a *civitas* ('city' or 'state'). This passage contains, I believe, an accurate summary of the whole of Hobbes's theory, and is worth quoting at length.

In the state of nature, where every man is his own judge, and differeth from other concerning the names and appellations of things, and from those differences arise quarrels, and breach of peace; it was necessary there should be a common measure of all things that might fall in controversy; as for example: of what is to be called right, what good, what virtue, what much, what little, what *meum* and *tuum*, what a pound, what a quart, &c. For in these things private judgements may differ and beget controversy. This common measure, some say, is right reason: with whom I should consent, if there were any such thing to be found or known *in rerum natura*. But commonly they that call for right reason to decide any controversy, do mean their own. But this is certain, seeing right reason is not existent, the reason of some man, or men, must supply the place thereof; and that man, or men, is he or they, that have the sovereign power . . .; and consequently the civil laws are to all subjects the measures of their actions, whereby to determine, whether they be right or wrong, profitable or unprofitable, virtuous or vicious; and by them the use and definition of all names not agreed upon, and tending to controversy, shall be established. As for example, upon the occasion of some strange and deformed birth, it shall not be decided by Aristotle, or the philosophers, whether the same be a man or no, but by the laws. (II.10.8)

This was the vision at the heart of Hobbes's moral and political philosophy, and whenever he had to summarize his theory (as, for example, in the *Critique of Thomas White*—see fo. 425v), he put some version of this idea in a central position.

But the obvious problem about it is this: if politics creates the moral consensus, how is political life possible in the first place? Surely the moral disagreements of the state of nature will overwhelm any attempt to set up a civil society or commonwealth? To answer this question, Hobbes (like Grotius) shifted from talking about 'the good', which had been the traditional subject for both ancient and Renaissance moralists, to talking instead about 'rights'—a subject which the ancient and Renaissance writers had barely tackled; indeed, there is arguably no word in classical Greek or Latin for a 'right'. It was much more the traditional material of medieval scholastic moralists, and its use in a central position by both Grotius and Hobbes marked a considerable break in appearances with the humanism of their youth, though the break in substance was much less striking. But within the language of rights, Hobbes first contrived a new sceptical doubt which seemed to render even the Grotian answer to relativism untenable, and which gave rise to the most famous aspect of Hobbes's theory: the picture of men as naturally and savagely at war with one another.

Put simply, Hobbes's argument begins in the following way. There is one thing on which even in a state of nature we can all agree, and that is that other people have a right to defend themselves against attack. We can also agree that if they wish to exercise that right, they will *have* to do certain things: they cannot, for example, exercise a right of self-preservation merely by sitting around and not responding when attacked. But we will also have to recognize that in a state of nature, there will be a larger number of cases where everyone must be their own judge of how and when to defend themselves.

The consequence of this last fact is that, despite our initial agreement about the general right of self-preservation, there will in practice still be a radical instability in the state of nature. There is not much point in my saying that I agree with you in principle about your right to preserve yourself, if I disagree about whether this is the moment for you to *implement* that right. Suppose I see you walking peacefully through the primitive savannah, whistling and swinging your club: are you a danger to me? You may well think not: you have an entirely pacific disposition. But I may think you are, and the exercise of my natural right of self-preservation depends only on *my* assessment of the situation. So if I attack you, I must be justified in doing so. We have all the instability of a wholly relativist world back again, despite our agreement that people are in general justified in protecting themselves. The state of nature thus becomes a state of war, savagery, and degradation— of which, Hobbes remarked, 'present-day Americans give us an example' (*De Cive* I.13).

As I said, this is Hobbes's argument put in a simple form. Before discussing how he proposed to get from the state of nature to civil society, it is worth enlarging on the details of the argument, all of which have proved contentious for genera- tions of Hobbes's readers.

First, what is involved in the claim that we can all agree that each of us possesses a right to defend ourselves? Hobbes expressed the claim in the following way in the *Elements of Law*:

> forasmuch as necessity of nature maketh men to will and desire *bonum sibi*, that which is good for themselves, and to avoid that which is hurtful; but most of all that terrible enemy of nature, death . . .; it is not against reason that a man doth all he can to preserve his own body and limbs,

173

> both from death and pain. And that which is not against reason, men call RIGHT, or *jus*, or blameless liberty of using our own natural power and ability. It is therefore a *right of nature*: that every man may preserve his own life and limbs, with all the power he hath. (I.14.6)

In both *De Cive* and *Leviathan* we find almost identical formulations. On the face of it, this passage might suggest that whatever we do, we must have the right to do it, since, according to Hobbes's general theory of action, we always act in such a way as to secure what we take to be good for us; so that the right to preserve ourselves is merely a special case of this general right. A philosopher later in the seventeenth century who did in fact say just this was the Dutchman Benedict de Spinoza, who drew in many respects on Hobbes's ideas. But Hobbes did not himself ever argue such a thing; indeed, on a number of occasions he specifically said that it is possible in a state of nature to do things, and to want to do things, which we have *no* right to do. In one of the explanatory footnotes to the second edition of *De Cive*, for example, he observed that it would be impossible ever to justify drunkenness or cruelty ('that is, revenge which does not look to some future good'), since they could never be seen as conducing to our preservation (III.27). It is clear that he believed that our only natural right is the right barely to preserve ourselves, and to use whatever means we take to be necessary for that purpose.

His reasons for thinking this are not set out straightforwardly anywhere, but the limitation of our 'natural' rights to self-preservation alone is something which makes very good sense against the background of Hobbes's pessimism about human mental and emotional malleability. If we are skilled at persuasion, for example, then for our own purposes we can get other people to believe and want almost anything; the one thing we will *not* be able to persuade them is that they want their own death. At that point their fundamental nature will rebel against us. Everyone, in turn, will have to recognize this fact about other people, and thus to accept that the one common and unmalleable belief to be found among men is the belief that their own preservation is a good. Beyond that, any belief is possible. Seen in this light, Hobbes's reasons for limiting our natural rights to the special case of self-preservation were precisely the same as Grotius's: the fact that whatever else people might believe, they will have to acknowledge that all men will always, whatever the circumstances, want to preserve themselves—and that this is the *one* thing which they will always want to do. If there is to be agreement among men, it will have to be on such a basis; if we were to acknowledge other people's right to do whatever they wanted, we would have no hope of leaving the world of moral conflict.

It should be said that Hobbes took seriously one possible exception to the universality of self-preservation, the case of martyrdom for religious reasons (see *Elements of Law* II.6.14, *De Cive* XVIII.13, and *Leviathan* ch. 43, p. 625). However, as we shall see later in the section on religion, Hobbes's attitude to martyrdom altered during his life as his views about the Christian religion changed. In the earlier works he had a good reason for supposing that Christian martyrdom was a special case; in *Leviathan* he no longer had such a reason, and the discussion of martyrdom in that work is appropriately muted: Christians, he now argued, have for their faith 'the licence that Naaman had, and need not put themselves into danger for it'.

The second claim which Hobbes made, and which has proved puzzling to many readers, was the one which I summarized earlier by saying that men in a state of nature can agree that if they wish to exercise their natural right to self-preservation, they will *have* to do certain things: they cannot, for example, exercise this right merely by sitting around and not responding when attacked. Hobbes expressed this claim by talking about the *law of nature*. In the *Elements of Law* he argued as follows:

> Forasmuch as all men, carried away by the violence of their passion, and by evil custom, do those things which are commonly said to be against the law of nature; it is not the consent of passion, or consent in some error gotten by custom, that makes the law of nature. Reason is no less of the nature of man than passion, and is the same in all men,

because all men agree in the will to be directed and governed in the way to that which they desire to attain, namely their own good, which is the work of reason. There can therefore be no other law of nature than reason, nor no other precepts of NATURAL LAW, than those which declare unto us the ways of peace, where the same may be obtained, and of defence where it may not. (I.15.1)

Once again, we find virtually identical formulations in *De Cive* and *Leviathan*.

What Hobbes meant was that if you wish to preserve yourself, then it is absurd—a logical error—to suppose that you could better preserve yourself in a situation of war than one of peace. The exercise of the right of nature requires as a matter of logic that men do whatever the law of nature requires. He did not mean that men *will* always follow the precepts of the law—as he said in *De Cive* (III.26), passions and perturbations of the mind can prevent people from apprehending the truth of the precepts; 'but there is no one who is not sometimes in a quiet mind', and when in that condition they will see clearly what they must do.

The puzzle which has sometimes arisen about this argument is, what is the point of differentiating between a *right* of nature and a *law* of nature, if the general theory is that we *have* to defend ourselves and *have* to follow certain rules in order to do so? The puzzle is made particularly teasing because Hobbes actually took some care to distinguish between rights and laws: in *Leviathan* he remarked that 'RIGHT, consisteth in liberty to do, or to forbeare; Whereas LAW, determineth, and bindeth to one of them: so that Law, and Right, differ as much, as Obligation, and Liberty; which in one and the same matter are inconsistent' (ch. 14, p. 189; cf. *Elements of Law* II.10.5 and *De Cive* XIV.3). Hobbes's first readers, friendly and hostile alike, were struck by this point. As Sir Robert Filmer, one of the hostile ones, said,

If the right of nature be a liberty for a man to do anything he thinks fit to preserve his life, then in the first place nature must teach him that life is to be preserved, and so consequently forbids to do that which may destroy or take away the means of life . . .: and thus the right of nature and the law of nature will be all one: for I think Mr. Hobbes will not say the right of nature is a liberty for a man to destroy his own life . . .

But this objection, and the similar ones made by more recent writers (see Part III), miss the point of Hobbes's definition of the right of nature. In the *Elements of Law*, he said that the right was for a man to 'preserve his own life and limbs, *with all the power he hath*' (my italics), and in *Leviathan* he said (even more clearly) that the right 'is the Liberty each man hath to use his own power, *as he will himselfe*, for the preservation of his own Nature' (ch. 14, p. 189; again, my italics). The thing which Hobbes was interested in, and which made this a *right* or a *liberty* and not a duty, was that in nature we are each to do what *we* want in order to preserve ourselves. It is this open-endedness, this dependence solely upon the will of the individual agent, which is important about a right, and it was this which Hobbes captured by describing our natural capacity to make our own decisions about how to protect ourselves as a right. The 'law' of nature tells us what we *ought* to decide if we are thinking rationally, but the 'right' tells us that it is we who have to decide, and that we are naturally and psychologically free to go any way we choose towards the necessary goal of our survival.

It is this fact, that is is each individual in the state of nature who decides on the route to take for his own preservation, which is captured in the third claim which I summarized above: that in the state of nature 'there will be a large number of cases where everyone must be their own judge of how and when to defend themselves'. This was the claim which split Hobbes off from Grotius (and which the Dutchman recognized as the issue between them when he read *De Cive* in 1643; Mersenne and Hobbes may even have sent him a copy). Hobbes expressed it by saying (in the words of the *Elements of Law*) that 'every man by right of nature is judge himself of the

177

necessity of the means, and of the greatness of the danger'. This too is repeated in *De Cive* and *Leviathan*, and it was a point upon which Sir Charles Cavendish, otherwise a very friendly reader of Hobbes's work, fastened critically when he first read *De Cive* (along with the point about the relationship between the right and the law of nature). He was right to do so, since virtually the whole of what is distinctive about Hobbes's political theory follows from this simple proposition.

For if men are to be their own judges of what conduces to their preservation, all the anti-sceptical advantages of the Grotian theory are immediately lost, since by virtue of Hobbes's general philosophy, it has to be the case that there is no clear and objective truth about the external world, and that all men will make different decisions about what counts as a danger to them. But if that is so, then there will still be no agreement about what should be done, and everyone will act on the basis of their own different assessments of the situation. Conflict will arise despite the apparent solution to the relativist problem contained in the idea of a natural and universal right of self-defence. The grimmest version of sceptical relativism seems after all to be the only possible ethical vision; and for ethics taken independently of politics, this is indeed Hobbes's conclusion.

Politics

However, Hobbes was able to provide a solution to his own version of ethical relativism, a solution which gave him in the end a genuine political theory. He tried various ways of expressing it; in each of the three major political works there is a slightly different formulation, but the general idea is essentially the same. It was that men in a state of nature will come to see, in their reflective moments, that the law of nature obliges them to renounce their right of private judgement over what is to count as dangerous in dubious cases, and to accept for themselves the judgement of a common authority. In the *Elements of Law* Hobbes tried to express this by talking about a renunciation of the right of nature *itself*; what he meant was the full right of nature, as defined in that work—that is, the right to use 'all the power' we have to defend ourselves—but it was a confusing way of putting the idea, since (as he conceded) a man cannot renounce the basic right to defend himself *in extremis*. In *Leviathan* he produced the most satisfactory formula: a common authority is created when everyone in a state of nature agrees 'to submit their Wills, every one to his Will, and their Judgements, to his Judgement (ch. 17, p. 227). Even in the *Elements of Law*, however, he had put the idea simply enough when he said that the 'sum' of the laws of nature 'consisteth in forbidding us to be our own judges, and our own carvers' (I.17.10).

By the terms of Hobbes's account of the state of nature, conflict arises because people judge differently about what is a danger to them, and the fact that they judge differently is enough to show that there is an inherent dubiousness about the cases in questions—a view similar to the attitude expressed in a remark he made in another context in the *Elements of Law*, that 'the infallible sign of teaching exactly, and without error, is this: that no man hath ever taught the contrary; not that few, how few soever' (I.13.3). There is no *fact of the matter* in these doubtful cases, and people therefore have no reason to prefer their own judgement to that of another person. Since they do have a most powerful reason for wanting their judgement aligned with other people's, it is a simple conclusion to draw that they should all find some single source of opinion whose view about the danger to each of them in doubtful or contentious cases they will accept. Its power will then protect its citizens, for it will be able to co-ordinate their judgements round the same dangers, and elicit common action against both criminals and other nations who pose a possible threat to the new 'commonwealth' which the citizens have thus brought into being. This common judge is by definition the *sovereign* over the commonwealth, though it need not be a single person: a single will, even if it is the decision of an assembly of some kind, is all that is necessary. Hobbes gave in all three of his political works some rather low-level reasons for preferring monarchy to other forms of government, but his theory applies indiscriminately to all types of government, including republics. Hobbes's theory is neatly summed up in a remark he made in Chapter 37 of *Leviathan* where he described the sovereign as 'Gods Lieutenant; to whom in all doubtfull cases, we have submitted our private judgements' (p. 477).

It remains true, however, that where it is absolutely clear to an individual citizen that his life is in danger—where no one could dispute it—then of course he must defend it himself, whatever the sovereign might say: 'A man cannot lay down the right of resisting them, that assault him by force, to take away his life; because he cannot be understood to ayme thereby, at any Good to himself' (*Leviathan* ch. 14, p. 192). This applies even if it is the sovereign himself, or his agents, who are assaulting him:

> for man by nature chooseth the lesser evill, which is danger of death in resisting; rather than the greater, which is certain and present death in not resisting. And this is granted to be true by all men, in that they lead Criminals to Execution, and Prison, with armed men, notwithstanding that such Criminals have consented to the Law, by which they are condemned. (Ibid., p. 199)

Hobbes found himself in something of a tactical quandary in his early formulations of this theory. In both the *Elements of Law* (II.1.2–3) and *De Cive* (VI.1) he claimed that the common submission of a disunited 'multitude' to a sovereign made the multitude one 'person', though it was a person only as long as it had a sovereign. He recorded in one of the footnotes to the second edition of *De Cive* (1647) that this had puzzled many readers, though he continued in that note to insist on it; but it was a dangerous position to take up, for it allowed the multitude a unity, albeit through the existence of a common sovereign, which might in principle be used *against* its sovereign. Hobbes wished to refute the idea repeatedly put forward in the English Civil War, that 'the People' had the collective right to limit their sovereign, but this early formulation in fact lent some credence to it. But in *Leviathan* he worked out an elaborate theory according to which all the members of a multitude are individually 'impersonated' or 'represented' by their sovereign, and the only unity is that possessed by the sovereign's will. 'For it is the *Unity* of the Representer, not the *Unity* of the Represented, that maketh the Person *One*. And it is the Representer that beareth the Person, and but one Person: And *Unity*, cannot otherwise be understood in Multitude' (ch. 16, p. 220; contrast particularly *De Cive* VI.1 note).

A question sometimes raised about Hobbes's theory of the origin of sovereignty is that it seems to rule out the possibility of men ever fighting for their sovereign, since it must always be better to avoid participating in a war than to run the risk of dying on the battlefield or being killed when trying to arrest a criminal. Yet Hobbes says (*Leviathan* ch. 21, p. 270) that 'when the Defence of the Common-wealth, requireth at once the help of all that are able to bear Arms, every one is obliged'. But if we think of the sovereign as making decisions for us in doubtful cases about what is a threat, then we can see that bearing arms for our country is rational: for it has just the same *rationale* as fighting against a presumed enemy in the state of nature. The only difference is that the sovereign is now doing the presuming, rather than us ourselves. This issue is, I think, one of the central issues with which Hobbes was originally concerned, for it was precisely the topic at issue during the Ship Money crisis of 1636 onwards: is it purely up to the sovereign to determine if, say, the Dutch are a threat to the English, or can individual Englishmen have an opinion on the matter? Hobbes's answer to this is clearly in line with that of the Royalist judges in the Ship Money case: only the King has the right to pronounce on the question of where England's vital interests lie, and his subjects must pay or fight as he decrees.

A similar problem, but one much harder to deal with, which is frequently raised about Hobbes's account of the generation of a commonwealth, is that he talks about it in terms of a *promise* or *contract* made by the inhabitants of the state of nature to co-ordinate their activities round a particular sovereign. But why should any of them keep this promise if it turns out to be to their advantage later to break it? This is made particularly problematical by Hobbes's general claim that in a state of nature no one could ever have a reason to keep their promises, 'because the bonds of words are too weak to bridle mens ambition, avarice, anger, and other Passions, without the fear of some coercive power' (*Leviathan* ch. 14, p. 196).

Hobbes's discussion of promising, at least in *Leviathan* (where it is most completely thought out), goes as follows. His fundamental point is that if two (or more) people promise each other to do something (in the case of the fundamental social contract, to respect the decisions of the same sovereign), then *if* one person keeps his word, the others have no good reason not to keep theirs. They have no good reason, because the only good reasons are those of self-preservation; and someone who has done what he said he would do is not a danger to other people. On these grounds, Hobbes argues in Chapter 15 of *Leviathan* (p. 203) that only a 'Foole' would say 'there is no such thing as Justice'—justice consisting precisely in keeping one's word if others have done likewise. The question then is simply, what can motivate someone in the state of nature into being the *first* person to keep his word? Hobbes himself seems to say that there can be *no* rational motive to do so: in a state of nature, 'he that performest first, has no assurance the other will performe after ... And therefore he which performeth first, does but betray himselfe his enemy' (ch. 14. p. 196). So the puzzle remains: how is the social contract possible?

There is, I think, no easy answer to this question to be extracted from the Hobbesian texts; the fact that Hobbes tried several slightly different ways of putting his idea about the construction of the commonwealth suggests that he found difficulties here too. What one might say is that Hobbes's remarks about the impossibility of making covenants or keeping promises in a state of nature are part of a very general account of promise-keeping. Clearly, for most promises it will indeed be true that one is delivering oneself into the hands of an enemy if one performs one's own side of a bargain before he does: but it is not too clear that this is true of the promise to regard the sovereign's judgement as one's own. This promise, it must be stressed, is made not to the sovereign but to the other prospective citizens, and one will presumably be no worse off in one's dealings with *them* after keeping one's word, even if they do not keep theirs, than one would have been in the state of nature anyway. All that has changed is that judgements about the threat posed by other men in doubtful cases are now made for me by another person; but precisely because they are doubtful cases, I have no reason to suppose that the judgements will be any worse than my own were, and therefore no reason to suppose that I will be worse off following my sovereign even if the others do not. So I may as well keep my word, and see what the others do.

But equally, it should be said, I will be no better off following him unless the others do likewise: I will effectively remain in the same state as I was before, surrounded by men with disparate judgements about when to exercise the right of self-preservation. If this is a situation which is likely to persist, then there is simply no point in transferring my right of private judgement to the sovereign, and I may as well go back to looking after myself in all instances. This is a point which Hobbes particularly stressed in the 'Review and Conclusion' he tacked on to the end of *Leviathan*, for it was what justified, in his opinion, the transference of allegiance by Englishmen from the Crown to the new republic. They were no longer 'protected' by the Crown, and there is 'a mutuall Relation between Protection and Obedience' (p. 728)—a slogan frequently used in the pamphlet literature in England during 1649–51 in relation to submission to the new regime.

This account of the foundational contract puts the matter in terms which Hobbes himself did not use, but it is arguably loyal to the general character of his idea. It enables us to accept that such a contract is possible, and we can now turn to the specifically political aspects of Hobbes's theory, and in particular to his discussion of the rights of sovereigns over their citizens.

The common impression of Hobbes is of a theorist of absolute state power, an impression fostered by the very title of *Leviathan* and by the description of the sovereign as 'that great LEVIATHAN, or rather (to speake more reverently) . . . that *Mortall God*' (p. 227). But there are some important qualifications to be introduced, which derive from Hobbes's conception of the fundamental character of sovereign power. As we have seen, the sovereign *represents* the citizens, in the sense that his judgement about dangers is (by and large) to count as their judgement. The considerations which govern the sovereign's actions are therefore the same as those which govern anyone's actions in the state of nature, namely, how best to secure a situation in which he will be at least risk from attack. His citizens' safety will, Hobbes believed, be caught up in his own; and he tended to gloss over the complexity of the actual relationship between a sovereign's preservation and that of his citizens. In *Leviathan*, at least, he frequently talks about the sovereign acting in some sense on behalf of his citizens, and seems to regard it as rational for a sovereign to do whatever he sincerely believes conduces to his own preservation and that of the people he represents. For the sovereign to do anything else, he repeatedly says (for example ch. 24, p. 297), would be 'a breach of trust, and of the Law of Nature'—though, as we shall see, he did not conclude from the fact that a sovereign might have no right to do something, that a subject might have the right to resist him.

What this meant was that many things which a conventional theory of absolute state power would allow are ruled out on Hobbes's account of the sovereign's rights. Perhaps the most striking example of this is the question of *private property*. It follows from Hobbes's account of the fundamental right of nature that everyone is entitled to the material objects necessary for their survival: food, water, housing, and so on. There is therefore a minimal level of private property, at least of a kind, in the state of nature; Hobbes further argued that men in a state of nature would not be entitled to amass more than was necessary for their own preservation, if by doing so they deprived others of the necessities of life:

> It is supposed to be incumbent upon everyone to acquire the necessities of life, not only by *right* but also by *natural necessity*. So if any one wishes to compete for more than this, he will be guilty of starting a war, since there was no

need for him to fight for anything; he will therefore be breaking *the fundamental law of nature.* (*De Cive* III.9; see also *Leviathan* ch. 15, p. 209)

As long as men teeter economically on the edge of survival, therefore, it is morally wrong (according to Hobbes) for some people to amass more than they need.

This general principle holds good in a commonwealth too. In *Leviathan* Hobbes argues that the particular distribution of land and resources in a society must be thought of as originally the decision of the sovereign. This was a frequently expressed view at the time, at least in the form of the claim that a particular property distribution is the consequence of a particular system of civil law. Grotius, for example, believed that to be the case. But Hobbes says that

> seeing the Soveraign, that is to say, the Common-wealth (whose Person he representeth,) is understood to do nothing but in order to the common Peace and Security, this Distribution of lands, is to be understood as done in order to the same: And consequently, whatsoever Distribution another shall make in prejudice thereof, is contrary to the will of every subject, that committed his Peace, and safety to his discretion, and conscience; and therefore by the will of every one of them, is to be reputed voyd . . . (ch. 24, p. 297) [the reading 'another' will not be found in any printed text, but is based on the manuscript of *Leviathan*]

So if the distribution of property works in such a way that people are physically endangered by it, and members of the commonwealth do not have access to the material necessities of life, then the sovereign is required to intervene and redistribute it; he must always ensure that everyone has at least the minimum necessary for survival. In Chapter 30 of *Leviathan*, Hobbes argues that the commonwealth must be responsible for the provision of maintenance for the destitute: 'they ought not to be left to the Charity of private persons; but to be provided for, (as far-forth as the necessities of Nature require,) by the Lawes of the Common-wealth' (p. 387). A corollary of this,

185

however, was that the sovereign must have the right to tax people to the level he thinks fit in order to protect the commonwealth: no 'right of private property' can be pleaded against his actions, as had been argued during the Ship Money controversy.

Furthermore, it seems that Hobbes's sovereign could not have the right to implement any policy (such as, say, a regime of strict egalitarianism) just because he thought it was a good idea. The only right of ours which the sovereign possesses, or which he exercises on our behalf, is the right to consider what means are necessary to our survival, and it would not therefore be on the basis of *our* rights that he would introduce any programme which went beyond the considerations of physical survival. Those considerations could take a sovereign a long way, it should be conceded: general economic prosperity, for example, might reasonably be thought to damp down civil conflict, so whatever made a nation prosperous would come to seem justified under the terms of Hobbes's theory. Hobbes indeed borrowed a great deal from contemporary accounts of how to increase a nation's prosperity—the literature of the movement subsequently known as 'mercantilism'. But at some point a sovereign might try to introduce policies which could not be justified in these terms, and at that point it would be possible to say that he had exceeded his rights. This would be particularly true if the policies were of a kind to arouse antagonism on the part of some section of the commonwealth, for the sovereign would then be endangering his own survival for no *necessary* reason. Accordingly, Hobbes, for example (*Leviathan* ch. 30, p. 386), while fully supporting a sovereign's right to level taxes without the consent of the taxed, argued against the legitimacy of egalitarian taxation, or income tax, preferring instead taxation on articles of consumption.

Hobbes's sovereign is thus, from the point of view of modern political assumptions, an ambiguous figure: possessed of great and apparently illiberal powers, there are nevertheless some things he cannot (or, more properly, *should* not) do which a modern state would regard as unquestionably legitimate. The vital point is that Hobbes's theory embodies the paradoxes of early or classical *liberalism* (and in this respect is not very different from, for example, John Locke's ideas). The primary responsibility of both citizens and sovereigns is to ensure the physical survival of themselves and their fellow citizens. Once this minimal requirement has been met, policies should not be enforced upon the community—though that requirement in fact implies a considerable degree of state power. Nineteenth- or twentieth-century exponents of *laissez-faire* in a sense took for granted the achievement of physical survival; for seventeenth-century liberals, both public order and a minimum level of subsistence were hard-won prizes. Nor should it be forgotten that it was only in Hobbes's lifetime that Western Europeans became more or less the first people in the history of our planet who could reasonably expect not to face devastating famine at some point in their lives.

A similar paradox is to be found in the last area of the sovereign's power which I want to consider, his rights over public debate and doctrine. More than anything else in Hobbes's theory, it has been the sovereign's total right to legislate on intellectual matters which has alarmed his readers, from the seventeenth century to our own time. Hobbes was absolutely clear that the sovereign had this right:

> it is annexed to the Soveraignty, to be Judge of what Opinions and Doctrines are averse, and what conducing to Peace; and consequently, on what occasions, how farre, and what, men are to be trusted withall, in speaking to Multitudes of people; and who shall examine the Doctrines of all bookes before they be published. For the Actions of men proceed from their Opinions; and in the well governing of Opinions, consisteth the well government of mens Actions, in order to their Peace, and Concord. And though in matter of Doctrine, nothing ought to be regarded but the Truth; yet this is not repugnant to regulating of the same by Peace . . . (*Leviathan* ch. 18, p. 233).

As this passage illustrates, the rationale for Hobbes's position was drawn straightforwardly from his fundamental presuppositions—that the alignment of opinion and judgement upon which the commonwealth rests cannot take place unless the sovereign is to be fully the judge of what men should be taught or might hear (for what they hear might persuade them). This seems on the face of it to be diametrically opposed to the most basic liberal assumptions.

However, once again we have to remember that we are dealing with the seventeenth century—and that what alarmed some of his readers then may have been very different from what would alarm us today. As I shall show in the next section, Hobbes's primary object in arguing like this was to elevate the power of the sovereign over the *churches*—bands of fanatics (in his eyes) who wished to enforce absurd opinions upon their fellow citizens, and whose activities were primarily responsible for the civil wars of Europe. They could only be controlled if the sovereign was empowered to determine public doctrine and silence disputes. But his was essentially a *negative* role: to align opinions, not to work hard in order to secure the acceptance of any *particular* point of view. The modern liberal fear of totalitarianism (especially after the experiences of the twentieth century) is primarily that the State will have its own ideological axe to grind, that it will force racist doctrines or particular economic theories upon its citizens. But for Hobbes and his contemporaries, the State was almost definable as the body in a society which has no ideological axe of its own. Though surrounded by dogmatists, there was no reason why the State itself should be wedded to any dogma other than the need to secure the survival of its citizens.

Apart from the churches, there was one other group of people whose views Hobbes wished to see the sovereign regulate; ironically, this was the group to which he himself had belonged in his youth, the *humanists*. *Leviathan* in particular is full of denunciations of the evil effects of studying the Greek and Roman classics, which, he said, had led their readers into mistaken ideas about *liberty*. Athens and Rome were republics, and to bolster their sovereignty they had appropriately taught their citizens the superiority of republican government; but reading the ancient classics out of this context had misled people into praising republican liberty as a universal value, and into seeking to reconstruct their own societies on republican lines—so that 'I think I may truly say, there was never any thing so deerly bought, as these Western parts have bought the learning, of the Greek and Latine tongues'. Hobbes conceded that 'the libertie, whereof there is so frequent, and honourable mention, in the Histories, and Philosophy of the Antient Greeks, and Romans' (*Leviathan* ch. 21, p. 266), did have a value, but only when understood as the liberty of the commonwealth from external pressure, rather than the liberty of the subject. This concession in fact reveals his disinclination fully to slough off his early humanism, for it was a view shared by many humanists (including, arguably, Machiavelli)—though those humanists had also argued that the citizens of a free commonwealth would *ipso facto* be freer themselves, and it was this claim which Hobbes repudiated. Hobbes summed up his view in a memorable passage about the Italian city of Lucca, which he must have visited, and which still displays the inscriptions he noticed:

> There is written on the Turrets of the city of *Luca* in great characters at this day, the word LIBERTAS; yet no man can thence inferre, that a particular man has more Libertie, or Immunitie from the service of the Commonwealth there, than in *Constantinople*. Whether a Commonwealth be Monarchicall, or Popular, the Freedome is still the same (p. 266)

Though in the regulation of public doctrine, trade, and private property, there might (according to Hobbes) be limitations on a sovereign's right to pursue his own programme beyond what the laws of nature prescribe, these limitations have to be understood as moral duties upon the sovereign, rather than as rights which his subjects can enforce against him. The distinction was an important one for Hobbes, for it was a key part of his theory that though one might say that a sovereign had broken the laws of nature in some way, one could not thereby claim the right immediately to resist him. Again, we have to draw a precise parallel with the ethical features of the state of nature. In that state, the fact that another person had broken the laws of nature (had, for example, got drunk) would not have given us some extra right to attack him: it would have been foolish and self-destructive conduct on his part, but irrelevant to the question of our own rights and duties. The same is true of the citizens' relations with their sovereign: until he actually starts to attack them, or until all government breaks down, what he does is irrelevant to the question of whether they ought to obey him. As a matter of fact, persistent incompetence by a sovereign is likely to antagonize people so much that they will eventually be led to rebel—though such a rebellion would be morally unjustified unless the actual survival of the rebels was at stake.

The narrowness of the right which the citizen possesses against the sovereign—a narrowness which seems (and indeed is) so markedly against fundamental liberal assumptions—is thus a function of the general narrowness of the rights which people possess under any circumstances; and that in turn, as we have seen, is a function of the impossibility of finding an agreed, coherent, and compelling moral theory of any elaborateness or complexity. In this area more than any other, perhaps, we have to face the fact that moral relativism—which is something to which many modern liberals would instinctively subscribe—may well issue in illiberal politics, and was almost universally taken by its first major exponents actually to do so. It may well be that Locke, who is the most obvious example of someone at the time who managed to avoid these political conclusions, was only able to avoid them because he had a more extensive and dogmatic ethical theory, which most of his modern readers are inclined to ignore; but whether liberalism of his kind can survive without such a theory remains an open question.

Religion

Only the politically radical in the seventeenth century read Hobbes as a fearsome theorist of state power; it was also quite possible to see his work instead as being corrosive of existing regimes—many conservatives, in fact, objected to it on just these grounds. But what made Hobbes almost uniformly alarming to his contemporaries, as I have already remarked in Part I, were his views on *religion*; and there is little doubt that it is his reputation for atheism, whether covert or overt, which has fuelled most discussion about his work since then. In this section I want to assess the real character of Hobbes's religious beliefs, and explain why they seem to have changed in the course of his life. We must distinguish, however, between his views on religion *in general*—the existence and character of a God—and his views on the *Christian* religion. While the former changed very little during his life, the latter changed markedly, and it seems to have been this change which most alienated his readers.

As we saw in the first section of Part II, the issue of the existence and character of a God was central to the debate about Descartes in which Hobbes was immersed in the late 1630s, and his writing from 1640 to 1643 make his own theological position perfectly clear. To understand it, we have first to remember that Hobbes argued in his metaphysics that the material upon which (so to speak) the mind works is made up of 'fantasies' or mental images, caused by inscrutable external forces. We can deduce from the existence of these fantasies something of the general character of the world—in particular, that it is composed of material objects interacting causally with one another—but we can know with certainty nothing else. Hobbes's fundamental claim about God was that it is absolutely impossible to form such a mental image of him. As he said in his Objections to Descartes's *Meditations* of 1641,

> to say that God is *independent* [i.e. uncaused] is simply to say that God belongs to the class of things such that I cannot image their origin. Similarly, to say that God is *infinite* is the same as saying that he belongs to the class of things such that we do not conceive of them as having bounds. It follows that any idea of God is ruled out. For what sort of idea is it which has no origin and no limits?

The same could be said, he observed in the *Elements of Law*, about all the conventional qualities attributed to God: 'all his attributes signify our inability and defect of power to conceive any thing concerning his nature' (I.10.2).

191

Since philosophy, according to Hobbes, can only concern itself with mental images and their implications, there is no place for God in philosophy—with one exception. Hobbes's metaphysics presupposed a sequence of causal relations, with each change in the world being brought about by some earlier moving body. At some inconceivably remote point in time— an 'infinity' ago—that sequence must have begun, and the 'first cause' could be described philosophically as 'God'. Hobbes, it should be said, believed that 'infinity' meant simply a quantity which human beings as a matter of fact could not count or measure. 'When someone says something is 'uncountable' we believe we understand that term. We do not, on hearing it, go mad or play the metaphysician, as we do on hearing the word 'infinite', yet both mean the same thing' (*Critique of Thomas White* fo. 330). So he accepted the possibility of a really existing first cause some uncountable number of years ago, though what it might have been like he could not say—modern astrophysicists' 'Big Bang' might have played the same role as 'God' for him. The crucial point is that all the conventional attributes of God such as benevolence and omnipotence were excluded from the *philosophical* concept of God.

But an impersonal, philosophical God of this kind still had an important role to play in Hobbes's theory. First, Hobbes argued in all his major works that there is a 'natural religion'. Whatever made the universe and therefore ourselves must be incomparably more powerful than anything else we can imagine, and it is a psychological truth that power of this kind necessarily elicits worship (*De Cive* XV.9; this whole chapter is the main discussion by Hobbes of natural religion). As part of our worship, we can use any language which tends to express our feelings; but this language (the language of any conventional religion) 'pertains not to the explanation of philosophical truth, but to proclaiming the states of mind that govern our wish to praise, magnify and honour God' (*Critique of Thomas White* fo. 396). All religions, Hobbes claimed, are simply ways of worshipping this inscrutable creator, and their doctrines and practices are whatever are deemed culturally appropriate as acts of worship. The institution responsible for deeming them was of course the commonwealth: 'the commonwealth [*civitas*] (that is, those who possess the power of the whole commonwealth) by right decides which *names* or *appellations* give honour to God and which do not; that is, which doctrines about the nature and works of God should be publically held and professed' (*De Cive* XV.16). But though the specific religion available in a society was a civil matter, and though Hobbes clearly aligned himself with those theorists such as Machiavelli who argued for a 'civil religion'—a tradition culminating in Rousseau—he was equally clear that it is rational to have a religion. Atheism, as he made clear in *De Cive* XIV.19, is a 'sin'; but it is a sin of 'imprudence or ignorance' only, by which he meant that it is like the denial of any other philosophically compelling argument.

Furthermore, this inscrutable creator could be thought of as the progenitor of the laws of nature. Thus Hobbes remarked in the *Elements of Law*, 'forasmuch as law (to speak properly) is a command, and these dictates, as they proceed from nature, are not commands; they are not therefore called laws in respect of nature, but in respect of the author of nature, God Almighty' (I.17.12). Hobbes was always slightly troubled by the fact that the principles which men ought rationally to follow in order to secure their preservation were termed 'laws', since 'law' normally implies the existence of a law*giver*; the modern use of the terms 'scientific law' or 'law of nature', as in the 'law of gravity', which carries of course no religious implications, lay some way in the future in Hobbes's lifetime. But he never advanced the view (which some modern scholars have attributed to him) that the *reason* for doing what the laws prescribe is that they are the commands of God: our reason for following them is that they are general principles which tell us how to preserve ourselves effectively. We do not have to know that there is a God in order to know that we must follow the laws of nature, because we obviously do not *need* to know that there is a first cause in order to believe any other true propositions about the world, and no other idea of God is admissible into philosophy. Hobbes registered this fact when, in addition to describing atheism as a sin of ignorance, he denied that it was a sin of 'injustice', or 'against the law of nature'. It should be said that he accepted this would not be true if God happened to be a civil sovereign, as had been the case for the Jews; but that was obviously a special case.

Hobbes's idea of a natural religion can fairly be described as 'deist', and his blend of deism and civil religion was to prove prophetic of much Enlightenment thinking. Like the Enlightenment writers, he took ancient religions to be paradigmatic, remarking in the *Elements of Law* that 'among the Grecians, Romans, or other Gentiles . . . their several civil laws were the rules whereby not only righteousness and virtue, but also religion and the external worship of God, was ordered and approved; that being esteemed the true worship of God, which was κατὰ τὰ νόμινα [*kata ta nomina*] (*i.e.*), according to the laws civil' (II.6.2). Religion in antiquity was thus like morality, the preserve of the State, with only the minimal 'natural religion' of God the creator as a common core to the different religions.

Such a narrow definition of natural or philosophical religion was contentious in Hobbes's own time, but it was by no means unusual or heretical: many contemporary theologians would have concurred that philosophical reasoning could tell men little about God. The idea that reason could deliver a full theology was primarily held by Aristotelians, committed by their general philosophy to the claim that rational common sense could tell men all truths about the world (a claim we have already seen being made in the context of discussions about sense-perception). By 1640 plenty of orthodox theologians, both Catholic and Protestant, were critical of Aristotle and sympathetic to the general sceptical case against him; but they reconciled this scepticism with their theology by insisting that belief in a Christian God, with all the properties conventionally attributed to him, must rest exclusively on *faith*.

But this tendency, which the nineteenth century dubbed 'fideism', took various forms, and to understand Hobbes's theology we need to see the difference between him and the fideists. Broadly speaking, there were three different fideistic ideas among orthodox theologians. The first and most implausible (though probably the commonest, at least among an older generation) was simply that to be a Christian was to believe in a Christian God, in the Incarnation and Redemption, etc., and that no reason could be given for this faith, though it could be explained within its own terms (by talking about God's good will in granting the believer his beliefs). This is rather like the approach to ethics which holds that everyone simply makes their own ethical commitment, and no reasons can be given for making one kind of commitment rather than another; like that approach, it most plausibly ends in relativism and pluralism. But religious pluralism was the last thing most orthodox theologians wanted, and two other kinds of fideism were advanced to meet this objection.

One was associated particularly with an early seventeenth-century follower of Montaigne, the Frenchman Pierre Charron. In many respects Charron was a pure sceptic, whose criticisms of Aristotelian philosophy were among the most cogent produced by the Renaissance sceptics. But he coupled this scepticism with an argument for a belief in Christianity (and, specifically, Catholic Christianity) which utilized one of the basic sceptical ideas. As we saw in Part I, the scepticism of men like Montaigne or Lipsius issued in a recommendation to men to do whatever was necessary to preserve themselves, from physical attack or emotional turmoil; Charron simply argued that religious belief is psychologically very sustaining and cheering. One will feel more content, and less troubled by the world, if one is religious; and in a Catholic country, one will be physically as well as mentally safer adopting Catholicism. The *truth* of the belief was irrelevant, since truths of this sort could not be determined; so Charron's argument presupposed that the content of religion was a matter of faith rather than reason. But there could be a good reason for having faith.

Charron's approach remained popular with a number of Christians, particularly in his native country—perhaps the most famous is Blaise Pascal who, later in the seventeenth century, elaborated a similar argument for Christianity. But, like the earlier form of fideism, it was basically relativist: in different countries and at different times, Charron's argument implies, man will rightly choose different religions. His argument could justify the existing distribution of religious beliefs and practices, but it could not help anyone faced by a stark choice between evenly balanced doctrines. Moreover, it was itself vulnerable to scepticism: Paolo Sarpi, leader of Venice during the Interdict Crisis (with whose circle of followers Hobbes was familiar, as we saw in Part I), argued in a series of unpublished reflections that political and psychological considerations of this kind would not necessarily lead to people adopting a religion of *any* kind; the states of the ancient world, he argued, had managed perfectly well by instilling a wholly secular sense of honour and patriotism into their citizens. Sarpi has some claim to be the first systematic thinker who denied any social efficacy for religion: even Hobbes was unwilling to go so far, though it is quite possible that he was influenced to some extent by his ideas.

The last variety of fideism was intended to avoid the problems which the other two approaches raised. This version is associated mainly with England, and a group of English theologians in the 1630s, among whom Hobbes had many friends. It was expressed particularly well in a classic of Anglican theology, William Chillingworth's *The Religion of Protestants* (1638). (Chillingworth was a close friend of Hobbes before the Civil War; he died in a Parliamentary prison in 1644). Chillingworth argued that we have as good reason to believe many of the stories about Christ as we do to believe in any historical events which we have not ourselves witnessed. It is a mistake to think that we need some special and mysterious kind of faith to be religious; it is true that we cannot demonstrate logically and philosophically the existence of a God or the truth of the Christian revelation, but nor can we demonstrate the former existence of Henry VIII. We do, however, have reasons of a universal, cross-cultural kind for taking some things on trust.

Chillingworth and his friends aligned themselves on this issue very much with Grotius, who devoted the last twenty years of his life before his death in 1645 to arguing that

Christianity was not a mysterious matter and that it could be defended against critics from other religions. A belief in 'at least one God' who made the world and cares for it was, Grotius said, as universal a human phenomenon as the principle of self-preservation, and therefore as unquestionable; this was the foundation of Grotius's 'natural religion', which was very close in spirit to Hobbes's. But this natural or primitive religion should be supplemented by Christianity, which had an advantage over all competing religions in that it was both more soundly based on a historical record, and required—or should require—fewer contentious beliefs on the part of its adherents. Grotius compared it in this respect particularly with the complicated ritual prescriptions of Judaism, and the military dogmas of Islam. The 'Grotian Religion' (as it was termed by one of his opponents) became popular in the most advanced Anglican circles on the eve of the Civil War, and the goal of a minimalist Christianity was set alongside the goal of a minimalist ethics as a solution to relativism.

As one might have expected, it is this English strain of fideism which is prominent in Hobbes's early works. In the *Elements of Law* he distinguishes clearly between *knowledge* and *opinion*, that is, between beliefs which are certain and those which are not; he describes faith as an opinion 'admitted out of trust to other men' (I.6.7). The critical issue, for Hobbes as for everyone else, was the status of belief in the validity of the Christian religion, particularly as set out in the Scriptures; and he explained faith in the truth of Scripture in terms of our confidence in the accurate transmission of the record:

> Seeing then the acknowledgement of the Scriptures to be the word of God, is not evidence [i.e. evident to natural reason], but faith; and faith . . . consisteth in the trust we have in other men: it appeareth plainly that the men so trusted, are the holy men of God's church succeeding one another from the time of those that saw the wondrous works of God Almighty in the flesh . . . (I.11.9)

A number of obvious problems immediately pose themselves about this position, all of which Hobbes tried to answer. The first is, does his general metaphysics not rule out at least some of the traditional dogmas of Christianity? How can a denial of the possibility of incorporeal objects, for example, square with the frequent references in the Bible to 'spirits'? Hobbes argued here that, on the one hand, talk of God as a 'spirit' was merely a result of our incapacity to think of him in material terms, and on the other that 'though the Scripture acknowledge spirits, yet doth it nowhere say, they are incorporeal' (I.11.5): a materialist explanation of all the events in the Bible was possible, and such an explanation would not, Hobbes claimed, deny the fundamentals of Christianity.

The second problem is, then, what are the fundamentals of Christianity? What are we believing if we take the Scriptures to be authoritative? Hobbes's answer here remained the same throughout his life: under the terms of our Christian faith, we are required to believe only 'that Jesus is the Messiah, that is, the Christ (II.6.6). Hobbes understood by this that Jesus is the Saviour—that the former existence of Christ on earth will cause those who believe in his existence to have eternal life. In his early work he did not explain how eternal life might be compatible with a materialist metaphysics, but in *Leviathan* (as we shall see presently) he went to some trouble to show that the two things were compatible. Hobbes's view of the fundamentals of Christianity broadly resembled Grotius's: once again, he was following the Dutchman along the path towards minimalism.

Thirdly, but in some ways the crucial problem, who is to be authoritative in the interpretation of Scripture? We can have a general confidence that the scriptural record is historically accurate, but there are difficulties in understanding such a complex document, and we need a source of confidence in one reading rather than another. This source could be our own private judgement, but Hobbes was always very opposed to this—naturally enough, since it restored exactly the randomness of opinion which plagued the state of nature. In both the *Elements of Law* and *De Cive*, however, the authoritative interpretation of the Scriptures is not left (as one might have expected) to the *sovereign*, but to the *Church*:

Seeing our faith, that the Scriptures are the word of God, began from the confidence and trust we repose in the church; there can be no doubt but that their interpretation of the same Scriptures, when any doubt or controversy shall arise, by which this fundamental point, that Jesus is come in the flesh, is not called into question, is safer for any man to trust to, than his own, whether reasoning, or spirit; that is to say his own opinion. (I.11.10)

The last problem is the relationship between the Church and the State. Here, Hobbes argued two things in his earlier works. First, in matters of natural reason or philosophy, the sovereign must have absolute power to determine the meanings of words and the content of public belief (for the reasons set out in the previous section). Secondly, where the Christian faith is concerned, though the sovereign's pronouncements are also to be authoritative for his citizens, a Christian sovereign is himself *obliged* to interpret the Scriptures 'through properly ordained Clergymen' (*De Cive* XVII.28). This is because Christ himself promised an 'infallibility' in the interpretation of those doctrines which are necessary to salvation to 'his *Apostles* until the day of judgement, that is to the *Apostles* and the *Priests* following the Apostles and consecrated by the laying-on of hands' (ibid).

Hobbes thus compromised the unity of his theory in this one respect, for he allowed (albeit in a kind of advisory position) a crucial role to the Church in the formation of public doctrine. With the one difficult and contentious exception of his materialism, in fact, Hobbes's religious ideas as set before his public by 1642 were extremely close to orthodox Anglicanism. Like the English Grotians, he wanted a minimalist Christianity; like Chillingworth he treated faith as a matter of confidence in a historical record; like all Anglicans he combined a belief in the supremacy of the sovereign in doctrinal matters with a commitment to the special role of the apostolic church in prescribing what dogmas the sovereign should enforce upon his citizens. It is not surprising, therefore, that many of his friends in the 1630s should have been devout clergymen, and that there was little hostility from them towards either the *Elements of Law* or *De Cive*.

But, as we saw in Part I, all this changed with the appearance of *Leviathan*, when the serious possibility was raised of regarding Hobbes as an atheist—the charge which was to plague his later years. As we also saw in Part I, the reason for the shift probably lay partly in Hobbes's enthusiasm for the anti-Presbyterian struggle, in which he saw Independency as having the best chance of winning; but another part of the reason lay, I think, in Hobbes's increasing awareness of the real implications of his general philosophical position.

The change came about through Hobbes's abandonment of his old view about the interpretation of Scripture; yet this apparently technical move was sufficient to make a dramatic difference in his religious theory. The fundamental distinction between philosophy and faith went through unaltered into *Leviathan*, as did the philosophical understanding of God as a first cause. But at great length and in minute detail, Hobbes now sought to show that the only interpreter of Scripture could be the civil sovereign, and that there was nothing special about a *church* at all. The apostolic succession from Christ through the sequential laying-on of hands, upon which he had placed so much stress in *De Cive*, was now dismissed as unimportant (ch. 42, pp. 571–5), on the basis of elaborate scholarship (much of which, it should be said, he owed to some of Grotius's recently published theological works—though characteristically he failed to acknowledge this fact). What form a church took, therefore, and what doctrines its clergy taught, were now to be determined solely and entirely by the *fiat* of the sovereign; there was no authoritative body beside him, obliging him to promulgate a particular interpretation of Scripture. The general rights of the sovereign over the meanings of words now extended to include all the meanings of all God's word also.

In many ways, of course, this position made much better sense than his earlier one, for it now aligned religious beliefs with other contentious beliefs in the domain controlled by the sovereign. But it had two particular consequences, both of which were disturbing to his old friends. The first concerned the question of ecclesiastical organization, and the second the question of theological dogma.

As regards the first, Hobbes now drew the natural conclusion that if there was nothing special about an apostolically ordained church, then there was no reason why a sovereign should in general be interested in maintaining a unified church in his commonwealth *at all*. All his passionate resentment at the power and influence of churches came to the fore in a remarkable series of chapters, and especially in Part Four of the book, subtitled 'Of the Kingdome of Darkness', in which the evil machinations of the clergy throughout the ages, and the pernicious consequences of their alliance with false philosophers (such as the Aristotelians), were exposed with savage irony. He put forward a vision of ecclesiastical history which was actually very close to a story Sarpi had told in some of his published works: free congregations of believers had been deceived into submitting their judgement to the pastors set over them, those pastors had then submitted to bishops, and finally the Pope had established an imperial sway over all ('the *Papacy*, is no other, than the *Ghost* of the deceased *Romane Empire*, sitting crowned upon the grave thereof' (ch. 47, p. 712)). But, at least in England, this structure had been dismantled in reverse order, beginning with the Reformation and culminating in the victory of the Independents. Hobbes celebrated their victory in a passage which, if one had not read it in *Leviathan*, one would attribute to Locke or one of the other great theorists of toleration:

And so we are reduced to the Independency of the Primitive Christians to folow Paul, or Cephas, or Apollos, every man as he liketh best: Which, if it be without contention, and without measuring the Doctrine of Christ, by our affection to the Person of his Minister, (the fault which the Apostle reprehended in the Corinthians,) is perhaps the best: First, because there ought to be no Power over the Consciences of men, but of the Word it selfe, working Faith in every one, not alwayes according to the purpose of them that Plant and Water, but of God himself, that giveth the Increase: and secondly, because it is unreasonable in them, who teach there is such danger in every little Errour, to require of a man endued with Reason of his own, to follow the Reason of any other men, or of the most voices of many other men; Which is little better, than to venture his Salvation at crosse and pile ... (ch. 47, p. 711)

The point is that, as I observed at the end of the previous section, in Hobbes's eyes the sovereign would not have the same kind of reasons for enforcing particular dogmas upon his citizens as churches historically had acted on in controlling their members. His right to enforce doctrine was essentially negative, and was intended above all to stop *non-sovereigns* from claiming such a right. As an example of what happened if churches (in this instance, the Church of Rome) got power over people, Hobbes referred to the most disturbing modern incident, the trial of Galileo:

Our own Navigations make manifest, and all men learned in humane Sciences, now acknowledge there are Antipodes: And every day it appeareth more and more, that Years, and Days are determined by Motions of the Earth. Neverthelesse, men that have in their Writings but supposed such Doctrine, as an occasion to lay open the reasons for, and against it, have been punished for it by Authority Ecclesiasticall. But what reason is there for it? (ch. 46, p. 703)

This freedom of philosophical enquiry would be safer under a regime of separate churches, ruled by a doctrinally omnipotent civil sovereign, than under the traditional balance between Church and State.

But the theological implications of Hobbes's theory were even more radical than its implications for ecclesiastical organization. As we have seen, religious belief was for him a matter purely of faith. As long as this faith was a matter of believing in the independent validity of the historical record of Christianity, it could be seen as a reasonably conventional religious commitment. But as soon as faith became exclusively a matter of believing what the civil sovereign said, then, on most understandings of religion, Hobbes had ceased to have one at all. It was precisely this which the men who accused Hobbes of atheism picked on; as one of them said in 1669, 'if once it be taken for granted that the Scriptures have no Authority but what the Civil Power gave them, they will soon come, upon a divine account, to have none at all.' We can best express the change which had come over Hobbes by saying that for him all religion, including Christianity, had now become civil religion; whereas in his earlier works the Christian Church had offered an alternative to civil religion, the arguments of *Leviathan* destroyed that alternative.

Contemporaries were particularly sensitive to this because, as we have seen, they already had before their eyes the example of someone who argued that a society's religion should be purely a matter of civil politics, namely Machiavelli. He had horrified an earlier generation by claiming that Christianity was not a particularly satisfactory religion from a political point of view, and implying that something more like the religions of the ancient world would be better. Hobbes now seemed to be giving a philosophical justification for this cavalier treatment of religious dogma. There were also plenty of people around in the 1650s and 1660s who were happy to read Hobbes in this way; a good example is Henry Stubbe, Hobbes's loyal follower at Oxford, who seriously considered the question of whether Islam might not on political grounds be a better religion for Western countries to adopt than Christianity.

Like Machiavelli or Stubbe, and unlike (say) Sarpi, Hobbes did not, however, argue that it might be desirable for a civil society to have *no* religion. In the Appendix to the Latin *Leviathan* (which was, admittedly, designed to meet his critics' objections), he argued that some religion was necessary for civil life, because of the utility of oath-taking (that is, promising to one's God) in order to maintain contracts and political allegiances (app. II, p. 352). But oath-taking, though important, was expressly presented in the body of the work as adding nothing to the force of contracts, so this argument must be treated with some reserve. What Hobbes consistently claimed was that a rational sovereign would organize *some* religion for his citizens as a means of worshipping the 'natural' God; but since that natural God was an impersonal creator about whom nothing could be truly predicated, this was as close to atheism as most contemporary readers could imagine. Hobbes's religious views were in the end most similar to those of Rousseau, the Jacobins, or the early nineteenth-century socialists.

But there was of course a certain irony in Hobbes's position. His general theory committed him not to any particular religious belief, but to the belief enforced by his sovereign (or to a free choice between the beliefs which his sovereign allowed to compete for support). But in seventeenth-century England, Hobbes alleged, the civil religion enforced by his sovereign was a Christianity based solely on the Scriptures. To demonstrate the coherence of his own intellectual position, therefore, Hobbes had fully to document the consistency of his general theory with Scripture. He had done this before, relatively superficially; but in *Leviathan* he tried seriously for the first time to wrestle with the problems posed to his metaphysics by the Christian belief that an eternal life awaited the true believer, and eternal damnation the ungodly.

His argument, as set out in Chapter 38 of *Leviathan*, is essentially that Christianity does not imply that there can be incorporeal existence. If Adam had not sinned, men would have lived on earth for ever; his sin (in some way Hobbes did not choose to analyse) caused mortality to fall upon the human race, but Christ's death redeemed mankind (again, Hobbes does not specify any of the mechanisms involved). Christ will return to earth at some time, to raise the dead and grant them back their material existence; he will then allow the godly to live for ever, but the ungodly he will condemn to a second, and this time final, death. There can be no independent life for men's 'souls': eternal life must require a body and a place of habitation. Such a view was not in fact completely outside the pale of Christianity: some early Christians believed something very similar, and in Hobbes's own time the heresy known as 'mortalism', which also asserted the impossibility of souls 'living' outside a body, had a number of adherents among radical Protestants (including, probably, John Milton).

But Hobbes's old friends greeted the theology of *Leviathan* with derision, and it is hard not to feel sympathy with them. A materialist apocalyptic vision of the kind set out in Chapter 38 is just about compatible with Christianity; but so much is left unexplained about what kind of physical process could possibly produce this result that it cannot be regarded as well integrated into Hobbes's general philosophy. As we have seen, Hobbes believed himself to be under a political obligation to produce a materialist Christianity, but the strain of the enterprise illustrates vividly the central dilemma of his (and, perhaps, *any* relativist or sceptical) approach.

This dilemma can be put in the following way. Hobbes's particular post-sceptical theory, like the sceptical theories of Montaigne and his followers, issued in the conclusion that one must obediently follow the laws and customs of one's country; Hobbes went further than Montaigne, in a way, since he argued in effect that one should *internalize* the laws and customs, and *really* believe them, or at least accept them as *intellectually* authoritative. But the laws and customs might include doctrines which were fundamentally incompatible with the principles upon which one was a relativist in the first place: what, then, should one do? Hobbes never resolved this dilemma, and it found expression in the deeply paradoxical fact that the great theorist of absolute submission to the power of the State lived the last years of his life in fear of being branded a heretic and atheist by that same State, while men who had taken up arms against it lived untroubled lives.

III Interpretations of Hobbes

Hobbes as a modern natural law theorist

Obviously, any philosopher of the stature of Hobbes plays a part in the construction of all subsequent philosophies. No successor can thoroughly ignore him, and even where they appear to do so (as, it has been argued, John Locke did) their silence is deeply expressive. Nevertheless, Hobbes's importance for later philosophers has fluctuated, and his works have not been read with the same care and attention throughout the 300 years between his death and our own time. In this part of the book, I shall survey the more important interpretations of Hobbes since his death, but I shall not attempt to give a complete history of his influence in modern philosophy, for such a history would amount in the end to a history of modern philosophy itself.

The first generation of serious and sympathetic readers of Hobbes were clear about his historical position. In the later seventeenth and early eighteenth centuries there were many attempts to write histories of modern philosophy, the first such works since antiquity. Their appearance signalled the fact that many contemporaries were conscious that something special and new had happened in the intellectual world, which could not be captured by using the categories left over from antiquity—categories such as 'Aristotelianism'. The first sketch of a history of modern moral philosophy was actually produced in Hobbes's lifetime by the German Samuel Pufendorf, who in 1672, in his *Law of Nature and Nations*, defended his own contentious ethical ideas by outlining what he took to be their origins. His sketch was then elaborated, largely by German and French writers, during the next fifty years, until it took the form of an absolutely standard account embodied in various textbooks and taken for granted by virtually everyone throughout Europe.

According to this history, modern moral philosophy began

with Hugo Grotius; he was 'the first to break the ice', in the words of one of these writers, after the long winter of Aristotelianism. Not only Aristotle, but all the theorists of antiquity and the Middle Ages, were flawed in central respects: as Pufendorf said, Aristotle's *Ethics*, 'which deals with the principles of human action, apparently contains scarcely anything other than the duties of a citizen in some Greek *polis*', and a similar charge of localism could be brought in some degree against other philosophers such as Cicero. The sceptics of antiquity, such as Carneades, and of modernity, such as Montaigne, all made this flaw abundantly clear, and it was Grotius's great merit that he was the first moral philosopher who fully engaged with the sceptical challenge and sought to answer it in a non-dogmatic way.

Grotius was followed in his enterprise, these histories continued, initially by two Englishmen. The first was John Selden, who published a vast and complex work on theories of natural law among the Jews; the second was Hobbes. The view of Hobbes put forward in these histories was, on the whole, a balanced and careful one. Pufendorf, for example, was critical of Hobbes's theology and of some of his ethics; but, he observed, many of the fundamental principles of modern moral philosophy 'would never have occurred to anyone had they not been in Hobbes's works' (Pufendorf was himself branded a Hobbist by some of his opponents for such remarks). The interpretation of Hobbes in the histories inspired by Pufendorf concentrated on what seemed to their authors to be the obvious facts that Hobbes took 'Self-Preservation, and Self-Interest, to be the original Causes of Civil Society' and that 'the Will of the Sovereign alone constitutes, not only what we call Just and Unjust, but even Religion; and that no divine Revelation can bind the Conscience, till the Authority, or rather Caprice, of his *Leviathan* . . . has given it the Force of a Law' (These quotations are from an early eighteenth-century history by the Swiss Protestant Jean Barbeyrac). Consequently, there was general agreement that Hobbes was close to being an atheist, and was certainly at least a deist rather than a true Christian.

Despite all this, Hobbes was placed firmly in the middle of

the sequence of writers beginning with Grotius, and continuing through Pufendorf himself to culminate (revealingly) in John Locke. All these men were seen as in some sense working on a common enterprise. As will be apparent, this early account of seventeenth-century moral philosophy is close to the account put forward earlier in this book. It *is* in many ways reasonable to view Hobbes as someone who was trying to provide a persuasive theoretical foundation to the ethical ideas put forward by Grotius, and in the process transforming those ideas (at least to some extent); it *is* plausible to see Pufendorf and Locke as engaged on a similar task. Moreover, the late seventeenth- and early eighteenth-century view of Hobbes's religion has much to commend it. Though, as we have just seen, there was caution and ambiguity on the subject, no one regarded him as a conventional theist; in fact his underground reputation as an atheist led to the circulation in eighteenth-century France of avowedly atheistical tracts under his name. But such a reputation did not shift him from the pantheon of modern philosophers: considerable religious heterodoxy was virtually the norm among all the writers saluted in the eighteenth-century histories of modern moral philosophy.

On the other hand, there was no question in the minds of these historians that Hobbes argued for anything other than unlimited sovereign power. Though opponents of such untramelled authority might sympathize with the other figures in this 'modern natural law' tradition—notably, of course, Locke, but also Grotius and Pufendorf to some extent—they could never sympathize on this issue with Hobbes. We can see this in the different responses to Hobbes of eighteenth-century Englishmen. The Whig party which dominated eighteenth-century English politics saw itself as heir to the seventeenth-century radical tradition of opposition to absolute monarchy, and few Whigs enthused about Hobbes; their Tory opponents, on the other hand, were wedded to Anglican orthodoxy and were equally hostile to him. The one group who read Hobbes with open enthusiasm were the men who sought in some way to be 'above party', particularly the associates of the young King George III; and it was one of these, John Campbell (later to make his name as the chief propagandist for George's favourite, the Earl of Bute), who first collected Hobbes's English language moral and political works together in a handsome new folio edition (1750), with an introduction defending their author from calumny.

But such men were a relatively weak force; much more representative of the attitude to Hobbes, even among people who more than shared his religious heterodoxy, were the remarks of David Hume in his *History of England* (Hume was a supporter of the 'Rockingham Whigs', the administration which ousted Bute):

> In our time he is much neglected . . . Hobbes's politics are fitted only to promote tyranny, and his ethics to encourage licentiousness. Though an enemy to religion, he partakes nothing of the spirit of scepticism; but is as positive and dogmatical as if human reason, and his reason in particular, could attain a thorough conviction in these subjects.

There was more, however, to this criticism of Hobbes than mere Whig prejudice. In the late eighteenth century the whole pantheon of modern philosophy was demolished, and on its ruins was erected quite another structure; and Hume was the man who began the process of demolition. His contemporary and (briefly) friend, Jean-Jacques Rousseau, continued it, and the final ground-clearing was accomplished by Immanuel Kant. Hume, in his *Treatise of Human Nature* (1739–40), was critical of all his natural law predecessors on the grounds that they had mistakenly tried to answer the sceptic by pointing to the actual universality of certain beliefs and practices—notably, the propensity to defend oneself and the belief that self-defence is morally legitimate. As Hume emphasized, no *evidence* of that kind could be relevant to the formation of anyone's own moral attitudes: it cannot follow from the fact that everyone else thinks or acts in a particular way, that *I* should do likewise. So the whole enterprise of modern natural law theory, with its emphasis on the facts of human psychology and culture, was itself vulnerable to a new kind of sceptical critique which denied the relevance of facts to ethical thinking. Not only

209

Hobbes, but also Grotius, Pufendorf, and Locke, shared in this new vulnerability. A similar point was made, though less explicitly, by Rousseau in his *Social Contract* (1762); as he said, men in a 'state of nature' could not be thought of as possessing moral rights or being under moral duties: morality was an invention of men in political communities, and could be authoritative only if those communities were properly founded democratic republics. Naturalistic ethics was thus a contradiction in terms.

Kant drew on both Hume and Rousseau to complete the criticism of eighteenth-century naturalism in all fields; but, far more than them, he explicitly repudiated the history of modern philosophy. In his eyes, Grotius and Pufendorf were 'sorry comforters' without any special intellectual role; the history of philosophy from antiquity down to his own time formed a single story, of a contest between what were later termed 'empiricists' and 'rationalists'—the former basing their arguments on sense-experience, the latter on mental concepts formed independently of experience. Kant's own philosophy was intended to locate this debate within a new context, and in particular to insist on the rigidity of the distinction between moral judgements and matters of fact. According to Kant, all the seventeenth-century writers thoroughly confused this distinction, mixing anthropology or psychology with ethics in an unjustifed way. Our moral judgements must come to us pure and uncontaminated by our beliefs about the material character of the world, including the character of human psychology.

The consequence of the rise of Kantianism (for Kant quickly became the model for the whole of Continental philosophy) was that the old history of moral philosophy was soon forgotten, the importance of Grotius and Pufendorf was overlooked, and the resemblance between Hobbes and the other natural law writers was disregarded. In post-Kantian histories (including, most strikingly, the *Lectures on the History of Philosophy* by Hegel), Hobbes is treated as a relatively minor contributor to an English 'empiricist' school of philosophers of which the most illustrious member was Locke. It should also be said that the seriousness with which Kant and his successors took the

Christian religion (in contrast to the insouciance of early eighteenth-century intellectuals) helped make them less impressed by Hobbes than the men of Pufendorf's and Barbeyrac's generation had been.

In England Kant's influence was far less; but here too the old heroes of modern philosophy were subjected to severe criticism, this time by the Utilitarians led by Jeremy Bentham, whose strictures on Grotius and Pufendorf in fact resemble those of Kant. Bentham chose Hume and Rousseau as his philosophical heroes, barely mentioning Hobbes; but later Utilitarians, and particularly Bentham's follower James Mill, came to see some of Hobbes's philosophy as anticipating their own. What the Utilitarians argued was that the different amounts of 'pleasure' or 'utility' which people get out of particular situations can be compared, and that public policy should be directed towards securing (in the famous phrase) 'the greatest happiness of the greatest number'. A necessary implication of this is that some people's interests or happiness might be sacrificed in the interests of wider utility, and that they might therefore have to be compelled politically to subordinate their concerns to those of the rest of the community.

It was this sense of the need for an omnipotent and neutral sovereign to bend citizens' wills to a Utilitarian norm which led the Utilitarian writers to read Hobbes with appreciation: Hobbes's own *moral* theory was very different from theirs, for there is no suggestion in Hobbes that one can meaningfully compare the utilities of different people, let alone subordinate one person's utility to a wider collective benefit. Hobbes was, as we have seen, a kind of liberal—that is, he believed that public policy should secure a particular level of welfare for all citizens (in his case, the level of bare survival), and that once that level is secured there should be no attempt to force policies upon the citizenry—though, as we have seen, extensive intervention in people's lives might in fact be necessary to secure the goal of universal survival. Moreoever, no one should be morally obliged to sink below that level (that is, to die) simply to allow more people the chance of living; yet the possibility of such a moral obligation is the essence of Utilitarianism. The

211

Utilitarian admirers of Hobbes thus borrowed his account of the right of the State to secure a social goal, but inserted their own account of what the social goal should be.

It was this Utilitarian interest that generated the first serious modern studies of Hobbes. What is still the standard edition of Hobbes's works (though a new edition is now gradually being put together at Oxford) was produced between 1839 and 1845 by William Molesworth, an MP and follower of the leading Utilitarian politicians of his day, George Grote and James and John Stuart Mill. The real relevance of Hobbes's ideas is shown strikingly by the fact that after Molesworth had supported the grant by the British government of an endowment for the Irish Roman Catholic college at Maynooth—a famous issue in the struggle against the remains of Anglican dominance of British public life—he was greeted by his Tory opponents when he stood for election at Southwark in 1845 with the cry of 'No Hobbes'! Grote and J. S. Mill were also mentors of the man who wrote the first scholarly modern biography of Hobbes, George Croom Robertson; his *Hobbes* (1886) is still well worth reading.

However, though (as Molesworth's experience at Southwark illustrates) the British State still encountered some opposition in its task of destroying the vestiges of *ancien régime* politics with which it was faced, its difficulties were as nothing compared to the problems faced by modern states on the Continent. It was an awareness of the relevance of Hobbes to these problems which led to a great revival of interest in him in Germany, in particular, and to the development of what is to this day the most authoritative and detailed study of Hobbes's intellectual development, that contained in the work of Ferdinand Toennies. In the years immediately after Bismarck's unification of Germany in 1870, many German socialists welcomed the new State as something which could in principle be used to advance the cause of socialism; whereas earlier socialists (such as Robert Owen in England) had been more like anarchists, highly wary of any incursions by the State into their socialist utopias, these German socialists thought that they could use the State to smash the forces of capitalistic exploitation, just as Bismarck had used it to smash artistocratic and ecclesiastical privileges.

Toennies was a follower of Ferdinand Lasalle, who argued along these lines, and he perceived that Hobbes could be used to provide a theoretical defence of using the State in this way: capitalistic enterprises and their competitiveness endangered social peace and individual liberty as surely as old religious feuding had done. From 1877 onwards he worked on Hobbes, making many manuscript discoveries in England (including notably the original manuscripts of the *Elements of Law*), and publishing the results of his labours in a series of articles and in a book of 1896. Gradually, like many other Germans, he came to lose confidence in the potential role of the State in promoting socialism, and he turned instead to a critique of the modern State in which Hobbes was the villain rather than the hero—he had ushered in a world of rationalistic, contractual relationships and had seen out a world of spontaneous communities. Socialism would now have to look back to the communities, and eschew the State. The sense that Hobbes was the genius of modernity, who invented the attitudes of what is called in German the *Gesellschaft*, the world of contract, and repudiated those of the *Gemeinschaft*, the world of community, has remained pervasive since Toennies—though Toennies also recognized that Grotius might equally qualify for this role. His approach to Hobbes was thus much closer in spirit to that of Hobbes's early readers than had been the case for more than a century.

Though Toennies himself concentrated on Hobbes's moral and political thought, his work on the Hobbesian manuscripts exposed the considerable range and power of Hobbes's philosophy of science. The first person to follow this up and carefully analyse the relationship between Hobbes and the other great early modern philosophers of science was a Dane, Frithiof Brandt, who published his work on *Thomas Hobbes's Mechanical Conception of Nature* in 1928 (Toennies read it in draft form and approved of it). Just as Toennies's studies have remained the basis of modern scholarship on Hobbes's political

ideas, so Brandt's book has been the foundation for all subsequent work on Hobbes's philosophy of science. It was not
until our own time that scholarship of this kind—the close
investigation of Hobbes's relationships with his contemporaries and of the historical circumstances in which he composed
his works—was applied once again to Hobbes. In this respect
his fate resembles that of other great political theorists, for the
period from about 1930 to about 1965 was remarkable for the
widespread lack of interest in the kind of detailed and scholarly
historical enquiry which had occupied the previous generation.

Hobbes as the demon of modernity

This is not to say, however, that the writers of the period
1930–65 had no interest in historical issues: the project of
understanding Hobbes, and his relationship with broadly
defined traditions of thought, continued, and produced most of
the current interpretative literature on Hobbes. Indeed,
Hobbes's allegedly special role in the creation of modernity,
and what that might tell us about modern thought in general,
has been at the heart of all these more recent discussions—
though by no means all twentieth-century commentators on
Hobbes have agreed that Hobbes was a characteristic representative of 'modern' thought.

The most striking examples of people who did think this are
provided by two very different figures. One is the German (and,
later, American) Leo Strauss, whose ideas on Hobbes were first
put forward in a volume on *The Political Philosophy of Hobbes*
(1934) and then in a series of lectures published under the title
Natural Right and History (1953). The other is the Canadian
C. B. Macpherson, who published an article on 'Hobbes's
Bourgeois Man' (originally entitled 'Hobbes Today') in 1945, a
book called *The Political Theory of Possessive Individualism*
in 1962, and what is now the standard edition of *Leviathan* in
1968. I will deal with Strauss first.

Strauss had a vision of European intellectual history of some
complexity and subtlety; put simply, he believed that there
had always been a fundamental conflict between moral relativism, of the kind embodied in the ancient sceptical texts and in

Renaissance writers such as Montaigne, and the belief in 'natural right'. This latter belief was expounded most cogently by the post-Socratic ancient philosophers, who held, according to Strauss, that relativism could be combated through a process of philosophical reflection which sought to go beyond the superficial variety of belief and custom to an underlying unity of some kind. Strauss himself only hinted at what that unity might consist in, for it was part of his argument that only 'the wise' could see it; indeed it was this aspect of his theory, with its disconcerting implications about the role of 'the wise' in a community, which attracted both most support and most criticism from his readers.

The natural science of antiquity, Strauss argued, had assisted the anti-relativists by giving an account of human beings' natural ends which validated their moral duties. But the justifiable and inevitable collapse of that science in the seventeenth century had left the highest form of philosophy, scientific enquiry, detached from ethics, and allowed relativism a free rein once again. Hobbes's philosophy was thus the first modern moral philosophy, for it was the first fully to accept the implications of modern natural science. It restated ancient relativism in the form of a rights theory according to which men's natural rights express what they *want* to do, and natural law becomes derivative from the rights and barely a matter of duty at all.

However, Hobbes, according to Strauss, retained one 'single, but momentous idea' from the anti-relativists, namely the idea that a political philosophy is necessary and that there can be a 'best regime': he was not content merely to say that everyone as a matter of fact seeks to get what they want; he also wished to show that conduct of that kind is compatible with a 'good' social order. He made them compatible through his Leviathan State, just as Adam Smith later made them compatible through the hidden hand of the market; but this State rested on the 'fundamental fiction' that the will of the sovereign is the will of all, so it cannot really provide the answer to relativism.

Setting aside the highly contentious historical and moral background against which Strauss read Hobbes, there is undoubtedly some cogency to his interpretation. In particular, Strauss in my view correctly recognized that Hobbes subordinated natural laws to natural rights, taking the laws of nature to be general principles for the wise exercise of our rights. He also had a correct instinct for the central importance in this story of the relativistic or sceptical challenge, and for the ambiguity in Hobbes's relationship to that challenge—on the one hand seeking an answer to it, and on the other wishing to incorporate its basic insights into his own theory. The weakness in Strauss's argument lies in his often highly fanciful readings of the ancient writers rather than in his better grounded reading of Hobbes; but it has proved hard for modern scholars to disentangle that reading from its distasteful surroundings.

Strauss represents in a fairly extreme form the claim that Hobbes is the demon-king of modernity, but others have argued similar cases. The most interesting of these is, as I have said, C. B. Macpherson, who tried to argue that the distinctive character of Hobbes's political thought is due to his role as in some sense the spokesman for 'bourgeois' values. The congruence between some of Hobbes's philosophy and some of the attitudes of competitive mercantile capitalism has often been remarked on: in a way it was implied in Toennies's handling of Hobbes's historical role, and Strauss too observed (in opposition to Max Weber's well-known argument about the connection between Calvinism and the rise of capitalism) that it was Hobbes rather than his Calvinist opponents who appeared first to give voice to capitalistic attitudes. Put very broadly, there is an obvious plausibility about this position (if, again, we subsume Hobbes into a wider European tradition alongside Grotius and Locke): thus, for example, these writers *were* interested in breaking up associations within the State which might dominate or terrorize their members, and capitalists *were* often also interested in seeing such associations broken up if they hampered their own economic activities. Hobbes's polemic against guilds was part of a general polemic against particular associations or professional bodies, but it echoed similar complaints made by many prospectively competitive manufacturers.

The snag about Macpherson's view (which became even

more obvious when he tried to apply a similar argument to Locke) is that he regarded 'modern' man as *essentially* bourgeois, whereas the more wide-ranging and flexible historical sense of someone like Toennies recognized that some anti-bourgeois attitudes may also be part of modernity. As we saw, Toennies at one point proffered a socialist reading of Hobbes, and similar socialist readings of Locke were given in the nineteenth century. This is not to say that such readings are correct; it is rather to illustrate that the reading of Hobbes or Locke as capitalists is as plausible (or implausible) as the reading of them as socialists. Both capitalism and its critics have been part of modernity from the beginning, and a general philosophy of Hobbes's kind could—and did—appeal to both. Keith Thomas, in an article of 1965 ('The Social Origins of Hobbes's Political Thought'), pointed this out forcefully, observing, for example, that Hobbes's requirement on the sovereign to ensure the survival of the poorest in society, if necessary by taking away the property of the wealthier, runs counter to the most obviously 'bourgeois' enthusiasm, for inviolable private property.

Hobbes as a social scientist

While both Strauss and Macpherson wished (in their different ways) to emphasize the special modernity of Hobbes, most other writers in the later twentieth century have been dubious about this claim. Roughly speaking, there are two other traditions of thinking about Hobbes; we can understand both if we go back to the change introduced by Kant into the European sense of what philosophy is and has been. Whereas Strauss and Macpherson were in a way pre-Kantian in their view of the history of philosophy, those who have smoothed away Hobbes's modernity have been much more post-Kantian. (This might have been expected, given the way in which Kant himself dismissed the special character of seventeenth-century thought.)

The first of these two traditions has argued that Hobbes's theory was a theory of *prudence* or purely psychological motivation without any clear moral implications, and that this theory was simply the application to human conduct of principles of scientific enquiry well established long before Hobbes. According to this view, Hobbes's philosophy stands in the same relationship to modern ethical ideas as (say) Freudian psychology does: it provides a 'scientific' account of how men do, and perhaps how they must, behave, which the moralist has to take into account when making what used to be called 'value judgements'. But it does not itself supplant those ethical ideas, nor, fundamentally, was it intended to do so; though Hobbes, these writers have argued, may have thought that no value judgements were as a matter of fact possible. The second tradition has argued that Hobbes was a moralist, and what is more a moralist of the Kantian kind: that is, he really believed in moral judgements independent of factual assumptions about man's psychology.

As will have been clear from this book so far, I myself regard both these traditions as fundamentally mistaken; but writers within them have made a number of interesting and important interpretative points about Hobbes which must be taken seriously. I shall deal with the former tradition first.

Effectively, this tradition began with a book by Richard Peters in 1956 entitled *Hobbes*, and was carried on notably by J. W. N. Watkins in his *Hobbes's System of Ideas* (1965). Three propositions tended to be put forward by these writers. First, that Hobbes's political theory was intimately connected with his general scientific philosophy. Second, that his scientific method was the same as Galileo's, which was in turn a well-established principle of scientific enquiry (particularly popular at the University of Padua), namely the so-called 'resolutive-compositive method'. And third, that this was a method of empirical enquiry designed to elicit a moral or political science in the modern sense—something which could be used to explain human social behaviour.

Few people (other than those in the second of the post-Kantian traditions) would now disagree with the first of these propositions. It is true that Strauss, in his early book on Hobbes, devoted some scholarly effort to breaking the link between Hobbes's scientific writings and his political theory;

but given the general argument which he put forward later in *Natural Right and History*, it is not clear that he needed to make this break. As we have just seen, an interpretation of the rise of modern science is a key feature of that book. On the other hand, the actual account of the link which Peters and his successors gave is radically flawed by their universal reliance on the 'Short Tract', which they took to have been written c. 1630 and therefore to antedate any of Hobbes's political writings: as we saw earlier, there is no reason to suppose that the 'Tract' is by Hobbes. Their reliance on the 'Tract' also skewed their account of Hobbes's philosophy of science, for that work is not concerned to answer the sceptics, and it presents a much cruder materialism than anything found in Hobbes's non-contentious works.

The second point (which J. W. N. Watkins particularly stressed) was derived ultimately from the work of a great late nineteenth-century German neo-Kantian, Ernst Cassirer. He argued (in a book of 1906) that sixteenth-century late scholastic philosophers at Padua developed a scientific method in which objects were to be 'resolved' down to their component parts, the behaviour of those parts studied in a simplified form, and then the pieces 'composed' to make the whole again (the idea is roughly that to find what makes, say, a watch work, you take it to pieces and then put it together again). Cassirer argued that this was Galileo's experimental method, and following him these Hobbes scholars have claimed that it was Hobbes's also, resting their argument on one or two passages in his works where he speaks of explaining phenomena by 'resolving' them down into their parts, or by 'composing' them from basic principles. The most notable such passage, perhaps, is in the preface to *De Cive*, where Hobbes compares investigating 'the authority of the state and the duties of citizens' to examining the workings of a watch by dismantling it.

The view that this was Hobbes's method can be criticized on two fronts. First, it is not clear to modern scholars that Galileo's own method owed as much to this basically scholastic tradition as Cassirer thought; second, it is clear that it was not the most important way in which Hobbes approached the task of explaining physical events. As we have seen repeatedly, Hobbes did not believe that it was possible to have more than conjectural or hypothetical knowledge of the physical causes of any phenomenon; though mentally dismantling an object or event might help to generate or test such a hypothesis, it cannot ultimately give a better kind of knowledge of what is going on than one would gain simply by thinking about what might cause such objects or events in the first place.

The most important claim put forward by this group of writers was, however, the last one, that Hobbes's enterprise was in some way 'value-free'. Speaking of Hobbes's 'prescriptions'—that is, the rules derived from the laws of nature—Watkins, for example, wrote that 'my thesis is that Hobbes did derive his prescriptions from factual premisses but without committing a logical fallacy: for his prescriptions are not *moral* prescriptions—they are like "doctor's orders" of a peculiarly compelling kind' (*Hobbes's System of Ideas*, 1973). And he used Kantian categories to analyse Hobbes's laws of nature in this way.

In 1969 David Gauthier added a particular twist to this line of argument by analysing Hobbes's theory partly in terms of what is known as 'games theory', in his book *The Logic of Leviathan* (1969). Since the Second World War, economists and mathematicians have been interested in the formal analysis of a variety of 'games'—situations where two or more players try to get the best result they can for themselves by responding tactically in various ways to what the other players do. Some situations of this kind (as had long been recognized in informal discussions) present a paradoxical aspect, and the example of this paradox which has become standard in the literature is known as the 'Prisoners' Dilemma'. The idea is that two suspects are arrested by the police and put in separate cells. Each is then told that if both confess, they go to prison for a short period; if neither confesses, they will have to be released. But if only one confesses and incriminates the other, then he will be rewarded and his companion will go to gaol for a long time. The problem about this is that *whatever* each one of them does, it is in the interests of the other to confess: for if one confesses, it is better for the other also to confess and go to prison for a short time than to keep silent and be sentenced to a long imprisonment; while if one keeps silent, it is better for the other to confess and reap the reward than to keep silent and merely be released. So if the prisoners act rationally, they will both confess—but then they are both worse off than if they had each kept silent.

Gauthier was the first person to suggest that Hobbes's state of nature could be represented as a kind of Prisoners' Dilemma. Voluntary co-operation is not possible for men in a state of nature because they will always be better off defecting from a contract and seizing a unilateral advantage than sticking to the agreement. Only if their co-operation can be *compelled* in some way will they be motivated to abide by their agreements. Recognizing this fact about themselves and their fellows, men in a state of nature establish a sovereign who will, Gauthier argued, act on their behalf and exercise their natural rights to enfore obedience to contracts. The agreement to erect a sovereign is different from other agreements, since if everyone else abides by the contract, it is not in my interest to defect, since I will now be punished for doing so: we are thus no longer faced with the Prisoners' Dilemma which was characteristic of the state of nature. (We could draw an analogy with the prisoners: if they believed in the power of their Mafia boss to punish them for treachery, they would keep quiet.) It does however, remain the case that if we can get away with it, it must be in our interests to defect or break the sovereign's law; Gauthier acknowledged that this is a difficulty, particularly since Hobbes remarked in *Leviathan*, as we have seen, that only a 'foole' would hold that it could be right to do so.

The problem about this line of argument is partly that Hobbes was not actually concerned with explaining human conduct. As we have seen, Hobbes recognized that men can behave in ways quite contrary to the laws of nature, and these laws cannot therefore be explanatory in any straightforward sense. But we cannot take the other 'value-free' route of regarding the laws as prescriptions which tell us how (in modern terms) to 'maximize our utilities'. They are prescriptions which tell us how to exercise our right of self-preservation, but not how to do anything else; and self-preservation is

221

important not simply because we all want to survive, but because it is the one thing we can be said to have the indubitable *right* to do—though the reason for that being the case is a fact about human psychology. If Hobbes is thereby indictable for having confused 'facts' and 'values' in some way, so be it: as we have seen, that very distinction was introduced partly as a criticism of writers like Hobbes. But it is not as obvious or as easy a distinction to make as these post-Kantian commentators have thought, and to reconstruct Hobbes's philosophy in such a way as to make him apparently aware of it may be as insensitive philosophically as it undoubtedly is historically.

To see the point of these remarks, we need only consider the difference between the account of the state of nature which I gave in Part II, and the account which Gauthier gave. According to my account, the problems of the state of nature arise, for Hobbes, *in the sphere of rights*: the state of war is the consequence of everyone implementing their right of self-preservation. Correspondingly, once a sovereign is established to co-ordinate the exercise of these rights, no one has the right to defect unless they believe incontrovertibly that their preservation is endangered by sticking to the contract (as in the case of the prisoner on his way to the gallows). They might want to defect, and their utility might be greater if they did so (for example, a burglar might be better off breaking the law than keeping it); but this is not the problem with which Hobbes was primarily concerned, nor were these the terms in which people were yet ready to write political theory.

For Gauthier, the state of nature involves the calculation of utilities by each inhabitant, and a choice between the best course of action, the next-best, and so on. On his view, there remains a puzzle about why, if we could be reasonably sure of not being caught, we should not break the sovereign's laws. On my view, this is not a problem for Hobbes, since we would have no *right* to break the law unless it was necessary for our preservation that we did so. Though we might benefit by breaking it, it would be an act *without right*, since rights (for

Hobbes) are limited to acts performed in the interests of self-preservation and do not extend to those rights which may satisfy our other wants. His objective was not to deliver a science of human behaviour of a non-moral kind, and many of the puzzles which have surfaced in the course of the modern discussions of such 'sciences' (like the Prisoners' Dilemma) are irrelevant to his inquiry.

Hobbes as a moralist

The idea that Hobbes was a moralist and not a value-free scientist was, of course, integral to the other tradition of thinking about Hobbes in the twentieth century; but the particular view of what a moralist must be which was enshrined in this tradition was highly misleading. It began with A. E. Taylor, in an article of 1938, 'The Ethical Doctrine of Hobbes', explicitly arguing that Hobbes was a kind of Kantian, as the Hobbesian laws of nature represent moral requirements upon men which are not founded in any way on the facts of human psychology; but the most famous and controversial statement of it was by Howard Warrender in a book published in 1957 entitled *The Political Philosophy of Hobbes: His Theory of Obligation*. Warrender's argument required him first to deny the connections between Hobbes's general philosophy and his moral or political theory; having narrowed his focus in this way, he turned to consider the distinction which Hobbes made in a number of passages, notably in Chapter 14 of *Leviathan*, between a *right* ('the liberty to do, or to forbeare') and a *law* (which 'determineth, and bindeth to one of them'). On the basis of this undeniable fact about Hobbes's terminology, Warrender then argued that since self-preservation is consistently described as a *right*, it could not be the foundation of the natural *law* to 'seek peace', since if we are free to protect ourselves *or to forbear from protecting ourselves*, no *obligation* can arise on us to protect ourselves.

Warrender then looked for some other source of obligation in Hobbes, and found it in the stray remarks which Hobbes made about the laws of nature being the commands of God. He concluded that according to Hobbes, we are morally obliged to obey God's commands simply because he is God (not because he has material power over us), and his commands require us above all to seek peace. If fulfilling God's instructions threatens our own survival, we are entitled to plead our natural right of self-preservation against the commands; but that right is not the foundation of our obligation to seek peace.

This subtle argument occasioned an immense amount of criticism in the 1950s and 1960s, much of which made the obvious but compelling point that on Warrender's account, Hobbes should have been the toast of seventeenth-century theists rather than the object of their deep suspicion. Yet these critics found it surprisingly difficult to provide an alternative explanation of the Hobbesian distinction between rights and laws. However, as we saw in Part II, an alternative explanation can be given, namely that our right of self-preservation is properly speaking a right *rationally to use our judgement about what conduces to our preservation*, and this right is indeed something we can 'forbear' from exercising—indeed, we partly forbear from exercising it when we establish a sovereign, for we then agree *not* to use our own judgement in a wide variety of cases. This is compatible with it being the case that the laws of nature provide (so to speak) permanent and incontrovertible judgements about what will lead to our preservation, and that they therefore in effect structure the way in which we rationally choose to exercise our right. If we put at the heart of our own reading of Hobbes's work his consuming interest in the disparities between different human beings' judgements and perceptions of the world, then Warrender's difficulties tend to disappear.

A somewhat different account of Hobbes as a moralist, though one of comparable or even greater subtlety, was provided by Michael Oakeshott, first in an introduction to an edition of *Leviathan* in 1945, and subsequently in an essay on 'The Moral Life in the Writings of Thomas Hobbes' (1960). What Oakeshott argued was essentially that Hobbes *defined* what is morally obligatory as *the commands of the sovereign*. The reason why men create a sovereign is that they are in some sense 'necessitated' or 'obliged' to do so by the laws of nature, given their natural fear of death; but this is not a 'moral' obligation—that is, it does not in any way take away natural moral rights. These natural rights are moral in character from the beginning: 'the natural Right of each man to all things . . . [is] inherent in the will, which is limitless in its claims.' But men are not by nature under any moral *obligation*. However, once the sovereign has been constituted, his will becomes a moral law for his subjects. Even the laws of nature, Oakeshott repeatedly said, could only become moral laws if the sovereign ordered his subjects to act upon them. What the sovereign says his subjects must do is not necessarily the same as their naked (non-moral) self-interest would have led them to do; his commands are therefore the same kind of thing as conventional moral principles—they depend for their force upon people's conviction about what they *ought* to do.

Thus, according to Oakeshott, Hobbes did not confuse facts and values; he simply had a rather unexpected view of what constituted the sources of morality, namely (for rights) the will of each person and (for laws) the will of a civil sovereign. In a sense, Oakeshott took seriously the description by Hobbes of the Leviathan as 'that *Mortall God*', for like God's will in what is called the 'voluntarist' tradition of medieval (and later) theology, the Leviathan's will constitutes right and wrong, and no further criterion is required. In another sense, Oakeshott's interpretation would make Hobbes very like Rousseau—for Rousseau undoubtedly did argue that the 'general will' of the civil association is the touchstone of moral truth, and that prior to their formation of the city, men in a state of nature are under no moral duties and have no moral rights. In a review of Strauss, Oakeshott did indeed link Hobbes to Rousseau, while in the introduction to *Leviathan* he linked him to the 'sceptical, late scholastic tradition' of voluntaristic nominalism.

The problem with Oakeshott's interpretation was partly, as a number of early critics observed, that it is hard to find clear textual evidence for it, but mostly that Hobbes does *not* base rights, either of individuals or of the sovereign, on 'limitless' wills. As we saw in Part II, Hobbes is very clear that 'the right to all things' is simply the right to do anything which is thought to be necessary for self-preservation; many things we might *will* to do (such as getting drunk) are straightforwardly prohibited by the laws of nature, even in the state of nature. Oakeshott said of the laws of nature that they may put an internal, psychological 'impediment' upon a person, but that the person's 'natural Right to act in any way he chooses has suffered no impediment; fear and reason may limit a man's power, but not his Right'. But Hobbes said (in one of his clarificatory footnotes to *De Cive*) that

> there are some natural laws whose exercise does not cease even in war. For I do not understand how drunkenness or cruelty (that is, revenge which does not look to some future good) can conduce to peace, or the preservation of anyone. Briefly, in the state of nature, what is Just and Unjust is not to be assessed by the actions, but by the opinions and consciences of the agents. What is done out of necessity, in the interests of peace and one's own preservation, is done rightly. (III.27)

It seems clear that for Hobbes, natural rights can be limited by natural laws; or, more properly, that we do not have a natural right to act in any way we choose. It was in fact Spinoza who extended the idea of natural rights to cover all possible desires and actions, and he did so knowing that he was transforming Hobbes's theory.

Hobbes today

The current scholarship on Hobbes includes representatives, in various guises, of all the modern traditions dealt with above. But it has also begun to be more open to the historical peculiarities of Hobbes, and to be aware of the dangers of reading Hobbes too much through Kantian lenses. The process of recovering the historical Hobbes began, perhaps, with some influential essays by Quentin Skinner in the late 1960s, in which he argued among other things that Hobbes's theory had the same political *point* as those of a number of other (non-Hobbesian) writers who sought to defend allegiance to the new republic set up in England after 1649. These writers, known as

'Engagement theorists' after the 'Engagement', the oath to support the new regime which was required of people in 1650, argued that a new ruler in possession of the apparatus of government must be accorded the same obedience as the old ruler, whatever the route by which he had come to power; and Hobbes in the 'Review and Conclusion' to *Leviathan* did indeed clearly align himself with these theorists.

What Skinner's observation suggested was that a more detailed consideration of the actual interaction between Hobbes and the other theorists of his time, and their common response to political events, might repay examination, and much recent scholarship has followed his lead. Indeed, there is now a wealth of detailed work on Hobbes's life and writings not known since the time of Toennies and Brandt; the best indication of this is that Oxford University Press has begun to issue a new and properly based edition of all Hobbes's works (inspired to do so, it should be said, by Howard Warrender). At the same time, a general modern scepticism about the force of Kant's view of the history and task of philosophy has begun to affect interpretations of Hobbes; Skinner's work may indeed have been an intimation of this, and a recent book by Tom Sorell (though superficially resolutely non-historical) treats Hobbes's enterprise as a quest for a *moral science* of a suitably pre-Kantian kind. As we move into a world where scepticism has more appeal than Kant's 'moral law', the writings of the greatest and most consistent post-sceptic are bound to be studied with ever greater attention.

Conclusion

Hobbes's reputation, even in his own time, was a paradoxical one. He was seen as a fierce controversialist and a brusque dogmatist, yet his chief anger was directed at dogmatism of every kind. He was hostile to the intellectual authority of the churches, as expressed for example in the universities, yet he wanted his own philosophical works to be the authoritative texts within the universities. He praised toleration, yet he advocated an absolute sovereign with total power over intellectual matters. In this book I have tried to explain something of this paradox, but I have done so by placing Hobbes within a wider paradox, one which may be inherent in scepticism or liberalism. What happens if, like the men of Hobbes's generation and the generation immediately preceding, we lose all confidence in the truth of most existing beliefs? How do we actually *live*? This was a question which was put even in antiquity to the sceptics of the Graeco-Roman world, and it has remained the central question for sceptics ever since. The answer given by the writers of both the ancient world and the late sixteenth century was, essentially, live according to the laws and customs of your country; these laws and customs have no universal validity, but that is no reason for denying their practical hold upon you. Their scepticism thus became part of a deeply conservative, indeed timorous attitude to the ideological storm in which they found themselves.

As I have stressed, Hobbes's philosophy dealt with just these issues, and ended with broadly the same conclusion. Instead of scepticism, he offered *science*; but when one looks closer, one finds that his science is of an extremely exiguous kind. By clearing away all that he thought was doubtful, he was left with a bare a priori materialism, according to which the universe must consist of material objects causally interacting with one another, but the real character of these objects and their interactions is unknowable. Similarly in ethics: by clearing away all the complicated ethical theories of his orthodox predecessors (whether Aristotelians or humanists), he was left with nothing but the bare principle that we are morally entitled to preserve ourselves. Hobbes was left with little more to stand on as a guide to living than the sceptics like Montaigne, for they too had always acknowledged the practical force of the principle of self-preservation.

So it should come as no surprise that his conclusions were also close to theirs: that the laws of one's country are constitutive of one's general morality, and that whatever is necessary for one's preservation must be morally acceptable. He was prepared to take this position to remarkable lengths; for example, in one of the most outspoken passages in his entire works, he claimed (as we have already seen) that 'upon the occasion of some strange and deformed birth, it shall not be decided by Aristotle, or the philosophers, whether the same be a man or no, but by the laws' (*Elements of Law* II.10.8). Even the definition of what a human being is was thus put entirely at the disposal of the sovereign: there can be no objective 'fact of the matter' about it. The question of what a human being is, is still an urgent one: witness the intense debate about abortion. But we still appoint philosophers to head commissions to decide these issues, and are unwilling to take the implications of radical scepticism in these areas seriously, for, on Hobbes's account, it assigns to the State a kind of arbitrary power over the most important matters in our lives.

Yet many people would now pay at least lip-service to the sceptical relativism of Montaigne's generation. Scepticism about both science and ethics is more persuasive now than for many generations. Claims about the special validity of modern Western natural science have been undermined by the work of historians and philosophers of science, who have come to stress the culturally determined and unsubstantiated character of many scientific assumptions; while the literally ancient sense of the sheer multiplicity of human moral opinions, and of their incompatibility, has come once again to possess us. What is still not recognized sufficiently, however, is that Hobbes was one of the chief philosophers of our culture who faced both

229

these issues with intelligence and consistency; the only comparable figure is Hume, but it is not clear that Hume's answer to the question of how the sceptic ought to live is in the end more compelling than Hobbes's. Hume's answer was effectively, 'Do not take scepticism too seriously'—'A true sceptic will be diffident of his philosophical doubts, as well as of his philosophical conviction; and will never refuse any innocent satisfaction, which offers itself, upon account of either of them.' For that reason he accused Hobbes, as we have seen, of being really a dogmatist in the guise of a sceptic. But Hobbes did take both scepticism and philosophy seriously, and there was a kind of courage in his doing so which far outweighed his famous personal timorousness.

So if we do not like Hobbes's conclusions, we must still ask ourselves how far we have faced the full implications of the beliefs which we may well share with Hobbes. It is common nowadays for people to say that moral relativism should lead to a kind of liberal pluralism: that (say) the waning of religious dogmatism paved the way for modern religious toleration. But Hobbes's work illustrates that there is no reason why this should be so. Moral relativism, thought through properly, might lead instead to the Leviathan; and the Leviathan, while it will destroy older intolerances, may replace them by newer ones. We might baulk at that prospect, but we cannot by an act of will reinstate ourselves into the condition of firm belief, though (as Job found) it may be the only thing which can counteract the Leviathan. The sceptics of antiquity lived under the rule of absolute emperors; those of the Renaissance under absolutist monarchs. The rigid and alienating state structures of the modern world may also be an appropriate landscape for sceptics, and it is Hobbes who shows us why.

Notes on sources

The editions of Hobbes's works cited in the text are as follows:

The Elements of Law, Natural and Politic, ed. Ferdinand Toennies, 2nd edn by M. M. Goldsmith (London, 1969).

De Cive. The Latin Version, ed. Howard Warrender (Oxford, 1983). In view of the fact that the seventeenth-century English translation published as *De Cive. The English Version* (Oxford, 1983), and also ed. Warrender, is neither by Hobbes nor particularly accurate, I have used my own translations of the Latin text.

Thomas White's De Mundo Examined, tr. H. W. Jones (Bradford, 1976). This is a translation of the Latin text contained in *Critique du De Mundo*, ed. Jean Jacquot and H. W. Jones (Paris, 1973).

Leviathan, ed. C. B. Macpherson (Harmondsworth, 1968).

Extended quotations in the text from other than these works are from the following sources.

p. 120 C. Cornelius Tacitus, *Opera quae exstant*, ed. Justus Lipsius (Antwerp, 1574), the dedicatory letter to the Emperor Maximilian (my translation).

p. 121 Justus Lipsius, *Six bookes of politickes or civil doctrine . . . done into English by William Iones* (London, 1594), p. 62.

p. 122 Justus Lipsius, *Epistolarum Selectarum III Centuriae* (Antwerp, 1601), p. 234 (my translation).

p. 122 Michel de Montaigne, *Essayes*, tr. John Florio (Modern Library, London, n.d., p. 524).

p. 123 Pierre Charron, *Of Wisdome* (London, n.d. (before 1612)), sig. a7v.

p. 124 Francis Bacon, *Essays* (Everyman's Library, London, 1906), p. 52.

p. 132 Hobbes to the Earl of Newcastle in Historical Manuscripts Commission, *13th Report II. Manuscripts of His Grace the Duke of Portland preserved at Welbeck Abbey* (1893), p. 130.

p. 150 Aubrey to Locke in *The Correspondence of John Locke*, vol. i, ed. E. S. De Beer (Oxford, 1976), p. 376.

p. 152 White Kennet, *A Sermon Preach'd at the Funeral of the Right Noble William Duke of Devonshire* (London, 1708), p. 107.

p. 155 Hobbes, *Critique du De Mundo*, ed. Jean Jacquot and H. W. Jones (J. Vrin, Paris, 1973), p. 449

p. 157 Descartes, *Philosophical Writings*, vol. ii, tr. John Cottingham, Robert Stoothoff, and Dugald Murdoch (Cambridge, 1984), pp. 122–3.

p. 161 'The Questions concerning Liberty, Necessity, and Chance' in Hobbes, *The English Works*, vol. v, ed. William Molesworth (London, 1841), p. 55.

p. 164 'Considerations upon the Reputation, Loyalty, Manners, and Religion of Thomas Hobbes', in Hobbes, *The English Works*, vol. iv, ed. William Molesworth (London, 1840), p. 437.

p. 176 Sir Robert Filmer, *Patriarcha and Other Political Works*, ed. Peter Laslett (Basil Blackwell, Oxford, 1949), p. 242.

p. 191 Descartes, *Philosophical Writings*, vol. ii, tr. John Cottingham, Robert Stoothoff, and Dugald Murdoch (Cambridge, 1984), p. 131.

p. 207 The description of Grotius is from Jean Barbeyrac's 'An Historical and Critical Account of the Science of Morality', annexed to his edition of Samuel Pufendorf's *The Law of Nature and Nations*, tr. Basil Kennet (London, 1749), p. 67. Pufendorf's remark about Aristotle is from his *Specimen controversiarum circa jus naturale ipsi nuper motarum* (Uppsala, 1678), p. 9 and his remark about Hobbes from ibid. p. 13 (my translations).

p. 207 Barbeyrac, 'An Historical and Critical Account,' pp. 67 and 68.

p. 209 Hume, *The History of England*, vol. vi (Liberty Classics, 1983), p. 153.

p. 220 J. W. N. Watkins, *Hobbes's System of Ideas* (2nd edn, Hutchinson & Co., London, 1973), p. 51.

p. 225 Hobbes, *Leviathan*, ed. by Michael Oakeshott (Basil Blackwell, Oxford, n.d.), p. lviii.

p. 226 Ibid. p. lix.

p. 226 Hume, *A Treatise of Human Nature*, ed. L. A. Selby-Bigge (2nd edn revised by P. H. Nidditch, Oxford, 1978), p. 273.

Further reading

Hobbes's own writings

Although Oxford University Press is now producing a modern edition of Hobbes's collected works, it is a long way from completion: only *De Cive* has so far appeared. The only collected editions are thus *The English Works of Thomas Hobbes*, ed. Sir William Molesworth (11 vols., London, 1839–45) and *Thomae Hobbes . . . opera philosophica quae Latina scripsit omnia*, also ed. Molesworth (5 vols., London, 1839–45). There are also a number of important editions of particular works; in addition to those mentioned in the note on p. 117 above, there are the *Tractatus Opticus*, ed. F. Alessio, in *Rivista critica di storia della filosofia* 18 (1963), pp. 147–288; *De Homine*, partially translated in *Man and Citizen*, ed. Bernard Gert (Humanities Press, 1972); *Physical Dialogue*, tr. Simon Schaffer in S. Shapin and S. Schaffer, *Leviathan and the Air-Pump* (Princeton, 1985), pp. 345–91; *Behemoth*, ed. Ferdinand Toennies, 2nd edn by M. M. Goldsmith (London, 1969); *A Dialogue between a Philosopher and a Student of the Common Laws of England*, ed. Joseph Cropsey (Chicago, 1971); Quentin Skinner, 'Hobbes on Sovereignty: an unknown discussion', *Political Studies* 13 (1965), pp. 213–18; and Samuel I. Mintz, 'Hobbes on the Law of Heresy: A New Manuscript', *Journal of the History of Ideas* 29 (1968), pp. 409–14.

His letters

Hobbes's letters, often a very revealing source, have not yet been collected, but some of the more important are to be found in the following places: Historical Manuscripts Commission, *13th Report II. Manuscripts of His Grace the Duke of Portland preserved at Welbeck Abbey* (1893), pp. 124–30; Ferdinand Toennies, 'Siebzehn Briefe des Thomas Hobbes an Samuel Sorbiere', *Archiv fur Geschicte der Philosophie* 3 (1889–90), pp. 58–71, 192–232, 'Hobbes-Analekten', *Archiv fur Geschicte der Philosophie* 17 (1903–4), pp. 291–317, 'Hobbes-Analekten II', *Archiv fur Geschicte der Philosophie* 19 (1905–6), pp. 153–75, and 'Contributions à l'Histoire de la Pensée de Hobbes', *Archives de philosophie* 12

(1936), pp. 73–98; G. R. De Beer, 'Some Letters of Thomas Hobbes', *Notes and Records of the Royal Society* 7 (1950), pp. 195–206; and Marin Mersenne, *Correspondance* Vol. X, ed. Cornelis de Waard (Paris, 1967), pp. 210–12, 420–33, 487–506, 568–77, 588–91. Important letters connected with Hobbes are to be found in 'Illustrations of the State of the Church During the Great Rebellion', *The Theologian and Ecclesiastic* 6 (1848), pp. 161–75 (these include Payne's letters, referred to in Part I above), and Vittorio Gabrieli, 'Bacone, le Riforma e Roma nella versione Hobbesiana d'un carteggio di Fulgenzio Micanzio', *English Miscellany* 8 (1957), pp. 195–250.

His life

The account of Hobbes's life and the chronology of his writings presented in Part I is based in part on my own research, some of which is reported in 'Hobbes and Descartes' in G. A. J. Rogers (ed.), *Hobbes's Fourth Centenary* (Oxford, 1988). The most entertaining life of Hobbes is John Aubrey's in *Brief Lives*, ed. Oliver Lawson Dick (Harmondsworth, 1962), but a fuller account is given by G. C. Robertson's *Hobbes* (London, 1886). A. Rogow, *Thomas Hobbes* (New York, 1986), is more up to date, but should be used with some caution. Useful material about particular episodes in Hobbes's life is to be found in J. Jacquot, 'Sir Charles Cavendish and his Learned Friends', *Annals of Science* 8 (1952); J. J. Hamilton, 'Hobbes's Study and the Hardwick Library', *Journal of the History of Philosophy* 16 (1978); N. Malcolm, 'Hobbes, Sandys and the Virginia Company', *Historical Journal* 24 (1981); Q. R. D. Skinner, 'Thomas Hobbes and his Disciples in France and England', *Comparative Studies in Society and History* 8 (1966), and 'Thomas Hobbes and the Nature of the Early Royal Society', *Historical Journal* 12 (1969). The interesting iconography of Hobbes's works is discussed in M. M. Goldsmith, 'Picturing Hobbes's Politics?', *Journal of the Warburg and Courtauld Institutes* 44 (1981) and Keith Brown, 'The Artist of the *Leviathan* Title-page', *British Library Journal* 4 (1978).

His intellectual context

The intellectual context in which I have located Hobbes is best studied through the writings of Descartes, *Philosophical Writings*,

Further reading

tr. John Cottingham, Robert Stoothoff, and Dugald Murdoch (Cambridge, 1984); Hugo Grotius, *De Iure Belli ac Pacis* tr. F. W. Kelsey (Oxford, 1925); and John Selden, *Table Talk*, ed. Frederick Pollock (London, 1927). I have discussed the context in my 'The "Modern" Theory of Natural Law' in *The Languages of Political Theory in Early-Modern Europe*, ed. Anthony Pagden, (Cambridge, 1987) and, in a somewhat different way, in my *Natural Rights Theories* (Cambridge, 1979).

His general philosophy

There are not many reliable accounts of Hobbes's general philosophy; the best are probably Richard Peters, *Hobbes* (Harmondsworth, 1956); Tom Sorell, *Hobbes* (London, 1986) and J. W. N. Watkins, *Hobbes's System of Ideas* (2nd edn, London, 1973). Two useful collections of essays on various aspects of Hobbes's thought are K. C. Brown (ed.), *Hobbes Studies* (Oxford, 1965); M. Cranston and R. Peters (eds.), *Hobbes and Rousseau: A Collection of Critical Essays* (New York, 1972).

Scientific ideas

On Hobbes's specifically scientific ideas, see above all F. Brandt, *Thomas Hobbes's Mechanical Conception of Nature* (Copenhagen, 1928) and A. Pacchi, *Convenzione e ipotesi nella formazione della filosofia naturale di Thomas Hobbes* (Florence, 1965). S. Shapin and S. Schaffer have discussed Hobbes's disputes with Boyle and Wallis in *Leviathan and the Air-Pump* (Princeton, 1985), and A. E. Shapiro has given a careful account of Hobbes's optics in 'Kinematic Optics: A Study of the Wave Theory of Light in the Seventeenth Century', *Archive for the History of the Exact Sciences* 11 (1973).

Ethics and politics

Modern writers on Hobbes's ethics and politics fall largely into the groups discussed in Part III above. Those who take Hobbes to be representative of modernity include C. B. Macpherson in his edition of *Leviathan*, his essay 'Hobbes's Bourgeois Man', repr. in Brown, *Hobbes Studies*, and his *The Political Theory of Possessive Individualism: Hobbes to Locke* (Oxford, 1962), and Leo Strauss: his chapter on Hobbes in *Natural Right and History* (Chicago,

1953) is also reprinted in *Hobbes Studies,* and he earlier devoted an entire book to Hobbes, *The Political Philosophy of Hobbes. Its Basis and Genesis* (Oxford, 1936).

Writers who look on Hobbes as a kind of social scientist include Peters, and Watkins; M. M. Goldsmith in his *Hobbes's Science of Politics* (New York, 1966); F. S. McNeilly in *The Anatomy of Leviathan* (London, 1968), and David Gauthier in *The Logic of Leviathan* (Oxford, 1969). An elegant recent work influenced by Gauthier is Jean Hampton, *Hobbes and the Social Contract Tradition* (Cambridge, 1986).

The principal writers who look on Hobbes as a moralist are A. E. Taylor, whose essay on Hobbes is reprinted in Brown's *Hobbes Studies;* F. C. Hood in *The Divine Politics of Thomas Hobbes* (Oxford, 1964); M. Oakeshott in *Hobbes on Civil Association* (Oxford, 1975), a collection of his earlier essays on Hobbes, including his famous introduction to *Leviathan;* and Howard Warrender in *The Political Philosophy of Hobbes. His Theory of Obligation* (Oxford, 1957). Warrender also published a useful summary of his views in Brown's *Hobbes Studies.* The controversy about Warrender is best studied in that collection, with the addition of Thomas Nagel, 'Hobbes's Concept of Obligation', *Philosophical Review* 68 (1959), and Q. R. D. Skinner, 'Hobbes's Leviathan', *Historical Journal* 7 (1964). A careful work on Hobbes's ethics which stands somewhat apart from these arguments is D. D. Raphael, *Hobbes. Morals and Politics* (London, 1977).

Useful studies of particular issues in Hobbes's political thought include R. Ashcraft, 'Hobbes's Natural Man', *Journal of Politics* 33 (1971); M. Missner, 'Skepticism and Hobbes's Political Philosophy', *Journal of the History of Ideas* 44 (1983); two related essays by Q. R. D. Skinner, 'The Ideological Context of Hobbes's Political Thought', *Historical Journal* 9 (1966), and 'Conquest and Consent: Thomas Hobbes and the Engagement Controversy' in *The Interregnum,* ed. G. E. Aylmer (London, 1972); and C. D. Tarlton, 'The Creation and Maintenance of Government: A Neglected Dimension of Hobbes's *Leviathan*', *Political Studies* 26 (1978). David Johnston has published an important study of Hobbes's attitude towards the political implications of rhetoric in *The Rhetoric of Leviathan. Thomas Hobbes and the Politics of Cultural Transformation* (Princeton, 1986).

Further reading

Religious ideas

So far, there is remarkably little of quality written on Hobbes's religious ideas. The four most useful essays are E. J. Eisenach, 'Hobbes on Church, State, and Religion', *History of Political Thought* 3 (1982); R. J. Haliday, T. Kenyon, and A. Reeve, 'Hobbes's Belief in God', *Political Studies* 31 (1983); J. G. A. Pocock, 'Time. History and Eschatology in the Thought of Thomas Hobbes' in *Politics, Language and Time* (London, 1972); and A. Ryan, 'Hobbes, Toleration, and the Inner Life' in *The Nature of Political Theory*, ed. D. Miller (Oxford, 1983).

His influence

Hobbes's influence on other writers, and his reputation among contemporaries, is traced by J. Bowles in *Hobbes and his Critics. A Study in Seventeenth-Century Constitutionalism* (London, 1951); F. M. Coleman, *Hobbes and America. Exploring the Constitutional Foundations* (Toronto, 1977); S. I. Mintz, *The Hunting of Leviathan. Seventeenth Century Reactions to the Materialism and Moral Philosophy of Hobbes* (Cambridge, 1962); and P. Russell, 'Hume's Treatise and Hobbes's *The Elements of Law*', *Journal of the History of Ideas* 46 (1985).

Mill

William Thomas

Preface

Mill's work is so widely read and has become the subject of such a vast literature that no book about him as short as this one can hope to be more than an interpretive essay. Most such books on Mill are by professional philosophers. This one is by a historian. I am of course heavily indebted to many recent critics, and cannot claim to have said anything on the following pages that has not been said by someone before me. My only claim to novelty is that I have taken seriously what Mill himself said about his education. When asked to give a short résumé of his life for a biographical dictionary he said he had been educated wholly by his father. If that is true (and it at least represents what he felt to be true at the close of his life) then a balanced assessment of Mill as a 'Past Master' must pay more attention to the formative influences on him than is usually paid. If this seems to diminish his originality in comparison with other thinkers, that may only be because other thinkers seldom state their debts so fully and so modestly. It certainly does not diminish his stature as a human being.

Many friends have helped me with this book. John Robson, Terence Ball, and Julia Annas read the manuscript and made many helpful suggestions. Alan Ryan's two books on Mill have been my constant aids, and he has cleared up a lot of my perplexities in discussion. I have learned a lot from colleagues who may not have realized what it was they were clarifying, especially Peter Pulzer, Colin Matthew, John Davis, Lucy Newlyn, and Ian Harris. Without the editorial labours of John Robson and his fellow editors in the *Collected Works*, no interpretation of Mill, least of all a historical one, can hope to avoid blunders, and those volumes have been really invaluable. I should like to thank my wife for compiling the index. Finally, I am most grateful to Keith Thomas for inviting me to contribute to the series and for being so patient with my delays.

Oxford   **WILLIAM THOMAS**
February 1985

Contents

Abbreviations

The following abbreviations are used in references to Mill's works:

E   J. S. Mill, *Three Essays: On Liberty, Representative Government, The Subjection of Women* (Oxford, 1912; reprinted as an Oxford University Press paperback 1978, with pagination unchanged)

W   J. M. Robson *et al.* (eds), *Collected Works of John Stuart Mill* (Toronto and London, 1963–   ). References are to volume and page. Where a number of references to the same volume appear close together in the text the reference is given in full only in the first instance; page numbers only are given thereafter.

1 Upbringing and education

John Stuart Mill was born in London in 1806. His father, James Mill, was a Scot of humble origin who, like many of his talented countrymen, had come south to earn his living as a writer. After trying journalism he decided to make a bid for fame and fortune by writing a *History of British India*. He hoped to finish it in three years, but it took eleven, and they were years of hardship, in which he had to provide for a wife and a growing family.

James Mill's work on India had a twofold significance for his son. It dominated his childhood, and it determined his career. In the Mill household everything revolved round the breadwinner and had to be subordinated to his requirements. John Mill took all his lessons from his father. He read the books his father was reading and shared the problems they raised. When he was eleven, he helped read the proofs of the *History of British India*. Soon after its publication in 1818, James Mill was appointed Assistant Examiner at the East India House, an appointment which was a tribute to his expert knowledge and a solution to his financial problems. He could now write on the philosophical and political problems which interested him. He could buy a house in the country. He could consider a liberal profession for his eldest son. For a time he thought of the law. But in 1823 there was a vacancy for another Assistant Examiner and James Mill obtained the post for his son. From then on until his retirement in 1858 John Mill served the British government of India. So while the dominant book of his boyhood was the history of the conquest of a supposedly backward people, his manhood's occupation was their administration. Between them they account for that preoccupation with backward and progressive social states which marks all his political writing and much of his thinking.

The most notable fact about John Mill's education was that

247

it was an isolating experience. This was due less to his father's poverty than his pride. James Mill had to be frugal, but he was never insolvent, and he had wealthy friends like the stock-broker economist David Ricardo and the philosopher Jeremy Bentham. John was born in the London suburbs of Pentonville, but James Mill's friendship with Bentham brought him into the centre of the city, and for a time they lived next to the old philosopher in Queen Square Place, Westminster. Between 1814 and 1819 Bentham chose to pass his summers at Ford Abbey in Somerset, and the Mills accompanied him. John Mill was later to feel grateful that he had experienced life in a medieval setting 'so unlike the mean and cramped externals of English middle class life' (W i 57).

The cramp he suffered was of a different sort. James Mill decided to teach his son himself, and he made few concessions to childish tastes. There were few children's books or toys, and no parlour games. Mrs Mill was an amiable but ineffectual woman who was quite unable to stand up to her husband's severity or make up for it in love and affection for her son. When he looked back on his boyhood many years afterwards, John could say nothing positive about her contribution and decided not to mention it at all. What he did recall was an unvarying regime of difficult books and daunting problems handed on to him by his father. He seems to have begun Greek at the age of three, Latin at eight. Before he was ten he had read through six of Plato's dialogues. He then began logic, in which his father had a special interest. There were breaks for lighter, but hardly for frivolous reading. John Mill read a great deal of history, he enjoyed *Robinson Crusoe*, and he was encouraged to read and even write poetry. But there was no unforced innocent saturation in imaginative literature for the sake of mere enjoyment; everything was subordinated to James Mill's didactic plan.

The manner of teaching was as demanding as the matter. Father and son worked at their respective tasks in the same room, and John was left to struggle with problems by himself, interrupting his father for help only when he dared. At the end of the day, they would take a walk, during which James Mill expected his son to give an account of what he had read and how much he had understood. Soon he had to put his knowledge to practical use. As his younger brothers and sisters grew up, John was required to supervise their lessons, and if they failed, to share their punishment. At a very early age he was being treated by his father as a sort of secretary. At thirteen he was introduced to political economy, with the *Principles* of David Ricardo. This James Mill expounded on walks, and John was expected to write up the discussion for his father's correction. The result was an introductory textbook, the *Elements of Political Economy*, published in 1820 . By his late teens, John was participating in all his father's literary work. By 1823, when he took the post at the India House, he must have seemed a mere replica of James Mill.

An education of this sort would hardly have been possible if John Mill had not been quite unusually gifted. Probably the boy's quickness and capacity for mastering tough problems by himself encouraged his father to load him with more. And for all its severity this method did bring real benefits. It wasted no time on trivia. At twenty, John Mill was a generation ahead of his contemporaries. He was not daunted by large and intractable subjects, but trusted his own capacity to worry out their meaning patiently and systematically. He early assumed that the best way to master a subject was to write his own 'treatise' on it. His logical training prevented him from becoming a pedant, a mere repository of recondite information. 'The first intellectual operation in which I arrived at any proficiency, was dissecting a bad argument, and finding in what part the fallacy lay ... an intellectual exercise in which I was most perseveringly drilled by my father' (W i 23). The daily *compte rendu* was a training in tenacity of memory and lucidity of exposition. He wrote clearer prose than his father from a very early age, and one of the most attractive things in his writings is the lucid presentation of difficult and abstract ideas. To the end of his life he wrote of the Socratic dialogue, not merely as a training in dialectical skill, but as the foundation of all scientific knowledge. His father's reliance on it, he insisted, had prevented his education from being one of mere 'cram'. His father had striven ' to make the understanding not only go along with every step of the teaching, but if possible, precede it' (W i 35). So John Mill's convictions were not mere dogmas, but carefully founded, defensible positions. He was, as one of his contemporaries noted, 'armed at all points'.

Of course this training brought its problems. Many people who met the younger Mill in his teens thought him a prig. Here was a boy who had no doubt that he was going to be a reformer of the world. Certain that he could expose the reasoning behind traditional beliefs and institutions he had gathered converts to his views, first through little discussion groups and societies, later in the wider forum of a debating society of young men of his own age. He was already, before the age of twenty, pouring out articles of considerable sophistication in newspapers and periodicals.

Some of his contemporaries called him 'a manufactured man'. He himself once made the moving admission: 'I never was a boy, never played at cricket: it is better to let nature have her own way.' Many of Mill's readers have wondered if Nature did not have her own way, since Mill experienced a reaction against this too intellectual regimen, which led him to revise his views. But Mill's mature judgement in the *Autobiography* was that his case showed that difficult subjects can be thoroughly taught at a time of life when most children are taught nothing at all. The implication of this is that what he was taught so early, he retained. We cannot decide how far Mill departed from his training until we have sketched at least its main elements. If this seems to take up too large a part of a short book, we have the support of Mill's own example. By far the largest part of the *Autobiography* deals with the influences upon him before he was twenty-four, nearly half of it with those he experienced before he was twenty.

Describing the creed which he and his friends adopted, John Mill was careful to say that it 'was not characterized by Benthamism in any sense which has relation to Bentham as a chief or guide, but rather by a combination of Bentham's point of view with that of modern political economy, and with the Hartleian metaphysics' (W i 107) . Let us consider these in turn, and examine the ethical and legal thought of Bentham, the political economy of Ricardo, and the psychological theory (then called metaphysics) and educational policy of his father James Mill.

Utilitarian ethics

John Mill first read Bentham in 1821, on his return from a year's stay in France. His father gave him the *Traité de Legislation*, the translation into French, by the Genevan Étienne Dumont, of Bentham's introductory view of a legal system. Reading this was a turning-point. 'I felt taken up to an eminence from which I could survey a vast mental domain, and see stretching out into the distance intellectual results beyond all computation' (W i 69). He learned for the first time of the 'principle of utility', which 'gave unity to my conceptions of things'.

The principle of utility (from which the popular name of the whole outlook rather confusingly derives) embraced both an ethical and a psychological theory. Bentham thought that the only things men desire for their own sakes are pleasure and the avoidance of pain. Men are egoists. The happiness they aim at *is* a preponderance of pleasure over pain. The same principle also provides them with a standard of conduct. An act is good if it produces or tends to produce more pleasure than pain. He who can calculate this most accurately is the most virtuous man: moral action is in fact the calculation, in units of pleasure and pain, of the consequences of an act. But of course men differ according to their circumstances in their conceptions of pleasure, and even the most far-seeing cannot predict all the consequences of a given act. What is needed, therefore, is a legislator who, taking self-interest as the universal motive, so orders men's relations in society that in benefiting himself each benefits the community of which he is a member. The legislator can assume that men in their private lives will regulate their conduct according to the principle of utility; his task is to extend this principle to society at large and show that it can produce 'the greatest happiness of the greatest number'. 'Private ethics', says Bentham, 'teaches how each man may dispose himself to pursue the course most conducive to his own happiness ... the art of legislation teaches how a multitude of men, composing a community, may be disposed to pursue that course which upon the whole is most conducive to the happiness of the whole community, by means of motives to be applied by the legislator.'

Bentham devoted his whole life to this 'art of legislation'. The enterprise began in a coolly scientific spirit, but gathered more fanciful elements as it went on. Originally he had hoped, like Hobbes before him, to show that individual self-interest was perfectly consistent with law and order, indeed their only safe foundation. His basic assumption was a simple empiricism: 'The only objects which have any real existence are those which are corporeal. 'To understand reality we had to reduce things to their smallest divisible components. Of course, for convenience, men grouped many things together under the same name, but these names were strictly speaking names for 'fictions'. There could be useful fictions, which conveniently described many things of the same sort, such as property, society, or nation. There were other misleading fictions which were not names for things but were commonly used as if they were. Such were duty, right, obligation, honour, community— dangerous words if used as if they stood for things with autonomous life. A community was nothing more than the sum of the individuals composing it. Individuals as a rule of their nature sought their own good, and so a community could have no interest at odds with the interests of its component members. Bentham thought that most social problems could be resolved, or at least a start made in their resolution, if such fictions could be shown for what they were. If by analysis general terms could be 'decomposed' into their elements, a rational vocabulary of political obligation could at last be devised, and a stable 'fabric of felicity' built upon it. Men had hitherto quarrelled over invulnerable nothings: teach them to give their attention to proven reality, and they could not fail to find a progressively larger measure of agreement.

At first this reductionism, this habit of decomposing things into their smallest elements, was directed at the fallacies, as

Bentham conceived them, of contemporary liberalism. It was absurd, Bentham thought, to suppose states originated in some contractual agreement: that idea only generated confusion. A state was only a convenient device, best defined as a number of persons in the habit of obeying a governor. Law was the will or command of this governor. Obedience was acting in pursuance of that will. Law created both duties and rights. A duty was an expectation of punishment for not doing something; rights were powers for enforcing duties. These definitions Bentham used against what he considered the most fruitful source of dangerous fictions, the theory of natural rights proclaimed by the American and French revolutionaries, which he called, in a famous phrase, 'nonsense on stilts'. A state founded on the principle of utility would not need such fictions, because in such a state there could be no conflict between a man's duties and his interests. All law was in one way or another an infringement of liberty, and the best way of preserving such liberty as was compatible with order was to define the law, analysing its elements and thereby delimiting its functions. 'We must first know what are the dictates of legislation', says Bentham, 'before we can know what are the dictates of private ethics.' Personal liberty would be that area of conduct which the laws could not reach. This reversed the procedure of the theorists of natural rights. The security of the subject was best obtained, not by vague declarations of natural rights but by an exact, scientific reduction of law to its essentials.

It was here that Bentham sought to apply his analytical method to the language of the law. To obtain a rational legal system, he thought, we must first describe its subject-matter as a science does, by accurate, simple, yet exhaustive classification. The constituent elements of a legal system were the physical acts of individuals. These could be sorted into classes of act, so that one law would apply to one class. Legal penalties would be determined according to a utilitarian calculus, of the pain caused by the act in question. They would be preventive, threatening just so much pain as would deter the would-be malefactor from committing a crime, not retributive, for revenge was pain that could not be rationally calculated. It was the inconsistency and capriciousness of English law which Bentham most disliked, and he thought its technicalities were only a screen for exploitation and chicane. By giving different names to essentially similar acts (murder and manslaughter, for example) it introduced a confusing subjectivity into the assessment of punishment. Bentham's plan sought to eliminate these abuses. Its classification would be as clear and objective as the classification of the elements in chemistry. Its penalties would follow the great rule of utility. The law might thus be condensed into a single book, of which a man might say, 'Within this cover is the sole basis of my rights, the sole standard of my duties. 'Armed with such an aid, the citizen would not need to buy a lawyer's specialist knowledge, for no knowledge would be needed that would not be available to all. Judges' discretion would be much reduced, and the common law, which Bentham regarded as a vast system of abuse, based on the fallacy that judges distilled a wisdom peculiar to themselves, would be replaced by a clear legal code.

That was the plan. Its application proved more difficult. Having thrust contemptuously aside the theorists of natural rights, Bentham failed to win over the lawyers with his scheme to recast the entire language of the law. The negative side of this, the purely destructive critique of current legal jargon, was very powerful. The positive side, the creation of a new and more accurate terminology, was largely a failure. Bentham had oddly anticipated this himself. 'Change the import of the old names', he had written, 'and you are in perpetual danger of being misunderstood: introduce an entire new set of names, and you are sure not to be understood at all.' This is what happened, especially with his later writings. There, one suspects, readers have usually made a straight utilitarian choice, and judged the pains of mastering the new terminology to be greater than the pains of abiding by the old. Nor was this just a matter of literary taste, though that had much to do with it. A more fundamental objection to the new names was that they did not correspond to new things. As a science discovers new phenomena, it must invent new names to describe them. But Bentham's terminology did not work like this; it invented the names first. For a professed empiricist, he had a surprising disdain for the actual practice of the law, and for the social system in which it operated. The multiple categories into which he divided his subject were his own invention; they followed from his basic utilitarian purpose, to show how a self-interested man would work in a legal system which took self-interest to be universal. The professed aim was the reform of the law, but no one could credit the conclusions who did not accept the assumptions. So the logical culmination of the system was the construction of an elaborate but wholly imaginary model of a state, the *Constitutional Code*.

The *Code* was never completed, and it was read, if at all, only by members of Bentham's immediate circle. He seems to have realized that his demands were too radical for his country-men, and as his plans ramified he developed his own forbidding jargon, quite as barbarous as the legal cant it was to replace, only less familiar. Originally meant as a more accurate and emotion-free terminology, its elaboration became a self-indul-gent game and private refuge. It made his later writings so impenetrable that he came to rely on 'translators' to present his ideas to the public. This was not wholly his fault. It took a series of disappointments (routine reverses to a politician, but crippling to a man of Bentham's sensibilities) to turn this reputedly tough-minded social reformer into a fantasizing recluse. At first he had seen himself as an inventor, every bit as practical as an Arkwright or a Watt. He had planned a utilitarian system in miniature, a reformatory prison called the Panopticon, in which the prisoners were housed in insulated cells each open to the scrutiny of the gaoler. In this way, the operation of self-interest combined inexorably with the princi-ple of publicity to reform the criminal, or at least convert him into a profit-making operative. Bentham had even dreamed of extending the principle and becoming the master of all the paupers and criminals in Britain, in a vast system of supervision and control. The Panopticon had been offered to the politicians, who toyed with it for a time and then turned it down. This was a turning-point for him. He concluded that society was so arranged that the men in power had no motive to recognize, much less pursue, the common good. The ruling groups—the aristocracy, the Church, and the lawyers—were leagued together in a common conspiracy against improvement, a network of 'sinister interests'. This explained why his arguments were ineffectual. He now took up the extreme radical programme of universal suffrage, annual parliaments and vote by ballot, and attacked the Church of England for its obscurantist attitudes. His friends feared, reasonably enough, that he would harm his reputation if he became associated with the radical movement at a time of popular violence.

They need not have worried. Bentham's later style was a form of censorship in itself. But in any case, he was never a simple radical republican. 'He merely passed', as the French historian Halévy pointed out, 'from a monarchic authoritarianism to a democratic authoritarianism, without pausing at the intermediary position, which is the position of Anglo-Saxon liberalism. 'He was always more fascinated by the machinery for controlling men than by the men themselves. For the prisoners in the Panopticon, and the paupers in the national scheme for poor-relief, he had planned a horrifying routine of unremitting supervision and direction. Accused of dehumanizing them and turning them into machines, he replied, 'Call them machines; so they were but happy ones, I should not care. 'Absorbed in the elaboration of machinery which would convert men's self-love into general benefit, he gave little attention to the psychological needs of the individual. The conversion to republicanism was not therefore as great a change as might be supposed. The same publicity which he had proposed for the reformation of his prisoners pervaded every area of the democratic state of his imagination. 'Official aptitude' (that is, the probity and efficiency of the rulers) depended on their responsibility to those they ruled. The operation of this principle could be made still more certain if every official was required to work in the perpetual glare of public attention. So officials became the new prisoners, the public itself was vested with the task of gaoler, and a complex web of bureaucratic rules replaced the cell walls to prevent

official collusion against the general good. It was the Panopti‑
con turned inside out.

It was just this faith in rational planning, which to us makes
Bentham the prophet of the modern bureaucratic state, which
made him seem to his radical contemporaries so irrelevant or
incomprehensible. Popular radicals misunderstood him, mod‑
erate reformers despaired of him, lawyers made fun of him. He
became an eccentric recluse. 'In my country, of course, less
said of me than in any other. 'The 'of course' has a hint of
complacency. Quite logically, he looked for the realization of
his plans to revolutionary regimes abroad. A virgin territory,
whose simple-minded inhabitants, without memories, would
submit to the new set of institutions imposed by a revolution‑
ary coup d'état, would be ideal. He considered Portugal, Spain,
Greece, the New World.

But while his ambitions to be the legislator of these new
republics brought him strange new followers and some public
ridicule, it was his earlier disciples who ensured his enduring
fame. Dumont's French versions probably gained Bentham a
wider readership abroad than he ever enjoyed in Britain. James
and John Mill applied his doctrines to the government of India,
and it was through the latter's sympathetic criticism that most
Victorians became acquainted with Bentham's ethical and legal
doctrines.

Ricardian economics

Utilitarianism claims to judge the morality of an action by its
consequences in pleasure and pain. But a knowledge of *all* the
consequences of an act is hardly possible for the agent to
achieve. However deliberately and scrupulously he commits an
action, he may still be totally unprepared for its major conse‑
quences, which may even be the reverse of what he intends.
We may be tolerably certain what effects an act will have in
our own circle of intimates; but outside that, in our wider
social relations and our behaviour as citizens, we need the help
of more technical knowledge. In other words, a consequential‑
ist theory of ethics like utilitarianism, if it is to be more than a
rough rule of thumb, needs to be supplemented by the findings

257

. In Mill's youth the social science which
／e attained the greatest prestige and scientific
.s economics—or political economy as it was then
d in the Mill circle, while Adam Smith was revered
.ounder of the science, Ricardo was thought to have
.ht it near perfection. In so far as John Mill's education
w.s directed at making him a reformer of society, it was
Ricardo's method that provided the model of social enquiry,
and Ricardo's *Principles* the foundation of his economic
theory.

It was a very different method from Bentham's. Ricardo was
a self-taught stockbroker, not much given to theorizing about
what he was doing, but James Mill, who did much to persuade
him to complete the *Principles*, and whose advice he took
about form and method, certainly had in mind Newtonian
mechanics. Ricardo sought to describe the economic system of
his day in a highly schematic and simplified form (what modern
economists would call a model) in which a few premisses were
assumed, and from these certain long-term trends projected. To
make the demonstration clearer, distracting details which
might qualify the original hypothesis, and any statistical confirmation of its predictions, were ruthlessly pared away. 'My
object', said Ricardo, 'was to elucidate principles, and to do this
I imagined strong cases that I might show the operation of
those principles. 'The language was plain and spare; there was
the greatest economy of illustration and example; the argument
was highly condensed. The *Principles* is a forbiddingly abstract
book. Its conclusions nevertheless served a clear political
purpose.

There are three classes in Ricardo's system: the labourers,
the landlords, and the capitalists, each with its characteristic
form of gain, wages for labour, rent for land, and profit for
capital advanced. Of the three, the labourers are in the least
favourable position. For they, as the most numerous class, are
most affected by the law, which Ricardo derived from the work
of Malthus, that population increases much faster than subsistence. They live on the edge of destitution, and as soon as they
experience an improvement in wages, they improvidently beget

more children and so are soon reduced to want again. These fluctuations in their condition lead Ricardo to the chilling observation that the natural price of their labour is that which will enable them 'to subsist, and to perpetuate their race, without either increase or diminution'. But the capitalist is not much more favourably placed. He has capital to start with, but as the value of a commodity is determined by the amount of labour which has gone into producing it, this capital is in a sense not his own. It represents the rewards of past labour, or 'hoarded labour' as James Mill was to call it, and it must be advanced to the labourer in the form of wages, tools, machinery and raw materials, the profit being what is left. This profit moreover is precarious, being threatened first by competition from other capitalists eager to imitate any example of success-ful investment, and next by the constant demands of the labourer for higher wages. These demands it is not in the power of the capitalist to limit or control. For they are determined by the price of food, or more precisely by the price of bread. The only gainer in all this is the landowner. For he draws his rent from his land, and while his land will vary in its fertility, the market price of the grain it yields will be determined by the cost of producing grain on the poorest soils in cultivation. Wages being the same on fertile or infertile soil, the greater profit will accrue to the owner of the fertile soil, because there the yield costs less labour to obtain. While therefore the pressure of population leads to the cultivation of poorer and poorer lands, it is the capitalist who has to pay higher wages and receive lower profits. The landowner merely enjoys higher and higher rents. He is the only gainer from a world moving rapidly to economic stagnation, as wages rise, costs increase, and the incentive to investment flags.

Set out in crude outline in this way, the political purpose of the system is clear. Its main thrust was directed at the Corn Laws, which by imposing duties on foreign corn, kept up the home price and made it worthwhile for farmers to grow wheat on inferior upland soils. This might suit the country's needs while the war lasted, but with the coming of peace it seemed merely a cynical way of keeping up the high price of food in the teeth of industrial depression and popular distress. Ricardo's argument blamed the landed interest (dominant in parliament, as the 1815 Corn Law showed) both for the high price of the poor man's food and for the industrialist's sagging profits. Repeal the Corn Laws, allow imports of cheap foreign corn, and the price of bread would fall and profits would recover. 'I contend for free trade in corn', Ricardo wrote, 'On the ground that while trade is free, and corn cheap, profits will not fall however great the accumulation of capital. If you confine yourself to the resources of your own soil, I say, rent will in time absorb the greatest part of that produce which remains after paying wages, and consequently profits will be low.' The landlords who received the rent, in other words, were inhibiting the investment of capital, and hastening the advent of the stationary state in which industry would stagnate. It was an argument both against the landed interest and the unreformed state of the parliamentary representation which gave landowners so much political power.

The mechanical rigidity of Ricardo's logic, and the political conclusion to which the argument pointed, seem all the more obvious to us now, because we know none of his predictions came about. The expansion of British industry was spectacular despite the Corn Laws. Population did not increase so fast that large numbers starved, even before the Laws were repealed. Living standards rose, and the birth-rate fell. But of course these developments lay in the future. To Ricardo's contemporaries what was convincing about his analysis was precisely its aloofness from politics. It seemed to penetrate the confusing welter of facts on the surface, to bypass the clamour of conflicting claims which various interested parties made from a partial appreciation of the facts, and to show, very clearly and objectively, the laws according to which the whole machine worked. Those laws had a political aspect, but that was not what made them authoritative so much as their simplicity, their logical consistency, and the indifference to party considerations of those who had found them out.

The political economists were hostile to state intervention. The economy should be allowed to work as its laws showed it would work best. Such political action as was needed should be limited to the removal of impediments to its working, not the creation of more. But that did not mean that the individual was to stand passively by and watch a process which might reduce him to destitution. When you know how a machine works, you can use it more effectively. If people could be shown the laws of political economy, they could learn how to use them to improve their lot. The laws were both explanations of complex phenomena and guides to action, principles as well as precepts. A good example is the 'principle of population', which Ricardo took from Malthus. Malthus claimed that while population increased in a geometrical ratio (1, 2, 4, 8, 16, 32 . . .), food did so only in an arithmetical one (1, 2, 3, 4, 5 . . .). There was no statistical evidence for this claim, which was in fact made before the first British population census. Though successive censuses provided the evidence of a spectacular rise in Britain's population, Malthus did not remove his chapter on the ratios from successive editions of his book. Not that Malthus thought that men were in the grip of a process over which they had no control. Rather he thought that if they knew about the principle they would see the point of controlling their appetites and having fewer children, or at least no more than they could support. This stress upon the individual's capacity to know the laws governing his own prosperity, pervades the whole Ricardian system. It is the core of what we call economic liberalism. The theory was at once individualistic, in leaving the individual master of his own destiny, and scientific, in claiming to find out by dispassionate, impartial enquiry, laws that lay in the nature of things.

In a famous passage, J. M. Keynes claimed that Ricardo's doctrine 'conquered England as completely as the Holy Inquisition conquered Spain'. He went on to describe the ingredients of this success.

That it reached conclusions quite different from what the ordinary uninstructed person would expect, added, I suppose, to its intellectual prestige. That its teaching translated into practice, was austere and often unpalatable, lent it

261

virtue. That it was adapted to carry a vast logical superstructure, gave it beauty. That it could explain much social injustice and cruelty as an inevitable incident in the scheme of progress, and the attempt to change such things as likely on the whole to do more harm than good, commended it to authority. That it afforded a measure of justification to the free activities of the individual capitalist, attracted to it the support of the dominant social force behind authority.

Historians of economic thought would now disagree with the last two sentences. Actually Ricardo's doctrines were being contested within a few years of his death. Even James Mill admitted that he and McCulloch were the only two men who could be truly called Ricardo's pupils, and later McCulloch came to differ sharply from his master. But the other ingredients Keynes noticed, the austerity, the unpalatable conclusions and the logical coherence of the system, certainly do explain its appeal to young men like John Mill.

Now this appeal had two most important consequences for utilitarianism; one political, the other theoretical. The political consequence was that for John Mill's generation, it neutralized the authoritarian element in Bentham's thinking. Utilitarianism is not necessarily a libertarian doctrine. If the goodness or badness of an action depends on its consequences, moral rectitude lies with the man who most accurately assesses those consequences. As governments are often better informed about the likely effects of certain activities, they must, at least in some areas, be better judges of what is right than the individual (who is usually misled by the will o' the wisp of conscience or the moral sense). Governments also have much more power than the individual to put their knowledge to effective use, so that even if they do not pursue the greatest happiness of the greatest number, they enlist the support of those who think they ought to.

Though Bentham paid lip service to the economic liberalism of Smith and Ricardo, his own economic writings show that he wanted the State to intervene in economic life in a manner contrary to their teaching. He wanted the Bank of England nationalized; he wanted governments to control education and research; he even wanted them to fix prices and guarantee a minimum wage, because 'insurance against scarcity cannot be left with safety to individual exertion'. The fact that these views remained unpublished and the divergence unnoticed has given a false impression of unanimity. Bentham's own fatuous remark that he was, through James Mill, the spiritual father of Ricardo, is typically misleading. In fact, he was at best a critical ally, and the main tendency of his thought lies in a different direction. His whole concern was with the mechanism of a legal and bureaucratic system which would so arrange its penalties or 'sanctions', that the individual would always be induced to pursue the public good. He would act in his own interest spontaneously within a limited sphere, under legal sanctions outside that. The political economists were not concerned with devising elaborate legal disciplines. They thought that the competing selfishness of individuals created its own discipline, in the operation of a free market, and that the study of this market revealed the prevalence of laws which worked, whether men knew it or not, for the ultimate benefit of society. Both agreed that governments could do little in the economic sphere. But for Bentham this was because they could do more in the spheres of law and order, education and administration, whereas economic activities could regulate themselves. For the economists the economic activities formed the centre of the picture and the institutions of government were secondary; not because the latter were not indispensable, but because their economic pretensions had usually been harmful and there was no point in rendering them more efficient. Bentham wanted to remodel government with exactly that aim of greater efficiency, and the existing political instruments were mere obstacles to his plans of reconstruction. So he supported radical democrats at home and revolutionary dictators abroad. The Mills reconciled the contradiction rather better, because it fitted their double roles as imperial administrators and radical publicists. In his writings on India James Mill was a utilitarian interventionist, loading Benthamic plans on to the baggage-train of military conquest; but in British politics he favoured individualism and the free play of market forces. He justified this with a theory of history, according to which societies were destined to pass through successive phases of development, the more advanced being justified in showing the less advanced what was good for them, if necessary by force. We shall see the same tension between interventionism and *laissez-faire* in John Mill's thought, though there the reconciliation is much more subtle.

The theoretical consequence of the prestige of Ricardian economics was that it encouraged a deductive a priori approach to social and political problems. In principle, at least, one would expect a utilitarian social science to be experimental and inductive. The utility of existing institutions would be measured according to the pain and pleasure they promote; a proposed change would be held to advance the greatest happiness of the greatest number because it would bring about what most people actually want. To a large extent Bentham's mechanical assumptions about human nature and his growing aversion to reality prevented him from founding such a science. But the prestige of Ricardianism inhibited it still more. It presented exactly what those who hankered after a Newtonian science of society thought they wanted most: a reduction of human activity to a bare, skeletal set of laws, deduced logically from certain supposedly dominant traits of human nature, and owing their persuasiveness to the theoretical coherence of the system rather than its capacity to accommodate the variety of social life. The search for such laws, which were to stand in the same relation to society and the task of the politician as the laws of mechanics stood to the materials and projects of the engineer, became a distinguishing feature of the utilitarian outlook.

A famous example of the application of the Ricardian method to a practical problem, that of parliamentary reform, is James Mill's *Essay on Government*. Mill's argument actually starts with a rejection of historical evidence. As history provides no certain principles in such an enquiry, he says, we must go deeper, and look at human nature. Here we find that man is everywhere self-seeking and rapacious. The point of government, indeed, is that it keeps this rapacity in check. As there is no limit to men's appetite for 'the objects of desire' all governments in which power is vested in one man or in a few, will tend to oppress their subjects. The only way to secure good government is to identify the rulers with the whole community. Modern States cannot assemble all their citizens like ancient Athens, but they have something more practicable in 'the grand discovery of modern times, the system of representation'. But will not representatives, once vested with power, abuse it and oppress the community they are supposed to represent? James Mill agrees that they will, unless they are made answerable to the community by the devices of a wide suffrage and regular elections. These conditions echo the radical demand for universal suffrage and shorter parliaments, and there has been much argument about how far Mill wanted the vote extended, whether he wanted universal suffrage or something more restricted. The important point however is that he did not feel obliged to spell out what precise measures he wanted, any more than Ricardo had done. He was enunciating the basic principles of good government, and leaving it to others to draw the correct conclusions. He thought he had set out his argument so clearly that no one could fail to draw from it conclusions favourable to reform. But to have given his proposals in the form of legislative measures would not only have put him in the awkward position of agreeing with this or that brand of radical politician, but would have derogated from the self-appointed role of the austere philosopher who despised 'practical politicians'.

Associationist psychology

Bentham's and Ricardo's works do not seem, to put it mildly, written to secure a wide popular appeal, however democratic they were in principle. Their views needed another ingredient before they could be made part of a popular movement for reform. This was the psychological theory of associationism, which derived from Locke and David Hartley, was broadened in the following century by Rousseau and narrowed by Helvetius, and which finds its most uncompromising expression in the work of James Mill. In his hands it had the look of a doctrine deliberately chosen to fill a political need. He had been an enthusiastic supporter of a whole series of schemes for popular education, from primary schools based on the monitorial system to the tract-distributing Society for the Diffusion of Useful Knowledge, and finally the new London University. In all these activities, Mill had felt the need for a philosophical argument which would discredit those who held that popular education involved propagating 'dangerous' ideas subversive of established institutions, and which would at the same time give encouragement to his fellow reformers. He found this in associationism. Originally intended by Locke to combat the theological dogma (by no means dead in the early nineteenth century) that our ideas of good and bad are implanted in our minds by the Creator, it could be used more generally to support the reformers' contention that the differences between men in society are due to environmental factors and not to innate abilities. Already in 1817 Mill had projected a book in which he would 'make the human mind as plain as the road from Charing Cross to St. Paul's'. In 1820 he sketched its outline in the *Essay on Education*, in which he called for further philosophical work, but declared provisionally: 'this much, at any rate, is ascertained, that all the difference which exists, or can be made to exist, between one *class* of men and another, is wholly owing to education'. In 1822 he began the book which was to become the *Analysis of the Phenomena of the Human Mind*, and he found the investigation surprisingly straightforward. His arguments were vetted by his son, 'whose mind however is perfectly ripe to judge of them; and to him the expositions appear easy of comprehension, and perfectly satisfactory'. The book was finally published in 1829 and was discussed at the morning seminars by John Mill and his friends.

The theory in James Mill's hands is a mixture of psychology and philosophy. That is, it purports to describe how the mind works, but also to show that only certain forms of mental activity constitute real knowledge. It claims to be experimental, but by this is meant merely that the enquirer describes what passes in his mind through introspection, not that he uses experimental methods to show the nature of mental processes such as learning, memorizing, and so on. The mind is conceived, as it was by Locke, as a dark room, the senses being the windows which alone provide its knowledge of the external world. All we know therefore is dependent on the experience of our senses. Our knowledge of composite objects or complex ideas is really the stored knowledge of particular examples grouped together by association. The laws of association tell us how this grouping takes place, by contiguity, succession, and so on. Our abstract-conceptions of good and bad, justice and injustice, are likewise resolvable into separate impressions, bound together by the experience of pleasure and pain. This is why moral convictions are susceptible to proof and disproof. The mind cannot resist the evidence of fact, any more than a mirror can resist reflecting an image of the object in front of it. A mere exposure to fact will precipitate a conviction. Moral convictions are more fallible, because the experience of pleasure and pain can be artificially associated with different objects. Put Oliver Twist among Fagin's pick-pockets, and he will come in time to approve of theft. But the educated mind has two functions. It can recover past impressions and it can analyse them. Analysis of the sequences or 'trains' of association by which the mind received a particular idea, can separate certain sensations from the pain or pleasure with which they had originally been fused. In this way a rational man dissolves his prejudices, by showing them to be nothing more than factitious associations of certain feelings with certain facts.

No theory could put more stress on the importance of the environment in mental development. But 'the doctrine of the formation of character by circumstances', as John Mill called it, cuts two ways. On the one hand it points to complete control of the learning environment for the most effective teaching. It implies that a child's perceptions are unselective, and that in the development of the intelligence the vital role is played by the teacher, in arranging the environment so as to make the 'right' associations in the pupil's mind. This is not flattering to the original intelligence. One of John Mill's most vivid memories was of being told by his father that he would find he was ahead of other boys in his reading and information, but that this was not something to be conceited about, as it was due 'to the very unusual advantage which had fallen to my lot, of having a father who was able to teach me, and willing to give the necessary trouble and time' (W i 37). He adds that this opinion was 'exactly the truth and common sense of the matter', as if in the learning process the mentor was all-important and the pupil a mere receptacle of impressions.

On the other hand, the environmentalist doctrine presents the political reformer with an almost insuperable obstacle in society at large. James Mill admitted that the earliest impressions were the deepest, and that this confirmed the common opinion about the special susceptibility of 'the tender mind'. But if that is so, then adult minds must be set in a pattern of prejudices which will be harder to change. If education includes, as James Mill said it did, 'every thing which operates from the first germ of existence to the final extinction of life', then it must be a progressively more futile enterprise.

James Mill would not accept this conclusion, because it led to the kind of conservatism which he disliked in Burke. Burke claimed that our moral values are set long before we learn to consider them critically. Men did not derive their moral ideas direct from their own experience, and it was dangerous and impious to claim that they did. Prejudices represented the accumulated moral wisdom of the race and their prevalence in society, far from being a thing to be deplored, was a source of stability: 'Prejudice makes a man's virtue his habit, and not a series of unconnected acts.' For James Mill virtue was precisely a series of unconnected acts. A utilitarian must judge the goodness of an act by its consequences: 'To act, without regard to consequences, is the property of an irrational nature. But to act without calculation is to act without regard to consequences.' He did not deny that men made use of general moral rules in the ordinary business of life. But he did deny that these rules should be allowed to become a sort of second nature and override the duty to calculate consequences. When faced by a conflict between a general rule and a course leading to the greatest happiness, one should follow the latter.

James Mill thought that the fundamental task of the teacher was to associate pleasure with the general good. But as his son noted, he had scarcely any belief in pleasure, and tended to identify it with what a man deliberately approves. He therefore gave Bentham's utilitarianism a very puritanical twist. Bentham wanted to harness men's egoism to drive an intricate political machine: James Mill wanted to eradicate egoism altogether, by a careful education, which was aimed to produce an alert, critical, and altruistic frame of mind. The principle of utility in his hands sheds it hedonistic elements and becomes almost an ascetic ideal. It 'marshals the duties in their proper order', Mill declares, 'and will not permit mankind to be deluded', as so long they have been, sottishly to prefer the lower to the higher good, and to hug the greater evil, from fear of the less'.

Was there not a rather undemocratic élitism lurking in this attitude of high-minded distaste for the 'sottish' preferences of the bulk of mankind? Certain passages in James Mill's works may suggest this. He was, for instance, a great admirer of Plato, and in the work just quoted he praises *The Republic* as a masterly development of his own principle, that the only security for good government is the identity of interest between rulers and ruled. It is clear that he admires the sort of education that Plato planned for his guardian class. But he goes on to say that the only reason Plato was forced to advocate a special status and a condition of propertyless celibacy for this class, was that he lived before the discovery of representative government. The implication of this seems to be that if Plato's guardians could become rulers in Mill's society, they would be good ones, but that a wide franchise would ensure their integrity quite as effectively as devices like celibacy or community of property. In other words, provided you have rulers accountable to the public, there is no need to fence their virtue with such artificial devices as Plato envisaged.

This faith in representation rested on the belief that all men were equally capable of receiving and understanding the truth.

What prevented them from acting on that understanding was the fact that men were grouped in classes or interests. The aristocracy, with its supports, the Church and the Law, represented the three great threats to enlightenment, being essentially accretions of what Bentham had called 'interest-begotten prejudice' which corrupted men's opinions. Their baneful influence was artificially prolonged by an unrepresentative political system. Their long sway accounted for the moral backwardness, the 'sottishness' of mankind.

James Mill sometimes wrote as if this system could only be overthrown by political means, but in general (and especially as he rose in official rank and acquired more knowledge of the world of politics) he trusted to the influence of education which, slowly but inexorably, would persuade the ruling classes that their own best interests lay in pursuing the general good. He always remained, in spite of his official duties, a teacher rather than a politician, keeping aloof from political agitations and preferring to give his energies to education and the Press. It was in fact his pedagogic attitude which made him so naïve in his political pronouncements. He had the teacher's characteristic failing of favouring those who agreed with him, and his didacticism biased his whole view of the political process. Those who agreed with him were the children of light. They had taken pains with their understandings; they did not live on the labour of others; they held the corrupting aristocracy at arm's length; and with their own hoarded labour (also called capital) they advanced good causes in such a way as to evoke the trust of their inferiors. They were the 'middle rank' who Mill thought formed the opinions of 'a large proportion of the whole body of the people'. James Mill would have denied that this middle rank was a class held together by an 'interest-begotten prejudice' of a new sort. Theirs was the legitimate influence of science and moral worth, and it could only grow with the growth of virtue; whereas the influence of the aristocracy was illegitimate, being based in the last resort on ignorance and deception, and would give way, as society improved 'under the guidance of educated intelligence' (W i 109).

James Mill used to be considered a mere popularizer of

Bentham's work, and John Mill's eventual divergence from the doctrines of his youth as essentially a disillusionment with 'Benthamism'. But this picture now needs revision. James Mill may not have been a very original thinker, but he was a great systematizer and teacher. His debt to Bentham was no greater than his debt to Ricardo or even Locke and Hartley. But the important thing was that he tried to weld these influences into a coherent social and political philosophy, which was made more formidable by his powerful didacticism. This philosophy, it is sometimes forgotten, loomed so large in John Mill's education that it left very little room for any other sorts of influence. There cannot be much doubt that his boyhood views were identical with his father's. What is less often admitted is that when he came to diverge from his father on particular issues, the ideal remained very similar. He may have developed a more indulgent view of the aristocracy and a more subtle one of the Church. He certainly came to question his father's faith in democracy. But on the central ideal, of a society ruled by its wisest and most virtuous members, father and son were at one.

2 Mental crisis and aftermath

At first, in the period of 'youthful propagandism' before he was twenty, John Mill was all confidence in the creed in which he had been brought up. He wrote and spoke with the dogmatism of a precocious adolescent, and he enjoyed the feeling of belonging to a movement with other young men who admired the work of Bentham and his father. They formed a little party of zealots, and Mill summarizes their views in his *Autobiography*. Their basic principles were a belief in representative government and freedom of discussion. They did not advocate a democratic system from a belief in natural rights, but because it seemed to them the only sure way to have good government. Their chief enemy was aristocracy, which they regarded as more formidable than monarchy, because it was more pervasive, and was abetted by the two great systems of corruption, the Established Church and the Law. Only if the general interest was mobilized against these two systems could they be destroyed, and the first step was to expose their pretensions by challenging them to open debate. The young utilitarians had no doubt that their own mentors gave them the advantage in argument. The two ancient universities, after all, where the aristocracy and clergy were mostly educated, taught archaic curricula full of exploded superstitions and narrow classical learning, and so could never present a serious intellectual opposition. Already Cambridge had produced notable converts to utilitarianism. The walls of the citadel had been breached. Once deprived of the support of the Church and the Law, the landed aristocracy would be easier to convert to the truth that their best hope of survival lay in the pursuit of the general good.

Mill and his friends were not democrats in feeling. They respected property as an institution, and none of them was poor. Some, like George Grote the banker, were very wealthy.

All were liberally educated and this, along with the recondite reading of the utilitarian canon, made it hard for them to reach down to the popular mind. They did not, like the Russian intelligentsia later in the century, sentimentalize the masses; their democratic faith consisted more of a dislike of aristocracy than a positive love of the common man. They hoped that the common man would be able at least to grasp the main conclusions of political economy and utilitarianism, and without presuming to interfere in the deliberations of his betters, be capable of distinguishing the honest from the dishonest among public men. They trusted in an enlarged electorate (covering at least the classes which could be reckoned to have the public good at heart) as a critical audience inducing probity in politicians, but hardly providing them itself. They wanted secret voting because that would at one stroke deprive 'the Few' of the means of intimidating 'the Many', and foster the independent judgement of the latter. Education for them did not mean only the spread of literacy, but also a heightening of political consciousness. Their empiricism led them to look on this as an irresistible process: as knowledge was diffused, people would become clearer about the choices before them, and the more these choices were made in the light of scientific fact, the more irreversible moral advance would be. They all agreed that this called for a programme of popularizing the new sciences of political economy, ethics, and jurisprudence. They were less good at putting this into effect. Their philosophic habit of mind, and their puritanical distaste for the more popular forms of literature (fiction was frivolous and poetry was misrepresentation) restricted their range as propagandists. They were strongest in abstract argument, and the journals in which they wrote were heavy going, dealing in matters which would nowadays be confined to academic periodicals. They saw themselves as playing a role like that of the Encyclopaedists in eighteenth-century France; but they had less variety and originality, and they came from a narrower stratum of society. Their fierce theoretical hatred of the aristocracy excluded them from the worlds of fashion and high politics, and seminars were no

273

substitute for salons. But what they lacked in literary finesse they made up in zeal.

No one threw himself into the common cause with more energy than John Mill. He was their most gifted theorist and their standard of utilitarian orthodoxy. Then, quite suddenly, he lost all zest for the fray. One day he asked himself if it would make him happy to see realized all the ideals he had been brought up to consider right, and was horrified to find that his answer was 'No'. This plunged him into the deepest depression, for it seemed to show that his education had failed. He tried various remedies in vain. His favourite reading had lost its savour. So had music: he was even distressed by the thought of 'the exhaustibility of musical combinations' (W i 149). He could confide in no one, least of all his father. Walks did no good. He managed to carry on with his duties and even with his writing, but felt no enthusiasm for either. What oppressed him continually was the thought that he had lost all capacity to feel, that an analytical education had worn away his emotions. Finally, reading a book of French memoirs, and coming upon a particularly moving passage, he shed tears. This was a great relief, because it showed him that his feelings were not quite dead, and from that moment the depression began to lift.

The description of this 'mental crisis' is the most striking passage in the *Autobiography*. It has more depth and immediacy than the later encomium of his wife, which even Mill's admirers find rather excessive. It also contrasts so sharply with the dry complacency of Mill's account of the other intellectual influences upon him that many readers have concluded that the episode, so pivotal in the book, must represent a decisive break in his life, involving a strong emotional and intellectual revulsion against his education and traceable in all his later work. It seems likely that the depression was caused by overwork. The overwork involved not only writing learned reviews, debating and campaigning for birth-control, but editing from manuscripts the monumental five volumes of Bentham's *Rationale of Judicial Evidence*, a task which took him a year. Those who have groped about in the crepuscular world of Bentham's later writings, and know the sensation they give of systematic estrangement from the world of ordinary discourse, can readily imagine the impact of this dreary chore upon a youth buoyed up with the wish to better his society. It cannot, surely, have increased his relish for reforming causes.

But treating the 1826 crisis as the start of a 'revolt' against Mill's inheritance has its difficulties. For one thing, very little evidence has survived to amplify the account in the *Autobiography*. For a long time after 1826 he wrote little, and when he resumed writing, about 1830, he was not free to say exactly what he thought. He remained very much under his father's tutelage, submitting some of his views to James Mill's censorship, and carefully keeping other work anonymous. This means that, though in the ten years between the mental crisis and his father's death in 1836, Mill wrote a good deal about the work and opinions of his various mentors, it is very hard to be sure whether his comments are to be read as expressions of open rejection, covert criticism, or merely the reaffirmation of one part of his heritage against another. This last possibility, which is also the most likely, is usually ignored by those who assume that the ideas in which he was educated formed a logically coherent system, altering one part of which implied overhauling the whole. Through all his changes of mind, Mill remained remarkably faithful to his father's ideals, and in fact came increasingly to identify himself with them as he grew older. His criticisms of his heritage were sharpest in the 1830s; thereafter he became more and more convinced that the ideals he had been taught had been, at least in essentials, right. It is this that makes the *Autobiography* unreliable as an account of his feelings during and after the crisis. For all the signs are that it was written to vindicate the view which Mill sets out in Chapter 2, book VI of the *System of Logic*, that though we are in general shaped by circumstances, yet we can, if we wish, alter those circumstances to make ourselves what we want to be. Mill admitted some faults in his upbringing, but on the whole he came to believe that he had been taught to think for himself, and that the crisis of 1826, which he had once thought an indictment of his training, had led in the end to its vindication.

It is true that John Mill made something of a public renuncia- tion of 'Benthamism'. He resigned from the Debating Society in 1829 after a bitter debate in which his beliefs were attacked, and after that he often denied that he was a Benthamite or Utilitarian. There may have been an element of real disillusion- ment here. It was undoubtedly a shock to discover that the doctrines he had thought self-evidently true and socially rege- nerative in fact aroused passionate opposition from young men like himself whom he respected and wanted to like; and he must often have wanted time for reflection and reconsideration of his heritage. In the same year, he had the extra shock of reading a powerful attack by Macaulay on his father's *Essay on Government*, an attack which seems all the more conclusive for the relative feebleness of the published replies. But what prompted his resignation was not a wish to capitulate to his critics. It was the feeling that debating did not advance the truth, but was only a rhetorical battle in which the contestants had to caricature each others' views. As utilitarian champion he was called on to defend positions he did not always hold, with weapons he no longer liked to use, and so to make enemies of people he wanted to convert. The best and most honest thing to do was to shed the sectarian label, try to draw attention to the real views behind it, and advance these views by temperate discussion among friends, away from the unreal combat of the Debating Society. He did not give up his beliefs, but in the cooler atmosphere of the morning seminars he laid them on the table for discussion.

His name for this new course was 'practical eclecticism'. Later, borrowing a word from Goethe, he called it 'manysided- ness'. Of course it involved making friends with men who, a few months before, he had considered opponents. Some of his fellow-utilitarians shook their heads and sniffed desertion, and outwardly at least they had a case. Mill became intimate with two notable disciples of Coleridge, John Sterling and F. D. Maurice, who were outspoken critics of associationism and utilitarian ethics. He became fascinated by Thomas Carlyle, whose writings made vehement fun of 'Benthamism', and who was mainly responsible for making the connection, which became a romantic cliche and has remained a socialist one, between the utilitarian outlook and the faith in machinery characteristic of the early factory system. He made friends with the young disciples of the French sociologist Saint-Simon, which was to lead to a long-lasting interest in the work of the most famous of the group, Auguste Comte. Finally, there was Harriet Taylor, the young married bluestocking with whom he fell in love and eventually married, to whom he attributed an influence over his opinions far exceeding that of all the others put together.

All these friendships may suggest Mill was straying from the straight and narrow path of utilitarianism. In fact, they show something rather more subtle. He had come to believe that one cannot be really confident of the truth of one's opinions unless one has given a fair hearing to those who hold the opposite. Neither Bentham in his insulated studies, nor James Mill in his confident dogmatism seems to have entertained such an idea. But John Mill was so impressed with it that he took it to mean that he must meet an opponent more than half-way. His correspondence with both Carlyle and Comte shows this. He is at first so openminded, so self-deprecating, and so anxious to please that he is mistaken for a disciple. Seeing that he is in a false position he issues a qualified warning, but so diffidently that it is brushed aside. Presuming he has a captive audience the new friend avows still less guarded views. Horrified, Mill is driven to a more candid statement of their differences. The result is a mutual cooling of enthusiasm, the start of secret recrimination, which ripens into open hostility. It is not that Mill abandons his own views, but that with his acute impressionableness and naïve appetite for controversy he plunges in, taking no account of the differences of personality and temperament which promise later divergence. His former friends and allies, not sharing his complex reasoning but judging by the company he keeps, conclude that he has deserted to the enemy.

But Mill was much too thoroughly versed in the doctrines he had been taught to throw them over; even had he wanted to, he had no other vocabulary in which to express himself. The most he sought to do was to make his inherited opinions seem less dogmatic. Eclecticism was a device to gain more converts. As Alan Ryan puts it, he wanted 'to expand, not to renounce his inheritance'. The picture we should have is not that of a young dogmatist being dislodged by powerful attacks from a rigidly held position. It is rather a case of his holding the same general ground, but realizing that some parts of it were vulnerable, and seeking to make the defences more flexible and stronger as occasion arose. By the end he had fashioned a deeper and more subtle version of the whole inheritance, and come to feel that, armed with it, he could meet at least those critics who acknowledged the same rules of controversy as he did. The overall purpose remained the same, to be a reformer of the world.

In what ways then did Mill 'expand his inheritance'? There were three main problems to confront. The first concerned the rival claims of intuitionism and associationism, and centred on the place of poetry in an education. The second followed from this, and involved a revision of utilitarian ethics. The third was concerned with the problem of authority in politics, why some men rule others, and how their rule can be reconciled with progress. This took longest of all, for the practical business of pressing for greater popular participation in politics was constantly hampered by the logically prior problem, whether politics could be made a science which the common people could understand.

Poetry and intuition

One of Mill's discoveries during the crisis of 1826 was that his analytical education had been very one-sided, developing the critical powers at the expense of the feelings (W i 141). The recovery of his capacity to feel which marked the ending of the crisis was a relief to him because it showed that analysis had not been totally destructive. Thereafter the problem was, how to keep faint feelings alive and even strengthen them. This was where Mill turned to poetry. He read Wordsworth for the first time in 1828 and thought that in this 'poet of unpoetic natures' he had found that 'culture of the feelings' he needed. This was in itself a departure from the critical attitude of the utilitarians towards poetry and poets. Bentham had said poetry was as good as 'pushpin'. James Mill in his *History* had tried to show that Hindu culture was backward and corrupt in spite of its beautiful Sanskrit poetry, by arguing that poetry was the characteristic expression of barbarous people who 'feel before they speculate', and which must necessarily give way to prose as scientific knowledge advances. He did not think that the imagination of the poet worked in any special way which distinguished it from that of the lawyer or the businessman. Imagination was any train of associations not set in motion by an external stimulus. Because poets habitually misread the evidence of the external world Bentham thought they made bad moral guides: 'Homer is the greatest of poets: where shall we place him among the moralists?' From their mentors the younger utilitarians drew that mixture of captious literalness and moral disapproval which marks the treatment of poets in the *Westminster Review*.

The followers of Coleridge however gave a much more important role to the poet than the utilitarians. In conscious revolt against the mechanistic philosophy which had 'untenanted creation of its God', they spoke of the poet as a moralist and seer, whose imagination gave men back their wonder and awe and appreciation of beauty, in spite of science. The poet perceived truths intuitively, and set them out in a form which all mankind could perceive directly and take to heart. A poetic fancy was one of the salient characteristics they approved of in their friends, a sign that a person could rise above the merely materialistic apprehension of life. For Maurice and Sterling poetry came to have more importance than theology. They found Mill amazingly prosaic, a 'manufactured man', and they looked hopefully for the growth of his imaginative powers.

Mill met the same outlook in Carlyle, who gave it strongly Germanic overtones and tremendous ironic force. Mill had been taught to believe that for an idea to be grasped it had only to be set out in clear, consecutive argument, and that analysis could dissolve all obscurities. Carlyle on the contrary believed,

279

and with some success practised, the doctrine that elaborate philosophizing generated confusion and cant, and that for an opinion to be worth attending to it must be set down in a vivid and graphic way to match the immediacy of the original perception. His work was in manner and intention the antithesis of Mill's, and was replete with forceful criticisms and sardonic mockery of the latter's opinions.

As long as he felt he lacked a faculty which others had, Mill was very vulnerable to this sort of criticism. But meeting Harriet Taylor must have made him aware that his emotions no longer needed watering with the thin nutrient of Wordsworth, and he was encouraged to state his position in relation to the new influences. He could not repudiate his debt to poetry; he did not want to undervalue the writings of Carlyle and others, which he continued to feel were more vivid and inspired than anything he could manage. But he did want to assure himself that poetry must tell truth of some sort, and have some usefulness to mankind. Even if the poet reached the truth by a quicker route than other men, those others must have some warrant that it was the truth, even if it took them longer to grasp it. So he decided that what the poet did was describe his own emotions in language calculated to arouse similar emotions in others. A poet was a person with 'a peculiar kind of nervous susceptibility' which made his impressions particularly 'vivid and distinct' (W i 413). But he needed an interpreter and for this role Mill proposed himself. He told Carlyle that he conceived his own task to be that making the truths perceived by the higher natures available to the lower—through the unlikely medium of logic. Later he seems to have changed his mind and decided that the really great poets must not only deal in mellifluous language apt to convey emotion, but also be deep thinkers. In a review of Tennyson he admonished the poet to read more philosophy if he wanted to improve his poetry. Mill was not primarily a literary critic, and he did not reprint all these essays. They are of interest mainly in showing the relatively slight effect his romantic and poetic phase had upon his thought. It amounts to the rather meagre admission that poetry as the 'culture of the feelings' ought to have a larger place in a philosophic education, not because it was a source of knowledge, but because it could offer a counterweight to the dissolving effect of analysis. Mill never explicitly admitted that poets were born rather than made, or had any intuitive grasp of truth. Even their peculiar temperament he explained in associationist terms. There was another, minor, effect of his interest in poetry. It explains his extraordinary reverence for Harriet's mind. If the poet was a person endowed with a peculiar kind of nervous sensibility, the converse was also true. Hence his conviction that she resembled Shelley, though he, 'so far as his powers were developed in his short life, was but a child compared with what she ultimately became' (W i 195). This was because, in her mastery of practical issues and her swift decisiveness in domestic matters, he discerned the qualities of a great statesman.

Utilitarian ethics

Another effect of the mental crisis was the realization that Bentham's egoistic psychology and the ethics drawn from it were quite inadequate. This may reflect a growing sense of the divergence between Bentham's views and James Mill's, and a perception that shedding Bentham's egoistic hedonism did less damage to the whole system of utilitarianism than any other concession. But it was upon that part of James Mill's work which is most Benthamic that the heaviest blow fell. In his attack on the *Essay on Government* Macaulay had pointed out that the claim that men were actuated by self-interest was an identical proposition: it merely amounted to saying that a man would rather do what he would rather do. Men had different conceptions of their interests, according to their different experiences and situations in life, so any attempt to take this as the foundation of a political science was building on sand. In his 'Remarks on Bentham's Philosophy', John Mill echoed Macaulay's criticism, but of course as a point against Bentham: 'There is nothing whatever which may not become an object of desire and dislike by association' (W x 13). By saying that all men were governed by their interests Bentham was only saying that 'all persons do what they feel themselves disposed to do'.

281

The effect of this use of the word 'interest' only encourages the 'vulgar usage' which equated it with 'selfishness and miserable selfseeking'. A crude conception of motive led to an equally crude conception of moral good. Bentham's indifference to the way we acquire our moral standards accounted for the fact that he had no place in his system for conscience or duty. He ignored the fact that one factor in the calculus of consequences of an action might be the effect on the character of the agent himself. This was not a serious defect in his legal philosophy; for law is more concerned to deter crime than analyse the character of the criminal. But such a theory failed altogether in questions of national policy, let alone the grand design of carrying a community towards perfection (W x 9, 12–16) Five years later Mill elaborated the charge that Bentham's ethics applied only to *la petite morale*, the merely business side of human life. His idea of the world was 'that of a collection of persons pursuing each his separate interest or pleasure, and the prevention of whom from jostling one another more than can be helped, must be attempted by hopes and fears derived from three sources—the law, religion and public opinion'. Self-education, the training of the individual's affections and will, was 'a blank in Bentham's system' (W x 97–9). In other words, Mill rejected the Benthamic conception of a rational society as one operating on the principle of enlightened self-interest.

It was easier to blame Bentham for a crude and easily travestied version of utilitarianism than to show that the creed was compatible with high moral ideas and humane culture. Mill's new friends derived these from religious belief, and they thought the utilitarian philosophy was hostile to altruism in private ethics as well as the ideal of public service in politics. You could not be a utilitarian and a high-minded gentleman. Mill, too, valued an altruistic and cultivated ruling class, though he derived the ideal from classical Greece rather than Christianity: he wanted to keep the culture and shed the religion. He had fitted poetry into his programme without any concessions to 'mysticism' or intuitionism. Now he wanted the ethical standards which he admired in Greek philosophy to be shown to be amenable to proof. Bentham's felicific calculus would not do. His father's *History of British India* used the principle of utility as the measure of the progress of different peoples from barbarism to civilization, but while that might justify their joint efforts at the India House on the behalf of the backward subcontinent, it would not explain why highly culti-vated young Englishmen like Sterling repudiated utility as a guide to action. What Mill sought was a version of utilitarian-ism which would combine ethical refinement and sophistica-tion with an objective test of the morality of an act.

He was to find it eventually in the doctrine (essentially an elaboration of his father's version) of higher and lower pleasures which he first set out in *Utilitarianism*. There he held that the idealist who sought the good of mankind was still after pleas-ure, but of a higher order, and that an educated man faced with a choice between a refined pleasure like poetry and a coarse one like beer-drinking would always prefer the former. So it was, in a famous phrase, 'better to be Socrates dissatisfied than a fool satisfied' (W x 212). But that —Mill's major divergence from Bentham's utilitarianism—was a later development (the phrase first occurs in a diary entry for 1854). In the 1830s he was more concerned with another aspect of the Master's cultural legacy. This concerned the relation of utilitarianism to political economy. In his anxiety to show that utilitarians were not just concerned with 'the merely business side of human life', Mill had to contend with those who said, in effect, that the faith he and his friends expressed in political economy proved that they were. Again, this put him in a dilemma. He wanted to affirm his new-found sense of the value of a wide culture, but he did not want to question the value of political economy as a science. He therefore made a distinction between science and art. Science studies what is. Art studies how things are done. 'The language of science is, This is, or, This is not; This does, or does not happen. The language of art is, Do this; Avoid that. Science takes cognizance of a phenomenon, and endeavours to discover its *law*; art proposes to itself an *end*, and looks out for *means* to effect it' (W iv 312). So political economy, as a science, merely *describes* a particular area of human life and the laws which might prevail in it: it *prescribes* nothing, though its data might be essential to the prescriptions of morality. Morality is not a science, but a branch, with prudence and aesthetics, of the Art of Life. In this, morality is concerned with imperatives, prudence with self-regarding precepts, and aesthetics with beauty or loveableness. Mill did not elaborate this classification. It functions in his work as a way of acknowledging areas of experience which utilitarians were usually accused of neglecting, while he gave his main efforts to those sciences on which the Art of Life depended. It also explains how in his final verdict on Bentham he was able to condemn him for shortcomings as a moralist yet praise him as the scientist who first classified the phenomena of the law, a sort of Linnaeus of the legal system.

Authority and progress

The new stress on self-culture also brought about a revision of Mill's attitude to traditional institutions. Instead of deducing from the 'known laws of human nature' the evils of aristocracy, Church, and Law, as he had done in his propagandist days, he developed a new feeling for society as a historic fabric, and he began to look more sympathetically at what he had once considered its 'interest-begotten prejudices'. Here the two great influences were the work of Coleridge and of Saint-Simon and his disciple Auguste Comte. One was romantic and conservative, the other was scientific and what would later be called positivist. Both helped Mill reformulate what he had first imbibed from Plato, a concern with fostering an élite leadership, not in the traditional shape of an aristocracy, but in the more modern one a trained and cultivated body of experts. The main question for Mill was how this body of experts could be both free to use their knowledge and responsible to the wider public whom they served.

The main idea Mill took from Coleridge was that of the 'clerisy'. In his tract *On the Constitution of Church and State* (1830) Coleridge set out his version of the doctrine of the three estates of the realm. The first consisted of the possessors of landed property and provided the element of law or 'permanence'. Merchants and manufacturers made up the second, and provided the element of 'progression'. The third was the clergy, who were the guardians of civilization, and made sure that there was something to preserve. For them was reserved what Coleridge called the 'Nationalty'—that portion of the national wealth not owned by the other two estates and explicitly reserved for the clergy by the nation, not to serve the narrow interests of the priesthood, or to ensure a doctrinal orthodoxy, but to cultivate and extend knowledge. Coleridge pointed out that in medieval Christendom the word clerk was used for all men of learning, and he argued that the modern Church would be more easily defended if it could recover something of its former comprehensiveness. Hence 'clerisy', a term which he hoped would convey the range of concern which 'clerk' or 'clergy' had lost.

What attracted Mill in this view of the English past was, first, that it gave a new and flatteringly large role to the thinker and man of letters. Once he had admitted that some people's opinions could count for more than others', Mill became alarmed at the danger of majority-rule. A majority might be that of the most ignorant mass, and this would be a threat to the ideal of self-cultivation and its political corollary, rule by the best-informed. Coleridge offered a way of counterbalancing the strength of the numerical majority. His three estates were more plausible historically than the utilitarian view of the constitution as an aristocratic fraud, and more in tune with Mill's new mood. Set out with great learning, and calculated to soothe the antagonism of commerce towards landed wealth, and of dissent towards the established Church, Coleridge's theory offered an ideal of social harmony without denying the need for reform. Society so balanced would still change, but the monitors of the change would be the clerisy.

The Coleridgeans were more interested in re-educating the possessing classes than in the superficial crash-programme which the 'useful knowledge' school urged to prepare the property-less for political responsibility. Such attempts to popularize science would, Coleridge said, only ensure its 'plebification'. More urgent was a dialogue *within* the clerisy. In his new mood Mill welcomed this as a bridge between his own views and those of Sterling and Maurice, and a more congenial task than the 'diffusion of superficial knowledge' which was the educational element in the radical programme. That, he now said, so far from being the march of intellect, was 'rather a march toward doing without intellect, and supplying our deficiency of giants by the united efforts of a constantly increasing multitude of dwarfs' (W i 330). Mill now sounded a note of distaste for popularization which contrasts sharply with his father's view that the reformer's prime duty was to popularize what was known. 'When almost every person who can spell, can and will write, what is to be done?' (W xxi 53). The real purpose of education was to make people think for themselves, not to indulge them with bald summaries and crude slogans; fostering genius for future discovery was more important than spreading what was known (W i 337–8).

Some of the Saint-Simonians affected the costume and ritual of a religious cult, but this was primarily as a means of harnessing a popular following. The core of their doctrine was scientific, and it was aimed, even more than Bentham's, at the reorganization of society on the principles of physical science. Saint-Simon's ideal society is the utopia of the frustrated inventor. He thought that as scientists, engineers, industrialists, and the various craftsmen whom they directed, created society's wealth and ensured its progress, they should govern it, and they would do the job better than the kings, aristocrats, and higher clergy, who had traditionally wielded power. For the only true knowledge was scientific; and the only real advances in men's understanding of their situation (as against the fitful intuitions and lucky guesswork of moralists and preachers) had been achieved by the physical sciences. So the only authority which had a right to command men's allegiance was that of the man of science. All other claims were archaic, the relics of previous ages' attempts to identify authority with knowledge, which had succeeded only in vesting it in various personifications of superstition. One could indeed, by marking off the successive stages by which mankind had emerged from superstition, demonstrate the underlying historical law. There were, said Comte, three stages through which all societies were bound to pass: the theological in which men attribute changes in the world around them to the actions of their gods; the metaphysical, when they explain them by reference to abstract forces; and the positive, when they come to understand them according to the laws of cause and effect—that is, by science. This was the scheme of development which Comte was to elaborate in the next fifteen years, and it seems to have made relatively little impact on Mill in the period immediately following the crisis of 1826. What made more impact on him was the Saint-Simonian division of history into organic and critical periods. Organic periods were those in which a particular creed dominated men's minds, and the authority of its teachers was generally accepted. Critical periods were those ages of transition when a creed was being outgrown, and men, no longer able to believe the old doctrines, cast about to find new ones. The Saint-Simonians said that the present age was a critical one, and they were confident that the organic age to follow would be one in which their own doctrines would hold sway.

Mill was wary of the Saint-Simonians' claims to form a new priesthood He was not going to be identified with another 'sect'. But he liked the distinction between critical and organic periods, because, by identifying the present age as one of transition, it seemed to justify his interest in other creeds than his own, and fitted in with his preference for discussing principles rather than programmes. Some writers have seen this as a conversion to reactionary and conservative views, but it amounts to little more than a historical explanation of his current disillusionment with radical polemic. He still believed that his own views, suitably qualified but in essentials unchanged, would prevail; but he wanted to be open-minded rather than polemical about them, and he thought of the social changes he wanted as coming about, not by direct political action, but as a result of a long period of discussion. 'In the present age of transition', he told Sterling, 'everything must be subordinate to *freedom of enquiry*: if your opinions, or mine, are right, they will in time be unanimously adopted by the instructed classes, and *then* it will be time to found the national creed upon the assumption of their truth' (W xii 77). On his side Mill undertook to re-educate his fellow utilitarians, especially to a true appreciation of what was right in the creed of their opponents. The most enduring of his writings reflecting this desire are the essays on *Bentham* and *Coleridge*, written in 1838 and 1840. In each Mill tries to put the opposite view as clearly as his own. Bentham is severely criticized, often from a point of view congenial to the romantic critics of the Coleridgean persuasion, for his want of imagination and so on. Coleridge is highly praised as an equally profound thinker on the other side, and the sort of Tory whom Liberals need to know better if they are to attain a proper appreciation of their own shortcomings. These two essays are the supreme expression of Mill's ideal of many-sidedness, his practical application of what would be one of the main arguments of *On Liberty*, that 'he who knows only his own side of the case, knows little of that' (E 46).

From both Coleridge and the Saint-Simonians Mill acquired the habit of looking at past institutions and opinions in their historical context. A society's morality and its institutions formed a coherent whole, appropriate to the stage in human progress it had reached. It was facile and unhistorical to condemn a whole society for behaviour or opinions which, taken out of context, might seem barbarous or archaic. An organization now in the way of progress might once have represented the most advanced element in society. A doctrine now exploded might originally have been a great improvement on its first rivals. This view explains some of Mill's remarks which might otherwise seem odd in a sceptic and an anti-clerical, as when, reviewing some volumes of Michelet's *History of France*, he said of the Middle Ages that his own views were 'strongly Guelphic ... almost always with the popes against the Kings' (W xiii 505).

He did not adopt a complete historical relativism, nor the conservative attitude to current political changes that normally goes with it. The recurrent pessimism in his writings which is often taken for conservatism is rather the logical consequence of his utilitarian vision. He had been taught to believe that societies improve and progress as the individuals who compose them learn to sacrifice their immediate to their long-term interests. As their outlook expands, as it were, from the immediate gratifications of the moment, to take in the larger destinies of the human race, the old intellectual and institutional obstacles to progress are simply superseded by arrangements based on the permanent interests of mankind as revealed by science. But the corollary of this highly intellectual conception of social change is that the failure of reform, the successful resistance of entrenched interests and traditional institutions, are really symptoms of men's moral and intellectual failure, occasions for lamentation and reproach at the backwardness of contemporary society. So Mill's alternations of optimism and pessimism are quite consistent with his utilitarian beliefs.

Of course his reappraisal of his heritage baffled his friends. Mill himself added to the confusion by writing in different moods. When the cause of reform was going well, as in the years 1830–2, he yielded to the euphoria around him and wrote polemically as the theorist of a party. When it was going badly he turned back to the theory, and as he had an acuter sense than anyone else on his side of its doctrinal shortcomings, and little relish for the mere party battle, what he wrote to clarify the radical philosophy often seemed to be more critical of his friends than his opponents. When he edited the *London and Westminster Review* in the 1830s he sought to make it the organ of the party he himself called the Philosophic Radicals; but it is in this journal that we find him giving vent to some of the most serious reservations about his heritage, notably the essays on Bentham and Coleridge. The policy was too subtle for his friends, and when the dispersal of the Philosophic Radicals gave him the excuse to give up the uncongenial role of party journalist, Mill was clearly relieved that he could at last concentrate on what he was best at doing—the elucidation of a coherent philosophy of politics. This was the purpose of the *System of Logic*.

3 Science and social science

The *System of Logic* was begun in the late 1820s, in Mill's period of 'practical eclecticism', and it was completed as he grew more confident that he could reformulate the empiricism in which he had been brought up, so as to meet the objections of the intuitionists on the one hand and of Comte and the positivists on the other. At first he hoped it would be a reconciling book. As men's disagreements were in the last resort differences of method, he thought a book on the method of science would help on the 'alliance among the most advanced intellects and characters of the age' (W xii 78–9). This hope survives in the book's Introduction where we read that 'Logic is common ground on which the partisans of Hartley and of Reid, of Locke and of Kant, may meet and join hands' (W vii 14). But as the book progressed Mill met critics of his philosophical heritage whose attacks made him range himself more and more on the side of Hartley and Locke and, of course, of his father. The first was Macaulay, whose criticism of the *Essay on Government* made mockery both of scholastic logic and of James Mill's conception of a science of government. The final stimulus to completion was the work of William Whewell, who provided much of the first-hand-descriptions of the physical sciences and their method which Mill most needed, but whom he came to see as the chief pillar of the opposite philosophy of intuitionism and the embodiment of Anglican dominance of the ancient universities (W xiii 530). From its publication in 1843 the *System of Logic* drew criticism, and in successive editions Mill replied to his critics. The book therefore became more committed and less conciliatory in the course of his lifetime. By the 1850s when he wrote his *Autobiography* he held that it had all along been meant to combat intuitionism, 'the great intellectual support of false doctrines and bad institutions' (W i 233). This view is even more forcibly expressed in the writings of his last years. In 1865 he wrote the polemical *Examination of Sir William Hamilton's Philosophy* in which he attacked the heresy still more vigorously, and he altered the text of the last three editions of the *Logic* to make it more consistent with the case against Hamilton.

The *Logic* is radical and empiricist. Mill did not use the word 'empiricism' as we do: in his vocabulary it means observations not guided by scientific principles. But the word derives from the Greek word for experience, and as Mill thought that all our knowledge is derived from experience, he is rightly placed in the empiricist tradition of British philosophy which runs from Locke and Hume to Russell and A. J. Ayer. What is peculiar to Mill's contribution to this tradition is that he tries to combine the radical empiricism of associationist psychology with a conception of social science based on the paradigm of Newtonian physics. In one direction he had to maintain that all we know is from the evidence of the senses. In the other he sought to show that all the sciences were progressing towards the abstract and deductive character of classical physics.

The first part of this programme takes up the first two books of the *Logic*. From the start we are conscious of Mill's reliance on the psychology of his father's *Analysis* with its wholly philosophical account of how the mind works. Sensations are the raw material of our knowledge: 'All we can know of Matter is the sensations which it gives us, and the order of occurrence of those sensations' (W vii 76). This is the doctrine philosophers call phenomenalism. Mill's classic statement of it is in the *Examination of Hamilton* (Chapters 10 and 11), where he gives the famous definition of external objects as 'permanent possibilities of sensation'. But the *Logic* has the same doctrine (W vii 58).

It is an important part of the empiricist programme to deny that we can learn anything from propositions themselves, independently of the things they describe. A preliminary move is to subject 'class' names to a reductionist analysis in Bentham's manner. When we call an object by the name of a class, such as a chair, we are not describing anything essential to chairs, for it is the general name that makes them a class (W vii 175). Mill then proceeds to deal with the syllogism, denying that it is 'a means of coming to a knowledge of what we did not know before'. The stock form of the syllogism 'All men are mortal: Socrates is a man: therefore Socrates is mortal' proves nothing in itself. All the information we want (in this case about the mortality of men) lies in the major premiss. We do not, in such a case, really infer the mortality of Socrates from the major and minor premisses; our inferring ends with the major. We observe from numerous individual instances that men die, and infer men's mortality from these. So 'all inference is from particulars to particulars' (W vii 193). Mill claims that this is borne out by the fact that simple people can attain great skill in complex operations without any knowledge of syllogistic reasoning. A savage who throws his weapon unerringly to bring down his game owes his skill 'to a long series of previous experiments, the results of which he certainly never framed into any verbal theorems or rules' (W vii 189). His skill is built up by inference from particulars; and many people attain great manual dexterity without acquiring the habit of expressing what they do in general propositions. The major premiss of a syllogism is such a general proposition, a register of inferences already made, by which we reduce our experiences to a ready shorthand. What then is the syllogism for, if it tells us nothing new? Mill insists that it has a function, that of a collateral security for the correctness of the general proposition. The syllogism is a way of storing our experiences 'in a commodious and immediately available shape' (W vii 199).

It is worth noting that Mill is too radical to allow this argument to become a prop to blind convention. The bad thing about 'general language' he says, is that inferences made on insufficient evidence become 'hardened into general maxims; and the mind cleaves to them from habit, after it has outgrown any liability to be misled by similar fallacious appearances if they were for the first time presented; but having forgotten the particulars, it does not think of revising its own former decision' (W vii 199). He was to extend this point into a general attack upon conventional moral language in *On Liberty*. In the *Logic* he merely uses it to explain how we attain certainty in science. In complicated chains of reasoning, he allows, we do seem to proceed syllogistically. Suppose we say, for instance, that no government which earnestly seeks the good of its subjects is overthrown, and so the Prussian government will remain stable. Here, says Mill, what appears to be a series of syllogisms is really a series of inductions reduced, for brevity, to 'marks'. These marks are simply summaries to aid memory. If our memories were capacious enough to order a mass of detail we could reason without general propositions, but as they are not, we use 'marks of marks'. These enable us to build, as it were, upon previous inductions, and to turn sciences originally inductive and experimental into sciences of pure reasoning. Deduction is not a mode of reasoning opposed to induction, but the culmination of it.

> The opposition is not between the terms Deductive and Inductive, but between Deductive and Experimental. A science is experimental, in proportion as every new case, which presents any peculiar features, stands in need of a new set of observations and experiments—a fresh induction. It is deductive, in proportion as it can draw conclusions, respecting cases of a new kind, by processes which bring those cases under old inductions; by ascertaining that cases which cannot be observed to have the requisite marks, have, however, marks of those marks. (W vii 219)

The sciences which remained experimental were those, like chemistry, which had not discovered 'marks of marks'. Newton's explanation of planetary motion, on the other hand, was 'the greatest example which has yet occurred of the transformation, at one stroke, of a science which was still to a great degree merely experimental, into a deductive science' (W vii 220).

In what sense, then, are the wholly deductive sciences, like mathematics, considered to be true? Are they not really systems of necessary truth which owe nothing to experience or experiment? Mill saw quite clearly that to admit that they were was to concede the intuitionist case at its strongest point, and so he attacked this argument head-on. He began with geometry. Whewell and the intuitionists claimed that the axioms of geometry were true because we could not conceive of their falsity. Mill retorted that they were generalizations from our experience, and that our inability to conceive of their falsity was merely due to the strength of associative habit. Propositions like 'A circle has all its radii equal' or 'Two straight lines cannot enclose a space' were inductions from the evidence of our senses. The intuitionists said that axioms in geometry were not just true in this or that instance; they were true universally and necessarily. Mill's answer was that his opponents were mistaking an acquired capacity for an intuitive perception: the laws of association showed how men came to assume that certain truths were necessary. In mathematics too the existence of necessary truths was an illusion. 'All numbers must be numbers of something: there are no such things as numbers in the abstract. Ten must mean ten bodies or ten sounds, or ten beatings of the pulse' (W vii 254). Mill concludes that the superior accuracy of these so-called 'exact sciences' derives, not from their exactly describing real objects (for there is no such thing in nature as a straight line, and numbers are not real entities) but from their providing exact inferences—a point which will recur later when we look at Mill's conception of political economy.

Mill's account of geometry and mathematics is generally regarded as the weakest part of the *Logic*. It was Mill's own godson, Bertrand Russell, who recalled that even as a boy he could not see how $2 + 2 = 4$ was a generalization from experience, nor understand how a fresh instance of it could possibly strengthen one's belief that it was true. Subsequent developments in logic and mathematics have ensured that Mill's mistakes are now scarcely discussed. Even the layman is made uneasy by the way Mill buttresses weak arguments with the archaic assumptions of associationist psychology. But these assumptions are no less prevalent in the third book of the *Logic*, in which Mill deals with induction, and this is a section of the *Logic* which receives much more respect, perhaps because his arguments have a closer family resemblance to those of modern empiricists.

Mill defines induction as 'the operation of discovering and proving general propositions' (W vii 284) and he seeks to explain this operation in phenomenalist terms, that is, by describing the causal relations implicit in general propositions not as forces in nature but as statements of expectation. We all observe regularities in nature, and when we have seen the same thing occur a few times we expect it to recur. This Mill calls 'the observation of nature, by uncultivated intellects' (W vii 312). Such intellects will mistake a small number of coincidences for a law, which will lead them to believe that, for instance, comets cause calamities. How do we distinguish between casual uniformities and true laws? Simply by experience, which tells us some uniformities are more to be relied on than others. Experience refined by art enables the cultivated to see the need to distinguish between coincidences and true laws of nature. But what are laws of nature? Mill says that they are the strongest inductions, on which the weaker ones depend. We discover causes by induction. What we call 'cause' indeed is no more than the invariable antecedent, and what we call 'effect' is no more than the invariable consequent. The task of science is to move from weak inductions, which merely recognize regularities in nature, to stronger ones which record unvarying laws. So Mill rephrases the question to read: 'What are the fewest and simplest assumptions, which being granted, the whole existing order of nature would result?' (W vii 317).

Mill's phenomenalist analysis is directed against the idea of occult agencies in nature, of effects conceived as being part of the properties of objects, as when we say thoughtlessly that coal makes or produces a hotter fire than wood. The capacity given to objects of being the causes of other effects, says Mill, 'is not a real thing existing in the objects; it is but a name for our own conviction that they will act in a particular manner when certain new circumstances arise' (W vii 337). The difficulty about this paraphrase is that it makes the attribution of cause too compendious. Mill is clearly anxious to show that our understanding of the world around us need not be a difficult or recondite matter, which perhaps accounts for his mixing examples from social life and the natural world as if to convey

295

that the ways we understand each do not differ in kind. But in both social and physical science we need to distinguish, in the welter of antecedent conditions of an event, between those which were essential and those which were incidental in its production. In fact, we need to know what were the *necessary* and what the *sufficient* conditions of an event. Mill's idea of cause is stretched to cover all antecedent conditions, and it comes to look too cumbersome for explanations of human affairs, and too loose and general for explanations of physical events.

When we say that a man died because he ate a particular dish, Mill insists that we are speaking incorrectly, by designating one cause as the precipitant one; whereas we should give *all* the antecedents, including the facts of his constitution, his state of health, perhaps even of the weather. For our analysis of cause to be correct, our enumeration of the antecedents must be complete; and though in everyday explanations we do often single out a particular factor as the efficient cause, this is an illusion. It is like saying that the decision of an assembly was *caused* by the chairman's casting vote. Nobody could seriously claim that this was really the cause of the assembly's decision: it was merely the last condition which preceded the decision. What we call the cause of an event, Mill argues, is actually more complex; it is 'the sum total of the conditions, positive and negative, taken together; the whole of the contingencies of every description, which being realized, the consequent invariably follows' (W vii 332).

But as far as human behaviour goes, does not our habit of isolating one factor as more important than another mean rather more than Mill allows? In his example, the chairman's casting vote is not the sole cause of the assembly's decision, but it is undeniably more crucial in producing it than any previous vote on either side. What makes us more interested in it than the others is that it carries a heavier load of responsibility. We might think the chairman more responsible *by definition* than any other member, so that his abstention from voting was a graver abdication of responsibility than any of theirs, if only because it must have come after previous votes had clarified the issues. A full explanation of the assembly's decision, in other words, would have to discriminate between them: it could never be the same as a complete enumeration of causes. Mill's doctrine that we have no other notion of cause than that of antecedents and consequents is implausible, because it seems to have no room for human motive, and seems to minimize individual will.

Mill was aware of the strength of the intuitionists' case for the will, which he sets out very fairly. They claimed that our knowledge of our own wills was independent of experience, and so constituted knowledge a priori. On the contrary, says Mill, will is simply a physical cause like any other.

> Our will causes our bodily actions in the same sense, and in no other, in which cold causes ice, or a spark causes an explosion of gunpowder. The volition, a state of our mind, is the antecedent; the motion of our limbs in conformity to the volition, is the consequent. This sequence I conceive to be not a subject of direct consciousness . . . (W vii 355)

Mill's main target here is what he calls the 'original fetishism', by which primitive people extend the notion of agency to the non-sentient objects around them, a tendency which gives way as our knowledge of phenomena extends, and we realize that our own bodily and mental structures do not offer exceptions to the laws around us. As a caution against superstition this is very laudable, but Mill is so determined to prove the intuitionist wrong, that he deprives himself of any alternative account of individual identity. An individual for him is nothing more than the sum of the psychological events which compose a particular mind; he has no other way of describing a person than as a locus of sensations. What gives anyone the right to suppose he has experiences, thought, and expectations peculiar to himself, Mill cannot explain. He was in his later work to develop an acute, even frantic, sense of the threats which social developments posed to the individual, but his own associationist heritage tended to the belief that the environment was everything and the individual nothing.

If Mill's account of causation in human affairs seems unduly

297

ungenerous to the individual will, when he looks at natural processes he seems equally hampered by his psychological assumptions. He sees that to explain the causes of phenomena something stronger is needed than invariable sequence. Night invariably follows day, but that does not make day the cause of night. So he tries to offer a definition of cause which will go beyond invariable sequence yet stop short of occult agency. He sees that in any explanation of a physical event, we need to know which were the decisive and which the incidental factors. In his own example of the man who dies from food-poisoning, we want to know which food killed him rather more urgently than what was his general state of health. If we know it was a poisonous mushroom, we can help prevent similar deaths, but if we are supposed to enumerate all the factors contributing to that one death, we shall get nowhere. We need a distinction between necessary and sufficient causes; but, for reasons we shall come to, Mill disliked the word necessary, which he insisted only meant 'unconditionalness'. So he finally defined cause as 'the antecedent, or the concurrence of antecedents, on which [a phenomenon] is invariably and *unconditionally* consequent' (W vii 340).

On the whole Mill's critics have held that he equated cause with sufficient conditions, and that this is plausible when applied to the sort of explanations we make in everyday life when our own observation is all we have to go on but is too imprecise for natural science, where a more rigorous elimination and selection of the antecedents is supposed to lay bare the causal mechanisms behind phenomena. It is not merely that Mill seems to be asking us to translate the language of cause and effect into the more artificial language of sensations, but also that, as he himself admits, 'mere constancy of succession' does not seem 'a sufficiently stringent bond of union for so peculiar a relation as that of cause and effect' (W viii 837). It seems easier to conceive of 'forces in nature' than 'contingent future facts'.

Mill thought that by providing a careful tabulation of methods of induction he could fix the difference between truly scientific laws and merely empirical ones. He gives the four methods in Chapter 8 of Book III. They are the Method of Agreement, the Method of Difference, the Method of Residues and the Method of Concomitant Variations. The first two in combination are sometimes taken to make a fifth. There is no need here for an elaborate analysis of these. They amount to rules for the elimination of extraneous factors in a situation so as to assign causes, and we do actually use them in everyday life. When I want to find out why all but one of my roses are flourishing, I use the Method of Agreement; when I want to find out why my car won't start, the Method of Difference, and so on. But are these the methods actually used by the physical scientist to discover causal laws?

Mill's opponent Whewell said they were not, and modern discussion has tended to uphold him. Mill's view of the mind as an essentially passive receptacle of sensations implies that our knowledge of nature's laws is built up 'by successive steps of generalization from experience'. The emphasis is on the facts encountering the mind rather than the mind engaging with the facts. Regularities in nature suggest themselves. Whewell however held that we had to start with a theory first, for without it we could not see that they were regularities. We probed nature with a series of questions each embodying a hypothesis. There was 'a mask of theory over the whole face of nature'. To Mill this was too haphazard. He called a hypothesis 'a mere supposition', and said of Whewell's method that it recognized 'absolutely no mode of induction except that of trying hypothesis after hypothesis until one is found which fits the phenomena' (W vii 490, 503)

The modern case against Mill' s type of inductivism has been mainly associated with Karl Popper, but it goes back to Hume. Hume had pointed out that, however many times we observe that A is followed by B, we have no logical warrant to suppose B will *always* follow A. That we expect it to is a fact of our psychological make-up, not a matter of logical entailment. Popper has added a further claim. Many recurrent instances of a phenomenon are not enough to verify a general statement, but one contrary instance is enough to falsify it. Any number of instances of white swans cannot prove the truth of the statement 'All swans are white', but one black swan is enough to disprove it. So there is an asymmetry between verification and falsification, and as scientific proof cannot rest on the former, it must rest on the latter. Empirical evidence cannot verify a theory (though it may strengthen a conjecture or hypothesis); it can only falsify it. It follows that induction cannot build up a body of certain, empirically verified knowledge, and that the business of forming hypotheses is a central task of the scientific observer, and not, as Mill supposed, a mere form of guesswork. In short, Whewell was on the right lines. Scientific advance is concerned with intuition and imagination, and the war Mill envisaged between them and empiricism rests on a false antithesis.

Mill's view of the physical sciences was clouded by his commitment to associationist psychology and the extreme empiricism which it entailed. When he considered the science of society he had to reconcile this empiricism with a wholly deductive approach. Utilitarianism claimed to deduce its con-clusions from the facts of human nature, but it was a human nature conceived as it were in a historical void, as a residuum of qualities independent of space and time. How could a science of society be deduced from data no one had proved?

Mill first met this problem in Macaulay's attack upon his father's *Essay on Government*. James Mill assumed a few principles of human nature, and deduced a whole science from them, passing over as ambiguous and unreliable the lessons to be derived from actual historical examples. The result, Macau-lay said, was 'an elaborate treatise on Government, from which, but for two or three passing allusions, it would not appear that the author was aware that any governments actually existed among men'. The older Mill's method was a regression to the syllogistic logic of the Middle Ages, which had long since been discredited in the learned world by the experimental method advocated by Bacon. To found a true science of politics on experimental principles, on the method of induction, we must, Macaulay insisted, proceed 'by generalizing with judgment and diffidence,—by perpetually bringing the theory which we have constructed to the test of new facts,—by correcting, or rather altogether abandoning it, according as those new facts prove it to be partially or fundamentally unsound'.

This advice is impeccably empiricist and Mill might have been expected to agree with it. But he rejected it. In the *Autobiography* he is severe on Macaulay's idea of a social science. 'I saw ... that he stood up for the empirical mode of treating political phenomena, against the philosophical [that is, scientific]; that even in physical science, his notion of philosophizing might have recognized Kepler, but would have excluded Newton and Laplace' (W i 165). This comment is of course a résumé of the argument in the *Logic*, that sciences begin as experimental and advance to becoming systems of pure deductive reasoning. In Book III there is a clear rebuke to Macaulay for invoking the authority of Bacon (W vii 482). Macaulay's point, however, was not about how the sciences had evolved, but about whether the first principles of a science of politics were or were not derived from experience. How did James Mill arrive at the principles of human nature from which his science was deduced? Obviously by experience. But was that experience of human nature in politics or out of it?

> If it includes experience of the manner in which men act when intrusted with the powers of government, then those principles of human nature from which the science of government is to be deduced, can only be known after going through that inductive process by which we propose to arrive at the science of government.

In that case the study of politics would have to come before principles of human nature, and the latter would depend on the former. But John Mill was determined not to admit the case for empiricism even in an infant science of politics. The reason was that he could not afford to allow that Macaulay was right, without seriously damaging political economy; and he defended political economy not because it was a mature science (utilitarians liked to flaunt the fact that it was very new) but because it was abstract and deductive in its reasoning, like Newtonian physics.

This becomes clear from his first formal defence of his

father's a priori method—an essay, written in 1831 but not published till late 1836, 'On the Definition of Political Economy'. Mill's strategy is to shift the defence of the method from a science of politics, where it was weak, to political economy, from which we saw it had originally been borrowed, and for which a Whig like Macaulay might have more respect. The whole drift of this essay (which anticipates the *Logic*'s last book) is to deny the worth of empiricism in the moral or, as we would say, the social sciences.

Mill begins with the distinction already touched on, between science and art. ' Science is a collection of *truths*; art a body of rules, or directions for conduct' (W iv 312). So Adam Smith's definition of political economy as the science by which a nation is made rich, is actually a confusion of art and science. The strictly scientific part consists of 'the laws which regulate the production, distribution and consumption of wealth' (313). The art of becoming rich stands to these laws as the art of gunnery stands to the science of ballistics. To mark the boundary between the science of political economy and those sciences like botany, physiology, and metallurgy which are related to it, Mill draws another distinction, between physical and moral science. The former concerns the laws of matter; the latter those of mind. Few physical sciences depend on the moral sciences, but all the moral ones presuppose the physical. In the production of corn, for instance, there are many laws of matter (regulating the germination of seed, the climate, and so on) and one law of mind, 'that man desires to possess subsistence, and consequently wills the necessary means of procuring it' (317). Political economy differs from the physical sciences in involving laws of the human mind. So Mill completes his definition of it as 'the science which treats of the production and distribution of wealth, so far as they depend upon the laws of human nature' (318). He is careful to separate it from ethics, which is an art, not a science (319–20). It is also distinct from the laws relating to man as a social being, which are the province of ' social economy, speculative politics, or the natural history of society'. Political economy deals with man 'solely as a being who desires to possess wealth'. Not that the political economist thinks men really are merely acquisitive beings, but simply 'because this is the mode in which science must necessarily proceed' (322). Its method must be a priori: 'It reasons, and ... must necessarily reason, from assumptions, not from facts. It is built upon hypotheses, strictly analogous to those which, under the name of definitions, are the foundation of the other abstract sciences' (325–6). In the moral sciences, unlike the physical, there is no room for laboratory experiment. You cannot for instance experiment to decide whether or not a policy of agricultural protection makes a nation prosperous. So political economy is a deductive science, its scientific character lying in the accuracy of its deductions from the abstraction of economic man. Mill does have a role for empirical verification or confirmation a posteriori, but it is not large, because economic laws are not strictly predictive and therefore are not strictly verifiable. When we meet 'a discrepancy between our anticipations and the actual fact' (Mill does not say 'between our predictions and the actual event') it is because economic laws are subject to 'disturbing causes' which operate 'like friction in mechanics' (330, 332). For this reason we can only talk of tendencies: economic prediction is not a matter of saying what *will* occur, but rather of describing 'a power acting with a certain intensity in that direction' (337). But because the disturbing causes are so complex, there can be no sure way of verifying the laws.

The admission that political economy dealt only with a limited area of human activity made the elaboration of a general science of society all the more urgent, if the universality of scientific method was to be upheld. It was the promise of such a general science of society which drew Mill to Comte, whose enterprise he once called 'very nearly the grandest work of the age'. Yet his reception of Comte's philosophy only throws into relief his greater debt to Ricardo and his father. Even the political disagreement which led Mill eventually to declare that Comte aspired to 'a despotism of society over the individual, surpassing anything contemplated in the political ideal of the most rigid disciplinarian among the ancient philosophers' (E 19–20) had its roots deep in Mill's youth. No one as familiar as Mill was with Bentham's fantasies of central control could have contemplated Comte's system with complete surprise.

It is sometimes said that Mill adopted Comte's 'law of three stages', according to which societies go through three successive states, each with its specific mental attitude and the institutions appropriate to it. Mill did adopt this classification; but it was after all only a neater and more comprehensive solution to a problem which he had first met in his father's *History of British India*, and continued to confront in his work at the India House. Any utilitarian approach to human morality is vulnerable to the objection that different societies have different conceptions of what constitutes good or bad conduct. The Hindus thought it right to burn widows on the funeral pyres of their husbands. The British thought the custom barbarous and tried to stamp it out. James Mill's solution to this diversity of moral values was to say that, if you set societies on a scale of progress, it became clear that the measure of their advance was the degree to which they made utility the standard of conduct. It was his solemn application of this crude yardstick to Indian culture which makes his *History* a classic in the history of philistinism. He was unable to see, or at least to admit, that there could be different levels of achievement *within* a given society. Degrading religious superstition might coexist with art, sculpture, and building of great merit; great intellectual feats might be compatible with technological backwardness. James Mill used a two-edged argument to prove all Hindu achievements were on the same low level. If their morals were low, he said it was proof of their barbarism; but if their poetry and literature were remarkable, he said these attainments were not essential to civilization. The method did imply some account of how the different attainments which make up civilization evolve, but it was crude and incomplete. Comte's classification was more sophisticated, and explained within a historical framework how mathematics, astronomy, physics, chemistry, and biology had in turn become positive sciences, as they became more complex and more concrete.

Most concrete of all, and the culmination of the process, was sociology, the science of man in society.

Obviously Comte's work helped Mill bring together his reflections on the nature of scientific proof with his wider quest for a scientific foundation for politics. But Comte thought his system could lead to a reordering of society straight away, without too much regard for dissenting opinions. Mill thought of sociology as a larger, more general science, embracing more specific sciences like political economy and jurisprudence; and whereas Comte assumed his positive polity rendered these sciences obsolete, Mill insisted that they provided the methodological discipline without which the larger science of society could never be more than vague speculation. Beneath this difference of expectations there were more fundamental differences of principle.

They disagreed about the role of the individual in the new science. Comte thought that a positive social science would improve on its 'metaphysical' forebears in studying the actions of men from the outside, as one might a species of animals. 'Il ne faut pas expliquer l'humanité par l'homme, mais au contraire l'homme par l'humanité.' Comte omitted psychology altogether from his scheme of sciences, and dismissed political economy as metaphysical, the characteristic expression of lawyers and literary men who would be useless in any positive reordering of society. Mill however had always insisted on starting with the individual and the laws of his being. In his first brush with the positivist faith in the 1820s he had asked of the Saint-Simonians' conception of the *pouvoir spirituel* whether it meant anything other than 'the insensible influence of mind over mind' (W xii 41). In the *Logic* he elaborated this. 'The laws of the phenomena of society are, and can be, nothing but the laws of the actions and passions of human beings united in the social state' (W viii 879).

Mill and Comte also differed on the nature of the laws which governed the individual. Comte thought that the laws of mind would be found through anatomy and physiology, and he was particularly struck by the theories of the German phrenologist Franz Joseph Gall (1758–1828). Mill was suspicious of phrenol-

ogy with its deterministic implications, and in any case the
science of mind as he conceived it was 'more advanced than
the portion of physiology which corresponds to it' (W viii 851).
Least of all could he swallow Comte's claim that as women
had smaller brains than men, they were naturally inferior, or
his conclusion that society under the positivist dispensation
would forbid divorce. Of course in theory associationism
should have been as deterministic as classical physics. Sensations were to Mill's science of mind what atoms were in
physics; association playing the role in mental phenomena
which attraction plays in physical. Any human science really
modelled on the physical sciences must elucidate rigorous,
predictive laws, from which no individual could claim exemp-
tion. Mill certainly saw the point of Comte's claim that, as
there was no such thing as the freedom to disagree with the
laws of astronomy, so it would be absurd to allow dissent from
the laws of a positive science of society once they were
established. But he had strong personal reasons for rejecting
this argument.

During the crisis of 1826 he had been oppressed by the
deterministic implications of associationism, by the thought
that he might be 'the helpless slave of antecedent circumstances' (W i 175). On his recovery he needed to believe that
one may use a knowledge of the laws of association to alter
one's own character. In the last book of the *Logic* he asks
whether the actions of human beings are 'subject to invariable
laws'. (It is interesting that he puts the argument for necessity,
or, as we would say, determinism, into the mouth of a follower
of Robert Owen. In fact it was an argument advanced by James
Mill.) He first defines 'necessity' as the doctrine 'that, given
the motives which are present to an individual's mind, and
given likewise the character and disposition of the individual,
the manner in which he will act might be unerringly inferred'
(W viii 837). If we knew all the circumstances, we could foretell
a man's conduct as surely as we can predict any physical event.
Put thus, says Mill, the doctrine is unobjectionable, for we do
not in fact resent it when people we know well predict our
behaviour: we should conclude they thought poorly of us if

they could not do so. But many people, he admits, mean more by 'necessity' than this. They confuse it with fatalism. Instead of taking cause to mean 'invariable, certain, and unconditional sequence', they think it means 'some peculiar tie, or mysterious constraint'. They believe 'not only that what is about to happen, will be the infallible result of the causes which produce it . . . but moreover that there is no use in struggling against it; that it will happen however we may strive to prevent it' (840). This is clearly the view which had distressed him in 1826. His mature refutation of it is that, though our actions are indeed formed by circumstances, we can nevertheless alter the circumstances.

> We cannot, indeed, directly will to be different from what we are. But neither did those who are supposed to have formed our characters, directly will that we should be what we are. Their will had no direct power except over their own actions. They made us what they did make us, by willing, not the end, but the requisite means; and we, when our habits are not too inveterate, can, by similarly willing the requisite means, make ourselves different. If they could place us under the influence of certain circumstances, we, in like manner, can place ourselves under the influence of other circumstances. We are exactly as capable of making our own character, *if we will*, as others are of making it for us (840).

The language strongly suggests a sort of usurpation of his father's role. He adds, still more autobiographically, that the very fact of regretting the influences which have formed our characters belies the doctrine of fatalism, because 'A person who does not wish to alter his character, cannot be the person who is supposed to feel discouraged or paralysed by thinking himself unable to do it.' Moral freedom is the wish to alter our characters, and as virtuous action is action by conscious choice, this confirms the old adage that only the virtuous man is free.

If then we can alter our environment as we wish, what need have we of social science? That should tell us how society is developing and why; but if we have power to interfere with the process, it can never be an accurate or precisely predictive science. Mill's answer is to sketch a new science, which he calls 'Ethology', which would propound the laws of the formation of character, and would serve as a bridge between psychology and sociology.

> If . . . we employ the name Psychology for the science of the elementary laws of mind, Ethology will serve for the ulterior science which determines the kind of character produced in conformity to those general laws, by any set of circumstances, physical or moral. According to this definition, Ethology is the science which corresponds to the art of education; in the widest sense of the term, including the formulation of national or collective character as well as individual (869).

He calls it 'the Exact Science of Human Nature', but he does not say its laws will make possible reliable predictions, only that they will 'affirm tendencies'. Like political economy, its method is 'altogether deductive' (870). Of course its laws would not attain the predictive accuracy of astronomy 'for thousands of years to come', but that delay would be due not to the complexity of the laws but to the complexity of the data to which they are applied. In any case, 'an amount of knowledge quite insufficient for prediction, may be most valuable for guidance' (878).

Was this a *rapprochement* with Macaulay? If it was, Mill would not admit it. He calls Macaulay's conception of a science of politics a misunderstanding of 'the Chemical Method', a vulgar Baconianism typical of 'practitioners in politics, who rather employ the commonplaces of philosophy to justify their practice, than seek to guide their practice by philosophic principles' (887). His father's method he calls 'the Geometrical or Abstract Method', and he is very anxious to be kind about it. Though the 'interest philosophy of the Bentham school' erred in having too narrow a conception of human motive, this was at least an error 'peculiar to thinking and studious minds'. But he adds that these minds made the mistake of presenting 'as the scientific treatment of a great philosophical question what should have passed for the mere polemics of the day' (892–3). In other words, the *Essay in Government* was only a political pamphlet.

But having thrown out the evidence of history as Macaulay invoked it, Mill readmits it in the form of Comte's 'inverse deductive method'. He has all along insisted that a social science, whether political economy, or ethology, or sociology, must derive its laws from the laws of mind, that its accuracy must lie in the correctness of its deductions, and that the difficulty of prediction in such human sciences lies not in the complexity of the laws themselves but in the computation of their effects. It is hard enough to calculate the effects of two or three converging laws in physics; it is almost impossibly difficult to do so in sociology. The actions of individuals being governed by psychological and ethological laws (Mill is assuming the new science will provide them) we can know the social effects they *tend* to produce. The complex part is compounding the effects of many tendencies and coexisting causes, and this will be beyond human capacity. But, says Mill, there is hope. We can use the method of Verification to check the result. This inverts the usual inductive process as he has described it.

> Instead of deducing our conclusions by reasoning, and verifying them by observation, we in some cases begin by obtaining them provisionally from specific experience, and afterwards connect them with the principles of human nature by *à priori* reasonings, which reasonings are thus a real Verification. (897)

What this means becomes clear from an example further on, when Mill discusses the phenomenon of social progress. If we ask if there is one element in social man which predominates over others as 'the agent of social movement' we find, by 'a striking instance of consilience', that the evidence of history and the facts of human nature agree. Both show that this element is 'the state of the speculative faculties of mankind'. We know from human nature that a desire for greater material comfort is the impulse behind improvements in the arts of life. We know from history that great social changes have been produced by changes in opinion and modes of thought. The two together amounted to proof. So Comte's law of three stages seemed to Mill to have 'that high degree of scientific evidence, which is derived from the concurrence of the indications of history with the probabilities derived from the constitution of the human mind' (928).

Mill's confidence that the determinant of social progress is the state of the speculative faculties of men may seem so typical of Victorian liberal optimism as to make his differences with Macaulay seem relatively insignificant. But they are fundamental. He may have admitted that Macaulay was right in saying that James Mill's science of government was drawn from too narrow a conception of human nature, but he never admitted that the general procedure was faulty: *some* conception of human nature, resting on the fundamental laws of mind, remained for him an indispensable preliminary for any social science. To give that up was to weaken fatally the twin supports of his creed, associationism and political economy. He was prepared to take from Comte a philosophy of history which he failed to acknowledge in Macaulay or his antecedents, but even Comte's historicism had to be tried by the prior laws of mind. As he grew older Mill tended to put the emphasis more on the laws of mind than the evidence of history. In 1865 in his final estimate of Comte he declared that if a sociological theory based on historical evidence contradicts the laws of human nature 'we may know that history has been misinterpreted and that the theory is false' (W x 307).

This cramping loyalty to his inherited methodology accounts for the disappearance from Mill's later writings of that sense of the past which marks some of his earlier historical essays. His early ambition to write a history of the French Revolution, his enthusiasm for Carlyle's imaginative evocations of past societies, his eager response to the work of Michelet, are in the end displaced by the rigid schema of Comte's law of three stages and his own gloss upon it. That effectively meant confining his historical interest to those ages in which the 'progressive mind' seemed to anticipate his own values: fifth-century Athens, pre-Christian Rome, the Protestant Reformation, and the French

Enlightenment. Macaulay's optimism drew upon a rich and varied conception of a political tradition, and was expressed in a joyous appreciation of the material and moral improvements going on around him. Mill's appreciation of his age was by contrast so severely limited by his philosophical principles, his expectations of his contemporaries were so screwed up to his own pitch of high-minded virtue, that he was much more disposed to note decline than improvement.

4 Political economy

After the breach with Comte, Mill came to feel that a proper sociology lay so far in the future that his own efforts were best employed in expanding the traditional doctrines in such a way as to meet the objections aimed at its first practitioners. He later said that he wrote the *Principles of Political Economy* 'to rescue from the hands of such people the truths they misapply, and by combining these with other truths to which they are strangers, to deduce conclusions capable of being of some use to the progress of mankind' (W xiv 37). He wrote it rapidly, beginning late in 1846, and completing the first draft by March 1847. It is consistently lucid, sometimes vivid, and its argument has little of the strained quality of some parts of the *Logic*. In the *Logic* Mill was a lonely pioneer, except at the beginning, and the fact that he owed so much to an antagonist, Whewell, suggests that few people in his immediate circle were competent to follow or to criticize his arguments. But in the *Principles* he was summarizing a body of economic writing with which he had been familiar from his childhood, and which already contained a good deal of high-quality writing dissenting from the main orthodoxy of Smith and Ricardo. So he was in his element. He was a born teacher, who excelled at making difficult and intractable subjects plain to the ordinary reader, and the *Principles* is, among other things, an excellent textbook, possibly the best place to begin a study of Ricardian economics. Its success was immediate. It did what James Mill's *Elements*, and the dramatized lessons of the 'useful knowledge' school failed to do; it popularized political economy and removed the stigma of 'the dismal science'.

This did not mean any concessions of importance to Comte's theories. The *Principles* is a very Ricardian book, and was meant to be. On the eve of its publication Mill told a friend that he doubted if there would be 'a single opinion (on pure

312

political economy) in the book, which may not be exhibited as a corollary from his [Ricardo's] doctrines' (W xiii 731). Critics have reacted to this fidelity on Mill's part in different ways. Some are disappointed at Mill's failure to add anything significant to the basic theory he had imbibed in the 1820s, chiding him, for example, for the complacent remark on the theory of Value: 'Happily, there is nothing in the laws of Value which remains for the present or any future writer to clear up; the theory of the subject is complete' (W iii 456). Others have said that Mill failed to bring the theory up to date with developments in his lifetime; that though his book appeared thirty years after Ricardo's and went through seven editions before his death, during which time the predictions Ricardo had made were all falsified, Mill still stuck to the original scheme he had been taught. There is a vast and technical literature on Mill's economic theory. Here we need only note that, if what has been said already about Mill's conception of social science is right, neither charge is fair to Mill's intentions in the book. He thought the accurracy of political economy lay in its deductions from assumed premises, and its predictions were strictly conditional on the individual's choice. The laws of economics were not to be blindly obeyed, but intelligently used. If a man chose to act in a certain way, he must expect certain results; if he struck for higher wages, his real wages would decline, and so on. Political economy presupposed an individual willing to use the deductions of the science to help him understand his condition and improve his lot. It was not a predictive science so much as a logic of choice; for individuals in its smaller details, for governments in its larger prescriptions.

These assumptions make the *Principles* fundamentally at odds with the *dirigisme* of Comte, and even with the sort of interventionism made in the name of public utility which one might expect from a disciple of Bentham. It illustrates the point made earlier, that liberal individualism owes more to Ricardo's political economy than to Bentham's ethics and jurisprudence. We may note three ways in which Mill's liberalism is shaped by his allegiance to Ricardian economics. First, in trying to make Ricardo's system more congenial to the ordinary reader, he makes it much less deterministic. Secondly, he on the whole preferred *laissez-faire* as a principle to State intervention in matters of economic and social policy. Finally, even his qualified approval of socialism was made in the context of a free-market system.

Undoubtedly, Ricardo's 'strong cases', and his aversion to actual examples, gave his system its air of inexorable gloom. It made popular radicals like Cobbett and romantic Tories like Southey claim that the political economists were merely cold-hearted calculators of human suffering. John Mill was torn between upholding the scientific pretensions of his teachers and denying their inhumane implications. Partly it was a question of style. He saw that Ricardo and his father had 'trusted too much to the intelligibleness of the abstract, when not embodied in the concrete', and that if their formulations were set out with historical evidence and illustrative detail, they could be made much more acceptable. But Mill also altered the character of the Ricardian laws. In Book I he deals with the laws of Production, in Book II with those of Distribution. The former he says 'partake of the character of physical truths. There is nothing optional or arbitrary about them.' But Distribution is 'a matter of human institution solely. The things once there, mankind, individually or collectively, can do with them what they like' (W ii 199). The distinction has been criticized as too rigid. In practice Mill did not apply it very stringently. In his exposition the Ricardian laws appear as tendencies, allowing of different responses according to situation. Few people believed more firmly than he did in the Malthusian law of population, for instance; but on the same page he can say *both* that improvements in the conditions of the labouring classes can rarely 'do anything more than give a temporary margin, speedily filled up by an increase of their numbers', *and* that England had seen steady increases in subsistence and employment along with smaller proportional increases in the population (W ii 159). In other words, the Malthusian law survives in the weaker form of a tendency, more or less prevalent according to the level of education in a given community.

He also blurred the stark contrasts between the three classes in Ricardo's system. The chief target is no longer the landowner idly receiving a steady increase of rent, while the capitalist faces diminishing returns and the labourer staggers along at a bare level of subsistence. Mill is as hostile to idleness and luxury as his father (in practice, perhaps more so), but it is the conspicuous consumption of the new-rich middle classes which he attacks, quite as much as the old landed aristocracy. In fact, because Mill is concerned to flesh out and clothe the Ricardian skeleton, and for this draws on his own observation and experience, the ordinary reader is made more aware of bourgeois vanity than of landowning arrogance. The landowner as such is no longer the enemy. The small landed proprietor comes in for a good deal of praise, perhaps because Mill had learned from Tocqueville about his importance in American democracy. The labourer's improvidence is still a threat to his living standards, but he is plainly seen to be winning the battle against the law of diminishing returns, because he benefits from every improvement in the 'arts of production' which tends to cheapen manufactured goods. His food may cost more, but other goods will cost less (W ii 184–5).

In all this, Mill's tone is more optimistic than Ricardo's. Even the stationary state which for Ricardo (though not for James Mill) was an imminent horror, as wages rose to provide for increased numbers and investment flagged, becomes in Mill a prospect to be positively welcomed. He could see no pleasure in expansion for its own sake. Increased production might be an important aim for poor countries, but for advanced ones a better distribution of existing wealth was more important still. For Mill, a happy society consists of

> a well-paid and affluent body of labourers; no enormous fortunes, except what were earned and accumulated during a single lifetime; but a much larger body of persons than at present, not only exempt from the coarser toils, but with sufficient leisure, both physical and mental, from mechanical details, to cultivate freely the graces of life, and afford

examples of them to the classes less favourably circum-
stanced for their growth. (W iii 755)

The image of an orderly classroom in which the older children
help the younger is never far from Mill's vision of the future.
He was not excited by the thought of a world spinning down
the ringing grooves of change. On the contrary, he wanted a
world in which one could still commune with nature in
solitude, and he saw that world under threat. In his youth he
had picked wild flowers in country lanes which in his middle
age became London streets, and he thought there would be no
satisfaction

> in contemplating the world with nothing left to the spon-
> taneous activity of nature; with every rood of land brought
> into cultivation, which is capable of growing food for human
> beings; every flowery waste or natural pasture ploughed up,
> all quadrupeds or birds which are not domesticated for man's
> use exterminated as his rivals for food, every hedgerow or
> superfluous tree rooted out, and scarcely a place left where a
> wild shrub or flower could grow without being eradicated as
> a weed in the name of improved agriculture. (W iii 756)

If that was what industrialism cost, then we would all gain if
industrialism ground to a halt. The stationary state in Mill's
work becomes a way of fusing the inexorable laws of the
political economists with the cult of nature in romantic poetry,
making the former seem less callous and the latter more useful.

Mill was consistently liberal in the powers he was willing to
grant the State. In the light of his views on the distribution of
wealth this is worth noticing. A utilitarian might be expected
to want to use the powers of government to overrule individual
or sectional interests for the sake of the greatest happiness of
the greatest number. Mill hints at something like this when he
says that 'the ends of government are as comprehensive as
those of the social union', and consist of 'all the good, and all
the immunity from evil, which the existence of government
can be made either directly or indirectly to bestow' (807). But
when he considers in detail particular functions of the State,

Mill is much more concerned to protect individual enterprise and initiative from State encroachment.

In the field of taxation, for instance, he shows a characteristic dislike of the prodigal spending of wealth. But when he considers a graduated property tax (that is, an income tax on which larger incomes pay a higher percentage) he is worried that the aim of equalizing wealth may tend to 'relieve the prodigal at the expense of the prudent'. 'To tax the larger incomes at a higher percentage than the smaller, is to lay a tax on industry and economy; to impose a penalty on people for having worked harder and saved more than their neighbours' (810–11). So he advocates taxing inheritances above a certain amount. 'No one person should be permitted to acquire, by inheritance, more than the amount of a moderate independence' (887). In cases of intestacy, the property should escheat to the State, after an adequate provision for descendants. Mill was against taxing income from investments, because this would harm those who could not work, and for whose security the provision had been originally made. He thought the current rate of income tax of 7d. in the pound involved an injustice, in that it took the same from the salary-earner as from the man who lived off his investments, and restricted the savings of the former. Here his argument actually favours the rich. He disliked a tax which fell both on income and on savings. But since the rich have most to save, exempting savings from taxation benefits them most. Mill defended this apparent partiality with the argument that the rich enjoy the advantage 'only in proportion as they abdicate the personal use of their riches', and prefer productive investments by which wealth is 'distributed in wages among the poor' (816). The thrifty and accumulating bourgeoisie in Mill's scheme therefore escape heavy taxation in so far as they refrain from conspicuous extravagance. But something of the old hostility to the landed aristocracy survives in Mill's proposals to tax increases in rent from land. The landlords, he says, 'grow richer, as it were in their sleep, without working, risking, or economizing' (819–20). For the same general reasons he was against primogeniture; and to McCulloch's argument for the great landed estates, that they were a standing incentive to 'the

317

ingenuity and enterprise of the other classes', Mill replies primly that people are more stimulated 'by the example of somebody who has earned a fortune, than by the mere sight of somebody who possesses one' (890).

Mill's concern to protect wealth energetically and conscientiously earned leads naturally to a fairly modest conception of what government can do to advance the welfare of its subjects. He shared the view of his teachers that governments, even in modern times, had been too anxious to interfere in the working of the economy and that their interference had been generally harmful. But in his youth he had assumed that these faults were characteristic of undemocratic governments, and that as a government really representing a majority of the people could have no interest at variance with the general interest, the reasons for opposing government intervention would diminish as democracy advanced. By the time he wrote the *Principles* he was more disillusioned. Experience, he says, shows that popular governments (and here he seems to have been influenced by Tocqueville's picture of the United States) are no less ready than oligarchical ones to encroach on private life, and the tendency in modern society for masses to prevail over individuals made it particularly urgent to protect that 'originality of mind and individuality of character' on which human progress depended (939–40).

He therefore criticized the sort of bureaucratic control Bentham had dreamed of and Comte brought so much nearer reality. His objection to Continental governments (which Bentham would hardly have considered a criticism) was that 'six or eight men, living at the capital and known by the name of ministers, demand that the whole public business of the country shall pass, or be supposed to pass under their individual eye' and that this meant the overruling of local interests and peculiarities. Mill wanted local administrators to have more share in initiating policy, and he thought that, though central government might be made more efficient, it was still true that individuals did things which affected themselves better than governments could (941). Above all, central government, by drawing talent to itself, was liable to inhibit what Mill calls the active energies of a people, 'labour, contrivance, judgment, self-control' (943). Even the central government of a democracy therefore would not be able to obviate the need for strong local institutions.

Mill concludes that the general rule should be *laissez-faire*: 'every departure from it, unless required by some great good, is a certain evil'. The exceptions to the rule were education, the care of children and the insane, planned colonization, poor relief, some public utilities such as water, and the regulation of hours of labour. Obviously the first of these, being bound up with maintaining the active energies of a people, interested him most, and he justified the departure from *laissez-faire* and the rule that the consumer is the best judge, with the argument that children are not competent judges. 'The uncultivated cannot be competent judges of cultivation' (947). A society has the right to provide for its own future and as the poor generally will not or cannot pay, government must. This is not to cosset the poor or encourage idleness, for education is 'help towards doing without help' (949). Moreover, government should confine itself to requiring some instruction, not specify what sort of instruction it should be. In a similar spirit Mill approved of the 'workhouse test' of the 1834 Poor Law. The State was not in a position to judge who deserved help and who did not; all it could ensure was that no one starved.

It may seem odd that Mill should have laid such stress on the principle that each individual is the best judge of his own interests, yet at the same time have written favourably of trade unions and even declared himself a socialist. The contradiction is explained partly by his puritanical dislike of mere accumulation, which we have seen led him to welcome the stationary state; and partly by his amiable habit of throwing his authority behind an unpopular cause in order to prevent too easy a victory to the opposite side. He did not have much experience of working-class life, nor any natural sympathy with the poor, being too concerned that they conform to his preconceptions about moral improvement for his comments on their conditions to have much warmth or vividness. The society he looked forward to was not a socialist one in the sense entertained by contemporaries like the French Socialists Louis Blanc or Pierre Joseph Proudhon. He had no plans for the abolition of property or its equalization. Rather his hope was for a general *embourgeoisement*, with everybody working for a living, enjoying a decent competence, and having leisure enough to improve his mind.

So his view of trade unions and their role is quite compatible with the free play of market forces. He was (like his teachers) against legal restraints on workmen combining in unions, but not because they could thereby raise their wages. The higher artisans, in skilled trades, might succeed in raising wages by combining, and this would probably do little harm to their employers, who would pass on the rise to the consumer in the form of higher prices. But they would harm the rest of the working class, by contracting the numbers the trade could employ and taking capital from other productive enterprises. They would also harm their own skilled trade by making its members narrow-minded and selfish. Strike action should not be forbidden by law, however, for if it were, workers would never find out the real causes of low wages. The market is the instructor:

> Experience of strikes has been the best teacher of the labouring classes on the subject of the relation between wages and the demand and supply of labour: and it is most important that this course of instruction should not be disturbed. (932)

Mill was also against making trade-union membership compulsory:

> No severity, necessary to the purpose, is too great to be employed against attempts to compel workmen to join a union, or take part in a strike by threats of violence. Mere moral compulsion, by the expression of opinion, the law ought not to interfere with; it belongs to more enlightened opinion to restrain it, by rectifying the moral sentiments of the people. (933)

320

On the question whether such unions, though voluntary, might still engage in some industrial malpractice, such as abolition of piecework, or securing equal pay for skilled and unskilled workers, Mill hesitated. In the end he concluded that it was best to leave to the sanction of public opinion acts which, though damaging in themselves, would occasion more trouble and pain if prohibited by law.

By socialism, Mill did not mean a political movement representing the working class, still less one dependent on trade unions. He meant rather the sort of experiments in cooperation which Marx called Utopian, and his experience of them was confined to what he had read of Owenite communities, the writings of the Saint Simonians and early French socialists like Cabet and Fourier. He did not distinguish as clearly as we would want to, between socialism and communism, but he implies that Owenism is communist and the plans of Saint Simon and Fourier socialist. He never envisaged an alliance between the latter and the centralizing plans of Comte. His views were further complicated by changes of mind prompted by political events. The *Principles* was published before the Revolutions of 1848, and Mill treated socialism in the chapter on Property in Book II, and in Book III, Chapter 7, 'On the Probable Futurity of the Labouring Classes' which he tells us was inspired by Harriet Taylor. He recast the first of these chapters, after the Revolutions of 1848 and the coup d'état of Napoleon III had given him much more sympathy with French socialists, and the change appears most fully in the third edition of 1852. The chapter on the working classes saw relatively few changes over that period. Finally in 1869 Mill wrote the *Chapters on Socialism*, which he never finished and which appeared after his death. If we consider Mill's views on socialism in three phases, represented by the first edition of the *Principles*, the third edition, and the posthumous *Chapters*, we can begin to understand the strange avowal in the *Autobiography*, where Mill says that he and Harriet were 'much less democrats' than he had been because they 'dreaded the ignorance and especially the selfishness and brutality of the mass' but also that their ideal of improvement 'went far beyond

321

Democracy' and would class them 'decidedly under the general designation of Socialists' (W i 239).

Throughout, Mill's concern is to compare communism or socialism on the one hand and private property on the other, with a view to deciding which is more favourable to energy, individuality, and public spirit. To begin with, his criticisms are mostly adverse to socialism and in line with the early political economists' criticisms of Owen. Socialist communities might be workable in a federal system, but are inconceivable on the scale of a modern State. They might be competitive in their products if only they could hold down population growth. They might manage without offering their members the incentive of private gain, but as they could not make full use of the division of labour their standards of invention and production would be low, and their communal lives dull. So Mill concludes that what is needed is that private property as a system should be improved rather than abolished, and this means enabling every individual to share in its benefits. By 1852 he has changed his mind on some of the disadvantages of communism. Public spirit might, by education, reach the required level. Public opinion could probably check reckless population growth. Men's mental progress could probably solve the problem of apportioning labour efficiently. If the choice were between communism with all its chances and private property with all its injustices, then the former would certainly win. But, says Mill cautiously, neither system has had a fair trial, and the issue will probably be finally decided by the criterion 'which of the two systems is consistent with the greatest amount of liberty and spontaneity'; and he adds a warning that, though private property may be unjust, communism may be intolerant. 'No society in which eccentricity is a matter of reproach, can be in a wholesome state. 'We still do not know whether communism will allow the variety of opinions and talents which are 'the mainspring of mental and moral progression' (W ii 209). This note of warning is echoed in the revision of Book III, Chapter 7, where Mill's dislike of the exploitation of one system and his fear of the uniformity threatened by the other impel him towards the syndicalist ideal of associations of workers pooling their own capital. These he hoped would bring about a 'moral revolution', involving

> the healing of the standing feud between capital and labour; the transformation of human life, from a conflict of classes struggling for opposite interests, to a friendly rivalry in the pursuit of a good common to all; the elevation of the dignity of labour; a new sense of security and independence in the labouring class; and the conversion of each human being's daily occupation into a school of the sympathies and the practical intelligence. (W iii 792)

The spirit is co-operative, but the machinery is competitive; and as we noted before, Mill, like a good schoolmaster, wants to maintain rivalry as a pedagogic device to ensure continuing progress.

Through the successive drafts of the *Principles* Mill assumes that socialism will be characterized by spontaneous choice and peaceful agitation. By the time he wrote the *Chapters on Socialism*, the first International had been founded, and its early congresses had seen the first glimmerings of a revolutionary movement. Mill knew some of the British trade unionists who were among the first delegates, and he thought they talked more sense than their European counterparts. They were moderate, practical, and more interested in peaceful agitation than revolutionary action. The revolutionaries, he thought, were doomed to failure. Their aim of seizing all the land and capital of a country was 'obviously chimerical' and could only plunge mankind back into the state of nature envisaged by Hobbes (W v 748–9). Mill may not have grasped the import of the theories behind the revolutionary movement, but he knew enough of it to feel inclined to qualify the concessions he had made in 1852. That meant tipping the balanced scales of self-interest and public spirit once more in favour of self-interest; in other words, sounding the alarm against the submergence of individuality:

> Already in all societies the compression of individuality by the majority is a great and growing evil; it would probably

be much greater under Communism, except so far as it might be in the power of individuals to set bounds to it by selecting to belong to a community of persons like-minded with themselves. (W v 746)

The last sentence shows how alien to Mill was the possibility that socialism or communism might override individual choice. He has little idea that he is dealing not with alternative experiments in living but with rival social systems, two giants who would one day divide the globe between them. Reading him is like watching the performance of a referee in a heavy-weight boxing contest. Frail and bow-tied and impeccable, he dances about, well clear of the punches, awarding points. In the first round (1848) he declares for private property. In the second (1852) he declares for socialism, but with a warning about keeping to the rules. In the final round (1869) socialism has committed a foul and private property wins on a disqualification. In the end, one feels the whole contest was staged primarily as a test and vindication of *laissez-faire*. Socialism, which Mill persistently conceives as a set of arguments rather than a portentous political force, is useful mainly because it keeps the advocates of free economic relations from too great complacency.

5 Schoolmaster of liberalism

With the completion of the *Principles of Political Economy* the main elements in Mill's mature philosophy were fixed. His writings in the last phase of his life, from his marriage in 1851 to his death in 1873, elaborate themes he had sketched before 1850. Had he written nothing after the *Principles*, he might have been remembered as a solid theorist who after some uncertain forays into politics and literature had buried his youthful radicalism in two heavy works of philosophy and economics in conscious abandonment of any hope of acquiring a political following. In fact, his fame rests very largely on what he wrote in his last years, and the popular idea of him as the 'saint of rationalism', the lonely and ascetic critic of Victorian complacency and convention, derives from *On Liberty* (1859), *Representative Government* (1861), and *The Subjection of Women* (1869). But for these works, it is quite likely that Mill would no longer be read outside the universities. Through them he became a household word. As they are the culmination of the earliest political thinking, we must first ask what makes them stand out from his earlier work.

Two major events helped produce a change of tone to something more urgent and polemical. The first was the French Revolution of 1848 and its aftermath, the short-lived Second Republic. For Mill this was not just a local event in a foreign country. France for him had, since his boyhood visit, been the country of his ideals, where social philosophy was more advanced and its opponents more readily identified than they were in England, where everything was befogged by compromise and goodwill. When Mill uses a phrase like 'the best writers on the Continent' he almost always means French writers. So when the French Revolution broke out in February 1848 he became very excited, predicting that a French republic would have the effect of republicanizing all Europe 'and England itself probably before we die' (W xiii 732). He admired the constitution of the Second Republic and defended it as 'a digest of the elementary doctrines of representative democracy' (W xx 358). While it flourished, he thought little of his own country. 'The whole problem of modern society . . . will be worked out, as I have long thought it would, in France and nowhere else.' And he added, 'As for England, it is dead, vapid, left quite behind by all the questions now rising' (W xiv 32, 34). Louis Napoleon's *coup d'état* in December 1852 was therefore a shock, the more so as it enlisted the peasantry and the mass of the middle classes against the liberal writers and theorists Mill so much admired. Thereafter Napoleon III was for Mill the epitome of wickedness, 'the most dangerous enemy of the future of humanity' (W xv 610). More important, the sort of alliance which he represented, of brutal power, frightened respectability and mass ignorance, had to be held out as a warning to contemporaries. Mill had always disliked the Catholic Church; but now his remarks on the lower classes became sharper and more contemptuous; while the middle classes, reproached in the *Principles* for their heartless hedonism, are henceforth castigated for their mental complacency as well.

The other event was Mill's marriage to Harriet Taylor in April 1851. During their long friendship they had considered they were victims of the institution of marriage. Rumours that they were the objects of gossip only gave them a sense of superiority to the narrow standards of society around them. When John Taylor died in 1849, their own principles did not require them to marry, but they did, preserving their consistency with an enhanced contempt for the insipidity of ordinary society, and making up for the company they missed by saying they were above it. Not that they flouted the canons of respectability. Harriet in particular was deeply sensitive to any hint that her connection with Mill had been improper, and she laid a ban on any she suspected of gossip.

Tocqueville is a notable specimen of the class which includes such people as the Sterlings Romillys Carlyles Austins—the gentility class—weak in moral [*sic*], narrow in intellect, timid, infinitely conceited, and gossiping. There are very few men in this country who can seem other than more or less respectable puppets to us.

The list, as Mill's biographer notes, included 'almost every man Mill had ever liked'. Mill's upbringing and education had given him an 'instinct of closeness' and an idiom which it had taken him years of effort to turn into a style accessible to a wide readership. His marriage, instead of widening his circle further, probably increased his sense of isolation and confirmed his highly intellectual view of human life. Once he had felt that, while he had the intellect, others had the emotion without which intellect remained ineffective. Now he had both, and the consciousness made him much more complacent about his heritage, and much less receptive to correction from outside.

The extent of Harriet's influence on Mill has been much debated. Some writers treat his claim that some of his later works were their joint productions as literally true. Others, contrasting his magisterial clarity with her breathless, unpunctuated letters have claimed that she merely gave him back his own measured and qualified views in a more opinionated and dogmatic form. Probably a definitive conclusion is not possible. But one effect of her influence is fairly clear. She made him recast his entire conception of social justice. He was led by her feminism to see the major division in society to be not that of the labouring classes and their masters, but simply that of women and men. The dominion of men over women, he came to feel, was the last vestige of 'the system of right founded on might'; women were 'the subject-class . . . in a chronic state of bribery and intimidation combined' (E 434, 439). So the old division of society into the oppressors and oppressed was given a new lease of life and the political imagery of radical agitation revamped to fit the battle of the sexes. Mill recovered a motive for engaging in polemic, this time with the advantage of an established reputation as a philosopher and economist, whose scientific caution was beyond dispute.

Illness gave urgency to what he had to say. Mill had caught

tuberculosis from his father and he seems to have given it to his wife. It was a common disease in Victorian England and it was thought to be fatal. Under its threat both showed great courage. The thought that most oppressed them was that they had works still to write which death might cut short. So they planned a series of essays to say what they had to say in a condensed form. If they lived they could add to them, if they died they would serve, as Mill put it (in words which one must remember were written privately to Harriet) as 'a sort of mental pemican which thinkers, when there are any after us, may nourish themselves with & then dilute for other people' (W xiv 141–2). The essays were to be prefaced by 'the Life', or what became the *Autobiography*, in which she wanted him to use his reputation to tell the world the truth about their relationship. In the event, Mill recovered his health with an extraordinary journey through France, Italy, and Greece, while Harriet's condition grew rapidly worse. The essay project was not completed. The only one which they were able to finish jointly before her death in 1858 was *On Liberty*, which Mill published the following year with a dedication to her memory. Their collaboration makes it in tone and manner quite unlike his other works.

These background factors explain *On Liberty*'s desperate urgency of tone. It is much more condensed than most of his works. It compares in style with the finest of the essays of his prime, deploying a complex argument in clear, calm prose, varied by passages of plangent eloquence. It is in itself a striking example of one of Mill's themes, the need to consider the opposing point of view. In fact Mill sometimes sets out objections to his case more eloquently than he puts the case itself, which may account for the fact that his critics often borrow their points from him. But the central principle, that we are justified in interfering with an individual's actions if they are harming others, but not if we merely wish to do him good, is so forcibly and memorably argued that it has passed into the public philosophy of all the great Western democracies.

The long-term influence is not so easy to explain. To anyone coming to the essay from Mill's previous writings, most of its ingredients will be fairly familiar. Its central contention, the 'single truth' of which Mill claimed it was the philosophic textbook, is a sharpened-up version of the political economists' view that certain activities are better left to the individual than the State, and that while the State may and should take the initiative in matters concerning the public good such as defence, public order, and welfare, there is a private area which may and should be left to the operation of self-interest. Adam Smith and Ricardo wanted to protect this area from the State in the name of commercial enterprise: Bentham was more concerned by the threat of religion enlisting the law to interfere in moral freedom. That there must be a private realm which the laws cannot reach was common to all Mill's mentors. His contribution was to try to reduce it to a simple working principle,

> that the sole end for which mankind are warranted, individ-ually or collectively, in interfering with the liberty of action of any of their number, is self-protection ... The only purpose for which power can be rightfully exercised over any member of a civilized community, against his will, is to prevent harm to others. His own good, either physical or moral, is not a sufficient warrant. (E 14–15)

Mill then makes the famous distinction between self—and other-regarding actions;

> The only part of the conduct of any one, for which he is amenable to society, is that which concerns others. In the part which merely concerns himself, his independence is, of right, absolute. Over himself, over his own body and mind, the individual is sovereign. (E 15)

Yet this distinction is sometimes said to be inconsistent with utilitarianism, especially in the light of Mill's disclaimer a little further on, that he does not want to avail himself of any theory of natural rights to defend liberty, but thinks utility is 'the ultimate appeal on all ethical questions' provided it is 'utility in the largest sense, grounded on the permanent inter-ests of man as a progressive being' (E 16). The principle of utility is supposed to measure happiness in units of pleasure and pain, in order to offer an objective justification for interfering in the individual' s conception of his own good. A course of action which promotes the general happiness might well have to sacrifice the liberty of the individual for the greater good of the whole. Did not Mill himself think that there should be laws forbidding marriage unless the parties to it showed they had the means to support a family (E 132–3)? Can there be, for the strict utilitarian, any area of private action inaccessible to constraints made in the name of the public happiness?

A similar point can be made from the viewpoint of the individual. It is said that there can be no such thing as a purely self-regarding action, even for a utilitarian. For utilitarianism is a consequentialist theory: the goodness or badness of an action lies in its consequences in pleasure and pain. To say that my misconduct is no concern of yours, though it might give you, and perhaps others too, a lot of distress, is to make an exception to the rule of utility. Mill argues that we should not interfere with a man merely for being drunk, but only if his drunkenness affects others, such as his dependants or his colleagues. But even solitary drunkenness affects others. A pledged teetotaller for instance might experience a physical revulsion equivalent to acute pain on seeing a man drunk, and a whole society which disapproves of alcohol might well enact measures against its consumption to secure the greatest happiness of the greatest number.

But Mill has a utilitarian answer to both these points. By specifying that he appeals to utility 'in the largest sense, grounded on the permanent interests of man as a progressive being' he is evidently appealing to his father's version of the doctrine rather than Bentham's. He specifies three exceptions to his 'very simple principle'. These are minors and invalids, both of whom must have their conduct regulated by others, and (more embarrassingly to modern readers) 'barbarians'. This is Mill the Indian administrator, invoking the cultural ladder of his father's *History*. Some peoples are so backward as not to know what is in their best interests. They represent a stage of development 'in which the race itself may be considered as in its nonage' (E 15). For such people, 'despotism is a legitimate mode of government ... provided the end be their improvement'. That means they are a proper object of interference on utilitarian grounds. The arguments of *On Liberty* are not for them, but only for people who have reached 'the capacity of being guided to their own improvement by conviction and persuasion' (E 16).

Mill's answer to the second point is also compatible with the principle of utility. It is very fairly set out in Chapter 4. He does not deny that a man's self-regarding actions may give pain to others. But he does deny that such pain always licenses their interfering with him. He does not (as some of his critics suppose) advocate letting an individual 'go to the devil in his own way'. He thinks that society ought to express its displeasure, without going to the length of actual penal sanctions, at foolish or disagreeable conduct, and that the individual citizen's duty to remonstrate with a wrongdoer in such cases is too little recognized or acted upon (E 95). He makes a very careful distinction between behaviour for which the agent is left to suffer the natural consequences such as unpopularity or even ostracism, and acts which so affect the interests of others that society must take a hand in the consequences with actual punishment. To the objection that 'no man is an island', that even minor follies do harm by example, Mill insists that a man may be punished for harming others, but not for harming himself. Should not individuals then be protected from themselves? Mill's reply is, not if they are adults; for more harm is done by interfering than by tolerating the fault. For 'the merely contingent, or, as it may be called, constructive injury which a person causes to society ... the inconvenience is one which society can afford to bear, for the sake of the greater good of human freedom' (E 100–1). He supports this with two further arguments: that society has in its educational system the means, anterior to the fault, of inculcating rational conduct, and if in spite of this its adult members continue to behave like children, it is itself to blame; and that when society does interfere for the individual's own private good, it will generally make mistakes. Mill then illustrates this last point with examples of societies in which a 'moral police' has enforced a principle which it ought to have left as a matter of private choice or taste. The examples are: the Moslem aversion to pork, the Catholic prohibition of a married priesthood, the temperance legislation in Maine, socialist demands for the equalization of wealth, the temperance agitation in England, sabbatarianism, and finally the Mormon practice of polygamy. Of the last, Mill is careful to express his deep disapproval; but he cannot resist a feminist point, that if women are brought up so ignorant as to think marriage 'the one thing needful', it is hardly surprising that some should prefer to be 'one of several wives, to not being a wife at all' (E 113). Throughout this part of the argument his concern is the utilitarian one that one learns morality, at least in part, from the experience of consequences, and that if one is denied that experience by well-meaning busybodies who assume they know what one's best interest is, one will remain morally immature.

Mill's argument for tolerating some morally objectionable behaviour is powerfully reinforced by his case for freedom of thought and discussion, in Chapter 2, the longest in *On Liberty*. Here too one is struck by his fidelity to his heritage, in this case the associationist psychology and the radical empiricism based on it which he set out in the *Logic*. Indeed most of the exaggerations of this chapter stem from this fidelity. Mill's main argument is that we cannot afford to suppress any opinion held by a minority, and he makes the case in three parts. If the received opinion is false and the minority opinion true, suppressing the latter involves an assumption of infallibility which will harm mankind. If the received opinion is true and the minority one false, then the suppression will deprive those who hold the received opinion of the means of knowing why it is true. If, as in the majority of cases, received and minority opinion are each a mixture of true and false, then suppression is an interference with the process of competing opinions by which one generation learns from another's errors. As a plea for fair treatment of minorities and for open-mindedness towards novel opinions, Mill's argument has become part of liberal orthodoxy; but the assumptions behind it have been largely forgotten, and so the most important section of the essay is actually the least discussed.

The guiding conception is the associationist view of the mind. The strength of human judgement depends on 'one property, that it can be set right when it is wrong' (E 27). Why do we trust a man's judgement? Because, Mill replies, he has observed 'the steady habit of correcting and completing his own opinion by collating it with those of others'. He is not merely asking for us to be fair to opinions which differ from ours: he is asserting that there is no other means available to the human mind of attaining truth: 'No wise man ever acquired his wisdom in any mode but this; nor is it in the nature of human intellect to become wise in any other manner' (E 28). There are several things to note about this. The first is that it confuses wisdom and open-mindedness. We often find that people who appreciate every side of a question find it hard to make a final decision, while those on whom we rely for wise, practical advice are not so much open-minded as experienced and without illusions. For Mill the acquisition of wisdom is so cerebral a process, embracing both an appetite for novelty and a suspicion of convention, that his wise man looks a little like a weathercock turning in every intellectual breeze.

He also seems to exaggerate the role of discussion in eliciting truth and keeping it alive. He does not make any clear distinction between polemical debate and temperate discussion. Writing militantly, his mind running on the struggle of rationalism with religious dogma and intolerance, he conveys the impression that only heretics can be discoverers and that those in authority are by definition opposed to new truth. But his choice of heretics is rather confusing. When he asks us to suppose cases where the received opinion is false and the minority opinion true, his examples of the latter are Socrates and Jesus Christ. This makes his argument hard to follow. For while Socrates provides an example of a teacher executed on the false charge of corrupting youth, the case of Jesus is quite different. Mill did not disapprove of Jesus's ethical teachings (which he was later to praise as including 'the ideal perfection of utilitarian morality') but he disliked Christianity, and seems to have shared Gibbon's view that the early experience of persecution taught it intolerance. Mill's case against Marcus Aurelius' persecution of the Christians seems to be, not that it delayed the eventual triumph of Christianity, but that, seeking to suppress it rather than improve it, he ensured that it was a worse religion which triumphed under his successor Constantine. So his examples carry him away from his stated intention. It turns out that he is not telling us what happens when falsehood in authority tries to stamp out truth, but rather illustrating the possibility that authority, though acting in good faith, may yet, by persecuting an opinion it thinks objectionable, make it still worse. Even when he goes on to discuss the case when the received opinion is true and the minority one false, his target is again Christianity, this time as an intolerant creed whose formularies tend to ossify the minds of its adherents, preventing the entry of fresh convictions, yet 'itself doing nothing for the mind or heart, except standing sentinel over them to keep them vacant' (E 51). It was natural that, in spite of Mill's evident admiration for Protestant heretics, many people took this part of his argument as a covert attack on the Christian religion. Under pretence of describing the survival of truth, Mill has actually been castigating the spread of creeds.

When Mill turns to consider open discussion in relation to other sorts of opinion, his strong dislike of dogmas or formularies raises problems. Much popular morality for instance takes the form of well-worn maxims and proverbs. Is a man who directs his actions by such unquestioned principles as 'Thou shalt not steal' or 'Honesty is the best policy' really allowing a part of his mind to go to sleep, or appointing a sentinel over it to keep it vacant? People hold to such principles habitually so as to free their minds and energies for other things: life would be intolerably complex if one had to keep one's most cherished principles under constant review. In *On Liberty*, Mill partly admits this, though he insists that such maxims would be more valuable if people could hear the arguments for and against before adhering to them. But in *Utilitarianism* he makes his position more clear. The stock case against utilitarian ethics, made by opponents from Burke to Whewell, was that there are relatively few cases of moral decision where the agent has time to make the calculation of consequences. When he came to deal with this objection in *Utilitarianism*, his reply was that there had been 'ample time, namely the whole past duration of the human species' to calculate and weigh the consequences; the results of the calculation were handed down in traditional moral maxims. But even this concession to convention he made reluctantly, calling the maxims so passed on 'the rules of morality for the multitude, and for the philosopher until he has succeeded in finding better' (W x 224). Only the vulgar cling to such maxims and the philosopher alone can leaven the lump of conventional opinion.

Mill's argument for continuous discussion is even more awkward in the case of scientific knowledge, for here he was committed to the eventual achievement of certainty. It may be plausible to say that a particular scientist's solitary researches are really an internal dialogue, in which he argues a case *pro* and *con* with himself. But can it be true that the resulting scientific truths have no better credentials than a 'standing invitation to the whole world to prove them unfounded' (E 28–9)? Mill himself sees that he has come near to saying that truths are useless once they are established and that 'the fruits of conquest perish by the very completeness of the victory' (E 54). His positivism commits him to the view that as men progress in knowledge, the area of possible dissent must contract. But would not mankind in that case have less and less of substance to disagree about and therefore to discuss? Yes, says Mill, and when that happens we shall have to invent matter for dispute; and he praises the Socratic method and even has a good word for the scholastic disputations of the Middle Ages as possible ways of keeping mankind intellectually alert once utopia has been reached. The idea that men may one day run out of matters for discussion is reminiscent of his worry during the mental crisis, that they would one day run out of musical tunes.

Mill then passes to a defence of individuality. 'Society', he says, 'has now fairly got the better of individuality' (E 75). Even men's occupational and regional differences are becoming assimilated:

> Comparatively speaking, they now read the same things, listen to the same things, see the same things, go to the same places, have their hopes and fears directed to the same objects, have the same rights and liberties, and the same means of asserting them. (E 90)

The lament sounds so much like a protest against twentieth-century conformity, that one has to remind oneself that Mill was talking about the golden age of private enterprise and *laissez-faire*. Contemporaries did not share his pessimism. Macaulay took the opposite view, that the age was marked by extreme eccentricity, and so Mill was 'crying "Fire" in Noah's Flood'. Whether meant as prophecy or description, Mill's claim provokes the question, Why should one suppose that people who see the same things, listen to the same things and visit the same places, should all react to them in the same way? Mill thinks they must, because (as we saw in the argument of the *Logic*) he holds a theory of the mind which leaves little room for the idea of personal identity. If the mind is a mere locus of sensations, then identical sensations will produce an identical mind. It is the different identities of different persons which prevent their assimilation by the same circumstances. Mill was more alarmed than his contemporaries at the prospect of the submergence of individuality because he was a more literal-minded environmentalist than most of them. The idea of 'Chinese stationariness' illustrates the difference. It was a common idea in early Victorian literature, and it usually appears as an argument to illustrate the virtues of free trade. The Chinese had reached the stationary state, in which returns on capital investment were too low to act as an incentive to improvement, and so none of them sought to exploit their great natural resources for more than the needs of the moment. Mill uses this argument in the *Principles* (W ii 167–70) in the usual way, to illustrate the benefits of free trade. He repeats it in *On Liberty* with the brief remark that if the Chinese are ever 'to be farther improved, it must be by foreigners' (E 89). But in 1848

Mill saw many compensations in the stationary state. In 1859 these were submerged in the all-pervasive fear of the despotism of custom. 'Chinese stationariness' is Mill's nightmare version of the stationary state, where custom has killed all originality of thought and behaviour by excluding not just foreign capital but foreign ideas.

To counter the deadening effect of convention and prejudice, Mill calls for more eccentricity, because that would encourage genius, which would in turn leaven the lump of mediocrity. This is sometimes taken as an élitist argument, but one must beware using a word which has since become a term of reproach. Mill used 'élite' (E 478, for example) more freely than a modern democrat would dare, but he would have claimed he was an egalitarian. The fact that he wanted to encourage talent does not mean that he thought all talent innate. He had no way of accounting biologically or physiologically for the emergence of genius. Whenever he speaks of men of outstanding ability, political or intellectual, he treats their occurrence as the result of external stimuli acting on physical and mental energies which would otherwise have remained dormant. But on his own principles, genius cannot result from severe external discipline, and so Calvinism is condemned as dwarfing and cramping the individual. This was not because it repressed 'human nature'. Elsewhere, Mill was concerned to show that the collections of attributes which generally went under that label were the result of social arrangements and not their cause. 'Nearly every respectable attribute of humanity is the result not of instinct, but a victory over instinct' (W x 393) . The best specimens of 'human nature' were products of education, being either those who had conquered their instincts, or those who had inherited the benefits of previous conquests.

This is perhaps why Mill combined a daring egalitarianism with the most old-maidish prudery. The mixture is well illustrated in *The Subjection of Women*. In arguing against the legal disabilities under which women then suffered, he refuses to credit any argument based on 'natural' differences between the sexes. 'What is now called the nature of women is an eminently artificial thing—the result of forced repression in some directions, unnatural stimulation in others' (E 450–1). Mill writes as if the position of women were wholly the result of a conspiracy by men bent on keeping them subordinate and ignorant. But when he deals with what he calls 'the sensual relation' he cannot suppress his disgust at the thought of the numbers of women, as he thought, enslaved against their inclinations to men, the vast number of whom 'are little higher than brutes'. It is puritanism rather than snobbery which accounts for Mill's distaste for 'the mass'. Rational behaviour for him necessarily involved a subordination of the passions, and it was the evidence of the pervasiveness of 'the animal instinct' which, more than any other factor, persuaded Mill that rational individuals were a small minority. *On Liberty* is full of phrases like 'those in advance of society in thought and feeling' or 'those who stand on the higher eminences of thought' (E 82). They express Mill's conviction, not so much that talent and ability were in short supply, as that the education and 'self-culture' which produced the 'developed' individual were insufficiently understood and practised. The science of ethology which was to underlie such educaton was unfortunately still to come; meanwhile, the best thing the reformer could do was to hold at bay the erroneous theories whose prejudiced devotees threatened to engulf those on 'the higher eminences of thought'.

Of course Mill valued individuality for its own sake. 'It really is of importance,' he says, 'not only what men do, but also what manner of men they are that do it' (E 73). But he did not want people to be left alone to develop their own nature, partly because he thought there was no such thing, and partly because he could only conceive of development as taking place in conditions of completely free choice. Custom and convention were, by definition, at odds with free choice. 'He who lets the world, or his own portion of it, choose his plan of life for him, has no need of any other faculty than the ape-like one of imitation' (E 73). That meant that the progress of mankind was in the hands of those who had broken free of convention, the developed, the initiators. Everyone should be equally free to choose, but the undeveloped choose only between one custom and another; the developed initiate new behaviour, experiments in living.

The driving impulse behind *On Liberty* is the sense that the available genius in society, which Mill carefully defines as 'originality in thought and action' (E 81), was not enough appreciated or used, and that if the surrounding mediocrity did manage to stifle it, progress would cease. It is a plea for the small thinking minority in contemporary England to be given more air and a wider hearing. Mill complains that

> With us, heretical opinions do not perceptibly gain, or even lose, ground in each decade or generation; they never blaze out far and wide, but continue to smoulder in the narrow circles of thinking and studious persons among whom they originate, without ever lighting up the general affairs of mankind with either a true or a deceptive light (E 41–2)

The effect was to discourage 'the open, fearless characters, and logical, consistent intellects, who once adorned the thinking world'. Without such intellects, no people could attain 'a generally high scale of mental activity'; but with them, there was hope that 'even persons of the most ordinary intellect' would be 'raised to something of the dignity of thinking beings' (E 44). Mill is not asking that the thinking minority be handed the levers of power to raise the mass to this level. He wants them to do so by teaching and example. He declares,

> No government by a democracy or a numerous aristocracy, either in its political acts or in the opinions, qualities, and tone of mind which it fosters, ever did or could rise above mediocrity, except in so far as the sovereign Many have let themselves be guided (which in their best times they always have done) by the counsels and influence of a more highly gifted and instructed One or Few. (E 82)

But he adds that he is not for hero-worship; all he wants is that the exceptional individual have 'freedom to point out the way', while it is 'the honour and glory of the average man' that he is capable of following 'with his eyes open' (E 82). More explicitly than in the *Principles*, Mill makes clear that his ideal is a pedagogic one, a society organized like a classroom, where the teachers justify their leadership by imparting their knowledge freely, and the pupils give obedience and respect to those who most deserve it, those from whom there is most to learn.

It is a distortion of Mill's argument to suppose that he advocates eccentricity of behaviour, or new 'experiments in living', from a mere dislike of conventional morality and in the name of a free, 'permissive' society. What he advocates, consistently with his vision of an educated minority giving an enlightened lead, is more argument and reasoned remonstrance. He says in Chapter 4 that the office of advising our neighbours about their conduct ought to be 'much more freely rendered than the common notions of politeness at present permit' (E 95). He wanted to see society's morals not merely diversified, but improved. Conservative critics have seen him as the apostle and forerunner of a modern type, the high-minded liberal who schools himself to tolerate distressing behaviour in his own circle for the sake of unspecified benefits to the species which he will not live to see. But Mill never envisaged the social changes which have produced this failure of moral nerve, and he would certainly not have approved of its effects.

On Liberty, then, may seem to be 'élitist' in the role it gives the thinking minority in society, but this minority owes its position to its own efforts, not to privilege or birth, and retains it in conditions of the freest enquiry. Its function is to educate and improve the mass, but it is given no special aids in this except the knowledge that its leadership depends on its openness and honesty. All this however is more implied than explicitly stated. Mill had still to show how the relationship of reciprocal respect might be made to work. This was the aim of *Considerations on Representative Government* (1861). There the argument of *On Liberty* is translated into what Mill saw as workable political arrangements. To form a just picture of Mill's mature political views the two works must be read together.

In fact they seldom have been. *Representative Government* is twice as long. It contains a wealth of reading and reflection, but diluted into general assertions which seem removed from reality. (In this respect it contrasts with a more popular contemporary work, Bagehot's *English Constitution*, which aims to be purely descriptive, but seems to be so rooted in actual observations of human behaviour that it has worn much better.) Mill's practical proposals too have embarrassed democrats and almost led to the book's being dropped (as *On Liberty* has never been) from the canon of liberal classics: for it advocated proportional representation and plural voting, discarded the secret ballot, and made the suffrage conditional on the literacy of voters. Only the first of these has promised a revival of interest in the book in recent years. But despite its relative unpopularity *Representative Government* amplifies the arguments of *On Liberty*.

The first assumption common to both works is that government cannot be morally neutral; it must improve its subjects or retard them, there was no such thing as simply governing. Those who said that governments were merely to keep order, and spoke of their institutions sometimes as machines to be judged by their efficiency, sometimes as organisms to be reverently left to grow by themselves, were really denying that institutions have an effect on the moral level of those who live under them. In backward states of society men might need to be coerced for their own good, but even paternalistic government must be judged by whether it improves men or keeps them backward. Equally, the institutions of an advanced society never work of their own accord; they too improve or stultify those who live under them. Both the mechanistic and the organicist views of political institutions underrate the power of human agency. 'It is what men think, that determines how they act' (E 156). Even if their thoughts proclaim a backward state, that too is a matter of education and therefore of human agency. So Mill steered between the blueprints of Bentham and the historicism of Comte to conclude that men can, within cultural and historical limits, shape the forms of government under which they live.

But what makes one form better than another? As in *On Liberty*, Mill eschews a theory of natural rights which might offer some universal yardstick. Instead he judges a government by the degree to which it is able to prepare its subjects for promotion to the next rung in the ladder of civilization. Proof of improving intentions legitimizes authority. By this standard the Greeks score higher marks (as one would expect from a classically-educated examiner) than the Chinese. The Greeks turned savage peoples into slaves, but being a Greek's slave was better than being a savage. Whereas the Chinese took their people up to a certain stage, and lacking the intellectual capacity to go further, froze them there. Clearly this is an elaboration of the sentiment we met in *On Liberty* that despotism is a legitimate government for dealing with barbarians. And just as there he dismisses backward peoples and their polities as irrelevant to this theme, so in *Representative Government* he tells us that he cannot deal with the complex questions of which governments suit which states of society, and passes immediately to a description of the ideally best form, which he has no doubt will be one or another variety of republicanism.

His case for representative government is of course that it is the form most calculated to call forth the energies of the largest number of individuals. Despotic or aristocratic governments, however well disposed, encourage passivity and self-regard in their subjects. Popular governments encourage activity, self-confidence and emulation. Mill, it is worth noting, does not follow his father in deriving democracy from the universal tendency in men to oppress one another. He points out that, though the working classes in England are excluded from power, no other 'rulers in history have been actuated by a more sincere desire to do their duty to the poorer portion of their countrymen' (E 188). His own case for popular participation in government is not that governments without it are oppressive, but that it is the best way of ensuring a self-reliant and public-spirited people. His father's concern was with minimizing oppression; his own is with maximizing responsibility.

But then why should not these benefits be extended to backward peoples without delay? Mill's answer, prophetic of the failure of constitutionalism among underdeveloped peoples in this century, is that a people must have reached a level of education and self-reliance before it can use representative institutions. Until it has, despotic or bureaucratic government would be more effective and even more just. Even as he wrote, the Russian autocracy's abolition of serfdom was illustrating his point. But Mill's old radical dislike of an aristocratic parliament comes out in his reasons for his preference. Representative assemblies, he says, reflect more faithfully than unrepresentative governments the faults of their society (E 206). Of course a monarch and his counsellors in a backward society might share its faults, but that is exactly what justifies bureaucratic rule over backward peoples by 'foreigners, belonging to a superior people or a more advanced state of society'. They are equipped to carry their subjects 'rapidly through several stages of progress' and clear away 'obstacles to improvement which might have lasted indefinitely if the subject population had been left unassisted to its native tendencies and chances' (E 207). Mill is obviously thinking of British rule in India.

When he considers advanced societies like his own, Mill shows the effects of two generations of official routine on utilitarian thought. Twenty years before he had criticized Bentham for exhausting 'all the resources of ingenuity in devising means for riveting the yoke of public opinion closer and closer round the necks of all public functionaries' (W x 108). Now he calls for an unhampered administration whose members apply their skills with the minimum of legislative interference. Every branch of public administration has its rules, evolved to meet peculiar problems, which members of the legislature often ignore and undervalue. When legislatures interfere in departmental matters, they represent 'inexperience sitting in judgement on experience, ignorance on knowledge' (E 217). Even when legislatures do contain experts, they are partial and concerned to mislead. Mill resents the way legislation carefully prepared by professionals is ruined because the House of Commons 'will not forgo the precious privilege of tinkering it with their clumsy hands'. Select committees were merely places where 'private crotchets', already once overruled by expert knowledge, get 'a second chance before the tribunal of ignorance'. Mill's solution to this amateurism is a Legislative Commission, embodying 'the element of intelligence', which will prepare bills which parliament, embodying the element of will, might pass or reject, but not amend (E 223). There is no mistaking the note of professional resentment in Mill's account of meddling by a parliament of gentleman amateurs.

But what should parliament's function be? It could not govern, nor administer, nor prepare legislation. Instead, it should check the executive by censure, discussion, and publicity, and be 'at once the nation's Committee of Grievances and its Congress of Opinions'. Its function is to talk, but for its talk to be valuable it must contain 'a fair sample of every grade of intellect among the people which is at all entitled to a voice in public affairs' (E 228). Mill is thus led, by his own high estimate of administrative expertise, to contrive a representative assembly talented enough to be an effective counterpoise. Bureaucratic skill will not by itself ensure good government, for following the professional maxims of officials is open to the same objection made in *On Liberty* to following custom: it encourages mental sloth. Bureaucracies 'perish by the immutability of their maxims' (E 234). (It is worth noting that Mill thought that entry by competitive examination would prevent the home civil service from hardening into a 'Chinese mandarinate'. He seems not to have known that China had had competitive examinations for its civil service for longer than any country in the Western world.)

Clearly administrative expertise must be balanced by popular control. The question Mill then asks is, How popular should this control be? We would not expect him to favour popular majorities, and in fact he applies to them exactly the same objection which he had made to aristocratic minorities in his youth; that they are likely to follow their selfish interests against the general good. So strongly does Mill express his fear of the legislative effects of popular ignorance that one wonders why he does not favour the existing representative system, with its high property qualification for the vote, not to mention the anomalous distribution of seats so unfavourable to the larger cities. In fact he does come near to this. He admits that it is 'roughly true' that the existing representation gives a voice to the opinions that matter, but he adds that this cannot continue if the qualification is lowered and the electorate enlarged (E 250). So it is to meet this threat that he favours the scheme of minority representation first devised by Thomas Hare.

The essence of Hare's scheme was that it sought to represent opinions rather than interests. Mill has a rather laborious chapter (VI) in which he explains his divergence from his teachers, who had always opposed the representation of interests. There are two sorts of interest, Mill tells us; immediate and selfish, or distant and unselfish. The virtuous man follows the latter, and is only liable to be diverted from this by the class or group to which he belongs in society. Separate him from this group and you will enable him to act virtuously. Allow him to vote with others who share his opinions, and he will (if those opinions are worth anything) see them represented in the legislature. At the moment they are not, because he is required to vote in a geographical constituency for a candidate whom he has not himself chosen, and whose views may not even overlap with his own. If he votes with the majority, his own views are submerged in the mass; if with the minority he is effectively disfranchised. But if we have notional constituencies, according to a quota system by which a given number of votes, in whatever district they are cast, ensures the return of one member, then every minority of any significance will have a voice. If moreover a voter is allowed a second preference, votes will not be 'wasted' on a very popular candidate who can easily fill up his quota of votes, but will be, so to speak, saved for another minority representative.

The great advantage of the scheme for Mill was that it would return to parliament exactly those people whose voices in *On Liberty* were in danger of going unheard or undervalued:

Hundreds of able men of independent thought, who would have no chance whatever of being chosen by the majority of any existing constituency, have by their writings, or their exertions in some field of public usefulness, made themselves known and approved by a few persons in almost every district of the kingdom; and if every vote that would be given for them in every place could be counted for their election, they might be able to complete the number of the quota.

A very pedagogic notion, nothing less than a constituency of readers. 'In no other way', Mill claims, 'would Parliament be so certain of containing the very *élite* of the country' (E 258).

Having sketched the two central elements of his representative system, standing for expertise in legislation and critical intelligence to check and ratify its proposals, Mill adds three further refinements, all of them designed to further the ideal of an alert and vigorous public led by enlightened legislators towards the common good.

The first of these was the suffrage. Mill had been most impressed in Tocqueville's description of American democracy by the educative effects of the vote, which made every American a patriot and 'a person of cultivated intelligence' (E 274). He admitted that their 'highly cultivated' citizens tended to stay out of politics because they were outnumbered by the ignorant majority, with the result that their democracy was a political school 'from which the ablest teachers are excluded' (E 275). But with Hare's scheme that need not recur in Britain. Instead, the ordinary labourers would have their horizons widened by the experience of real political discussion, conducted by the most educated. Ideally, Mill wanted this political education to extend to all, but his fear of ignorance led him to insist that no one should have a vote who could not read or write and do simple arithmetic. He also wanted to exclude those who paid no taxes, and anyone on parish relief. Even those provisions might produce an electorate with 'too low a standard of political intelligence', and so he proposed extra votes for those whose occupations indicated a higher level of instruction. He thought this would be less invidious than a property-franchise. Finally of course he asserts that there is no more reason for excluding women from the suffrage than for excluding people for their height or the colour of their hair (E 290).

Secondly, Mill declared against the ballot. This is not as sharp a break with his heritage as some of his critics imply. James Mill had favoured secret voting, but for a special reason. Seeing how frightened the propertied classes had been before 1830, by the radical pressure for a wider suffrage and shorter parliaments, he had sought to reassure them, by laying most weight on the ballot. He argued that this alone would bring about a moral change in the existing system of representation, because it would at once oblige the candidate to stand on his own merits, and free the elector to express a conscientious preference, free of threats or bribery. The Philosophic Radicals who took this up in parliament always treated the ballot as the most practicable of the various radical reforms of the electoral system, and one which, far from threatening the dominance of the propertied classes, would tend to strengthen it, by freeing it of the suspicion of bribery and corruption. They did not envisage the ballot as a mere adjunct to universal suffrage and shorter parliaments as the Chartists did, and in the event their disagreement with the latter delayed both secret voting and suffrage extension by a generation. By 1859 when he first abjured the ballot, John Mill maintained that the chief abuses which had made it seem desirable no longer existed. The middle classes were in the ascendant, tradesmen were prosperous enough to defy customer pressure at election times, landlords no longer threatened tenants who voted for their opponents. So the ballot was no longer needed as protection for the elector; indeed it would be a positive hindrance to his function of educating the mass by his example. If elections were to be lessons in political responsibility, voting must be open. Publicity would have the elevating effect upon electors which secrecy was to have had upon his candidates in James Mill's original proposal. 'The bare fact of having to give an account of their conduct, is a powerful inducement to adhere to conduct of which at least some decent account can be given' (E 309). John Mill would not even admit that the ballot would be useful when every man and woman had the vote, because the proposition that the community could have no interest at odds with the general interest (his father's contention) 'will be found on examination to have more sound than meaning in it' (E 311).

Finally Mill condemned the doctrine of pledges, which required a parliamentary candidate to pledge himself to particular policies favoured by his supporters as a condition of his election. This was in fact a position Mill had always held, and it may even have been more in harmony with his later than with his earlier views. Radicals in the 1830s had often demanded pledges from their candidates, and among those who opposed the doctrine with a fine aristocratic disdain was the MP for Westminster, Sir Francis Burdett, who managed to combine vast popularity with a consistent refusal to demean himself by canvassing. When Mill stood as candidate for Westminster in 1865 the constituency had long lost its reputation for turbulence, but he also refused to canvass or give pledges. His reasons were not as aristocratic as Burdett's, but they were hardly less exclusive. 'Superior powers of mind and profound study are of no use, if they do not sometimes lead a person to different conclusions from those which are formed by ordinary powers of mind without study' (E 326). Electors must learn that if they wish to be served in parliament by able men, they must not fetter them with conditions. 'A man of conscience and known ability should insist on full freedom to act as he in his own judgement deems best; and should not consent to serve on any other terms' (E 332). Mill as a candidate never had to face a mob as Burdett had, but in his works he had given some hostages to fortune. At a meeting of non-electors which he had, very reluctantly, consented to address, he was confronted with a placard bearing his own words: 'The lower classes, though mostly habitual liars, are ashamed of lying.' He was asked if he had written them. He replied calmly that he had. The audience rose and cheered.

There are other proposals in *Representative Government*, notably on second chambers and local government, which are of interest, but cannot detain us here. Enough has perhaps been said to show that the book closely follows and illustrates the argument of *On Liberty*. If the political system they both point to is élitist, it is so only in the tautological sense that any educational system comprising teachers and taught is élitist. Mill remained loyal to Bentham's and his father's conviction that politics could be made a science, but he could never consent to its being a recondite study inaccessible to the ordinary man or woman. He shared his father's powerful didacticism and could only reconcile himself to forms of expert guidance if the experts justified their leadership by teaching; and to popular compliance if the people were actively engaged in learning and improving themselves. Reading the two books against the background of Victorian politics one may wonder why Mill, fearing popular majorities and mass mediocrity as he did, was not more willing to acquiesce in a representative system which, as we now see, enjoyed a remarkably high level of political debate, high standards of probity among public men, and a record of earnest philanthropy and reform. A brief explanation, and a tentative one, would be Mill's intellectualism. He could not conceal his contempt for stupidity, but he had no great confidence in contemporary manifestations of intellect. To draw comfort from human stupidity and conservatism like Bagehot, or to exploit them like Disraeli, would have been unthinkable treachery to his own principles of energetic asceticism. But pursuing those principles meant a perpetual war against both the privileged and the poor, or what he now, reviving his father's phrase, called the Few and the Many. The Few must be persuaded to shed any arrangements which would shore up their power or perpetuate their influence beyond their strict deserts. The Many must consent to be placed in situations which would call forth their self-improving energies and help them spurn short-term gratifications. It was an uncomfortable programme which made few converts even in the Liberal party, where its puritanism was likely to have the strongest appeal.

Even in the cause of feminism, where he became something of a leader with a following, his views are a strange blend of abstract deduction and subjective feeling. The *Subjection of Women* was written in Avignon in the winter of 1860–1, and it belongs in mood with the essay *On Liberty*. But Mill did not publish it until events (notably the 73 votes for his amendment to the second Reform Bill proposing votes for women, in May 1867) made him feel opinion was turning his way. It was published in 1869. It is the most passionate and autobiographical of his pamphlets, his final attempt to reconcile utilitarianism with the most romantic experience of his life.

The first half of the essay is an environmentalist polemic against the view that women's legal and political disabilities stem from any kind of natural inferiority to men. Mill denies altogether the force of any arguments from experience, except indeed in the case of vigorous queens, where he claims the evidence is on his side. Men, he holds, have kept women in subjection down the ages, and what they call 'natural' feminine behaviour really means 'customary' (E 440). Until we know more of 'the laws of the influence of circumstances on character' (the unfinished ethology) the common opinions on female nature are merely reflections of male dominance and afford no justification for legal inequalities. Only in conditions of complete freedom of choice will it be possible to discover what each sex is best at doing. Meanwhile, as virtue only derives from experience of consequences, a situation in which only one of the parties enjoys freedom of choice, is morally bad for both. So the family, far from being a refuge of love and trust, is actually an arena for male dominance, a 'school of despotism'. If it is really to be a school of virtue, it must be more like a business partnership, which each party enters with a clear idea of the services owed and the benefits due. But that can never be achieved until women participate on equal terms in the making of the laws under which they live. This part of the argument is purely utilitarian: Mill demands votes for women in exactly the same way as James Mill demanded them for 'the Many', as the only security against oppression by 'the Few'.

When he turns to argue that women are fit for most of the jobs men do, however, Mill reveals a more romantic attitude, perhaps more calculated to have made converts among women themselves. He allows, as 'admitted points of superiority' of women over men, that they are more practical, and have greater nervous susceptibility, greater mental mobility (that is, they can do more things at once) and more intuition. This last Mill carefully defines 'a rapid and correct insight into present fact (E 494). It is obvious that the 'really superior woman' who possesses these qualities is modelled on Harriet Mill. But she needs a partner. Her intuition cannot be effective until a person whose mind has had the requisite discipline 'takes it in hand, tests it, gives it a scientific or practical form, and fits it into its place among the existing truths of philosophy and science' (E 511). It was an improved version of the partnership of poet and logician which Mill had envisaged in his relations with Carlyle.

But if women have special qualities, should they not have special roles too? Here Mill's romanticism is reined in by his utilitarianism. He warms to the idea of women offering men an ideal to strive for, and he calls medieval chivalry 'the acme of the influence of women's sentiments on the cultivation of mankind' (E 529); but he wants women not only passively to inspire men' s activities but to share them. So he argues that it is their exclusion from the benefits of education which has confined them to certain pursuits, and ensured that even in those they do harm. They are fond of philanthropy, for example; but conceive it to consist of religious proselytism and charity. The first generates religious discord; the other mistakes immediate for long-term benefit. A proper education will enable them to use their energies better. Mill's severest censure falls on the way a poorly educated woman married to a well-educated man will drag him down. (Here one is irresistibly reminded of the suppressed passage of the *Autobiography* about his mother.) This is why 'young men of the greatest promise cease to improve as soon as they marry, and, not improving, inevitably degenerate'. The only tolerable marriage is between equals, each enjoying 'the luxury of looking up to the other' and having 'alternately the pleasure of leading and being led in the path of development' (E 540–1). As children are mentioned only in passing as 'hostages to Mrs Grundy', Mill can skirt the whole contentious subject of divorce. For him the main purpose of the dowdy and ascetic partnership, and its sole gratification, is the mental improvement of the parties and of society at large.

351

Conclusion

Mill has often been treated as the quintessential Victorian liberal, but this is due more to his position in academic syllabuses than to his actual reception by his contemporaries. He was an assiduous and conscientious MP for the short time he was in parliament, but he was never a party man, and indeed political parties play no positive role in his writings. For the aristocratic Whig tradition, which gave liberal politics its constitutional experience and its historical pedigree, he had an inherited antipathy. But having, as he himself said, no religious belief, he was also cut off from the much larger number for whom liberalism chiefly meant membership of one of the many Protestant sects. So among the politicians he was always marked out by what Gladstone called 'the high independent thought of a recluse'.

Even as a political thinker he baffled as many liberals as he converted. No one in the Bentham circle had been more thoroughly imbued with its doctrine and outlook, and despite all the influences, reactionary and romantic, which modified individual doctrines, Mill retained the abstract, schematic cast of mind of his teachers. In fact, while other Philosophic Radicals shed their doctrine and were reconciled with the institutions they had once set out to change, Mill tended as he grew older to return to the aims of Bentham and his father. We find him in the 1860s defending the *History of British India* against the criticisms of its second editor, re-editing his father's work as if it was about to undergo a revival, and in the *Examination of Sir William Hamilton's Philosophy* engaging in a fierce polemic with a man long dead in a way reminiscent of his father's *Fragment on Mackintosh*. Here and there he would differ from his father's views, in general terms and without naming him, but the overall theme is the same in the writings of father and son: that the ideal government would be one of philosophers earnestly engaged in educating and improving their fellow-citizens.

352

This habit of rehearsing the theoretical debates of his youth gave his treatment of contemporary issues an odd slant which puzzled would-be allies who did not see to what extent he had cast his arguments in the form of a debate with his teachers. At the same time his vision of his youth as a heroic age when 'open, fearless characters, and logical, consistent intellects' had 'adorned the thinking world' (E 42), and his conviction that the society of his middle age was hopelessly timid and mediocre, cut him off from the preoccupations of the younger generation. He does not seem to have realized the importance for that generation of Darwin's *Origin of Species*, which appeared in the same year as *On Liberty* and not only did more than associationism to undermine religious belief, but also had wide implications for international relations. Not surprisingly therefore some of the younger liberals found his idiom strange and his proposals irrelevant. It is significant that the most penetrating critics of his views in his lifetime or shortly after his death, such as Bagehot, Goldwin Smith, J. F. Stephen, or W. S. Jevons, were all liberals.

Yet Mill's reputation survived these attacks, and it is not hard to see why. We may read James Mill's *Essay on Government* now mainly because it was attacked by Macaulay, but we do not read *On Liberty* because it was attacked by J. F. Stephen. The very abstraction which made it hard for Mill's contemporaries to know what line he would take on a particular issue, has helped give him a wider readership since, not merely in Britain but everywhere in the English-speaking world. Few English philosophers have been so accessible to the general reader. There are several reasons for this.

One is that Mill was a very self-conscious writer, for all the abstraction of his subject-matter. His *Autobiography* in its final form is so purged of feeling that it reads like an educational treatise; but his theoretical treatises contain passages which throb with feeling. The reason is that difficult problems in Mill' s work are seldom treated as mere matters of technical complexity, but always related to a wider moral or social issue. His supposed eclecticism is really no more than a reflection of the division of labour in academic life, which leads specialists to concentrate on particular aspects and neglect the rest. Recent work has shown pretty conclusively the unity of conception that underlies the whole, and this has reminded us what an individual writer he is. Not everyone will be attracted by the personality, but no one can deny one feature which accounts for Mill's appeal, his fair-mindedness. One lasting effect of that period of 'practical eclecticism' in his twenties was that Mill always practised the advice he gave to Bertrand Russell's father, to try to think of an opponent as a man climbing the hill on the other side. He often puts an opponent's case with such clarity and force as almost to weaken his own reply, and if in some of his later writings one finds a note of dogmatism now and again, that is surely because they date from a period when Mill's social circle was restricted and he was cut off from the intellectual variety on which he flourished and from which so much of his best work stems.

This brings us to the third reason for Mill's wide appeal. He had the intuitive (he would have said acquired) tact of a great teacher, which shows in his extraordinary skill at expounding difficult problems in a lucid and attractive way. His major works, *A System of Logic* and the *Principles of Political Economy*, though surrounded with an undergrowth of commentary which makes them look impenetrable, are in fact set out in a most inviting manner, like the best introductory courses of lectures. For some reason economists resent the fact that Mill sacrificed originality to the aim of making their subject attractive to generations of students, but the lay reader can have no doubt that this is an advantage. The *Logic* too had an enormous impact, which is best shown by its reception in those two strongholds of clericalism, Oxford and Cambridge. To young men perplexed by the waning authority of the Church on the one hand and the onset of democracy on the other, Mill's own quest for certainty had an obvious appeal. He was, as the legal writer A. V. Dicey put it, 'a teacher created for, and assured of a welcome in, an age of transition'. It was this function as a teacher which gave Mill his influence with the men of letters of the next generation, men like John Morley and Leslie Stephen. It was through them that Benthamic utilitarianism, which began its career as the creed of a small coterie, was brought into the mainstream of English liberalism.

Note on sources

Mill's remark on p. 250 is recorded by Caroline Fox, in H. N. Pym, *Memories of Old Friends* (1882), p. 85. The quotations from Bentham on pp. 251–5 are from *Introduction to the Principles of Morals and Legislation* [1789], edited by J. H. Burns and H. L. A. Hart (London, 1970), pp. 293, 188, and 292 and from *Of Laws in General*, edited by H. L. A. Hart (London, 1970), pp. 235 and 284. Bentham's comment on his prisoners (p. 256) is quoted by J. Dinwiddy in 'The Classical Economists and the Utilitarians' in E. K. Bramsted and K. J. Melhuish (eds), *Western Liberalism: a History in Documents from Locke to Croce* (1978), p. 21. Quotations from Ricardo on pp. 258 and 260 are from Ricardo's *Works*, edited by P. Sraffa (Cambridge 1962–6), viii, p. 184; i, p. 93; and viii, p. 208. James Mill's remark quoted on pp. 266 is from the same work, ix, p. 332. Keynes's remark on Ricardo's influence, quoted on p. 261, is from the *General Theory in Collected Writings* (1973), vii, pp. 32–3. James Mill's *Essay on Government* and Macaulay's criticism of it, on pp. 265, 270, and 300–1 are in J. Lively and J. C. Rees (eds), *Utilitarian Logic and Politics: James Mill's 'Essay on Government', Macaulay's Critique and the Ensuing Debate* (Oxford, 1978), pp. 73, 94, 101, 128, and 167. Other quotations from James Mill are: pp. 266 and 268, from the *Essay on Education*, in W. H. Burston (ed.), *James Mill on Education* (Cambridge, 1969), p. 71; pp. 269 and 270, from the *Fragment on Mackintosh* (2nd ed., 1876), pp. 164, 270, and 289–90; and p. 278, from my selection of the *History of British India* (Chicago, 1975), p. 190. The quotation from Bentham on p. 279 is from the *Rationale of Reward*, in *Works*, edited by J. Bowring, ii, p. 213. Coleridge is quoted on pp. 285 and 286 from T. Colmer's edition of *On the Constitution of the Church and State*, Vol. x of the *Collected Works*, edited by K. Coburn (Princeton and London, 1976), pp. 45 and 69. Whewell is quoted on p. 299 from *Philosophy of the Inductive Sciences* (2nd ed., 1847), p. 42. Harriet Mill's remark given on p. 327 is from M.

St.J. Packe's *The Life of John Stuart Mill* (London, 1954), p.338. Dicey's tribute to Mill in the last paragraph of this book is given in C. Harvie, *The Lights of Liberalism: University Liberals and the Challenge of Democracy 1860–86* (London, 1976), p. 40.

Further reading

For the serious student of Mill the great edition of the *Collected Works of John Stuart Mill* now being edited under the general direction of Professor J. M. Robson at Toronto is indispensable. The 21 volumes so far published include all Mill's letters and major works. Two offshoots of the Toronto edition offer as full a guide to writings about Mill as can be found: Michael Laine's *Bibliography of Works on John Stuart Mill* (Toronto, 1982) and the biennial *Mill News Letter*, the former listing everything of importance to 1978, the latter current work. What follows is a selection of work I have found useful.

The best biography of Mill is still M. St.J. Packe's *The Life of John Stuart Mill* (London, 1954), though it is better on the man than his work. A good general study of Mill's thought is J. M. Robson, *The Improvement of Mankind: the Social and Political Thought of John Stuart Mill* (Toronto and London, 1968). Alan Ryan's *J. S. Mill* in the Routledge Author Guides Series (1974) is excellent.

The background to the utilitarian movement is best studied in Élie Halévy's *The Growth of Philosophic Radicalism*, trans. Mary Morris (London, 1928). But Halévy was not strong on the Scottish background on which much recent work has been done. For this *That Noble Science of Politics: a Study in Nineteenth Century Politics* by Stefan Collini, Donald Winch, and John Burrow (Cambridge, 1983) is suggestive and important. Halévy's book hardly deals with the movement after 1815: that is the subject of W. Thomas, *The Philosophical Radicals: Nine Studies in Theory and Practice, 1817–1841* (Oxford, 1979). *The English Utilitarians and India* by Eric Stokes (Oxford, 1959) is a fine study. Bentham's work continues to baffle elucidation and absorb public funds, and there are no introductions to it which are both comprehensive and simple, but J. Steintrager's *Bentham* (London, 1977) is clear and brief, Ross Harrison's of the same title (London, 1983) more difficult. *Bentham and Bureaucracy* by L. J. Hume (Cambridge, 1981) is important. Hostile views of Bentham are G. Himmelfarb's essay in *Victorian Minds* (London, 1968) and Charles F. Bahmueller, *The National Charity Company: Jeremy Bentham's Silent Revolution* (Berkeley and Los Angeles, 1982). Ricardian economics is the subject of a vast literature. I have gained most from J. A. Schumpeter's grand, rambling *History of the Economic Analysis* (London, 1954), supplemented by D. P. O'Brien, *The Classical Economists* (Oxford, 1975). D. Winch's introduction to his selection of J. S. Mill's *Principles of Political Economy* (London, 1970) is excellent. P. Schwartz, *The New Political Economy of J. S. Mill* (London, 1968) is the most comprehensive study to date. Ricardian methodology is well analysed by M. Blaug, *The Methodology of Economics: or how Economists Explain* (Cambridge, 1980).

Mill's reception of romantic poetry is most fully dealt with by F. P. Sharpless, *The Literary Criticism of J. S. Mill* (The Hague, 1967). His debt to the Saint-Simonians is efficiently surveyed in I. W. Mueller, *J. S. Mill and French Thought* (Urbana, 1956). R. K. P. Pankhurst's *The Saint Simonians Carlyle and Mill* (London, 1957) is vivid and entertaining. F. A. Hayek's *The Counter-Revolution of Science: Studies in the Abuse of Reason* (Glencoe, Ill., 1952) is a classic if hostile treatment of Saint-Simon and Comte.

On the origins of Mill's *System of Logic*, Oskar A. Kubitz's *Development of J. S. Mill's System of Logic* (Urbana, 1932) is still of historical interest. On the *Logic*'s relation to recent work, Alan Ryan's *The Philosophy of John Stuart Mill* (1970) is brilliant. A pungently expressed view of Mill's inductivism against current conceptions of scientific method is Sir P. Medawar's in *Pluto's Republic* (Oxford, 1984), pp. 73–135.

On Liberty has been more studied than any of Mill's other works. The closest modern analysis is C. L. Ten's *Mill on Liberty* (Oxford, 1980). John Gray's *Mill on Liberty: a Defence* (London, 1983) is the best discussion to date of the relation of liberty to utilitarianism in Mill's thought. J. F. Stephen's *Liberty, Equality, Fraternity* (1873, repr. with introduction by R. J. White, Cambridge, 1967) is much the most readable attack. More acute but for some reason less well known is W. S.

Jevons's series of articles in the *Contemporary Review* for 1877 and 1878, reprinted in *Pure Logic* (1890). Bagehot's *English Constitution* (Oxford, 1928) is acute on Mill's views on the civil service and Hare's scheme. Dennis Thompson's *John Stuart Mill and Representative Government* (Princeton, 1976) is the only full study of the book. On Mill's *Subjection of Women*, I have learned most from Julia Annas's article, 'Mill and the Subjection of Women', in *Philosophy*, vol. 52 (1977), pp. 179–94. Two important collections of articles on Mill are J. B. Schneewind (ed.), *Mill: a Collection of Critical Essays* (London, 1969) and J. M. Robson and M. Laine (eds.), *James and John Stuart Mill: Papers of the Centenary Conference* (Toronto, 1976).

Marx

Peter Singer

Preface

There are many books on Marx, but a good brief introduction to his thought is still hard to find. Marx wrote at such enormous length, on so many different subjects, that it is not easy to see his ideas as a whole. I believe that there is a central idea, a vision of the world, which unifies all of Marx's thought and explains what would otherwise be puzzling features of it. In this book I try to say, in terms comprehensible to those with little or no previous knowledge of Marx's writings, what this central vision is. If I have succeeded, I need no further excuse for having added yet another book to the already abundant literature on Marx and Marxism.

For biographical details of Marx's life, I am especially indebted to David McLellan's fine work, *Karl Marx: His Life and Thought* (Macmillan, London, 1973). My view of Marx's conception of history was affected by G. A. Cohen's *Karl Marx's Theory of History: A Defence* (Oxford University Press, Oxford, 1979), although I do not accept all the conclusions of that challenging study. Gerald Cohen sent me detailed comments on the draft of this book, enabling me to correct several errors. Robert Heilbroner, Renata Singer and Marilyn Weltz also made helpful comments on the draft, for which I am grateful.

In the interest of clear prose I have occasionally made minor amendments to the translations of Marx's works from which I have quoted.

Finally, were it not for an invitation to take part in this series from Keith Thomas, the general editor of the series, and Henry Hardy, of Oxford University Press, I would never have attempted to write this book; and were it not for a period of leave granted me by Monash University, I would never have written it.

Washington, D.C.   PETER SINGER
June 1979

Contents

Abbreviations

References in the text to Marx's writings are generally given by an abbreviation of the title, followed by a page reference. Unless otherwise indicated below, these page references are to David McLellan (ed.), *Karl Marx: Selected Writings* (Oxford University Press, Oxford, 1977).

B	'On Bakunin's *Statism and Anarchy*'
C I	*Capital*, Volume I (Foreign Languages Publishing House, Moscow, 1961)
C III	*Capital*, Volume III
CM	*Communist Manifesto*
D	Doctoral thesis
EB	*The Eighteenth Brumaire of Louis Bonaparte*
EPM	*Economic and Philosophical Manuscripts of 1844*
G	*Grundrisse* (translated M. Nicolaus, Penguin, Harmondsworth, 1973)
GI	*The German Ideology*
GP	'Critique of the Gotha Program'
I	'Towards a Critique of Hegel's *Philosophy of Right*: Introduction'
J	'On the Jewish Question'
M	'On James Mill' (notebook)
MC	Letters and miscellaneous writings cited in David McLellan, *Karl Marx: His Life and Thought* (Macmillan, London, 1973)
P	Preface to *A Contribution to the Critique of Political Economy*
PP	*The Poverty of Philosophy*
R	Correspondence with Ruge of 1843
T	'Theses on Feurerbach'
WLC	*Wage Labour and Capital*
WPP	'Wages, Price and Profit' (in K. Marx, F. Engels, *Selected Works*, Foreign Languages Publishing House, Moscow, 1951)

1 A Life and its impact

Marx's impact can only be compared with that of religious figures like Jesus or Muhammad. Nearly four out of every ten people alive today live under governments which consider themselves Marxist and claim—however implausibly—to use Marxist principles to decide how the nation shall be run. In these countries Marx is a kind of secular Jesus: his writings are the ultimate source of truth and authority; his image is everywhere reverently displayed. The lives of hundreds of millions of people have been deeply affected by Marx's legacy.

Nor has Marx's influence been limited to communist societies. Conservative governments have ushered in social reforms to cut the ground from under revolutionary Marxist opposition movements. Conservatives have also reacted in less benign ways: Mussolini and Hitler were helped to power by conservatives who saw their rabid nationalism as the answer to the Marxist threat. And even when there is no threat of an internal revolution, the existence of a foreign Marxist enemy serves to justify governments in increasing arms spending and restricting individual rights in the name of national security.

On the level of thought rather than practical politics, Marx's contribution is equally evident. Can anyone now think about society without reference to Marx's insights into the links between economic and intellectual life? Marx's ideas brought about modern sociology, transformed the study of history, and profoundly affected philosophy, literature and the arts. In this sense of the term—admittedly a very loose sense—we are all Marxists now.

What were the ideas that had such far-reaching effects? That is the subject of this book. But first, a little about the man who had these ideas.

* * *

Karl Marx was born in Trier, in the German Rhineland, in 1818. His parents, Heinrich and Henrietta, were of Jewish origin but became nominally Protestant in order to make life easier for Heinrich to practise law. The family was comfortably off without being really wealthy; they held liberal, but not radical, views on religion and politics.

Marx's intellectual career began badly when, at the age of seventeen, he went to study law at the University of Bonn. Within a year he had been imprisoned for drunkenness and slightly wounded in a duel. He also wrote love poems to his childhood sweetheart, Jenny von Westphalen. His father had soon had enough of this 'wild rampaging' as he called it, and decided that Karl should transfer to the more serious University of Berlin.

In Berlin Marx's interests became more intellectual, and his studies turned from law to philosophy. This did not impress his father: 'degeneration in a learned dressing-gown with uncombed hair has replaced degeneration with a beer glass' he wrote in a reproving letter (MC 33). It was, however, the death rather than the reproaches of his father that forced Marx to think seriously about a career—for without his father's income the family could not afford to support him indefinitely. Marx therefore began work on a doctoral thesis with a view to getting a university lectureship. The thesis itself was on a remote and scholarly topic—some contrasts in the philosophies of Democritus and Epicurus—but Marx saw a parallel between these ancient disputes and the debate about the interpretation of the philosophy of Hegel which was at that time the meeting ground of divergent political views in German thought.

The thesis was submitted and accepted in 1841, but no university lectureship was offered. Instead Marx became interested in journalism. He wrote on social, political and philosophical issues for a newly-founded liberal newspaper, the *Rhenish Gazette (Rheinische Zeitung)*. His articles were appreciated and his contacts with the newspaper increased to such an extent that when the editor resigned late in 1842, Marx was the obvious replacement.

Through no fault of his own, Marx's editorship was brief. As interest in the newspaper increased, so did the attentions of the Prussian government censor. A series of articles by Marx on the poverty of wine-growers in the Moselle valley may have been considered especially inflammatory; in any case, the government decided to suppress the paper.

Marx was not sorry that the authorities had, as he put it in a letter to a friend, 'given me back my liberty' (MC 66). Freed from editorial duties, he began work on a critical study of Hegel's political philosophy. He also had a more pressing concern: to marry Jenny, to whom he had now been engaged for seven years. And he wanted to leave Germany, where he could not express himself freely. The problem was that he needed money to get married, and now he was again unemployed. But his reputation as a promising young writer stood him in good stead; he was invited to become co-editor of a new publication, the *German-French Annals* (*Deutsch-Französische Jahrbücher*). This provided him with enough income to marry and also settled the question of where to go—for, as its name implies, the new publication was supposed to draw French as well as German writers and readers.

Karl and Jenny Marx arrived in Paris in the autumn of 1843 and soon began mixing with the radicals and socialists who congregated in this centre of progressive thought. Marx wrote two articles for the *Annals*. The publication was, however, even more short-lived than the newspaper had been. The first issue failed to attract any French contributors and so was scarcely noticed in Paris; while copies sent to Prussia were confiscated by the authorities. The financial backers of the venture withdrew. Meanwhile, in view of the communist and revolutionary ideas expressed in the confiscated first issue, the Prussian government issued a warrant for the arrest of the editors. Now Marx could not return to Germany; he was a political refugee. Luckily he received a sizeable amount of money from the former shareholders of the *Rhenish Gazette*, so he had no need of a job.

Throughout 1844 Marx worked at articulating his philosophical position. This was philosophy in a very broad sense, including politics, economics and a conception of the historical processes at work in the world. By now Marx was prepared to call himself a communist—which was nothing very unusual in those days in Paris, for socialists and communists of all sorts could be found there then.

In the same year the friendship between Marx and Engels began. Friedrich Engels was the son of a German industrialist who also owned a cotton factory in Manchester; but Engels had become, through contacts with the same German intellectual circles that Marx moved in, a revolutionary socialist. He contributed an article to the *Annals* which deeply affected Marx's own thinking about economics. So it was not surprising that when Engels visited Paris he and Marx should meet. Very soon they began to collaborate on a pamphlet—or rather Engels thought it was going to be a pamphlet. He left his contribution, about fifteen pages long, with Marx when he departed from Paris. The 'pamphlet' appeared under the title *The Holy Family* in 1845. Almost 300 pages long, it was Marx's first published book.

Meanwhile the Prussian government was putting pressure on the French to do something about the German communists living in Paris. An expulsion order was issued and the Marx family, which now included their first child, named Jenny like her mother, moved to Brussels.

To obtain permission to stay in Brussels, Marx had to promise not to take part in politics. He soon breached this undertaking by organising a Communist Correspondence Committee which was intended to keep communists in different countries in touch with each other. Nevertheless Marx was able to stay in Brussels for three years. He signed a contract with a publisher to produce a book consisting of a critical analysis of economics and politics. The contract called for the book to be ready by the summer of 1845. It was the first of many deadlines missed by the book that was to become *Capital*. The publisher had, no doubt to his lasting regret, undertaken to pay royalties in advance of receiving the manuscript. (The contract was eventually cancelled, and the unfortunate man was still trying to get his money back in 1871.)

Engels also now began to help Marx financially, so the family had enough to live on.

Marx and Engels saw a good deal of each other. Engels came to Brussels, and then the two of them travelled to England for six weeks to study economics in Manchester, the heart of the new industrial age. (Meanwhile Jenny was bearing Marx their second daughter, Laura.) On his return Marx decided to postpone his book on economics. Before setting forth his own positive theory, he wanted to demolish alternative ideas then fashionable in German philosophical and socialist circles. The outcome was *The German Ideology*, a long and often turgid volume which was turned down by at least seven publishers and finally abandoned, as Marx later wrote, 'to the gnawing criticism of the mice'.

In addition to writing *The German Ideology*, Marx spent a good deal of these years attacking those who might have been his allies. He wrote another polemical work attacking the leading French socialist, Proudhon. Though theoretically opposed to what he called 'a superstitious attitude to authority' (MC 172), Marx was so convinced of the importance of his own ideas that he could not tolerate opinions different from his own. This led to frequent rows in the Communist Correspondence Committee and in the Communist League which followed it.

Marx had an opportunity to make his own ideas the basis of communist activities when he went to London, to attend a Congress of the newly formed Communist League in December 1847. In lengthy debates he defended his view of how communism would come about; and in the end he and Engels were commissioned with the task of putting down the doctrines of the League in simple language. The result was *The Communist Manifesto*, published in February 1848, which was to become the classic outline of Marx's theory.

The *Manifesto* was not, however, an immediate success. Before it could be published the situation in Europe had been transformed by the French revolution of 1848, which triggered off revolutionary movements all over Europe. The new French government revoked Marx's expulsion order, just as the nervous Belgian government gave him twenty-four hours to get out of the country. The Marxes went first to Paris and then, following news of revolution in Berlin, returned to Germany. In Cologne Marx raised money to start a radical newspaper, the *New Rhenish Gazette (Neue Rheinische Zeitung)*. The paper supported the broad democratic movements that had made the revolution. It flourished for a time, but as the revolution fizzled out the Prussian monarchy reasserted itself and Marx was compelled to set out on his travels again. He tried Paris, only to be expelled once more; so on 24 August 1849 he sailed for England to wait until a more thoroughgoing revolution would allow him to return to Germany.

Marx lived in London for the rest of his life. The family was at first quite poor. They lived in two rooms in Soho. Jenny was pregnant with their fourth child (a son, Edgar, had been born in Brussels). Nevertheless Marx was active politically with the Communist League. He wrote on the revolution in France and its aftermath, and attempted to organise support for members of the Cologne Committee of the League, who had been put on trial by the Prussian authorities. When the Cologne group were convicted, notwithstanding Marx's clear demonstration that the police evidence was forged, Marx decided that the League's existence was 'no longer opportune' and the League dissolved itself.

For a time Marx now lived an isolated existence, unconnected with any organised political group. He spent his time reading omnivorously and engaging in doctrinal squabbles with other left-wing German refugees. His correspondence is full of complaints of being able to afford nothing but bread and potatoes and little enough of those. He even applied for a job as a railway clerk, but was turned down because his handwriting was illegible. He was a regular client of the pawnshops. Yet Marx's friends, especially Engels, were generous in their gifts, and it may be that Marx's poverty was due to poor management rather than insufficient income. Jenny's maid, Helene Demuth, still lived with the family, as she was to do until Marx's death. (She was also the mother of Marx's illegitimate son, Frederick, who was born in 1851; to avoid scandal, the boy was raised by foster parents.)

These were years of personal tragedy for the family: their fourth child had died in infancy; Jenny became pregnant again, and again the child died within a year. The worst blow was the death of their son Edgar, apparently of consumption, at the age of eight.

From 1852 Marx received a steadier income. The editor of the *New York Tribune*, whom he had met in Cologne, asked him to write for the newspaper. Marx agreed, and over the next ten years the *Tribune* published an article by Marx almost every week (although some were secretly written by Engels). In 1856 the financial situation improved still further when Jenny received two inheritances. Now the family could move from the cramped Soho rooms to an eight-room house near Hampstead Heath, scene of regular Sunday picnics for all the family. In this year Marx's third daughter, Eleanor—nicknamed Tussy—was born. Although Jenny was to become pregnant one more time, the child was stillborn. From this time on, therefore, the family consisted of three children: Jenny, Laura and Eleanor. Marx was a warm and loving father to them.

All this time Marx was expecting a revolution to break out in the near future. His most productive period, in 1857–8, resulted from his mistaking an economic depression for the onset of the final crisis of capitalism. Worried that his ideas would be overtaken by events, Marx began, as he wrote to Engels, 'working madly through the nights' in order to have the outlines of his work clear 'before the deluge' (MC 290). In six months he wrote more than 800 pages of a draft of *Capital*—indeed the draft covers much more ground than *Capital* as it finally appeared. In 1859 Marx published a small portion of his work on economics under the title *Critique of Political Economy*. The book did not contain much of Marx's original ideas (except for a now famous summary of his intellectual development in the preface) and its appearance was greeted with silence.

Instead of getting the remaining, more original sections of his manuscript ready for publication, Marx was distracted by a characteristic feud with a left-wing politician and editor, Karl Vogt. Marx claimed that Vogt was in the pay of the French government. Lawsuits resulted, Vogt called Marx a forger and blackmailer, and Marx replied with a 200-page book of satirical anti-Vogt polemic. Years later, Marx was shown to have been right; but the affair cost him a good deal of money and for eighteen months prevented him writing anything of lasting value.

There was also a more serious reason for Marx's tardiness in completing his work on economics. The International Workingmen's Association—later known as the First International—was founded at a public meeting in London in 1864. Marx accepted an invitation to the meeting; his election to the General Council ended his isolation from political activities. Marx's forceful intellect and strength of personality soon made him a dominant figure in the association. He wrote its inaugural address and drew up its statutes. He had, of course, considerable differences with the trade unionists who formed the basis of the English section of the International, but he showed rare diplomacy in accommodating these differences while trying constantly to draw the working-class members of the association closer to his own long-term perspective.

In 1867 Marx finally completed the first volume of *Capital*. Again, the initial reaction was disappointing. Marx's friends were enthusiastic and did what they could to get the book reviewed. Engels alone wrote seven different—but always favourable—reviews for seven German newspapers. But wider recognition came slowly. In fact Marx became a well-known figure not because of *Capital*, but through the publication, in 1871, of *The Civil War in France*. Marx wrote this as an address to the International on the Paris Commune, the worker's uprising which, after the defeat of France at the hands of Prussia, took over and ruled the city of Paris for two months. The International had had virtually nothing to do with this, but it was linked with the Commune in the popular mind. Marx's address reinforced these early suspicions of an international communist conspiracy, and Marx himself immediately gained a notoriety which, as he wrote to a friend, 'really

does me good after the tedious twenty-year idyll in my den'
(MC 402).

The ruthless suppression of the Commune weakened the
International. Disagreements that had simmered beneath the
surface now rose to the top. At the Congress of 1872, Marx
found that he had lost control. A motion restricting the powers
of the General Council was carried over his strong opposition.
Rather than see the organisation fall into the hands of his
enemies, Marx proposed that the General Council should
henceforth be based in New York. The motion was passed by a
narrow margin. It meant, as Marx must have known it would,
the end of the First International; for with communications as
they then were, it was utterly impractical to run the largely
European organisation from across the Atlantic.

By this time Marx was fifty-four years old and in poor health.
The remaining ten years of his life were less eventful. Further
inheritances had by now ended any threat of poverty. In many
respects the Marxes' life now was like that of any comfortably-
off bourgeois family: they moved to a larger house, spent a
good deal on furnishing it, sent their children to a ladies'
seminary, and travelled to fashionable Continental spas. Marx
even claimed to have made money on the stock exchange—
which did not stop him asking for, and receiving, further gifts
of money from Engels.

Marx's ideas were spreading at last. By 1871 a second edition
of *Capital* was needed. A Russian translation appeared in 1872—
Marx was very popular among Russian revolutionaries—and a
French translation soon followed. Though *Capital* was not
translated into English during Marx's lifetime (like his other
books, it was written in German) Marx's growing reputation,
even among the untheoretical English, was indicated by his
inclusion in a series of pamphlets on 'Leaders in Modern
Thought'. Marx and Engels kept up a correspondence with
revolutionaries throughout Europe who shared their views.
Otherwise Marx worked desultorily on the second and third
volumes of *Capital*, but never got them ready for publication.
This task was left to Engels after Marx's death. The last
important work Marx wrote arose from a congress held in

Gotha, in Germany, in 1875. The purpose of the congress was to unite rival German socialist parties, and to do this a common platform was drawn up. Neither Marx nor Engels was consulted about this platform—known as 'the Gotha Program'—and Marx was angry at the many deviations it contained from what he considered to be scientific socialism. He wrote a set of critical comments on the Program, and attempted to circulate it among German socialist leaders. After Marx's death this *Critique of the Gotha Program* was published and recognised as one of Marx's rare statements on the organisation of a future communist society. At the time, however, Marx's critique had no influence, and the planned unification went ahead.

In his last years the satisfaction Marx might have gained from his growing reputation was overshadowed by personal sorrows. Marx's elder daughters, Jenny and Laura, married and had children, but none of Laura's three children lived beyond the age of three. Jenny's firstborn also died in infancy, although she then had five more, all but one of whom survived to maturity. But in 1881 the older Jenny, Marx's dearly beloved wife, died after a long illness. Marx was now ill and lonely. In 1882 his daughter Jenny became seriously ill; she died in January 1883. Marx never got over this loss. He developed bronchitis and died on 14 March 1883.

2 The Young Hegelian

Little more than a year after his arrival as a student in Berlin, Marx wrote to his father that he was now attaching himself 'ever more closely to the current philosophy'. This 'current philosophy' was the philosophy of G. W. F. Hegel, who had taught at the University of Berlin from 1818 until his death in 1831. Years later, Friedrich Engels described Hegel's influence in the period when he and Marx began to form their ideas:

> ... the Hegelian system covered an incomparably greater domain than any earlier system and developed in this domain a wealth of thought which is astounding even today ...
>
> One can imagine what a tremendous effect this Hegelian system must have produced in the philosophy-tinged atmosphere of Germany. It was a triumphal procession which lasted for decades and which by no means came to a standstill on the death of Hegel. On the contrary, it was precisely from 1830 to 1840 that 'Hegelianism' reigned most exclusively, and to a greater or lesser extent infected even its opponents.

The close attachment to this philosophy Marx formed in 1837 was to affect his thought for the rest of his life. Writing about Hegel in 1844, Marx referred to *The Phenomenology of Mind* as 'the true birthplace and secret of his philosophy' (EPM 98). This long and obscure work is therefore the place to begin our understanding of Marx.

The German word for 'Mind' is sometimes translated as 'Spirit'. Hegel uses it to refer to the spiritual side of the universe, which appears in his writings as a kind of universal mind. My mind, your mind and the minds of every other conscious being are particular, limited manifestations of this universal mind. There has been a good deal of debate about whether this universal mind is intended to be God, or whether Hegel was, in pantheistic fashion, identifying God with the world as a whole. There is no definite answer to this question, but it seems appropriate and convenient to distinguish this universal mind from our own particular minds by writing the universal variety with a capital, as Mind.

The Phenomenology of Mind traces the development of Mind from its first appearance as individual minds, conscious but neither self-conscious nor free, to Mind as a free and fully self-conscious unity. The process is neither purely historical, nor purely logical, but a strange combination of the two. One might say that Hegel is trying to show that history is the progress of Mind along a logically necessary path, a path along which it must travel in order to reach its final goal.

The development of Mind is dialectical—a term that has come to be associated with Marx because his own philosophy has been referred to as 'dialectical materialism'. The dialectical elements of Marx's theory were taken over from Hegel, so this is a good place to see what 'dialectic' is.

Perhaps the most celebrated passage in the *Phenomenology* concerns the relationship of a master to a slave. It well illustrates what Hegel means by dialectic, and it introduces an idea echoed in Marx's view of the relationship between capitalist and worker.

Suppose we have two independent people, aware of their own independence, but not of their common nature as aspects of one universal Mind. Each sees the other as a rival, a limit to his own power over everything else. This situation is therefore unstable. A struggle ensues, in which one conquers and enslaves the other. The master/slave relationship, however, is not stable either. Although it seems at first that the master is everything and the slave nothing, it is the slave who works and by his work changes the natural world. In this assertion of his own nature and consciousness over the natural world, the slave achieves satisfaction and develops his own self-consciousness, while the master becomes dependent on his slave. The ultimate outcome must therefore be the liberation of the slave, and the overcoming of the initial conflict between the two independent beings.

This is only one short section of the *Phenomenology*, the whole of which traces the development of Mind as it overcomes contradiction or opposition. Mind is inherently universal, but in its limited form, as the minds of particular people, it is not aware of its universal nature—that is, particular people do not see themselves as all part of the one universal Mind. Hegel describes this as a situation in which Mind is 'alienated' from itself—that is, people (who are manifestations of Mind) take other people (who are also manifestations of Mind) as something foreign, hostile and external to themselves, whereas they are in fact all part of the same great whole.

Mind cannot be free in an alienated state, for in such a state it appears to encounter opposition and barriers to its own complete development. Since Mind is really infinite and all-encompassing, opposition and barriers are only appearances, the result of Mind not recognising itself for what it is, but taking what is really a part of itself as something alien and hostile to itself. These apparently alien forces limit the freedom of Mind, for if Mind does not know its own infinite powers it cannot exercise these powers to organise the world in accordance with its plans.

The progress of the dialectical development of Mind in Hegel's philosophy is always progress towards freedom. 'The History of the World is none other than the progress of the consciousness of freedom,' he wrote. The *Phenomenology* is thus an immense philosophical epic, tracing the history of Mind from its first blind gropings in a hostile world to the moment when, in recognising itself as master of the universe, it finally achieves self-knowledge and freedom.

Hegel's philosophy has an odd consequence which would have been embarrassing to a more modest author. If all history is the story of Mind working towards the goal of understanding its own nature, this goal is actually reached with the completion of the *Phenomenology* itself. When Mind, manifested in the mind of Hegel, grasps its own nature, the last stage of history has been reached.

To us this is preposterous. Hegel's speculative mixture of philosophy and history has been unfashionable for a long time. It was, however, taken seriously when Marx was young. Moreover we can make sense of much of the *Phenomenology* even if we reject the notion of a universal Mind as the ultimate reality of all things. We can treat 'Universal Mind' as a collective term for all human minds. We can then rewrite the *Phenomenology* in terms of the path to human liberation. The saga of Mind then becomes the saga of the human spirit.

This is what a group of philosophers known as Young Hegelians attempted in the decade following Hegel's death. The orthodox interpretation of Hegel was that since human society is the manifestation of Mind in the world, everything is right and rational as it is. There are plenty of passages in Hegel's works which can be quoted in support of this view. At times he seems to regard the Prussian state as the supreme incarnation of Mind. Since the Prussian state paid his salary as a professor of Philosophy in Berlin, it is not surprising that the more radical Young Hegelians took the view that in these passages Hegel had betrayed his own philosophy. Among these was Marx, who wrote in his doctoral thesis: 'if a philosopher really has compromised, it is the job of his followers to use the inner core of his thought to illuminate his own superficial expressions of it' (D 13).

For the Young Hegdians the 'superficial expression' of Hegel's philosophy was his acceptance of the state of politics, religion and society in early nineteenth-century Prussia: the 'inner core' was his account of Mind overcoming alienation, reinterpreted as an account of human self-consciousness freeing itself from the illusions that prevent it schieving self-understanding and freedom.

During his student days in Berlin and for a year or two afterwards Marx was close to Bruno Bauer, a lecturer in theology and a leading Young Hegelian. Under Bauer's influence Mars seized on orthodox religion as the chief illusion standing in the way of human self-understanding. The chief weapon against this illusion was philosophy. In the Preface to his doctoral thesis, Marx wrote:

Philosophy makes no secret of it. The proclamation of Prometheus—in a word, I detest all the gods—is her own profession, her own slogan against all the gods of heaven and earth who do not recognise man's self-consciousness as the highest divinity. There shall be no other beside it. (D 12–13).

In accordance with the general method of the Young Hegelians, Bauer and Marx used Hegel's own critique of religion to reach more radical conclusions. In the *Phenomenology* Hegel referred to the Christian religion at a certain stage of its development as a form of alienation, for while God reigns in heaven, human beings inhabit an inferior and comparatively worthless 'vale of tears'. Human nature is divided between its essential nature, which is immortal and heavenly, and its non-essential nature, which is mortal, and earthly. Thus individuals see their own essential nature as having its home in another realm; they are alienated from their mortal existence and the world in which they actually live.

Hegel, treating this as a passing phase in the self-alienation of Mind, drew no practical conclusions from it. Bauer reinterpreted it more broadly as indicating the self-alienation of human beings. It was humans, he maintained, who had created this God which now seemed to have an independent existence, an existence which made it impossible for humans to regard themselves as 'the highest divinity'. This philosophical conclusion pointed to a practical task: to criticise religion and show human beings that God is their own creation, thus ending the subordination of humanity to God and the alienation of human beings from their own true nature.

So the young Hegelians thought Hegel's philosophy both mystifyingly presented and incomplete. When rewritten in terms of the real world instead of the mysterious world of Mind, it made sense. 'Mind' was read as 'human self-consciousness'. The goal of history became the liberation of humanity; but this could not be achieved until the religious illusion had been overcome.

3 From God to money

The transformation of Hegel's method into a weapon against religion was carried through most thoroughly by another radical Hegelian, Ludwig Feuerbach.

Friedrich Engels later wrote of the impact of the work that made Feuerbach famous: 'Then came Feuerbach's *Essence of Christianity* . . . One must himself have experienced the liberating effect of this book to get an idea of it. Enthusiasm was general; we all became at once Feuerbachians.' Like Bauer, Feuerbach in *The Essence of Christianity* characterised religion as a form of alienation. God, he wrote, is to be understood as the essence of the human species, externalised and projected into an alien reality. Wisdom, love, benevolence—these are really attributes of the human species, but we attribute them, in a purified form, to God. The more we enrich our concept of God in this way, however, the more we impoverish ourselves. The solution is to realise that theology is a kind of misdescribed anthropology. What we believe of God is really true of ourselves. Thus humanity can regain its essence, which in religion it has lost.

When *The Essence of Christianity* appeared, in 1841, the first meeting between Marx and Engels still lay two years ahead. The book may not have made as much of an impression on Marx as it did on Engels, for Marx had already been exposed to similar ideas through Bauer; but Feuerbach's later works, particularly his *Preliminary Theses for the Reform of Philosophy*, did have a decisive impact on Marx, triggering off the next important stage in the development of his thought.

Feuerbach's later works went beyond the criticism of religion to the criticism of Hegelian philosophy itself. Yet it was a curious form of criticism of Hegel, for Feuerbach continued to work by transforming Hegel, using Hegel's method against all philosophy in the Hegelian mode. Hegel had taken Mind as the moving force in history, and humans as manifestations of Mind. This, according to Feuerbach, locates the essence of humanity outside human beings and thus, like religion, serves to alienate humanity from itself.

More generally, Hegel and other German philosophers of the idealist school began from such conceptions as Spirit, Mind, God, the Absolute, the Infinite, and so on, treating these as ultimately real, and regarding ordinary humans and animals, tables, sticks and stones, and the rest of the finite, material world as a limited, imperfect expression of the spiritual world. Feuerbach again reversed this, insisting that philosophy must begin with the finite, material world. Thought does not precede existence, existence precedes thought.

So Feuerbach put at the centre of his philosophy neither God nor thought, but man. Hegel's tale of the progress of Mind, overcoming alienation in order to achieve freedom, was for Feuerbach a mystifying expression of the progress of human beings overcoming the alienation of both religion and philosophy itself.

Marx seized on this idea of bringing Hegel down to earth by using Hegel's methods to attack the present condition of human beings. In his brief spell as editor of the *Rhenish Gazette*, Marx had descended from the rarefied air of Hegelian philosophy to more practical issues like censorship, divorce, a Prussian law prohibiting the gathering of dead timber from forests, and the economic distress of Moselle wine growers. When the paper was suppressed Marx went back to philosophy, applying Feuerbach's technique of transformation to Hegel's political philosophy.

Marx's ideas at this stage (1843) are liberal rather than socialist, and he still thinks that a change in consciousness is all that is needed. In a letter to Arnold Ruge, a fellow Young Hegelian with whom he worked on the short-lived *German-French Annals*, Marx wrote: 'Freedom, the feeling of man's dignity, will have to be awakened again in these men. Only this feeling . . . can again transform society into a community of men to achieve their highest purposes, a democratic state.' And in a later letter to Ruge about their joint venture:

... we can express the aim of our periodical in one phrase: A self-understanding (equals critical philosophy) of the age concerning its struggles and wishes ... To have its sins forgiven, mankind has only to declare them for what they are. (R 38)

Up to this point Marx had followed Feuerbach in reinterpreting Hegel as a philosopher of man rather than Mind. His view of human beings, however, focused on their mental aspect, their thoughts and their consciousness. The first signs of a shift to his later emphasis on the material and economic conditions of human life came in an essay written in 1843 entitled 'On the Jewish Question'. The essay reviews two publications by Bruno Bauer on the issue of civil and political rights for Jews.

Marx rejects his friend's treatment of the issue as a question of religion. It is not the sabbath Jew we should consider, Marx says, but the everyday Jew. Accepting the common stereotype of Jews as obsessed with money and bargaining, Marx describes the Jew as merely a special manifestation of what he calls 'civil society's Judaism'—that is, the dominance in society of bargaining and financial interests generally. Marx therefore suggests that the way to abolish the 'problem' of Judaism is to reorganise society so as to abolish bargaining.

The importance of this essay is that it sees economic life, not religion, as the chief form of human alienation. Another German writer, Moses Hess, had already developed Feuerbach's ideas in this direction, being the first, as Engels put it, to reach communism by 'the philosophic path'. (There had, of course, been many earlier communists who were more or less philosophical—what Engels meant was the path of Hegelian philosophy.) Now Marx was heading down the same route. The following quotation from 'On the Jewish Question' reads exactly like Bauer, Feuerbach or Marx himself, a year or two earlier, denouncing religion—except that where they would have written 'God' Marx now substitutes 'money':

Money is the universal, self-constituted value of all things. Hence it has robbed the whole world, the human world as well as nature, of its proper value. Money is the alienated essence of man's labour and life, and this alien essence dominates him as he worships it. (J 60)

The final sentence points the way forward. First the Young Hegelians, including Bauer and Feuerbach, see religion as the alienated human essence, and seek to end this alienation by their critical studies of Christianity. Then Feuerbach goes beyond religion, arguing that any philosophy which concentrates on the mental rather than the material side of human nature is a form of alienation. Now Marx insists that it is neither religion nor philosophy, but *money* that is the barrier to human freedom. The obvious next step is a critical study of economics. This Marx now begins.

Before we follow this development, however, we must pause to note the emergence of another key element in Marx's work which, like economics, was to remain central to his thought and activity.

4 Enter the proletariat

We saw that when the Prussian government suppressed the newspaper he had been editing, Marx started work on a critique of Hegel's political philosophy. In 1844 he published, in the *German-French Annals*, an article entitled 'Towards a Critique of Hegel's *Philosophy of Right*: Introduction'. The critique which this article was to introduce remained unfinished, but the 'Introduction' stands alongside 'On the Jewish Question' as a milestone on the road to Marxism. For it is in this article that Marx first allocates to the working class a decisive role in the coming redemption of humanity.

The 'Introduction' starts by summarising the attack on religion made by Bauer and Feuerbach. This passage is notable for its epigrams, including the frequently quoted description of religion as 'the opium of the people', but it says nothing new. Now that human self-alienation has been unmasked in its holy form, Marx continues, it is the task of philosophy to unmask it in its unholy forms, such as law and politics. He calls for more criticism of German conditions, to allow the German people 'not even a moment of self-deception'. But for the first time— and in contrast to Bauer and Feuerbach—Marx suggests that criticism by itself is not enough:

> The weapon of criticism obviously cannot replace the criticism of weapons. Material force must be overthrown by material force. But theory also becomes a material force once it has gripped the masses. (1 69)

In his initial recognition of the role of the masses, Marx treats this role as a special feature of the German situation, not applicable to France. Whereas in France 'every class of the nation is *politically idealistic* and experiences itself first of all not as a particular class but as representing the general needs of society', in Germany practical life is 'mindless' and no class can be free 'until it is forced to be by its *immediate* condition, by *material* necessity, by its *very chains*'. Where then, Marx asks, is the positive possibility of German freedom to be found? And he answers:

> In the formation of a class with *radical chains* . . . a sphere of society having a universal character because of its universal suffering . . . a sphere, in short, that is the *complete loss* of humanity and can only redeem itself through the *total redemption of humanity*. This dissolution of society as a particular class is the *proletariat*. (i 72–3)

Marx concludes by placing the proletariat within the framework of a transformed Hegelian philosophy:

> As philosophy finds its material weapons in the proletariat, the proletariat finds its intellectual weapons in philosophy.

More explicitly:

> Philosophy cannot be actualised without the superseding of the proletariat, the proletariat cannot be superseded without the actualisation of philosophy. (i 73)

Here is the germ of a new solution to the problem of human alienation. Criticism and philosophical theory alone will not end it. A more practical force is needed, and that force is provided by the artificially impoverished working class. This lowest class of society will bring about 'the actualisation of philosophy'—by which Marx means the culmination of the philosophical and historical saga described, in a mystified form, by Hegel. The proletariat, following the lead of the new radical philosophy, will complete the dialectical process in which humans have emerged, grown estranged from themselves and become enslaved by their own alienated essence. Whereas the property-owning middle class could win freedom for themselves on the basis of rights to property—thus excluding others from the freedom they gain—the propertyless working class possess nothing but their title as human beings. Thus they can liberate themselves only by liberating all humanity.

Before 1844, to judge from his writings, Marx scarcely

noticed the existence of the proletariat; certainly he never suggested they had a part to play in overcoming alienation. Now, like a film director calling on the errand-boy to play Hamlet, Marx introduces the proletariat as the material force that will bring about the liberation of humanity. Why?

Marx did not arrive at his view of the proletariat as the result of detailed economic studies, for his economic studies were just beginning. He had read a great deal of history, but he does not buttress his position by quoting from historical sources, as he was later to do. His reasons for placing importance on the proletariat are philosophical rather than historical or economic. Since human alienation is not a problem of a particular class, but a universal problem, whatever is to solve it must have a universal character—and the proletariat, Marx claims, has this universal character in virtue of its total deprivation. It represents not a particular class of society, but all humanity.

That a situation should contain within itself the seed of its own dissolution, and that the greatest of all triumphs should come from the depths of despair—these are familiar themes in the dialectic of Hegel and his followers. (They echo, some have said, the redemption of humanity by the crucifixion of Jesus.) The proletariat fits neatly into this dialectical scenario, and one cannot help suspecting that Marx seized upon it precisely because it served his philosophical purposes so well.

To say this is not to say that when he wrote the 'Introduction' Marx knew nothing about the proletariat. He had just moved to Paris, where socialist ideas were much more advanced than in Germany. He mixed with socialist leaders of the time, living in the same house as one of the leaders of the League of the Just, a radical workers' group. His writings reflect his admiration of the French socialist workers: 'The nobility of man, he writes, 'shines forth from their toil-worn bodies' (MC 87). In giving so important a role to the proletariat, therefore, the 'Introduction' reflects a two-way process: Marx tailors his conception of the proletariat to suit his philosophy, and tailors his philosophy in accordance with his new-found enthusiasm for the working class and its revolutionary ideas.

5 The first Marxism

Marx had now developed two important new insights: that economics is the chief form of human alienation, and that the material force needed to liberate humanity from its domination by economics is to be found in the working class. Up to this stage, however, he had only made these points briefly, in essays ostensibly on other topics. The next step was to use these insights as the basis of a new and systematic world-view, one which would transform and supplant the Hegelian system and all prior transformations of it.

Marx began his critical study of economics in 1844. It was to culminate in Marx's greatest work, *Capital*, the first volume of which was published in 1867, later volumes appearing after Marx's death. So the work Marx produced in Paris, known as the *Economic and Philosophic Manuscripts of 1844*, was the first version of a project that was to occupy him, in one form or another, for the rest of his life.

The 1844 version of Marxism was not published until 1932. The manuscript consists of a number of disconnected sections, some obviously incomplete. Nevertheless we can see what Marx was trying to do. He begins with a Preface which praises Feuerbach as the author of 'the only writings since Hegel's *Phenomenology* and *Logic* containing a real theoretical revolution'. There are then sections on the economics of wages, profits and rent, in which Marx quotes liberally from the founding fathers of classical economics like J.-B. Say and Adam Smith. The point of this, as Marx explains, is to show that according to classical economics the worker becomes a commodity, the production of which is subject to the ordinary laws of supply and demand. If the supply of workers exceeds the demand for labour, wages fall and some workers starve. Wages therefore tend to the lowest possible level compatible with keeping an adequate supply of workers alive.

Marx draws another important point from the classical economists. Those who employ the workers—the capitalists—build up their wealth through the labour of their workers. They become wealthy by keeping for themselves a certain amount of the value their workers produce. Capital is nothing else but accumulated labour. The worker's labour increases the employer's capital. This increased capital is used to build bigger factories and buy more machines. This increases the division of labour. This puts more self-employed workers out of business. They must then sell their labour on the market. This intensifies the competition among workers trying to get work, and lowers wages.

All this Marx presents as deductions from the presuppositions of orthodox economics. Marx himself is not writing as an economist. He wants to rise above the level of the science of economics, which, he says, simply takes for granted such things as private property, greed, competition and so on, saying nothing about the extent to which apparently accidental circumstances are really the expression of a necessary course of development. Marx wants to ask larger questions, ignored by economists, such as 'What in the evolution of mankind is the meaning of this reduction of the greater part of mankind to abstract labour?' (By 'abstract labour' Marx means work done simply in order to earn a wage, rather than for the worker's own specific purposes. Thus making a pair of shoes because one wants a pair of shoes is not abstract labour; making a pair of shoes because that happens to be a way of getting money is.) Marx, in other words, wants to give a deeper explanation of the meaning and significance of the laws of economics.

What type of explanation does Marx have in mind? The answer is apparent from the section of the manuscripts entitled 'Alienated Labour'. Here Marx explains the implications of economics in terms closely parallel to Feuerbach's critique of religion:

The more the worker exerts himself, the more powerful becomes the alien objective world which he fashions against himself, the poorer he and his inner world become, the less there is that belongs to him. It is the same in religion. The more man attributes to God, the less he retains in himself. The worker puts his life into the object; then it no longer belongs to him but to the object ... The externalisation of the worker in his product means not only that his work becomes an object, an external existence, but also that it exists outside him, independently, alien, an autonomous power, opposed to him. The life he has given to the object confronts him as hostile and alien. (EPM 78–9)

The central point is more pithily stated in a sentence preserved in the notebooks Marx used when studying the classical economists, in preparation for the writing of the 1844 manuscripts:

It is evident that economics establishes an alienated form of social intercourse as the essential, original and natural form. (M 116)

This is the gist of Marx's objection to classical economics. Marx does not challenge the classical economists within the presuppositions of their science. Instead he takes a viewpoint outside those presuppositions and argues that private property, competition, greed and so on are to be found only in a particular condition of human existence, a condition of alienation. In contrast to Hegel, whom Marx praises for grasping the self-development of man as a process, the classical economists take the present alienated condition of human society as its 'essential, original and definitive form'. They fail to see that it is a necessary but temporary stage in the evolution of mankind.

Marx then discusses the present alienated state of humanity. One of his premises is that 'man is a species-being'. The idea is taken directly from Feuerbach, who in turn derived it from Hegel. Hegel, as we saw, told the story of human development in terms of the progress of a single Mind, of which individual human minds are particular manifestations. Feuerbach scrubbed out the super-Mind, and rewrote Hegel in less mysterious human terms; but he retained the idea that human beings are in some sense a unity. For Feuerbach the basis of this unity, and the essential difference between humans and animals, is the ability of humans to be conscious of their species. It is because they are conscious of their existence as a species that human beings can see themselves as individuals (that is, as one among others), and it is because humans see themselves as a species that human reason and human powers are unlimited. Human beings partake in perfection—which, according to Feuerbach, they mistakenly attribute to God instead of themselves—because they are part of a species.

Marx transforms Feuerbach, making the conception of man as a species-being still more concrete. For Marx 'Productive life . . . is species-life.' It is in activity, in production, that humans show themselves to be species-beings. The somewhat unconvincing reason Marx offers for this is that while animals produce only to satisfy their immediate needs, human beings can produce according to universal standards, free of any immediate need—for instance, in accordance with standards of beauty (EPM 82).

On this view, labour in the sense of free productive activity is the essence of human life. Whatever is produced in this way a statue, a house, or a piece of cloth—is therefore the essence of human life made into a physical object. Marx calls this 'the objectification of man's species-life'. Ideally the objects workers have freely created would be theirs to keep or dispose of as they wish. When, under conditions of alienated labour, workers must produce objects over which they have no control (because the objects belong to the employers) and which are used against those who produced them (by increasing the wealth and power of the employers) the workers are alienated from their essential humanity.

A consequence of this alienation of humans from their own nature is that they are also alienated from each other. Productive activity becomes 'activity under the domination, coercion and yoke of another man'. This other man becomes an alien, hostile being. Instead of humans relating to each other cooperatively, they relate competitively. Love and trust are replaced by bargaining and exchange. Human beings cease to recognise in each other their common human nature; they see others as instruments for furthering their own egoistic interests.

That, in brief, is Marx's first critique of economics. Since in his view it is economic life rather than Mind or consciousness that is ultimately real, this critique is his account of what is really wrong with the present condition of humanity. The next question is: What can be done about it?

Marx rejects the idea that anything would be achieved by an enforced wage rise. Labour for wages is not free productive activity. It is merely a means to an end. Higher wages Marx describes as 'nothing but a better slave-salary'. It would not restore significance or dignity to workers or their labour. Even equal wages, as proposed by the French socialist Proudhon, would only replace individual capitalists with one overall capitalist, society itself (EPM 85).

The solution is the abolition of wages, alienated labour, and private property in one blow. In a word, communism. Marx introduces communism in terms befitting the closing chapter of a Hegelian epic:

> Communism . . . is the genuine resolution of the antagonism between man and nature and between man and man; it is the true resolution of the conflict between existence and essence, objectification and self-affirmation, freedom and necessity, individual and species. It is the riddle of history solved and knows itself as this solution (EPM 89).

One might expect that Marx would go on to explain in some detail what communism would be like. He does not—in fact nowhere in his writings does he give more than sketchy suggestions on this subject. He does, however, gesture at the enormous difference communism would make. All human senses, he claims, are degraded by private property. The dealer in minerals sees the market value of the jewels he handles, not their beauty. In the alienated condition caused by private property we cannot appreciate anything except by possessing it, or using it as a means. The abolition of private property will liberate our senses from this alienated condition, and enable us to appreciate the world in a truly human way. Just as the musical ear perceives a wealth of meaning and beauty where the unmusical ear can find none, so will the senses of social human beings differ from those of the unsocial.

These are the essential points of 'the first Marxism'. It is manifestly not a scientific enterprise in the sense in which we understand science today. Its theories are not derived from detailed factual studies, or subjected to controlled tests or observations.

The first Marxism is more down-to-earth than Hegel's philosophy of history, but it is a speculative philosophy of history rather than a scientific study. The aim of world history is human freedom. Human beings are not now free, for they are unable to organise the world so as to satisfy their needs and develop their human capacities. Private property, though a human creation, dominates and enslaves human beings. Ultimate liberation, however, is not in doubt; it is philosophically necessary. The immediate task of revolutionary theory is to understand in what way the present situation is a stage in the dialectical progress to liberation. Then it will be possible to encourage the movements that will end the present stage, ushering in the new age of freedom.

Marx's writings after 1844—including all the works which made him famous—are reworkings, modifications, developments and extensions of the themes of the *Economic and Philosophic Manuscripts*. The number and bulk of these writings make it impossible to discuss each work adequately. (Their repetitiveness would make it tedious, anyway.) So from here on I shall depart slightly from a strict chronological account. I shall begin by tracing the development of the materialist conception of history, which Marx himself described as the 'guiding thread for my studies' (P 389), and Engels, in his funeral oration by Marx's grave, hailed as Marx's chief discovery, comparable with Darwin's discovery of the theory of evolution. This will occupy the next two chapters. I shall then consider Marx's economic works, principally of course *Capital*. Since *Capital* was written only after Marx had arrived at the materialist conception of history, the departure from chronological order in this section will be slight. It will be greater in the next and last of these expository sections, which will assemble from passages of varying vintage Marx's thoughts on communism and on the ethical principles underlying his preference for a communist rather than a capitalist form of society.

6 Alienation as a theory of history

Marx's first published book—and, incidentally, the first work in which Engels participated—attacked articles published in the *General Literary Gazette* (*Allgemeine Literatur-Zeitung*), a journal edited by Marx's former friend and teacher, Bruno Bauer. Since Bauer's brother was a co-editor, the book was mockingly entitled *The Holy Family*. The best comment on it was made by Engels: 'the sovereign derision that we accord to the *General Literary Gazette* is in stark contrast to the considerable number of pages that we devote to its criticism'. Nevertheless some passages of *The Holy Family* are interesting because they show Marx in transition between the *Economic and Philosophic Manuscripts* and later statements of the materialist conception of history.

One section is a defence of the French socialist Proudhon and his objections to private property. Marx is still thinking in terms of alienation:

> The propertied class and the class of the proletariat represent the same human self-alienation. But the former feels comfortable and confirmed in this self-alienation, knowing that this alienation is its own power and possessing in it the semblance of a human existence. The latter feels itself ruined in this alienation and sees in it its impotence and the actuality of an inhuman existence.

Then comes a passage in which the outlines of an embryonic materialist theory of history are clearly visible:

> In its economic movement, private property is driven towards its own dissolution but only through a development which does not depend on it, of which it is unconscious, which takes place against its will, and which is brought about by the very nature of things—thereby creating the

proletariat as proletariat, that spiritual and physical misery conscious of its misery, that dehumanisation conscious of its dehumanisation and thus transcending itself . . .

It is not a question of what this or that proletarian or even the whole proletarian movement momentarily *imagines* to be the aim. It is a question of *what* the proletariat is and what it consequently is historically compelled to do. Its aim and historical action is prescribed, irrevocably and obviously, in its own situation in life as well as in the entire organisation of contemporary civil society. (HF 134–5)

The structure of this and surrounding passages is Hegelian. Private property and the proletariat are described as 'antitheses'—the two sides of a Hegelian contradiction. It is a necessary contradiction, one which could not have been otherwise, for to maintain its own existence private property must also maintain the existence of the propertyless working class needed to run the factories. The proletariat, on the other hand, is compelled to abolish itself on account of its miserable condition. This will require the abolition of private property. The end result will be that both private property and the proletariat 'disappear' in a new synthesis that resolves the contradiction.

Here we have an early version of the materialist theory of history. The basis of the dialectical movement Marx describes is the economic imperatives that flow from the existence of private property. The movement does not depend on the hopes and plans of people. The proletariat becomes conscious of its misery, and therefore seeks to overthrow capitalist society, but this consciousness arises only because of the situation of the proletariat in society. This is the point Marx and Engels were to make more explicitly in a famous passage of *The German Ideology*: 'Consciousness does not determine life, but life determines consciousness' (GI 164).

According to Engels's later account of the relationship between German philosophy and the materialist conception of history, 'the first document in which is deposited the brilliant germ of the new world outlook' is not *The Holy Family* but the

'Theses on Feuerbach' which Marx jotted down in the spring of 1845. These 'Theses' consist of eleven brief remarks in which Marx distinguishes his own form of materialism from that of Feuerbach. Because of their epigrammatic form they have become among the most quoted of Marx's writings. Because Engels published them in 1888, long before any of Marx's other early unpublished writings appeared, they are also among the most misunderstood.

Despite Engels's accolade, the 'Theses' largely recapitulate points Marx had made before. They attack Feuerbach and earlier materialists for taking a passive view of objects and our perception of them. Idealists like Hegel and Fichte emphasised that our activities shape the way we see the world. They were thinking of mental activity. A child sees a red ball, rather than a flat red circle, only when it has mentally grasped the idea of three-dimensional space. Marx wants to combine the active, dialectical side of idealist thought with the materialism of Feuerbach: hence 'dialectical materialism' as later Marxists called it (though Marx himself never used this phrase).

By the active side of materialism Marx meant practical human activity. Marx thought that practical activity was needed to solve theoretical problems. We have seen examples of this. In 'On The Jewish Question' Marx wrote that the problem of the status of Jews, which Bauer had seen as a problem in religious consciousness, would be abolished by reorganising society so as to abolish bargaining. In 'Towards a Critique of Hegel's *Philosophy of Right*: Introduction', Marx argued that philosophy cannot be 'actualised' without the material weapon of the proletariat. And in the *Economic and Philosophic Manuscripts* Marx had referred to communism as 'the riddle of history solved'. This 'riddle of history' is of course a theoretical problem, a philosophical riddle. In Marx's transformation the contradictions of Hegelian philosophy become contradictions in the human condition. They are resolved by communism.

The 'Theses on Feuerbach' are the principal source of the celebrated Marxist doctrine of 'the unity of theory and practice'. This unity some think of as scribbling Marxist philosophy during quiet moments on the barricades. Others take it as meaning that one should live in accordance with one's theoretical principles—socialists sharing their wealth, for instance. The intellectual background of the 'Theses' makes it clear that Marx had neither of these ideas in mind. For Marx the unity of theory and practice meant the resolution of theoretical problems by practical activity. It is an idea which makes little sense outside the context of a materialist transformation of Hegel's philosophy of world history.

The eleventh thesis on Feuerbach is engraved on Marx's tombstone in Highgate cemetery. It reads: 'The philosophers have only interpreted the world in various ways; the point is, to change it' (T 158). This is generally read as a statement to the effect that philosophy is unimportant; revolutionary activity is what matters. It means nothing of the sort. What Marx is saying is that the problems of philosophy cannot be solved by passive interpretation of the world as it is, but only by remoulding the world to resolve the philosophical contradictions inherent in it. It is to solve philosophical problems that we must change the world.

The materialist conception of history is a theory of world history in which practical human activity, rather than thought, plays the crucial role. The most detailed statement of the theory is to be found in Marx and Engels's next major work, *The German Ideology* (1846). Like *The Holy Family* this was a polemic of inordinate length against rival thinkers. Marx later wrote that the book was written 'to settle our accounts with our former philosophic conscience' (P 390).

This time Feuerbach is included in the criticism, although treated more respectfully than the others. It is in the section on Feuerbach that Marx and Engels take the opportunity to state their new view of world history:

> The first premise of all human history is, of course, the existence of living human individuals ... Men can be distinguished from animals by consciousness, by religion, or by anything else you like. They themselves begin to distinguish themselves from animals as soon as they begin to

produce their means of subsistence, a step which is conditioned by their physical organisation. By producing means of subsistence men are indirectly producing their actual material life . . .

In direct contrast to German philosophy, which descends from heaven to earth, here we ascend from earth to heaven. That is to say, we do not set out from what men say, imagine, conceive, nor from men as narrated, thought of, imagined, conceived, in order to arrive at men in the flesh. We set out from real, active men, and on the basis of their real life-process we demonstrate the development of the ideological reflexes and echoes of this life-process. The phantoms formed in the human brain are also, necessarily, sublimates of their material life-process, which is empirically verifiable and bound to material premises. Morality, religion, metaphysics and all the rest of ideology and their corresponding forms of consciousness no longer seem to be independent. They have no history or development. Rather, men who develop their material production and their material relationships alter their thinking and the products of their thinking along with their real existence. Consciousness does not determine life, but life determines consciousness. (GI 160, 164)

This is as clear a statement of the broad outline of his theory as Marx was ever to achieve. Thirteen years later, summing up the 'guiding thread' of his studies, he used similar language: 'It is not the consciousness of men that determines their existence, but, on the contrary,their social existence determines their consciousness.' With *The German Ideology* we have arrived at Marx's mature formulation of the outline of historical materialism (though not the detailed account of the process of change).

In view of this, and Marx's later description of the work as settling accounts with his 'former philosophic conscience', it might be thought that his early interest in alienation has now been replaced by a more scientific approach. It has not. Henceforth Marx makes more use of historical data and less use of abstract philosophical reasoning about the way the world must be; but his interest in alienation persists. *The German Ideology* still describes the social power as something which is really nothing other than the productive force of individuals, and yet appears to these individuals as 'alien and outside them' because they do not understand its origin and cannot control it. Instead of them directing it, it directs them. The abolition of private property and the regulation of production under communism would abolish this 'alienation between men and their products' and enable men to 'regain control of exchange, production and the mode of their mutual relationships' (GI 170).

It is not the use of the word 'alienation' that is important here. The same point can be made in other words. What is important is that Marx's theory of history is a vision of human beings in a state of alienation. Human beings cannot be free if they are subject to forces that determine their thoughts, their ideas, their very nature as human beings. The materialist conception of history tells us that human beings are totally subject to forces they do not understand and cannot control. Moreover the materialist conception of history tells us that these forces are not supernatural tyrants, for ever above and beyond human control, but the productive powers of human beings themselves. Human productive powers, instead of serving human beings, appear to them as alien and hostile forces. The description of this state of alienation is the materialist conception of history.

7 The goal of history

We have traced the development of the materialist conception of history from Marx's earlier concern with human freedom and alienation, but we have not examined the details of this theory of history. Is it really, as Engels claimed, a scientific discovery of 'the law of development of human history', comparable to Darwin's discovery of the law of development of organic nature?

The classic formulation of the materialist conception of history is that of the Preface to *A Contribution to the Critique of Political Economy*, written in 1859. We have already seen a little of this summary by Marx of his own ideas, but it merits a lengthier quotation:

> In the social production which men carry on they enter into definite relations that are indispensable and independent of their will; these relations of production correspond to a definite stage of development of their material powers of production. The sum total of these relations of production constitutes the economic structure of society—the real foundation, on which rise legal and political superstructures and to which correspond definite forms of social consciousness. The mode of production of material life conditions the general character of the social, political and spiritual processes of life. It is not the consciousness of men that determines their existence, but, on the contrary, their social existence determines their consciousness. At a certain stage of their development the material forces of production in society come into conflict with the existing relations of production—or what is but a legal expression for the same thing—with the property relations within which they had been at work before. From forms of development of the forces of production these relations turn into their fetters.

Then comes the epoch of social revolution. With the change of the economic foundation the entire immense superstructure is more or less rapidly transformed. In considering such transformations the distinction should always be made between the material transformation of the economic conditions of production, which can be determined with the precision of natural science, and the legal, political, religious, aesthetic, or philosophic—in short, ideological—forms in which men become conscious of this conflict and fight it out. (P 389–90)

It is commonly said that Marx divided society into two elements, the 'economic base' and the 'superstructure', and maintained that the base governs the superstructure. A closer reading of the passage just quoted reveals a threefold, rather than a twofold, distinction. The opening sentence refers to relations of production, corresponding to a definite stage of the material powers of production. Thus we start with powers of production, or 'productive forces', as Marx usually calls them. The productive forces give rise to relations of production, and it is these relations—not the forces themselves—which constitute the economic structure of society. This economic structure, in turn, is the foundation on which the superstructure rises.

Marx's view may be clearer if made more specific. Productive forces are things used to produce. They include labour-power, raw materials and the machines available to process them. If a miller uses a handmill to grind wheat into flour, the handmill is a productive force.

Relations of production are relations between people, or between people and things. The miller may own his mill, or may hire it from its owner. *Owning* and *hiring* are relations of production. Relations between people, such as 'Smith employs Jones' or 'Ramsbottom is the serf of the Earl of Warwick', are also relations of production.

So we start with productive forces. Marx says that relations of production correspond to the stage of development of productive forces. In one place he puts this very bluntly:

The handmill gives you society with the feudal lord; the steam mill, society with the industrial capitalist. (PP 202)

In other words, when the productive forces are developed to the stage of manual power, the typical relation of production is that of lord and serf. This and similar relations make up the economic structure of society, which in turn is the foundation of the political and legal superstructure of feudal times, with the religion and morality that goes with it: an authoritarian religion, and a morality based on concepts of loyalty, obedience and fulfilling the duties of one's station in life.

Feudal relations of production came about because they fostered the development of the productive forces of feudal times—the handmill for example. These productive forces continue to develop. The steam mill is invented. Feudal relations of production restrict the use of the steam mill. The most efficient use of steam power is in large factories which require a concentration of free labourers rather than serfs tied to their land. So the relation of lord and serf breaks down, to be replaced by the relation of capitalist and employee. These new relations of production constitute the economic structure of society, on which a capitalist legal and political superstructure rises, with its own religion and morality: freedom of religious conscience, freedom of contract, a right to disposable property, egoism and competitiveness.

So we have a three-stage process: productive forces determine relations of production, which in turn determine the super-structure. The productive forces are fundamental. Their growth provides the momentum for the whole process of history.

But isn't all this much too crude? Should we take seriously the statement about the handmill giving us feudal lords, and the steam mill capitalists? Surely Marx must have realised that the invention of steam power itself depends on human ideas, and those ideas, as much as the steam mill itself, have produced capitalism. Isn't Marx making a deliberately exaggerated statement of his own position in order to display its novelty?

This is a vexed question. There are several other places where Marx says flatly that productive forces determine everything else. There are other statements which acknowledge the effect of factors belonging to the superstructure. Particularly when writing history himself, in *The Eighteenth Brumaire of Louis Bonaparte*, for instance, Marx traces the effects of ideas and personalities, and makes less deterministic general statements, for example:

> Men make their own history, but they do not make it just as they please; they do not make it under circumstances chosen by themselves, but under circumstances directly encountered, given, and transmitted from the past. (EB 300)

And what of the opening declaration of *The Communist Manifesto*: 'The history of all hitherto existing society is the history of class struggles'? If the forces of production control everything, class struggles can be no more than the superficial form in which these forces are cloaked. Like the images on a cinema screen they would be powerless to affect the underlying reality they reflect. So why describe history as the history of class struggles? And if neither thought nor politics has any real causal significance, what is the meaning of Marx's dedication, intellectually and politically, to the cause of the working class?

After Marx died, Engels denied that Marx had said that 'the economic element is the *only* determining one'. He and Marx, he conceded, were partly to blame for this misinterpretation, for they had emphasised the economic side in opposition to those who rejected it altogether. Marx and he had not, Engels wrote, overlooked the existence of interaction between the economic structure and the rest of the superstructure. They had affirmed only that 'the economic movement finally asserts itself as necessary'. According to Engels, Marx grew so irritated at misinterpretations of his doctrine that towards the end of his life, he declared: 'All I know is that I am not a Marxist.'

Was Engels right? Some have accused him of watering down the true doctrine; yet no one was in a better position to know what Marx really meant than his lifelong friend and collaborator. Moreover the relatively recent publication of Marx's *Grundrisse*—a rough preliminary version of *Capital* and other projects Marx never completed—reveals that Marx did, like

Engels, use such phrases as 'in the last analysis' to describe the predominance of the forces of production in the interacting whole that constitutes human existence (G 495). Right or wrong, one cannot help sympathising with Engels's position after Marx died. As the authoritative interpreter of Marx's ideas he had to present them in a plausible form, a form not refuted by commonsense observations about the effect of politics, religion or law on the productive forces.

But once 'interaction' between the superstructure and the productive forces is admitted, is it still possible to maintain that production determines the superstructure, rather than the other way round? It is the old chicken-and-egg problem all over again. The productive forces determine the relations of production to which correspond the ideas of the society. These ideas lead to the further development of productive forces, which lead to new relations of production, to which correspond new ideas. In this cyclical movement it makes no more sense to say that productive forces play the determining role than to say that the egg ensures the continued existence of chickens rather than the other way round.

Talk of the productive forces 'finally' or 'in the last analysis' determining the other interacting factors does not provide a way out of the dilemma. For what can this mean? Does it mean that in the end the superstructure is totally governed by the development of the forces of production? In that case 'finally' merely stretches the causal chain; it is still a chain and so we are back with the hard-line determinist version of the theory.

On the other hand, if 'finally' not merely stretches, but actually breaks, the chain of economic determinism, it is difficult to see that asserting the primacy of the productive forces can mean anything significant at all. It might mean, as the passage from *The German Ideology* quoted in the previous chapter appears to suggest, that the process of human history only gets going when humans 'begin to produce their means of subsistence'; or as Engels put it in his graveside speech: 'mankind must first of all eat, drink, have shelter and clothing, before it can pursue politics, science, art, religion, etc.' But if politics, science, art and religion, once they come into existence, have as much effect on the productive forces as the productive forces have on them, the fact that mankind must eat first and can only pursue politics afterwards is of historical interest only; it has no continuing causal importance.

Alternatively, describing the economic side as 'finally' asserting itself could be an attempt to say that although both economic and non-economic factors interact, a larger proportion of the causal impetus comes from the productive forces. But on what basis could one say this? How could one divide the interacting processes and say which played the larger role? We cannot solve the chicken-and-egg problem by saying that while the existence of the species is not due to the egg alone, the egg has more to do with it than the chicken.

In the absence of more plausible ways of making sense of the softening phrases used by Engels and—more rarely—Marx, the interpretation of the materialist conception of history seems to resolve itself into a choice between hard-line economic determinism, which would indeed be a momentous discovery if it were true, but does not seem to be true; or the much more pliable conception to be found in the *Grundrisse*, where Marx describes society as a 'totality', an 'organic whole' in which everything is interconnected (G 99–100). The view of society as a totality is no doubt illuminating when set against the view that ideas, politics, law, religion and so on have a life and history of their own, independently of mundane economic matters. Nevertheless it does not amount to 'the law of development of human history', or to a scientific discovery comparable to Darwin's theory of evolution. To qualify as a contribution to science, a proposed law must be precise enough to enable us to deduce from it certain consequences rather than others. That is how we test proposed scientific laws—by seeing if the consequences they predict actually occur. The conception of society as an interconnected totality is about as precise an instrument of historical analysis as a bowl of porridge. Anything at all can be deduced from it. No observation could ever refute it.

It still needs to be explained how Marx, though obviously aware of the effect of the superstructure on the productive forces, could so confidently assert that the productive forces determine the relations of production and hence the social superstructure. Why did he not see the difficulty posed by the existence of interaction?

The explanation may be that belief in the primacy of the productive forces was not, for Marx, an ordinary belief about a matter of fact but a legacy of the origin of his theory in Hegelian philosophy.

One way to see this is to ask why, if Marx's view is inverted Hegelianism, the existence of interaction between ideas and material life does not pose exactly the same problem for Hegel's view (that the progress of Mind determines material life) as it poses for Marx's inversion of this view. Hegel's writings contain as many descriptions of material life influencing consciousness as Marx's contain of consciousness influencing material life. So the problem of establishing the primary causal role of one set of factors over the other should be as great for Hegel as for Marx.

Yet Hegel's reason for believing in the primacy of consciousness is clear: he regards Mind as ultimately real, and the material world as a manifestation of it; accordingly he sees the purpose or goal of history as the liberation of Mind from all illusions and fetters. Hegel's belief that consciousness determines material life therefore rests on his view of ultimate reality and the meaning of history. History is not a chain of meaningless and often accidental occurrences, but a necessary process heading towards a discoverable goal. Whatever happens on the stage of world history happens in order to enable Mind to reach its goal. It is in this sense that what happens on the level of Mind, or consciousness, is the real cause of everything else.

Like Hegel, Marx has a view about what is ultimately real. His materialism is the reverse of Hegel's idealism. The materialist conception of history is usually regarded as a theory about the causes of historical change, rather than a theory about the nature of ultimate reality. In fact it is both—as Hegel's idealist conception of history was both. We have already seen passages from *The German Ideology* which indicate that Marx took material processes as real in a way that ideas are not. There Marx and Engels contrast the 'real life-process' of 'real, active men' with 'the ideological reflexes and echoes of this life-process'. They distinguish the 'phantoms formed in the human brain' from the 'material life-process, which is empirically verifiable'. The frequent reiteration of 'real' or 'actual' in describing the material or productive life of human beings, and the use of words like 'reflex', 'echo', 'phantom' and so on for aspects of consciousness, suggest a philosophical distinction between what is real and what is merely a manifestation or appearance.

Nor is this terminology restricted to Marx's early works. The contrast between appearance and reality is repeated in *Capital*, where the religious world is said to be 'but the reflex of the real world' (c 1 79).

Also like Hegel, Marx thought that history is a necessary process heading towards a discoverable goal. We have seen evidence of this in the *Economic and Philosophic Manuscripts*, where Marx criticised classical economists for saying nothing about the meaning of economic phenomena 'in the evolution of mankind' or about the extent to which 'apparently accidental circumstances' are nothing but 'the expression of a necessary course of development'. That this too is not a view limited to Marx's youthful period seems clear from, for instance, the following paragraph from an article of his on British rule in India, written in 1853:

> England, it is true, in causing a social revolution in Hindustan, was actuated only by the vilest interests, and was stupid in her manner of enforcing them. But that is not the question. The question is, can mankind fulfil its destiny without a fundamental revolution in the social state of Asia? If not, whatever may have been the crimes of England, she was the unconscious tool of history in bringing about that revolution.

The references to 'mankind's destiny' and to England as 'the unconscious tool of history' imply that history moves in a purposive way towards some goal. (The whole paragraph is reminiscent of Hegel's account of how 'the cunning of reason' uses unsuspecting individuals to work its purposes in history.)

Marx's idea of the goal of world history was, of course, different from Hegel's. He replaced the liberation of Mind by the liberation of real human beings. The development of Mind through various forms of consciousness to final self-knowledge was replaced by the development of human productive forces, by which human beings free themselves from the tyranny of nature and fashion the world after their own plans. But for Marx the progress of human productive forces is no less necessary, and no less progress towards a goal, than the progress of Mind towards self-knowledge is for Hegel.

We can now explain the primary role of the productive forces in Marx's theory of history in the same manner as we explained Hegel's opposite conviction: for Marx the productive life of human beings, rather than their ideas and consciousness, is ultimately real. The development of these productive forces, and the liberation of human capacities that this development will bring, is the goal of history.

Marx's suggestion about England's role in advancing mankind towards its destiny illustrates the nature of the primacy of material life. Since England's colonial policy involves a series of political acts, the causing of a social revolution in Asia by this policy is an instance of the superstructure affecting the economic base. This happens, though, in order to develop the productive forces to the state necessary for the fulfilment of human destiny. The superstructure acts only as the 'unconscious tool' of history. England's colonial policy is no more the ultimate cause of the social revolution in Asia than my spade is the ultimate cause of the growth of my vegetables.

If this interpretation is correct the materialist theory of history is no ordinary causal theory. Few historians—or philosophers for that matter—now see any purpose or goal in history. They do not explain history as the necessary path to anywhere. They explain it by showing how one set of events brought about another. Marx, in contrast, saw history as the progress of the real nature of human beings, that is, human beings satisfying their wants and exerting their control over nature by their productive activities. The materialist conception of history was not conceived as a modern scientific account of how economic changes lead to changes in other areas of society. It was conceived as an explanation of history which points to the real forces operating in it, and the goal to which these forces are heading.

That is why, while recognising the effect of politics, law and ideas on the productive forces, Marx was in no doubt that the development of the productive forces determines everything else. This also makes sense of Marx's dedication to the cause of the working class. Marx was acting as the tool—a fully conscious tool—of history. The productive forces always finally assert themselves, but they do so through the actions of individual humans who may or may not be conscious of the role they are playing in history.

8 Economics

Although Marx described the materialist conception of history as the leading thread of his studies, he was in no doubt that his masterpiece was *Capital*. In this book he presented his economic theories to the public in their most finished form. 'Most finished', not 'finished'; Marx saw only the first volume of Capital through to publication. The second and third volumes were published by Engels, and a fourth volume, entitled *Theories of Surplus Value*, by the German socialist Kautsky.

As with the materialist conception of history, so with the economics: the mature form is easier to appreciate in the light of earlier writings. So let us return to Marx's ideas in 1844, the point at which we ceased to follow their general development and went off in pursuit of the materialist conception of history.

By 1844 Marx had come to hold that the capitalist economic system, regarded by the classical economists as natural and inevitable, was an alienated form of human life. Under capitalism workers are forced to sell their labour—which Marx regards as the essence of human existence—to the capitalists, who use this labour to accumulate more capital, which further increases the power of the capitalists over the workers. Capitalists become rich, while wages are driven down to the bare minimum needed to keep the workers alive. Yet in reducing so large a class of people to this degraded condition, capitalism creates the material force that will overthrow it. For Marx, the importance of economics lay in the insight it provided into the workings of this alienation and the manner in which it could be overcome.

In the years immediately after 1844 Marx's major literary efforts went into polemical works: *The Holy Family*, *The German Ideology* and *The Poverty of Philosophy*. In the course of castigating his opponents Marx developed the materialist conception of history, but did not greatly advance his economic theories. His first attempt to work out these theories in any detail came in 1847, when he gave a series of lectures on economics to the Workingmen's Club in Brussels. The lectures were revised and published as newspaper articles in 1849, and later reprinted under the title *Wage Labour and Capital*.

Wage Labour and Capital is a lucidly written work, containing many echoes of the 1844 manuscripts, but without their Hegelian terminology. It is worth examining in some detail, because its clarity makes the more difficult *Capital* easier to grasp.

Marx starts with labour. Labour is described as 'the worker's own life-activity, the manifestation of his own life'. Yet it becomes, under capitalism, a commodity the worker must sell in order to live. Therefore his life-activity is reduced to a means to go on living, not part of his life, but 'a sacrifice of his life'. His real life only begins when his work ceases, 'at table, in the public house, in bed' (WLC 250).

Marx then asks how wages are determined and answers that the price of labour is determined like the price of any other commodity. It may rise or fall according to supply and demand, but the general tendency is for wages to level down to the cost of production of labour, that is, the cost necessary for keeping the worker alive and capable of working and reproducing.

Next Marx turns to capital. He states the view of classical economics, that capital consists of the raw materials, instruments of production, and means of subsistence which are used in further production. Since all these elements of capital are the creation of labour, even the classical economists hold that capital is accumulated labour.

What the classical economists overlook, however, is that all this is true only within a certain set of social relations. Just as a Negro is not, as such, a slave, but can become a slave in a slave-owning society, so accumulated labour becomes capital only in bourgeois society.

The classical economists see capital as natural, rather than socially conditioned, because they see it as material products—machines, raw materials etc. These material products, however, are also commodities. Commodities are items which can be exchanged against other items—for instance, a pound of sugar may be exchangeable for two pounds of potatoes, or half a pound of strawberries. They therefore have exchange-value. 'Exchange-value' is a key term in Marxist economics. It is contrasted with 'use-value'. The use-value of a pound of sugar is its power to satisfy people's desires for something sweet. The exchange-value of a pound of sugar is two pounds of potatoes or, expressed in terms of money, say, 20p. Use-values therefore exist independently of a market or any other system of exchange: exchange-values do not.

Now capital is really a sum of commodities, that is, of exchange-values. Whether it consists of wool, cotton, machines, buildings, or ships, it remains capital.

While all capital is a sum of exchange-values, however, not all sums of exchange-values are capital. A sum of exchange-values becomes capital only if used to increase itself by being exchanged for labour. Thus capital cannot exist without hiring wage labour. Nor can wage labour exist unless hired by capital. This is the basis of the claim made by bourgeois economists that the interests of the capitalists and the workers are one and the same.

Marx now examines this 'much-vaunted community of interests between worker and capitalist'. He takes the case most favourable for the bourgeois economists, the situation in which capital is growing, and hence the demand for labour, and the price of labour, is rising.

Marx's first point is one still made by critics of the modern consumer society:

A house may be large or small; as long as the surrounding houses are equally small it satisfies all social demands for a dwelling. But let a palace arise beside the little house, and it shrinks from a little house to a hut . . . however high it may shoot up in the course of civilisation, if the neighbouring palace grows to an equal or even greater extent, the occupant of the relatively small house will feel more and more uncomfortable, dissatisfied and cramped within its four walls. (WLC 259)

The reason for poverty and affluence being relative to the standard of our neighbours is, Marx says, that our desires are of a social nature. They are produced by our life in society, rather than by the objects we desire themselves. Thus rising wages do not produce greater satisfaction if the standard of living of the capitalist has risen even more. Yet this is exactly what happens when the growth of capital produces a rise in wages. Growth in capital means a growth in profit, but Marx, following the classical economist Ricardo, claims this can only happen if the relative share of wages is reduced. Wages may rise in real terms, but the gulf between workers and capitalists will increase.

There is also a more fundamental opposition between capitalists and workers. If capital grows, the domination of capital over workers increases. Wage labour 'produces the wealth that rules over it', and gets from this hostile power its means of subsistence, only on condition that it again assists the growth of capital.

Capital increases its domination by increasing the division of labour. This occurs because competition between capitalists forces them to make labour ever more productive, and the greater the scale on which they can produce, and the greater the division of labour, the more productive labour is. The increasing division of labour has several effects.

First, it enables one worker to do the work of ten, and so increases the competition among workers for jobs, thus driving wages down.

Second, it simplifies labour, eliminates the special skills of the worker and transforms him into 'a simple, monotonous productive force'.

Thirdly, it puts more small-scale capitalists out of business. They can do nothing but join the working class. 'Thus', says Marx, 'the forest of uplifted arms demanding work becomes ever thicker, while the arms themselves become ever thinner.'

Finally, Marx says, as the scale of production increases and new markets are needed to dispose of the production, economic crises become more violent. Initially a crisis of overproduction can be relieved by opening up a new market or more thoroughly exploiting an old one. This room for manoeuvre shrinks as production expands, and *Wage Labour and Capital* closes with an image of capitalism collapsing into its grave, but taking with it the corpses of its slaves, the workers, who perish in economic crises.

And all this, Marx ironically reminds us, when capital is growing—the most favourable condition for wage labour!

Wage Labour and Capital contains no answer to a crucial puzzle common to classical economists like David Ricardo and Marx in his own early theory. Both held that commodities are, on average, exchanged for their value. They also held a 'labour theory of value', namely the theory that the exchange-value of a commodity corresponds to the amount of labour it takes to produce it. (Value is, Marx was later to write, 'crystallised social labour' (WPP 379).) But labour is a commodity too. Like other commodities, it should, on average, be exchanged for its value. The capitalist who buys a day's labour should therefore, on average, have to pay the value of a day's labour. This will add the value of a day's labour to the production cost of the commodity the worker produces in that day. This commodity the capitalist will then sell for a price that, on average, corresponds to the value of the labour required to produce it. Where then does the capitalist get his profit from?

Marx first worked out his solution to this puzzle in unpublished notebooks written in 1857–8. These notebooks contain, in draft form, a good deal of material that was to appear in *Capital*, but the four fat volumes of *Capital* appear to be only a portion of the works projected in the notebooks. The notebooks were published only in 1953 and not translated into English until 1972. They are known as the *Grundrisse*, a German word meaning 'outlines' or 'foundations', since they were first published, in German, under the title *Foundations of the Critique of Political Economy (Rough Draft)*.

The most intriguing point about the *Grundrisse* is that although it was written well into Marx's maturity, it is closer, in both terminology and method of argument, to the 1844 *Manuscripts* than to any of the works published in Marx's lifetime after 1844. Even if it were not possible to trace transformed Hegelian themes in Marx's mature published works, the *Grundrisse* makes it plain that Marx did not make the decisive break with Hegelian philosophy that his reference to *The German Ideology* as 'settling accounts with our former philosophic conscience' has been taken to imply.

The key element of Marx's mature economic theory appears in the *Grundrisse*. The worker, Marx writes,

> sells labour itself as *objectified labour*; i.e. he sells labour only in so far as it already objectifies a definite amount of labour, hence in so far as its equivalent is already measured, given; capital buys it as living labour, as the general productive force of wealth; activity which increases wealth. (G 307)

What does Marx mean by this distinction between objectified labour and living labour? Objectified labour is the predetermined amount for which the capitalist pays—for instance, the worker's labour for twelve hours. This is labour as a commodity. The exchange-value of this commodity is the amount needed to produce it, that is, the amount needed to keep the worker alive and reproductive. But there is a dual nature to the exchange of labour and capital. The capitalist obtains the use of the worker's labour-power for the prescribed period—say, one day—and can use this labour-power to produce as much wealth as he is able to get out of it. This is what Marx means when he says that capital buys 'living labour'. The worker gets a fixed sum, regardless of what the capitalist can make out of his labour power.

Here we have what Engels in his funeral oration described as the second of Marx's great discoveries: 'the discovery of surplus value'. Surplus value is the value the capitalist is able to extract from the labour-power he buys, above the exchange-value of the labour that he must pay. It is the difference between labour-power as a creative, productive force, and labour-time as an objectified commodity.

Suppose that the cost of keeping a worker alive and reproducing for one day is £1, and suppose that a day's work consists of twelve hours. Then the exchange-value of twelve hours' labour will be £1. Fluctuations above this figure will be short-lived. Suppose, however, that the development of the forces of production means that a worker's labour-power can be used to add £1 to the value of some raw materials in only six hours. Then the worker effectively earns his wages in six hours. But the capitalist has bought twelve hours of labour-power for his £1, and can now use the remaining six hours to extract surplus value from the worker. This is, Marx claims, the secret of how capital is able to use the worker's creative power to increase its domination over the worker.

Marx published some of his new economic ideas in 1859, in *A Contribution to the Critique of Political Economy*. This work is justifiably famous for the succinct summary of the materialist view of history contained in its Preface, which we have already discussed; but the economic ideas were insignificant compared with those published eight years later in the first volume of *Capital*. So we shall go straight on to this pinnacle of Marx's writings.

Capital has a familiar-sounding subtitle—*Critique of Political Economy*—and once again the work criticises classical economic theories, both within their own presuppositions and from a broader point of view. But *Capital* also contains historical material on the origin of capital, and detailed descriptions, drawn from government publications like the reports of factory inspectors, of the horrific nature of factory labour. We can see how all this fits in with Marx's general theoretical system by examining the first chapter of *Capital*, on commodities, and particularly the final section of this chapter, intriguingly entitled 'The Fetishism of Commodities and the Secret thereof'.

According to Marx, commodities are mysterious things in which the social character of human labour appears to be an objective feature of the product of that labour. He illustrates this with religion. In religion, Marx says, the productions of the human brain seem to be independent beings. Similarly, with commodities, a social relation between human beings appears in the form of the value of a commodity, as if that value were objective and independent of human relations. Like religious believers bowing before an idol, we make a fetish of commodities by treating them as more than they really are.

How does this happen? It happens only when we begin to produce things not because they directly serve our wants, but in order to exchange them. Since the exchange-value of a product corresponds to the amount of labour required to produce it, when we produce in order to exchange, the value of our labour becomes its exchange-value, rather than its use-value. When we exchange our products we are, without being aware of it, taking as equal the different kinds of labour embedded in them.

In a society based on the production of commodities there is, Marx says, a 'mystical veil' over these 'life-processes of society' which would not exist if we produced 'as freely associated men', consciously regulating our production in a planned way. Then the value of a product would be its use-value, the extent to which it satisfies our desires. Classical economists like Adam Smith and David Ricardo lifted the veil far enough to see that the value of a product (i.e. its exchange-value) represents the labour-time it took to produce it; but they took this as a law of nature, a self-evident necessary truth. On the contrary, says Marx, it bears the stamp of a society 'in which the process of production has the mastery over man, instead of being controlled by him'.

The aim of *Capital*, then, is to rip aside this mystical veil over the life-processes of modern society, revealing these processes as the domination of human beings by their own social relations. Thus *Capital*, like Marx's other writings, is based on the idea that human beings are in a state of alienation, a state in which their own creations appear to them as alien, hostile forces and in which instead of controlling their creations, they are controlled by them.

Within this overall conception, the detail of *Capital* falls into place. The economic theory, contained mostly in the first nine chapters, is an attempt to display the real economic basis of production in a capitalist society. Here Marx debates with the classical economists, trying to show that, even on their own terms, he has a better account of the economic workings of capitalism.

Most of these first nine chapters prepare the ground for, and then introduce, the notion of surplus value. This involves a lengthy re-statement, in plain language, of the point made in more Hegelian terms in the *Grundrisse*. The dual nature of commodities, which can be seen as use-values or exchange-values, affects labour too. What is special about labour, though, is that it is the measure of exchange-value. Thus a new machine which makes it possible to produce two coats in the time it used to take to produce one will increase the use-value of an hour's labour (because two coats are more useful than one) but will not increase the exchange-value of the hour's labour (because an hour's labour remains an hour's labour, and if a coat only takes half as long to make as it used to, it will, in the end, be worth correspondingly less). Increasing the fruitfulness of labour therefore increases its use-value but not the exchange-value of its output.

This is how capitalism enslaves its workers. Through machinery and the division of labour, capitalism greatly increases the productivity of human labour; but this increased productivity does not benefit the producers. If in pre-capitalist times people had to work for twelve hours to produce the necessities of life, doubling the productivity of their labour ought to mean that they can now choose between an extra six hours of leisure, twice as many useful products, or some combination of the two. Under capitalism, however, labour is geared to the production of goods for exchange. Paradoxically, under these conditions increased productivity does not lead to the production of more exchange-value. Instead, the exchange-value per item of what is produced drops. Small independent producers are forced to become wage-labourers, since they cannot produce as many items in a day as the larger producers who obtain economies of scale by the use of wage-labourers. Since wages tend to fall to the level at which they barely sustain the labouring class, the overwhelming majority of human beings have lost, not gained, by the increased productivity of human labour. That, at any rate, is Marx's view.

But what happens to the increased productivity, if it does not improve the lives of the workers? Marx's answer is that it is skimmed off from the worker's output in the form of surplus value. The capitalist obtains the use-value of the worker's labour-power, and pays only the exchange-value. Because labour-power is a commodity which can be used to produce more value than it has itself, the capitalist is able to retain the difference between the two.

The fact that the worker obtains only the exchange-value, rather than the use-value, of his labour, means that in order to earn enough to support himself he has to work a full day—say, twelve hours—whereas his labour produces the use-values of the necessary food, clothing, shelter and so on in, say, six hours. The six hours in which the worker produces the value of the goods he needs Marx calls 'necessary labour' because it is labour that the worker would have to undertake in any economic system, given the level of development of forces of production; but the extra six hours are surplus-labour, which is in effect a form of forced labour for the benefit of the capitalist. The essential difference between a society based on slave-labour and one based on wage-labour lies, Marx says, only in the manner in which this surplus-labour is extracted from the real producer, the worker.

The significance of all this lies in the fact that Marx regards the period in which people must work to keep themselves alive as a period in which they are not free:

> The realm of freedom actually begins only where labour which is determined by necessity and mundane considerations ceases. (c iii 496)

In primitive societies property was held in common. People were not alienated from each other, or from the products of their labour, but at the same time human productive forces were so poorly developed that people had to spend much of their time providing for their needs, and for all that time were not free to choose what to do. The growth of the forces of production led to a feudal form of society in which the serf was subordinate to the feudal lord, and had to work a specified number of days on the lord's land rather than on his own. It was then perfectly obvious when the serf was working to feed himself and when he was working for his lord. At neither time was he free to choose his own activity.

The vastly greater development of productive forces that takes place under capitalism provides the means, Marx believes, to reduce the domination of nature over us to insignificant proportions and increase human freedom proportionately; but this cannot take place under capitalism, because the forced labour of the serf for the feudal lord still exists as the forced labour of the worker for the capitalist. The difference is that under feudalism the nature and extent of the forced labour is apparent; under capitalism the nature and extent of the coercion is disguised. Workers appear to be 'free labourers', voluntarily making agreements with capitalists. In fact the position of workers as a class in relation to capitalists as a class means that they are not free. They must take the terms the capitalists offer them, or starve; and capitalists will only employ them under terms which allow surplus-value to be extracted from their labour. This is not because capitalists are cruel or greedy—though some may be—but because of the economic laws inherent in capitalist production which, through free competition, coerce individual capitalists as much as individual workers. (Though equally coerced, capitalists suffer less from this coercion than workers.)

Marx sums all this up as the development of capitalism into

> a coercive relation, which compels the working class to do more work than the narrow round of its own life-wants prescribes. As a producer of the activity of others, as a pumper-out of surplus-labour and exploiter of labour-power, it surpasses in energy, disregard of bounds, recklessness and efficiency, all earlier systems of production based on directly compulsory labour. (C I 310)

The most gripping chapters of *Capital* are not those in which Marx expounds his economic theories, but those which record the consequences of capitalist efficiency. The tenth chapter, on 'The Working Day', chronicles the capitalists' attempts to squeeze more and more labour-time out of the workers, oblivious of the human costs of working seven-year-old children for fifteen hours a day. The struggle for a legally limited working day is, Marx writes, more vital to the working classes than a pompous catalogue of 'the inalienable rights of man' (c 1 302). Other chapters describe how the increasing division of labour eliminates intellectual and manual skill and reduces the labourer to a mere appendage to a machine; how industrialisation has ruined cottage industries, forcing hand-workers to starve, how capitalism creates an 'industrial reserve army' of unemployed workers, subsisting in the direst poverty, to keep the 'active labour-army' in check; and how the agricultural population of England had their land taken from them by landlords and capitalists, so that they could survive only by selling their labour-power. The documented evidence presented justifies Marx's description of capital as 'dripping from head to foot, from every pore, with blood and dirt' (c 1 760).

Near the end of the first volume of *Capital* the gloom lifts. Marx sketches how the laws of capitalism will bring about the destruction of capitalism. On the one hand competition between capitalists will lead to an ever-diminishing number of monopoly capitalists: on the other hand the 'misery, oppression, slavery, degradation, exploitation' of the working class grows (c 1 763). But the working class is, because of the nature of capitalist production, more numerous and better organised. Eventually the dam will burst. The ensuing revolution will be, says Marx, lapsing into the style of his earlier writings, 'the negation of the negation'. It will not mean a return to private property in the old sense, but to property based on the gains made under capitalism, that is, on cooperation and common possession of land and the means of production. Capitalism will make the transition relatively easy, since it has already expropriated all private property into its own hands. All that is now necessary is for the mass of the people to expropriate these few expropriators.

The second and third volumes of *Capital* are much less interesting than the first. The second volume is a technical discussion of how capital circulates. It also discusses the origin of economic crises. The third volume attempts to patch up some problems in the first volume, particularly the objection that prices do not reflect the amount of labour in a product, as one would expect them to do on Marx's account. More important is Marx's claim that under capitalism the rate of profit tends to fall. Marx argued that the surplus-value of the past accumulates in the form of capital. Hence capital is always increasing, and the ratio of 'living labour' to capital is always decreasing; but since capitalists only make profit by extracting surplus-value from living labour, this means that the rate of profit must fall in the long run. All this was part of Marx's attempt to show that capitalism cannot be a permanent state of society.

Marx, Engels and later Marxists treat *Capital* as a contribution to the science of economics. Taken in this way it is open to several objections. For instance, Marx asserts that all profit arises from the extraction of surplus value from living labour; machines, raw materials and other forms of capital cannot generate profit, though they can increase the amount of surplus-value extracted. This seems obviously wrong. Future capitalists will not find their profits drying up as they dismiss the last workers from their newly-automated factories. Many of Marx's other theories have been refuted by events: the theory that wages will always tend downwards to the subsistence level of the workers; the theory of the falling rate of profit; the theory that under capitalism economic crises will become more and more severe; the theory that capitalism requires an 'industrial reserve army' of paupers; and the theory that capitalism will force more and more people down into the working class.

Does this mean that the central theses of *Capital* are simply mistaken, and that the work is just another piece of crackpot economics—as we might have expected from a German philosopher meddling in a field in which he has not been trained? If this view seems at all plausible, Marx himself, with his emphasis on the scientific nature of his discovery, must bear the blame. It would be better to regard *Capital*, not as the work of 'a minor post-Ricardian' (as a leading contemporary economist has appraised Marx as an economist) but as the work of a critic of capitalist society. Marx wanted to expose the deficiencies of classical economics in order to expose the deficiencies of capitalism. He wanted to show why the enormous increase in productivity brought about by the industrial revolution had made the great majority of human beings worse off than before. He wanted to reveal how the old relationships of master and slave, lord and serf, survived under the cloak of freedom of contract. His answer to these questions was the doctrine of surplus-value. As an economic doctrine it does not stand up to scientific probing. Marx's economic theories are not a scientific account of the nature and extent of exploitation under capitalism. They nevertheless offer a vivid picture of an uncontrolled society in which the productive workers unconsciously create the instruments of their own oppression. It is a picture of human alienation, writ large as the dominance of past labour, or capital, over living labour. The value of the picture lies in its capacity to lead us to see its subject in a radically new way. It is a work of art, of philosophical reflection and of social polemic, all in one, and it has the merits and the defects of all three of these forms of writing. It is a painting of capitalism, not a photograph.

9 Communism

In his speech at Marx's funeral, Engels said that although the materialist conception of history and the doctrine of surplus value were Marx's crowning theoretical discoveries

> Marx was before all else a revolutionist. His real mission in life was to contribute, in one way or another, to the overthrow of capitalist society and of the state institutions which it had brought into being, to contribute to the liberation of the modern proletariat . . .

To complete our account of Marx's main ideas, therefore, we need to ask: what kind of society did Marx hope would take the place of capitalism? This question is easily answered in a single word: communism. It is difficult to answer it more adequately, that is, to say what Marx meant by communism.

There is a reason for Marx's reticence over the details of communist society. He believed that history owed its momentum to the development of the forces of production rather than the development of ideas. This did not mean that theory was unimportant. If Marx's mission in life was to contribute to the overthrow of capitalism and the liberation of the proletariat, his theories of history and of economics were intended to do this by showing the workers their role in history and making them conscious of the manner in which capitalism exploited them. While theory could describe existing reality in this way, however, for theory to reach ahead of its time was another matter altogether. Marx derided as 'Utopian' those socialists who sought to bring about communism by producing blueprints of a future communist society. His own form of socialism was, he claimed, scientific because it built on knowledge of the laws of history that would bring socialism into existence.

Along with Utopian views of socialism, and for the same reason, Marx condemned conspiratorial revolutionaries who wished to capture power and introduce socialism before the economic base of society had developed to the point at which the working class as a whole is ready to participate in the revolution. Utopian dreamers and revolutionary conspirators fancy that the laws of history will bend to their desires. Marx prided himself on his freedom from this illusion. He saw his role as raising the revolutionary consciousness of the workers and preparing for the revolution that would occur when conditions were ripe. He thought he could describe the underlying laws governing the past and his own time, but he knew he could not impose his own will on the course of history. Nor could he predict the form to be taken by the new society to be built by the free human beings of the new era.

That, at least, was Marx's official position. In practice he could not refrain entirely from hinting at the form communist society would take.

We have seen that in his first discussion, in the *Economic and Philosophic Manuscripts of 1844*, Marx described communism as 'the riddle of history solved' and as the resolution of various conflicts that have existed throughout all previous history: the conflicts between man and nature, between man and man, between freedom and necessity, and between individual and species. This conception of communism is thoroughly Utopian—though not in Marx's sense of the word. It sees communism as the goal of history and the answer to all problems, as a virtual paradise on earth.

A similarly Utopian conception of communism can be found in *The German Ideology*, where Marx suggests that in communist society the division of labour would not force us into narrow occupational roles. I could, Marx says, 'hunt in the morning, fish in the afternoon, breed cattle in the evening, criticise after dinner, just as I like, without ever becoming a hunter, a fisherman, a herdsman, or a critic' (GI 169). More important than this idyllic image of pastoral communism, however, is Marx's claim in the same passage that the split between the particular interests of the individual and the common interest of society would disappear under communism. This is in line with his earlier remarks about communism resolving such conflicts as that between man and man, and between the individual and the species. It is crucial to Marx's vision of communism. Marx immediately goes on to say that it is out of this very contradiction between the interest of the individual and the community that the state develops as an independent entity. So an understanding of how this contradiction can be overcome should enable us to understand the famous Marxist doctrine that under communism the state will be superseded.

In proposing a solution to the problem of the individual and the community, Marx was contributing to a tradition in moral philosophy going back at least to Plato. Plato had argued that personal happiness is to be found in virtuous conduct and in serving one's community. He thus found harmony between the individual's interest in happiness and the needs of the community. But Plato's arguments did not convince later philosophers.

Marx thought the division between individual interest and community interest was a feature of a particular stage of human development, rather than an inevitable aspect of social existence, a feature which had existed ever since the break-up of very simple societies which had lived communally, without private ownership and division of labour. Capitalism, however, heightened the conflict by turning everything into a commodity, leaving 'no other nexus between man and man than naked self-interest, than callous "cash payment"' (CM 223).

How did Marx think the opposition between private and communal interests could be overcome? Obviously the abolition of private property could play a part—it is not so easy to feather one's own nest if there is nothing one can call one's own to feather it with. But the change would have to go deeper, for even without private property people could pursue their own interests by trying to get as much as they could for themselves (for immediate consumption if the abolition of private property made hoarding impossible) or by shirking their share of the work necessary to keep the community going. To alter this, nothing short of a radical transformation of human nature would suffice.

Here the materialist conception of history underpins the possibility of communism. According to Marx's view of history, as the economic basis of society alters, so all consciousness alters. Greed, egoism and envy are not ingrained for ever in the character of human beings. They would disappear in a society in which private property and private means of production were replaced with communal property and socially-organised means of production. We would lose our preoccupation with our private interests. Citizens of the new society would find their own happiness in working for the good of all. Hence a communist society would have a new ethical basis. It has been claimed—by Lenin among others—that Marxism is a scientific system, free from any ethical judgements or postulates. This is obviously nonsense. Marx did not just predict that capitalism would be overthrown and replaced by communism. He judged the change to be desirable. He did not need to make this judgement explicit, as it was implied by everything he wrote about capitalism and communism, and by his unceasing political activity. Marx's ethical attitudes are woven into his conception of human progress through alienation to the final state of complete freedom.

The belief that Marxism contains no ethical judgements derives from some comments made by Marx and Engels. In *The Communist Manifesto*, for instance, morality is listed together with law and religion as 'bourgeois prejudices, behind which lurk in ambush just as many bourgeois interests' (CM 230). It is true that for Marx morality is part of the ideological superstructure of society, is determined by the economic basis and serves to promote the interests of the ruling class. But it does not follow from this that all morality is to be rejected. What has to be rejected is morality that serves the interests of the ruling class. This includes all dominant moralities up to now. Once communism has been established and classes have disappeared, however, we can pass beyond class morality, to what Engels called 'a really human morality'.

As with communism in general, so with communist morality one can only guess at its detailed content. Communism would differ from all previous societies in that there would be no false consciousness. False consciousness involves failing to see things as they really are. It comes about because a society's superstructure can conceal the real basis of the society—as the legal freedom of the worker to sell his labour to whomever he likes on whatever terms he likes conceals the fact that he is really no more able to avoid exploitation by capitalists than the feudal serf is free to avoid working on the land of his lord. Class morality adds an extra layer of false consciousness, leading the worker to believe that, for example, the capitalist has a moral right to the proceeds of his investment.

With communist production there would be no exploitation to be concealed. Everything would really be as it appeared to be. Moral illusions would crumble along with the religious illusions against which the Young Hegelians argued so fiercely. The new human morality would not hypocritically cloak sectional interests in a universal guise. It would genuinely serve the interests of all human beings. Its universal form would be matched by a universal content.

The new morality would have a character quite different from previous moralities, different even from moralities like utilitarianism which proclaim their equal concern for all. Though Marx was as scornful of utilitarianism as of any other ethical theory, his scorn was directed at the utilitarian conception of the general interest rather than at the basic utilitarian idea of maximising happiness—in fact Marx refers to this idea as 'a homespun commonplace', which does not imply that he disagrees with it (C I 609). But in capitalist society, to propose that people act for the general interest is often to propose that they work against their own interest, as they conceive it. Under such conditions the very idea of morality implies something burdensome and contrary to our own interests. Under communism this aspect of morality will vanish as the gulf between individual interest and universal interest vanishes. Morality will cease to be a dictate from without, and become an expression of our chief wants as social beings.

It has been said that later in life Marx developed a less Utopian view of communism, but it is difficult to find much evidence of this. There is one passage in the third volume of

Capital which, in contrast to the claim of the *Economic and Philosophic Manuscripts*, sees the conflict between freedom and necessity as ineliminable. This is the passage, already cited, in which Marx says that freedom begins 'only where labour which is determined by necessity and mundane considerations ceases'. He goes on to say that it is part of 'the very nature of things' that when we are producing to satisfy our needs we are not free. Shortening the working day is, therefore, the prerequisite of freedom (c III 496–7). This implies that the conflict between freedom and necessity cannot be overcome, and the best that can be done is to reduce the amount of necessary labour to a minimum, thereby increasing the time that we are free. It is a statement which contrasts oddly with what Marx says about communism in his comments on the Gotha Program—also a late work—which are as optimistic as any of the early statements. There Marx foresees the end of the 'enslaving subordination of the individual to the division of labour' and a time when labour will become 'not only a means of life, but life's prime want' (GP 569). The idea of labour as 'life's prime want' is very different from the clockwatching attitude that takes the shortening of the working day as the prerequisite of freedom.

It is, incidentally, in these comments on the Gotha Program that Marx proposes the celebrated principle of distribution for a communist society: 'from each according to his ability, to each according to his needs'. The principle is not original to Marx, and Marx places little emphasis upon it. He refers to it only in order to criticise those socialists who worry too much about how goods would be distributed in a socialist society. Marx thought it a mistake to bother about working out a fair or just principle of distribution. He was even prepared to allow that, given the capitalist mode of production, capitalist distribution was the only one that was 'fair'. His point was that production was what mattered, and once 'the productive forces have increased with the all-round development of the individual, and all the springs of cooperative wealth flow more abundantly', distribution will look after itself (GP 566).

Everything Marx says about communism is premised on

material abundance. Remember that it is the development of the forces of production that, according to the materialist theory of history, is the driving force behind historical change. The change from one form of society to another occurs when the existing structure of society acts as a fetter on the further development of the productive forces. But communism is the final form of society. Building on the dramatic advances so ruthlessly made by capitalism, communism allows the forces of production to develop to their fullest possible extent. Production will be cooperatively planned for the benefit of all, not wasted in socially fruitless competition between individual capitalists for their own private ends. There will be no crises of overproduction, as there are in unplanned economies. The reserve army of unemployed workers required by capitalism to keep labour cheap and available will become productive. Mechanisation and automation will continue to develop as they had developed under capitalism, though without their degrading effect on the workers (unfortunately Marx does not tell us how these effects would be avoided, but presumably it would be by a drastic reduction in the hours of necessary labour). No longer will surplus-value be extracted from the workers to line the pockets of the capitalists. The working-class will receive the full use-value of its labour, subject only to a deduction for future social investment. We will control our economy, instead of being controlled by it.

Material abundance and the transformation of human nature provide the basis for Marx's claim that the state as we know it would cease to exist under communism. This would not happen immediately, for at first the proletariat would have to assert itself over the other classes, in order to abolish capitalist forms of production. This would be the 'dictatorship of the proletariat'. But once capitalist production had been replaced by socialist production the division of society into classes would disappear, along with conflicts between individual and social interests. There would be no need for political power in the Marxist sense of the organised power of one class used to oppress another. Nor, given Marx's idea that communism would come first to the most industrially advanced societies, and would be international in character, would there be any need for the state in the sense of an organisation existing to defend the nation against attacks from other nations. Relieved from oppressive conditions that bring their interests into conflict, people would voluntarily cooperate with each other. The political state resting on armed force would become obsolete; its place would be taken by 'an association, in which the free development of each is the condition for the free development of all' (CM 238).

10 An assessment

Any exposition of Marx's ideas is also an assessment of them. In arguing that Marx's main achievements—his theory of history and his economics—are not scientific discoveries, I have already rejected the accolade bestowed on Marx by Engels, confirmed by Lenin and echoed by orthodox Marxist-Leninists ever since. But if Marx did not make scientific discoveries about economics and society, what did he achieve? Is his system now only a historical curiosity? In this concluding section I shall state my view of which elements of Marx's thought remain valuable, and which need to be revised or scrapped.

First, though, it is necessary to say a little more about Marx as a scientist; for it cannot be denied that Marx thought of his own theories as 'scientific', and based predictions about the future of capitalism on them. He predicted that:

The income gap between capitalists and workers will increase

More and more independent producers will be forced down into the proletariat, leaving a few rich capitalists and a mass of poor workers

Workers' wages will, with short-lived exceptions, remain at subsistence level

The rate of profit will fall

Capitalism will collapse because of its internal contradictions

Proletarian revolutions will occur in the most industrially advanced countries

More than a century after Marx made these predictions, most of them are so plainly mistaken that one can only wonder why anyone sympathetic to Marx would attempt to argue that his greatness lies in the scientific aspects of his work. Throughout the industrialised world, the gap between rich and poor has narrowed. This is largely because real wages have risen. Factory workers today earn considerably more than they need in order to remain alive and reproducing. The rate of profit has not gone into a steady decline. Capitalism has gone through several crises, but nowhere has it collapsed as a result of its alleged internal contradictions. Proletarian revolutions have broken out in the less developed nations, rather than the more developed ones.

Nevertheless, the fate of Marx's predictions is not a ground for disregarding his ideas as a whole, any more than the fact that Jesus thought the second coming would take place in the lifetime of those he addressed is a reason for taking no further heed of Christianity. Such errors merely show that those who made them are fallible. It is better to think of Marx as a philosopher—in the broadest sense—rather than as a scientist. We have seen how Marx's predictions were derived from his application of Hegel's philosophy to the progress of human history and the economics of capitalism. No one now thinks of Hegel as a scientist, although Hegel, like Marx, described his work as 'scientific'. The German term they both used includes any serious, systematic study, and in that sense, of course, Marx and Hegel were both scientists; but we now regard Hegel as a philosopher, and we should think of Marx primarily in the same way.

As a philosopher, Marx's work endures. It has altered our understanding of our own nature, and deepened our grasp of what it is to be free.

Let us take the second of these first, for freedom was Marx's central concern (paradoxical as this may seem when we look at the regimes that profess to follow his ideas). The significance of Marx's idea of freedom is best appreciated by contrasting it with the standard liberal notion of freedom accepted—in Marx's time and in our own—by those who oppose government interference with the free market. According to this view, I am free so long as I am not subject to deliberate interference from other people. Of course, there have to be limits to this freedom. The government may properly interfere with me if, for instance, I assault my neighbours; then I am deliberately interfering with others and my own freedom can be restricted to ensure greater freedom for all. This is consistent with holding that freedom is at its maximum when each individual is able to act without deliberate interference from others.

This liberal conception of freedom fits perfectly with the economic theories of defenders of unrestrained capitalism, for they portray capitalism as the outcome of the free choices of millions of individuals. The capitalist merely offers people work at, say, £1 an hour, for forty hours a week. Anyone can choose, without interference from others, to accept or reject this offer. If some accept it, the capitalist uses their labour for his own purposes, say, to make shirts. He offers these shirts for sale at a certain price, and again anyone can freely choose whether or not to buy them at this price. And anyone who thinks he can do better than the capitalists now in business is free to set up his own enterprise.

This is not how capitalism really works, of course, but it shows how the liberal view of freedom can be used to provide a defence of capitalism which is immune to objections along the line that capitalists are greedy people who exploit the poor by selling at exorbitant prices. Defenders of capitalism can readily admit that some capitalists may be greedy, but they can also point out that no one is forced to work for or buy from any individual capitalist. So the greed of individual capitalists is not a reason for condemning the free enterprise system.

Marx saw that within its own terms this defence of capitalism is coherent; but he also saw that from a broader, historical perspective, the liberal definition of freedom is open to a fundamental objection. To explain his objection, I shall switch to a more homely example. Suppose I live in the suburbs and work in the city. I could drive my car to work, or take the bus. I prefer not to wait around for the bus, and so I take my car. Fifty thousand other people living in my suburb face the same choice and make the same decision. The road to town is choked with cars. It takes each of us an hour to travel ten miles.

In this situation, according to the liberal conception of freedom, we have all chosen freely. No one deliberately interfered with our choices. Yet the outcome is something none of us want. If we all went by bus, the roads would be empty and we could cover the distance in twenty minutes. Even with the inconvenience of waiting at the bus stop, we would all prefer that. We are, of course, free to alter our choice of transportation, but what can we do? While so many cars slow the bus down, why should any individual choose differently? The liberal conception of freedom has led to a paradox: we have each chosen in our own interests, but the result is in no one's interest. Individual rationality, collective irrationality.

The solution, obviously, is for us all to get together and make a collective decision. As individuals we are unable to bring about the situation we desire. Together we can achieve what we want, subject only to the physical limits of our resources and technology. In this example, we Can all agree to use the bus.

Marx saw that capitalism involves this kind of collective irrationality. In pre-capitalist systems it was obvious that most people did not control their own destiny—under feudalism, for instance, serfs had to work for their lords. Capitalism seems different because people are in theory free to work for themselves or for others as they choose. Yet most workers have as little control over their lives as feudal serfs. This is not because they have chosen badly. Nor is it because of the physical limits of our resources and technology. It is because the cumulative effect of countless individual choices is a society that no one—not even the capitalists—has chosen. Where those who hold the liberal conception of freedom would say we are free because we are not subject to deliberate interference by other humans, Marx says we are not free because we do not control our own society. Economic relations between human beings determine not only our wages and our prospects of finding work, but also our politics, our religion and our ideas. These economic relations force us into a situation in which we compete with each other instead of cooperating for the good of all. These conditions nullify technical advances in the use of our resources. Rationally organised, industrialisation should enable us to enjoy an abundance of material goods with a minimum of effort; under capitalism, however, these advances simply reduce the value of the commodity produced, which means that the worker must work just as long for the same wage. (In saying this, Marx was supposing that real wages would remain around subsistence level; in fact the increase in productivity has allowed real wages to rise.) Worse still, the absence of any overall planning or direction in the economy leads to crises of overproduction—that overproduction can cause a crisis is in itself a clear indication of an irrational system—and to recessions in which the economy operates in a manner that neither workers nor capitalists desire. (Here Marx's point remains valid, as the failure of government after government to overcome unemployment, recession and inflation indicates.)

Economic relations appear to us blind natural forces. We do not see them as restricting our freedom—and indeed on the liberal conception of freedom they do *not* restrict our freedom, since they are not the result of deliberate human interference: Marx himself is quite explicit that the capitalist is not individually responsible for the economic relations of his society, but is controlled by these relations as much as the workers are (C I 10). Yet these economic relations are our own unwitting creations, not deliberately chosen but nevertheless the outcome of our own individual choices and thus potentially subject to our will. We are not truly free until, instead of letting our creations control us, we collectively take control of them. Hence the significance of a planned economy. In an unplanned economy human beings unwittingly grant the market control over their lives; planning the economy is a reassertion of human sovereignty and an essential step towards true human freedom.

Marx's penetrating insight into the nature of freedom remains a challenge to any liberal political philosophy. It is the core of Marx's attack on alienation in the 1844 *Manuscripts*, as it is the core of his critique of the free market in *Capital*. It earns Marx a place alongside Hobbes, Locke, Rousseau and Hegel as a major figure in Western political thought. All the same, the alternative conception of freedom Marx espoused contains within it a difficulty Marx never sufficiently appreciated, a difficulty which can be linked with the tragic mutation of Marx's views into a prop for murderously authoritarian regimes. This is the problem of obtaining the cooperation of each individual in the joint endeavour of controlling our society.

Return for a moment to our example of the commuters. They hold a meeting. All agree that it would be better to leave their cars at home. They part, rejoicing at the prospect of no more traffic jams. But in the privacy of their own homes, some reason to themselves as follows: 'If everyone else is going to take the bus tomorrow, the roads will be empty. So I'll take my car. Then I'll have the convenience of door-to-door transportation and the advantage of a traffic-free run which will get me to work in less time than if I took the bus.' From a self-interested point of view this reasoning is correct. As long as most take the bus, a few others can obtain the benefits of the socially-minded behaviour of the majority, without giving up anything themselves.

What should the majority do about this? Should they leave it up to the individual conscience to decide whether to abuse the system in this manner? If they do, there is a risk that the system will break down—once a few take their own cars, others will soon follow, for no one likes to be taken advantage of. Or should the majority attempt to coerce the minority into taking the bus? That is the easy way out. It can be done in the name of freedom for all; but it may lead to freedom for none.

Marx was devoted to the cause of human freedom. When asked, in a Victorian parlour game, to name the vice he most detested, he replied: 'Servility'; and as his favourite motto he put down: 'De omnibus dubitandum'—'You must have doubts about everything' (MC 456–7). Though his own personality had an authoritarian streak, there can be little doubt he would have been appalled at the authority Lenin and Stalin wielded in his name. (Marx would probably have been an early victim of the purges.) Marx thought that under communism the state would cease to exist as a political entity. Coercion would be unnecessary because communism would end the conflict between individual interests and the common good. The end of this conflict would bring with it the end of any threat of a conflict between the freedom of the community to control its own economic and social life, and the freedom of the individual to do as he or she pleases.

Here Marx's second lasting contribution to modern thought—his view of human nature—ties in with his idea of freedom. Marx's theory that human nature is not for ever fixed, but alters in accordance with the economic and social conditions of each period, holds out the prospect of transforming socity by changing the economic basis of such human traits as greed, egoism and ambition. Marx expected the abolition of private property and the institution of common ownership of the means of production and exchange to bring about a society in which people were motivated more by a desire for the good of all than by a specific desire for their own individual good. In this way individual and common interests could be harmonised.

Marx's view of human nature is now so widely accepted that a return to a pre-Marxist conception of human nature is unthinkable. Though Marx's own theory is not scientific, it laid the foundations for a new social science which would explore the relations between such apparently unconnected areas of life as the tools people use to produce food and their political and religious beliefs. Undoubtedly this is a fruitful area for historians and social scientists to investigate. In opening it up, Marx shattered the assumption that our intellectual and spiritual lives are entirely independent of our economic existence. If 'Know thyself' is the first imperative of philosophy, Marx's contribution to our self-understanding is another reason for ranking him highly among philosophers.

Once Marx has been given due credit for making us aware of the economic and social forces that may influence us, however, it has to be added that his own view of human nature is probably false. Human nature is not as pliable as he believed. Egoism, for instance, is not eliminated by economic reorganisation or by material abundance. When basic needs are satisfied, new 'needs' emerge. In our society, people want not simply clothes, but fashionable clothes; not shelter, but a house to display their wealth and taste. It is not just advertising that kads to these desires, for they emerge in the non-capitalist world as well, often in the face of disapproval from the official ideology. Unless rigid uniformity is imposed—and perhaps even then—these desires will find an outlet. And it will never be possible to satisfy everyone's material desires. How could we provide everyone with a house in a secluded position overlooking the sea, but within easy reach of the city?

In different societies, egoistic desires will take different forms. This does not show that they Can be abolished altogether, but only that they are the expression of a more basic desire. There is, for instance, more than simple greed behind our insatiable urge for consumer goods. There is also the desire for status, and perhaps sometimes a desire for the power which status can bring. No doubt capitalism accentuates these desires. There are societies in which competition for status and power are much more restrained. There may even be societies lacking any such competition. Yet desires for status and power exist in many human beings, in a range of different societies. They tend to surface despite repeated efforts to suppress them. No society, no matter how egalitarian its rhetoric, has succeeded in abolishing the distinction between ruler and ruled. Nor has any society succeeded in making this distinction *merely* a matter of who leads and who follows: to be a ruler gives one special status and, usually, special privileges. Important officials in the Soviet Union have access to special shops selling delicacies unavailable to ordinary citizens; in China travelling by car is a luxury limited to tourists and those high in the party hierarchy (and their families). Throughout the 'communist' nations, the abolition of the old ruling class has been followed by the rise of a new class of party bosses and well-placed bureaucrats, whose behaviour and life-style comes more and more to resemble that of their much-denounced predecessors.

I point to these failings of the allegedly communist world not in order to say that this is the kind of society Marx wanted—obviously, it isn't—but to ask what there is to be learnt from these historical experiments. Before answering this question, however, we should note that the prevalence of hierarchy is not limited to human societies. There are clear hierarchies among most social birds and mammals, including those species most nearly related to human beings. Farmers have always known that barnyard flocks of hens develop a 'pecking order' in which each hen has a rank, allowing her to peck at and drive away from food birds below her in rank, but to be pecked by, and forced to give up food to, those above her. More careful studies have shown that similiar hierarchies exist among wolves, deer, lions, baboons and chimpanzees, to name only a few of the species studied.

So we have evidence that was not available to Marx—evidence of the failure of deliberate attempts to create egalitarian societies on the basis of the abolition of private ownership of the means of production and exchange; and evidence of the hierarchical nature of non-human societies. The evidence is not yet all in; but we have enough to reach the provisional judgement that it will not be as easy as Marx thought to bring the conflicting interests of human beings into harmony.

If this is right, it has far-reaching consequences for Marx's positive proposals. If changing the economic basis of society will not bring the individual to see that his own interests and the interests of society are the same, communism as Marx conceived it must be abandoned. Except perhaps for the brief period in which the economic structure of the society was in the process of transformation to social ownership, Marx never intended a communist society to force the individual to work against his or her own interests for the collective good. The need to use coercion would signify not the overcoming of alienation, but the continuing alienation of man from man; a coercive society would not be the riddle of history resolved, but merely the riddle restated in a new form; it would not end class rule, but would substitute a new ruling class for the old one. While it is absurd to blame Marx for something he did not foresee and certainly would have condemned if he had foreseen it, the distance between Marx's predicted communist society and the modern reality of 'communism' may in the end be traceable to Marx's misconception of the flexibility of human nature.

It is both sad and ironic to read today some marginal jottings Marx made in 1874, while reading Bakunin's *Statism and Anarchy*. Marx copied out passages from this work by his anarchist rival from the days of the first International, and then made his own comments on each passage. Thus the jottings read like a dialogue, one section of which goes like this:

Bakunin: Universal suffrage by the whole people of representatives and rulers of the state—this is the last word of the Marxists as well as of the democratic school. They are lies behind which lurks the despotism of a governing minority, lies all the more dangerous in that this minority appears as the expression of the so-called people's will.

Marx: Under collective property, the so-called will of the people disappears in order to make way for the real will of the cooperative.

Bakunin: Result: rule of the great majority of the people by a privileged minority. But, the Marxists say, this minority will consist of workers. Yes, indeed, but of ex-workers who, once they become only representatives or rulers of the people, cease to be workers.

Marx: No more than a manufacturer today ceases to be a capitalist when he becomes a member of the municipal council.

Bakunin: And from the heights of the state they begin to look down upon the whole common world of the workers. From that time on they represent not the people but themselves and their own claims to govern the people. Those who can doubt this know nothing at all about human nature.

Marx: If Mr Bakunin were familiar just with the position of a manager in a workers' cooperative, he could send all his nightmares about authority to the devil. He should have asked himself: what form can administrative functions take, on the basis of this workers' state—if he wants to call it that? (B 563)

The tragedy of Marxism is that a century after Marx wrote these words, our experience of the rule of workers in several different countries bears out Bakunin's objections, rather than Marx's replies. Marx saw that capitalism is a wasteful, irrational system, a system which controls us when we should be controlling it. That insight is still valid; but we can now see that the construction of a free and equal society is a more difficult task than Marx realised.

Note on sources

The quotations from Engels on pp. 379 and 384 are from 'Ludwig Feuerbach and the End of Classical German Philosophy', in K. Marx, F. Engels, *Selected Works* (Foreign Languages Publishing House, Moscow, 1951), vol. 2, pp. 365–8. The description of Moses Hess as the first to reach communism by 'the philosophic path' (see p. 386) comes from 'Progress of Social Reform on the Continent', an article Engels wrote for *The New Moral World*, a small English journal, in 1843; it is quoted in Robert Tucker's *Philosophy and Myth in Karl Marx* (Cambridge University Press, Cambridge, 1961), p. 107. Engels refers to 'Marx denying that he is a Marxist (see p. 407) in a letter to Starkenburg, 25 January 1894; Engels's letters to Schmidt (5 August 1890), to Bloch (21 September 1890) and to Mehring (14 April 1893) also deal with the interpretation of historical materialism. All are reprinted in L. S. Feuer (ed.), *Marx & Engels: Basic Writings on Politics and Philosophy* (Doubleday Anchor, New York, 1959). The expression 'a really human morality' cited on p. 431 comes from Engels's *Anti-Dühring*, also reprinted in Feuer, at p. 272.

The quotation from Hegel on p. 381 is from *The Philosophy of History* (trans. J. Sibree, ed. C. J. Friedrich, Dover, New York, 1956), p. 19.

The contemporary economist quoted on p. 426 is Paul Samuelson, writing in the *American Economic Review*, vol. 47 (1957), p. 911.

Further reading

Writings by Marx

Marx wrote so much that the definitive edition of all the writings of Marx and Engels, now in the process of publication in East Germany, will take twenty-five years and a hundred volumes to complete. A more modest English edition of *Collected Works* began appearing in 1975, published by Lawrence and Wishart; it will eventually contain about fifty volumes. Meanwhile the English reader must make do with complete editions of the major works, and selections from others. As the list of abbreviations on p. 367 suggests, I regard *Karl Marx: Selected Writings* edited by David McLellan (Oxford University Press, Oxford, 1977) as the best single-volume collection. Lewis Feuer's *Marx & Engels: Basic Writings on Politics and Philosophy* (Doubleday Anchor, New York, 1959) has a good selection of the 'classic' writings of the mature Marx, but for a comprehensive picture it needs to be supplemented by a collection of Marx's earlier writings, like Loyd Easton and Kurt Guddat (eds.), *Writings of the Young Marx on Philosophy and Society* (Doubleday Anchor, New York, 1967).

There are many editions of Marx's most famous works. The *Communist Manifesto* is a good place to begin reading Marx. It is available in a Penguin edition, edited by A. J. P. Taylor (Harmondsworth, 1967); and is reprinted in its entirety in McLellan's and many other volumes of selected writings. Having read the *Manifesto* and some selections from other texts, the reader may like to try the first volume of *Capital*. It is not as difficult as one might imagine, and is again available in a number of different editions, of which the Moore and Aveling translation published in Moscow is the most commonly used.

For those who want something in between one and fifty volumes, the Marx Library, published by Penguin in Britain and Vintage in the U.S.A., is an eight-volume collection that includes the complete *Grundrisse* and a good selection of Marx's journalism and political writings.

Writings about Marx

If the writings by Marx and Engels take up a hundred volumes, those about Marx must run into the tens of thousands. Below is a *very* brief selection of some better recent books. Although older works are interesting because they enable us to see how earlier generations conceived Marx, their ignorance of his unpublished early writings and of the *Grundrisse* make them an unreliable guide to the basis of Marx's views.

For books on Marx's life, there is little need to go beyond David McLellan's outstanding *Karl Marx: His Life and Thought* (Macmillan, London, 1973). A slightly less sympathetic alternative is Saul K. Padover, *The Man Marx* (McGraw-Hill, New York, 1978). Jerrold Seigel's *Marx's Fate* (Princeton University Press, Princeton, 1978) may appeal to those who favour psychoanalytic biographies. Among older works, Isaiah Berlin's *Karl Marx: His Life and Environment* (first edition 1939, fourth edition, Oxford University Press, Oxford, 1978) has lost none of its flowing style in several updatings.

On Marx's thought, as distinct from his life, Robert Tucker, in *Philosophy and Myth in Karl Marx* (Cambridge University Press, Cambridge, 1961) was among the first to emphasise the continuity of Marx's ideas, from his earliest Hegelian essays to *Capital*. Tucker's interpretation is novel, if at times too dramatic. David McLellan's *The Young Hegelians and Karl Marx* (Macmillan, London, 1969) gives useful background to Marx's intellectual development. Bertell Ollman, *Alienation: Marx's Conception of Man in Capitalist Society* (second edition, Cambridge University Press, Cambridge, 1977) is more readable than most works on alienation.

To balance the Hegelian emphasis of these works, G. A. Cohen's *Karl Marx's Theory of History: A Defence* (Oxford University Press, Oxford, 1979) argues brilliantly for a more old-fashioned interpretation of Marxism as a scientific theory of history, an interpretation often known—disparagingly—as 'technological determinism'. Melvin Rader's *Marx's Interpreta-*

tion of History (Oxford University Press, New York, 1979) presents a wider range of possible interpretations.

Finally, those interested in the entire sweep of Marxist theory, from the founders through its 'Golden Age' to its dissolution into Soviet ideology, should not miss *Main Currents of Marxism* by Leszek Kolakowski (3 vols, Oxford University Press, Oxford, 1978).

Index

451

OXFORD

MORE OXFORD PAPERBACKS

This book is just one of nearly 1000 Oxford Paperbacks currently in print. If you would like details of other Oxford Paperbacks, including titles in the World's Classics, Oxford Reference, Oxford Books, OPUS, Past Masters, Oxford Authors, and Oxford Shakespeare series, please write to:

UK and Europe: Oxford Paperbacks Publicity Manager, Arts and Reference Publicity Department, Oxford University Press, Walton Street, Oxford OX2 6DP.

Customers in UK and Europe will find Oxford Paperbacks available in all good bookshops. But in case of difficulty please send orders to the Cash-with-Order Department, Oxford University Press Distribution Services, Saxon Way West, Corby, Northants NN18 9ES. Tel: 01536 741519; Fax: 01536 746337. Please send a cheque for the total cost of the books, plus £1.75 postage and packing for orders under £20; £2.75 for orders over £20. Customers outside the UK should add 10% of the cost of the books for postage and packing.

USA: Oxford Paperbacks Marketing Manager, Oxford University Press, Inc., 200 Madison Avenue, New York, N.Y. 10016.

Canada: Trade Department, Oxford University Press, 70 Wynford Drive, Don Mills, Ontario M3C 1J9.

Australia: Trade Marketing Manager, Oxford University Press, G.P.O. Box 2784Y, Melbourne 3001, Victoria.

South Africa: Oxford University Press, P.O. Box 1141, Cape Town 8000.

PAST MASTERS

A wide range of unique, short, clear introductions to the lives and work of the world's most influential thinkers. Written by experts, they cover the history of ideas from Aristotle to Wittgenstein. Readers need no previous knowledge of the subject, so they are ideal for students and general readers alike.

Each book takes as its main focus the thought and work of its subject. There is a short section on the life and a final chapter on the legacy and influence of the thinker. A section of further reading helps in further research.

The series continues to grow, and future Past Masters will include **Owen Gingerich** on *Copernicus*, **R G Frey** on *Joseph Butler*, **Bhiku Parekh** on *Gandhi*, **Christopher Taylor** on *Socrates*, **Michael Inwood** on *Heidegger*, and **Peter Ghosh** on *Weber*.

P A S T

MASTERS

KEYNES

Robert Skidelsky

John Maynard Keynes is a central thinker of the twentieth century. This is the only available short introduction to his life and work.

Keynes's doctrines continue to inspire strong feelings in admirers and detractors alike. This short, engaging study of his life and thought explores the many positive and negative stereotypes and also examines the quality of Keynes's mind, his cultural and social milieu, his ethical and practical philosophy, and his monetary thought. Recent scholarship has significantly altered the treatment and assessment of Keynes's contribution to twentieth-century economic thinking, and the current state of the debate initiated by the Keynesian revolution is discussed in a final chapter on its legacy.

P A S T

MASTERS

RUSSELL

A. C. *Grayling*

Bertrand Russell (1872–1970) is one of the most famous and important philosophers of the twentieth century. In this account of his life and work A. C. Grayling introduces both his technical contributions to logic and philosophy, and his wide-ranging views on education, politics, war, and sexual morality. Russell is credited with being one of the prime movers of Analytic Philosophy, and with having played a part in the revolution in social attitudes witnessed throughout the twentieth-century world. This introduction gives a clear survey of Russell's achievements across their whole range.

Oxford
Paperback
Reference

THE OXFORD DICTIONARY OF PHILOSOPHY

Edited by Simon Blackburn

* **2,500 entries covering the entire span of the subject including the most recent terms and concepts**

* **Biographical entries for nearly 500 philosophers**

* **Chronology of philosophical events**

From Aristotle to Zen, this is the most comprehensive, authoritative, and up to date dictionary of philosophy available. Ideal for students or a general readership, it provides lively and accessible coverage of not only the Western philosophical tradition but also important themes from Chinese, Indian, Islamic, and Jewish philosophy. The paperback includes a new Chronology.

'an excellent source book and can be strongly recommended . . . there are generous and informative entries on the great philosophers . . . Overall the entries are written in an informed and judicious manner.'
Times Higher Education Supplement

Oxford Paperback Reference

THE CONCISE OXFORD DICTIONARY OF POLITICS

Edited by Iain McLean

Written by an expert team of political scientists from Warwick University, this is the most authoritative and up-to-date dictionary of politics available.

* Over 1,500 entries provide truly international coverage of major political institutions, thinkers and concepts

* From Western to Chinese and Muslim political thought

* Covers new and thriving branches of the subject, including international political economy, voting theory, and feminism

* Appendix of political leaders

* Clear, no-nonsense definitions of terms such as veto and subsidiarity

Oxford
Paperback
Reference

THE CONCISE OXFORD COMPANION
TO ENGLISH LITERATURE

Edited by Margaret Drabble and Jenny Stringer

Derived from the acclaimed *Oxford Companion to English Literature*, the concise maintains the wide coverage of its parent volume. It is an indispensable, compact guide to all aspects of English literature. For this revised edition, existing entries have been fully updated and revised with 60 new entries added on contemporary writers.

* **Over 5,000 entries on the lives and works of authors, poets and playwrights**

* **The most comprehensive and authoritative paperback guide to English literature**

* **New entries include Peter Ackroyd, Martin Amis, Toni Morrison, and Jeanette Winterson**

* **New appendices list major literary prize-winners**

From the reviews of its parent volume:

'It earns its place at the head of the best sellers: every home should have one'
Sunday Times

OPUS

General Editors: Walter Bodmer,
Christopher Butler, Robert Evans,
John Skorupski

CLASSICAL THOUGHT

Terence Irwin

Spanning over a thousand years from Homer to Saint Augustine, *Classical Thought* encompasses a vast range of material, in succinct style, while remaining clear and lucid even to those with no philosophical or Classical background.

The major philosophers and philosophical schools are examined—the Presocratics, Socrates, Plato, Aristotle, Stoicism, Epicureanism, Neoplatonism; but other important thinkers, such as Greek tragedians, historians, medical writers, and early Christian writers, are also discussed. The emphasis is naturally on questions of philosophical interest (although the literary and historical background to Classical philosophy is not ignored), and again the scope is broad—ethics, the theory of knowledge, philosophy of mind, philosophical theology. All this is presented in a fully integrated, highly readable text which covers many of the most important areas of ancient thought and in which stress is laid on the variety and continuity of philosophical thinking after Aristotle.

PHILOSOPHY IN OXFORD PAPERBACKS
THE GREAT PHILOSOPHERS
Bryan Magee

Beginning with the death of Socrates in 399, and following the story through the centuries to recent figures such as Bertrand Russell and Wittgenstein, Bryan Magee and fifteen contemporary writers and philosophers provide an accessible and exciting introduction to Western philosophy and its greatest thinkers.

Bryan Magee in conversation with:

A. J. Ayer	John Passmore
Michael Ayers	Anthony Quinton
Miles Burnyeat	John Searle
Frederick Copleston	Peter Singer
Hubert Dreyfus	J. P. Stern
Anthony Kenny	Geoffrey Warnock
Sidney Morgenbesser	Bernard Williams
Martha Nussbaum	

'Magee is to be congratulated . . . anyone who sees the programmes or reads the book will be left in no danger of believing philosophical thinking is un-practical and uninteresting.' Ronald Hayman, *Times Educational Supplement*

'one of the liveliest, fast-paced introductions to philosophy, ancient and modern that one could wish for' *Universe*

THE OXFORD AUTHORS

General Editor: Frank Kermode

THE OXFORD AUTHORS is a series of authoritative editions of major English writers. Aimed at both students and general readers, each volume contains a generous selection of the best writings—poetry, prose, and letters—to give the essence of a writer's work and thinking. All the texts are complemented by essential notes, an introduction, chronology, and suggestions for further reading.

Matthew Arnold
William Blake
Lord Byron
John Clare
Samuel Taylor Coleridge
John Donne
John Dryden
Ralph Waldo Emerson
Thomas Hardy
George Herbert and Henry Vaughan
Gerard Manley Hopkins
Samuel Johnson
Ben Jonson
John Keats
Andrew Marvell
John Milton
Alexander Pope
Sir Philip Sidney
Oscar Wilde
William Wordsworth